A Handbook of
Software and Systems Engineering

Empirical Observations, Laws and Theories

The Fraunhofer IESE Series on Software Engineering

Whereas software technology is concerned with individual techniques, methods and tools for developing software, such as programming languages, design notations, or test techniques, software engineering takes a holistic view of the entire software development process, regarding it as an integral part of a given organizational, technical and business context. Software engineering does not focus on individual projects only, but treats development activities as steps in an evolutionary process improvement. Like other engineering disciplines, software engineering rests on three pillars:

- "Architectural principles" that can be applied to reduce the complexity of systems
- "Process technology" for modeling individual process steps and their interaction, and for measuring and controlling their impact
- "Precise methods" for describing software

Software is developed by humans, so the effects of the application of techniques, methods and tools cannot be determined independent of context. A thorough understanding of their effects in different organizational and technical contexts is essential if these effects are to be predictable and repeatable under varying conditions. Such process–product effects are best determined empirically. Empirical software engineering develops the basic methodology for conducting empirical studies, and uses it to advance the understanding of the effects of various software engineering approaches.

Frustrated by the apparent lack of progress in the discipline, with repeated examples of major software projects overrunning on budgets and deadlines, the software community realizes the importance of empirical software engineering. The 2001 ICSE conference in Toronto made it quite clear that software measurement and empirical studies are considered a major driver of the faster integration of academic research and industrial practice. Unfortunately, books about measurement and empiricism are scarce and scattered across numerous book series. This makes it hard to achieve the necessary thrust and visibility. The Fraunhofer IESE Series on Software Engineering helps by providing an open forum for all important books in the area of software engineering that contribute to the advancement of the empirical view. This series will contain books on empirical infrastructures in software engineering, and on all software engineering topics that include empirical validation.

Titles in the series
Endres, A. and Rombach, D. *A Handbook of Software and Systems Engineering* (2003)

Fraunhofer Institute for Experimental Software Engineering, Sauerwiesen 6, D-67661 Kaiserslautern, Germany

A Handbook of Software and Systems Engineering

Empirical Observations, Laws and Theories

Albert Endres

Dieter Rombach

PEARSON

Addison
Wesley

Harlow, England • London • New York • Boston • San Francisco • Toronto
Sydney • Tokyo • Singapore • Hong Kong • Seoul • Taipei • New Delhi
Cape Town • Madrid • Mexico City • Amsterdam • Munich • Paris • Milan

Pearson Education Limited
Edinburgh Gate
Harlow
Essex CM20 2JE
England

and Associated Companies throughout the world

Visit us on the World Wide Web at:
www.pearsoneduc.com

First published 2003

ISBN 0 321 15420 7

British Library Cataloguing-in-Publication Data
A catalogue record for this book can be obtained from the British Library

Library of Congress Cataloging-in-Publication Data
A catalog record for this book is available from the Library of Congress

10 9 8 7 6 5 4 3 2 1
07 06 05 04 03

Typeset by 30 in 10/12pt Sabon
Printed and bound in Great Britain by Biddles Ltd, Guildford and King's Lynn

'Ma, why is this and why is that?'
'Would you please stop asking those why-questions!'
'Why?'

Conversation between a three-year-old girl and her mother.

* * *

This book is dedicated to all those colleagues who have
preserved their innate passion for theory, revealing itself
by continually asking 'Why?'

Contents

Chapter 1: Introduction   1

Chapter 2: Requirements definition, prototyping, and modeling   10

Chapter 6: Testing or dynamic verification — 123

Chapter 7: System manufacturing, distribution, and installation — 150

Chapter 8: System administration, evolution, and maintenance 160

Chapter 11: Technology, architecture, and industry capabilities   242

This book is about the empirical aspects of computing. We believe that the fields of computer science, information technology (IT), systems, and software engineering do not emphasize enough the fundamental knowledge needed by practitioners. Moreover, the four fields are diverging more than is necessary. Practitioners have to rely on all of them whenever modern information systems have to be planned, developed, evaluated, or introduced. A unified approach based on empirically derived knowledge from all four fields is helpful for this task.

Instead of arguing in favor of individual methods and techniques, we intend to look for rules and laws, and their underlying theories. We shall do that by repeatedly asking 'Why?'. We shall ask, 'What are the fundamental rules, why do they work, and why are they useful? We will not always find the correct answer or even a satisfying one, but we want to motivate other people to take the same route. We do not claim that this is the only possible approach for an engineering discipline. It certainly is more demanding than a purely phenomenological approach, namely a listing of interesting features and relevant techniques. Above all, we have included as laws only those rules which, in our view, have stood the test of time, either being supported by direct experimentation, documented case studies, or by the collective experience of practitioners. The latter are important, since much of conventional engineering practice arose in this way.

We believe that our approach has advantages for both students and practitioners. Basic concepts are easier to remember than a plurality of features. It is our opinion that this type of knowledge has a longer lifetime than knowledge of passing trends and their manifestations. The rules presented here can serve as checklists with respect to the state of the art. No doubt the knowledge of applicable methods, tools, and products is indispensable for every practitioner, but it has to be complemented by more basic knowledge.

This book was not possible without the help of several colleagues. We are particularly indebted to Calvin Arnason, Lucian Endicott, Jürgen Münch, Karl Reed, Toru Takeshita, Walter Tichy, and several unnamed reviewers for valuable comments, be it on the content or the style. We also thank David Hemsley for carefully editing our text and improving our English.

Albert Endres
H. Dieter Rombach
Stuttgart and Kaiserslautern, August 2002

ACM	Association for Computing Machinery
AFM	Atomic force microscope
AI	Artificial Intelligence
B	Byte
BNF	Backus–Naur Form
CBO	Coupling between objects
CD	Compact Disk
CERT	Computer Emergency Response Team
CMM	Capability Maturity Model
CORBA	Common Object Request Broker Architecture
COTS	Commercial off-the-shelf (software)
CSI	Changed source instructions
CTSS	Compatible Timesharing System
DBMS	Database management system
DB2	IBM's relational DBMS
DCOM	Distributed Common Object Model
DFD	Dataflow diagram
DIT	Depth of inheritance tree
DVD	Digital Versatile Disk
ERD	Entity relationship diagram
FNF	Functional normal form
G	Giga ($\approx 10^9$)
GQM	Goal-Question-Metric
GUI	Graphical user interface
HP	Hewlett Packard
HTTP	Hypertext Transfer Protocol
IEEE	Institute of Electrical and Electronic Engineers
ISERN	International Software Engineering Research Network
IS	Information systems
ISO	International Organization for Standardization
IT	Information technology
K	Kilo (1024)
Kbit/s	Kilobit per second
KLOC	Kilo (= thousand) lines of code
KPA	Key process area
LAN	Local area network
LCOM	Lack of cohesion in methods
LOC	Lines of code
M	Mega ($\approx 10^6$)

Mbit/s	Megabit per second
MLOC	Million lines of code
MTTF	Mean time between failures
Multics	Multiplexed Information and Computing Service
NLS	Natural Language System
NOC	Number of children
OOA	Object-oriented analysis
OOD	Object-oriented design
OOP	Object-oriented programming
PBE	Programming by example
RFC	Response for a class
PDL	Program design language
PL/I	Programming Language/I
PSP	Personal software process
RMI	Remote method invocation
QIP	Quality improvement program
SDL	System design language
SE	Software engineering
SEI	Software Engineering Institute (at Carnegie Mellon University)
SEL	Software Engineering Laboratory (of NASA)
SQL	Structured Query Language
SSI	Shipped source instructions
STM	Scanning tunneling microscope
T	Tera ($\approx 10^{12}$)
Tbit/s	Terabit per second
V&V	Validation and verification
VOD	Violations of Demeter
WAC	Weighted attributes per class
WMC	Weighted methods per class
XML	Extensible Mark-up Language

The following designations are trademarks or registered trademarks of the organizations whose names follow in brackets:

ABAP/4 and SAP (SAP); Apache (Apache Software Foundation); CERT (Carnegie Mellon University); CICS, DB2, MVS, and OS/2 (IBM Corporation); CORBA and UML (Object Management Group, Inc.); DBase II (Borland International, Inc.); Intel, Pentium, and Pentium Pro (Intel Corporation); Java (Sun Microsystems, Inc.); LINUX (Linus Torvalds); Microsoft, Visual Basic, and Windows (Microsoft Corporation); Motif and UNIX (The Open Group); PeopleSoft (PeopleSoft, Inc.).

Supplementary material

Case study material and code to support this book are available to download at:
www.booksites.net/endres

chapter 1

Introduction

Building software will always be hard. There is inherently no silver bullet.

F.P. Brooks, Jr [Broo87]

1.1 Computing as empirical science

Computing is a broad field at whose core we find the academic discipline called computer science. We consider computing largely as an empirical science. This is particularly true for two of its major application areas, namely software and systems engineering. Systems engineering deals with the planning, development, and administration of complex systems, particularly of computing systems. Software engineering is that part of systems engineering that deals with the systematic development, evaluation, and maintenance of software. In practice, new people are constantly entering the field of computing. Not all of them have been trained as either computer scientists or software engineers. Even if they have computing degrees, they may never have learnt about what has been done by people before them. Many people purposely ignore the lessons of the past. It may take a major project failure before these people realize that the problems they encountered were neither new nor unique.

Academics have often complained that software and systems engineering operate without a scientific basis. It is customary to reproach the practitioners for this. For 30 years, theorists have demanded that practitioners should be re-educated in order to make better use of available theoretical results. In our opinion, this is a biased view. We believe that the problem sometimes lies with the theorists. Rather than developing theories, they frequently argue in favor of specific methods and tools, many of which demonstrate technical virtuosity. They often do this without sufficient regard to their usefulness in practice nor after validating them by meaningful trials. Practice should be the true measure of a method's usefulness, however, because this is where daily problems are solved. The knowledge that helps us master practical tasks should have our highest attention. In computing, a new approach is therefore needed if we want to close the gap between theory and practice. We call this approach empirical software and systems engineering.

1.2 From observations to laws and theories

The key terms used throughout this book are observation, law, and theory. In science and general human life, we often go from observations to laws and then to theories. All three are important. *Observations* may be facts, or simply subjective impressions. We make observations all day long using all our senses. In more recent times we can even make observations of signals that are not detectable to our senses. Electrical waves or radioactive particles have become very important. However, we can't always find regularities or recurring patterns in the observations and often consider non-repeatable observations as accidents, or put them aside as observation errors. There are no apparent laws that govern them, no observable systematic behavior.

Whenever we make reoccurring observations we might want to react on them, whether that means adjusting to them or taking advantage of them. Examples are the symptoms of a widespread disease, the beginning of the rainy season, or the re-appearance of a planet. Repeatable observations can often be stated as a *law*. Using this law, we can then make predictions about further observations. Laws are generalizations from one situation to others, or from one time period to another. A law tells us *how* things occur, but not *why*. Kepler's laws describe how the planets move, but not *why*. If there is a law, we like to know why it is true – we like to have a *theory*. Theories explain and order our observations. We get at them the same way children do, by asking 'Why?'. Fig. 1-1 depicts this relationship.

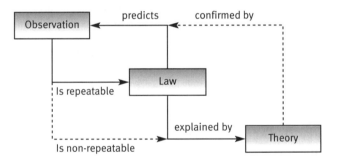

Fig. 1-1 Relationship between observations, laws and theories

Theories may exist first. They may predict observations or even laws. In an empirical science, theories should always be verified through observations. Until adequately confirmed by observations, such a theory (or potential law) is called a hypothesis. An empirical science looks at the world as it exists around us and in us. It not only looks at the objects created or manipulated, but also at the people involved in doing this. Rather than assuming that all objects that are dealt with have mathematical properties only, a much broader view is required. All kinds of important properties need to be taken into account. These may be cognitive, economic, technical, or sociological properties. They are all subjects of study.

Observations can be made during all kinds of daily work, but most intensively in the framework of projects, surveys, case studies, or experiments. In software and systems engineering, *projects* are organizational efforts to develop, introduce, or evaluate new applications, tools, or methods. The development of new knowledge is not their primary purpose. Projects may succeed, partially succeed, or fail. Projects that fail, in total or in part, can be more important from a learner's perspective than successful ones. Lessons are learned during the course of a project, and may be summarized at the end as a post mortem. *Surveys* and *case studies* are usually done to complement projects, frequently as peripheral activities. They are less expensive and less risky but may produce limited information. If they cover multiple projects and different organizations, they may give a broader picture, however, than a single project.

An *experiment* is an intentional exercise, carried out to gain new knowledge. To do this, a hypothesis is set up that has to be verified or falsified by the experiment. A special form of experiments are controlled experiments. To conduct experiments with real systems or real users can be very expensive or socially undesirable. Nevertheless, this source of knowledge should not be neglected. Unfortunately, in the early decades of computing, experiments seldom took place. However, their number has significantly increased over the last decade. Most experiments in software engineering make use of statistical methods to assure that the results obtained are meaningful. Many experiments reported in the literature, however, were done with small or toy systems and with students. Some of them, nevertheless, produced results that seem to be applicable to real systems and real users, and could easily be followed up by case studies in realistic environments.

1.4 Laws as lessons learned by the profession

If project participants achieve new and significant results worth remembering, we usually talk of 'lessons learned'. These are the nuggets that must be captured to improve future performance. This is true both for individuals and organizations, and applies to the entire profession. The results may be communicated in several forms. The simplest form is oral or written transmission between individuals within an organization. It may also take the form of lessons taught by senior professionals and specialists, or may end up in handbooks or knowledge databases that compile and structure available knowledge. It is the recognition and dissemination of widely applicable laws with defined applicability that will strengthen the development of software engineering as an effective discipline.

Electronic computing is about 50 years old. The lessons that have been learned by our profession during this period are the essence of our empirical knowledge. It will be complemented by other knowledge, even if it is much older and stems from seemingly unrelated disciplines. Which lessons are most valuable depends partially on the situations we later encounter. Not all lessons learned are applicable to the entire profession, while some of them stand out and have been stated clearly before. We will call the essential lessons *laws* in this book. By using this term, we are exaggerating a little: the less exacting term 'rule' may be more appropriate, but several authors have already used the term 'law' for these lessons, and we will abide by this convention.

Of the different meanings associated with the term law, we mean law in the sense of 'law of nature'. According to Webster's definition, a *law of nature* is a statement of an order or relation of phenomena that, so far as is known, is constant under certain conditions. Certainly, the laws we cite can be better compared with laws in economics, than with laws in physics or biology. To quote Lehman [Lehm80], whose laws we will discuss later, our laws are 'certainly weaker than those formulated in the biological sciences, where regularity stems from the collective behavior of cellular systems that, even though alive, are non-intelligent'. Laws represent firm knowledge upon which people can rely, and are a proven way to summarize knowledge that needs to be conveyed to large communities. Of course, it is always possible to construct situations where a certain law does not apply. These situations, however, usually deviate from the environments typical for professional software and systems development and evaluation.

We distinguish here between laws, hypotheses and conjectures. By quoting a certain rule as a law, we mean that there is strong empirical evidence supporting it, and that it represents an important insight. As in science, a *hypothesis* is a proposition that is only tentatively accepted. If we call something a hypothesis, this does not necessarily mean that we are in agreement with it; sometimes we have doubts about its validity. Otherwise, we might have looked harder for more good evidence, so that we could turn it into a law. With *conjectures* it is different again. A conjecture is a guess only. We usually believe in it, but have not found too many people (yet) who share our view. If we elevate something to a law, we are suggesting that it be accepted as truth, at least for the time being, and that future studies should be directed at something else, maybe at our hypotheses and conjectures. That is exactly the fine line we are trying to follow in this book.

Some of the laws we cite became popular because the projects or studies leading to them were landmark events at their time. They were convincing because several people made similar observations in different environments, or the experiments were done repeatedly. The professional community had (and still has) the same interpretation of the facts that were observed and agreed with the conclusions that were drawn. In Shaw's [Shaw90] terms, this knowledge somehow became part of our folklore. Our criterion for expressing knowledge by a law is quite stringent: firstly, there is a clear underlying hypothesis that has been validated in the context of systematic studies (with a few exceptions as indicated). Secondly, the study may have been performed as an experiment, a case study, or as an afterthought or byproduct of a regular project. Thirdly, some experiments were repeated, achieving consistent results across different groups or environments.

By selecting a set of 50 laws, we want to express our opinion that, in the field of software and systems engineering, there is a significant body of agreement among experts. We also believe that these insights will remain true for a long time. In this book, some of the laws have been slightly reworded, so that the long-term significance becomes more obvious. To some people, our list may seem arbitrary and incomplete. However, if laws have not been discovered yet, we do not attempt to invent them. We also exclude many areas where good results have been achieved or are considered as 'best practice'. We shall try to compensate for this to some extent by quoting a number of hypotheses and conjectures, which in our opinion, should fill the most significant gaps. By doing this we want to say that these insights are shared by many people but have not been validated by a systematic study. In fact, we want to challenge both researchers and practitioners to work together to turn these hypotheses or conjectures into laws or to replace them. Even a law can be challenged, whether because the problem it addresses has became irrelevant, or that the circumstances leading to a certain conclusion have changed over time.

We will mainly cite laws that have a certain surprise value, i.e. are not considered as obvious or common sense by everybody, particularly people who are new to the field. It is no coincidence that many of our laws were first formulated decades ago. In empirical science, if something has survived the test of time, it is a sign of quality. In fact, some of the laws we cite originate from the very beginning of the computer age. The dates when a particular law was first formulated express somewhat the changing emphasis of the field. The older laws deal with implementation and test; newer ones are more concerned with design and requirement issues. If, in our selection, requirements, design and testing seem to be over-represented, this reflects our assessment that these activities are really 'intellectually demanding tasks', as Brooks [Broo87] calls them.

Laws and hypotheses are given both names and numbers in this book. Names are easier to memorize than numbers, and we will usually refer to them using the name. We would like to give credit for these important contributions to our field by naming the laws and hypotheses after the authors who first formulated them. Advancements in many disciplines are due to those people who see order where others see only disorder. This is the same in astronomy, biology, and physics, as well as in the social sciences.

1.5 On principles, methods and tools

Not all experiences are such that they can be called laws. They may be less universal or may not have been sufficiently validated. They are frequently at a rather detailed level. They are useful, nevertheless, and we will refer to them as *principles*. Most books on computing science try to outline at least some principles, from which in conjunction with laws, *methods* have been derived. We will use the term 'method' to include what other people may call a 'technique' or 'practice'. Methods are supported by *tools*. Typical tools are a stopwatch, a measuring tape, or a microscope. In our case, tools are frequently computer programs. Fig. 1-2 illustrates this relationship.

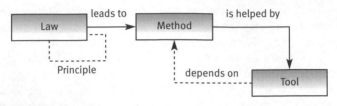

Fig. 1-2 From laws to methods and tools

There is a feedback from tools to methods: the preferred methods are those for which good tools exist. Tools take over repetitive tasks and assure the reliability of results. As every practitioner knows, decisions regarding methods and tools are not always made in a rational way: sometimes tools are bought before knowing that they require the introduction of a new method.

It is symptomatic of the state of the art in systems and software engineering that handbooks abound with methods, including practices and techniques. The market for tools is mushrooming in its own right, as a glance into any bookstore will show. This is, in some respect, an advancement when compared to the hopes of those naïve optimists looking for a single all-encompassing cure, referred to as a 'silver bullet' in Brooks' quote above. Typical examples of such catalogs of methods are Davis [Davi95], Jones [Jone00] and the Software Engineering Body of Knowledge (SWEBOK[1]). The latter is the laudable attempt by a professional society (IEEE Computer Society) to collect an agreed-on body of knowledge. All list many principles, techniques, and best practices, but give little explanation of *why* they should be used. This is similar to medieval medicine: there were hundreds of ointments and tinctures that seemed to work, but no-one knew why. Such medicine is difficult to teach and, more significantly, difficult to improve. Many of the laws presented here can be used in exactly this way, as direct guides to action and as predictors of outcomes in a broad but specific sense, hence they are of direct value to practioners and managers alike.

Software and systems engineering are no different in this respect to most other branches of engineering. Engineering cannot wait until all phenomena can be explained. Electrical engineering is a typical example. It existed about a 100 years before the phenomenon of electric current could be explained. Engineers may work effectively, often for centuries, with heuristics. These are rules ('rules-of thumb') of the form: if such a condition exists, do such and such. They exist in most fields of engineering and cannot be ignored.

1.6 Search for theories

Using the definition of an economist, a *theory* is a deliberate simplification (abstraction) of factual relationships that attempts to *explain how* these

---

[1] http://www.swebok.org

relationships work [Baum01]. It is an explanation of the mechanisms *behind* observed phenomena. Our laws are such observed phenomena. If we accept something as a law, the salient question is, '*Why* is this so?' Understanding why something is happening puts a given phenomenon onto another level; it helps to demystify it. For all laws quoted in this book, we therefore try to come up with an explanation or a theory. In fact, we will try to answer two types of question: (1) 'What is the reason or the rational explanation for this phenomenon?' and (2) 'Why will it reoccur elsewhere, or why can it be generalized?' This is the key characteristic, and the defining value, of this book. It is not presently possible to give a theory for all rules and methods that are important or seem to work. This is work for several generations, but we want to make a start.

Any theory is an attempt to explain observed laws with current knowledge. Following Popper [Popp63], all that we have are preliminary theories only, i.e. theories that have not yet been rejected. In other words, a theory is assumed to be true (or similar to truth) if no observations have been made that are in conflict with it. As an example, the Ptolemaic theories of the world explained sufficiently the movement of heavenly bodies for centuries. Only when more precise observations were possible did they become questionable. They were good, or useful, theories up to that point.

Theories are helpful to researchers in order to design their experiments. They are useful (although not mandatory) for practitioners as well. It allows them to cope more effectively with the situations they encounter. It is of secondary importance, whether those theories are easily expressible in some formal notation. Theories may come from either hard or soft sectors of science. Hard science observes that part of nature that is considered to be non-intelligent and thus more predictable. The more established disciplines in this respect are physics, chemistry, and parts of biology (those that are not concerned with human beings). In earlier times they were all branches of physics. The soft sciences have to take into account mental and social processes. Examples are medicine (sometimes considered as a part of biology), economics, psychology, and sociology. Developing a good theory is mainly an intellectual effort. In physics or astronomy, observations or measurements may require expensive set-ups, time, and equipment. Therefore, theories are often the inexpensive part. The proper attitude to get at them is to lean back and let our imagination play.

Mathematics does not normally produce scientific theories (in the sense defined above), as it cannot *explain* the reasons behind natural phenomena, although it can certainly help to describe them. As an example, mathematics does not give the reasons why the sun rises, but it can help to predict the timing with high precision, provided a physical theory is available. Mathematics provides theorems. Theorems are basically different from the theories discussed here. They cannot be validated even by millions of observations, but can be falsified by a single observation. If proven to be correct, they are valid forever.

1.7 About this book

This book is intended as a handbook for students and practitioners alike. The information contained is largely independent of particular technologies or tools, application areas or geographical regions, fashions or fads. It takes into account only what we consider as basic insights. It represents the fundamental knowledge for any professional in computing or information processing. This type of knowledge is required and valuable for an entire career. Without it, one should not assume responsibility for developing or evaluating business- or mission-critical systems. Indeed, we would dare to say that without this state-of-the-art knowledge, practitioners today would perform with the same effectiveness as those of 50 years ago.

The goals and ideas pursued in this book were excellently expressed by Boehm and Basili [Boeh00a] in their report on two workshops in 1999. They recommended the development of an 'empirical science of software' as soon as possible. We also support their plea not to separate information technology (IT) from software engineering (SE). 'Great systems require both great IT components and great SE elements' is a maxim we fully agree with. We therefore want to extend their idea by outlining an empirical science of software and *systems* engineering. With this we come closer to their goal of unifying software and systems engineering [Boeh00a].

The type of tasks that practitioners confront determined the structure of this book. These tasks or activities are reflected in the chapter headings. The first seven chapters (after the introduction) follow roughly the sequence encountered in practical studies or development projects. In different process models, these tasks have varying importance or are applied in a different sequence. In an iterative or cyclic model they may be applied repeatedly. The subject of quality assurance is treated together with each individual activity. This reflects the authors' opinion that it should be closely interwoven with development. The chapters towards the end deal with tasks that are not development related. They are, nevertheless, important for most practitioners.

If the book is used as a handbook, each chapter can be referred to individually and repeatedly. Therefore, not all 50 laws need to be memorized. A small subset that is relevant for the current task, as given in each chapter, will suffice. When presenting a law, we shall discuss applicability, evidence and relevant theory. For hypotheses and conjectures, no theory is given. For each chapter, additional activities are discussed in detail. Each chapter also contains examples and exercises. All laws, hypotheses and conjectures are summarized in the Appendices, along with short biographies of the people contributing to the results presented, and a list of groups doing research in empirical software and systems engineering.

Many books on computer science are structured similarly to books on mathematics. They start out with some theoretical concepts, for example, fuzzy logic or lattice theory, and list at the end a few situations where they may apply. That approach asks a lot of most readers; it requires considerable effort to place these kinds of result into a practical context. Our approach builds on practical situations and activities. However, the reader still has to translate the general conclusions to his or her specific context. This we cannot replace.

Finally, we hope that our book will provide a guide for researchers. There are experiments still to be done, experiences to be collected and investigations to be made to develop specific methods based on some of our laws, to validate some of the theories and to determine the truth of various conjectures. In some cases, the laws as we now know them raise challenges which, if they can be overcome, will provide significant advances.

chapter 2

Requirements definition, prototyping, and modeling

Requirements engineering is more difficult now, because all systems that were easy to specify have been built some time ago.

T. DeMarco [DeMa01]

In this chapter, we explain why the definition of requirements can be a very critical aspect of any project. Recognizing its limitations and pitfalls, and taking the proper precautions, can reduce the risks of any development project. For this, more than any other activity, a purely technical view is not sufficient.

2.1 Definitions and importance

Requirements definition is the process that determines the properties a particular system should have. The requirements process generates the information on which the design will be based. For this, you have to know where a system is to be used, by whom, and what services it should provide. It is also important to determine what trade-offs can be made in case of conflicting requirements. We assume that each system has a set of useful functions that are crucial for its success.

The concern for the importance of requirements definition arose rather late in our industry. Firstly, there was the concern for implementation languages, then for verification and testing, and finally for design and requirements definition. This corresponds to the personal evolution of most people. Only after they feel that they have the final activities under control do they look for potential problems in the early activities. As biologists say, 'Ontogeny repeats phylogeny', the development of the individual repeats that of the species.

The parties participating in the requirements definition process are collectively referred to as *stakeholders*. If the system is being built for a known customer, requirements may be the basis for a development contract. If the customer is initially unknown, the marketing organization may assume this function. At first, requirements are discussed at the application level. It is not always initally clear whether they will be implemented in hardware or in software, or performed by humans. Requirements should therefore always be considered as *system* requirements. Software requirements are only a part of them. They are determined after the system requirements, or derived from them. The results of the requirements definition process are documented in the *requirements specification*. Sometimes the term 'objectives' is used for this document. The requirements definition process is frequently referred to as 'systems analysis' or 'requirements engineering'.

Prototyping is an activity intended to build a partial replica of a system comprising a subset of functions and using methods and materials that may be inappropriate for the final product. A prototype is executable and will usually accept the same type of inputs as the actual system and will produce the expected output. The development of a prototype should be considerably faster and less expensive than the actual product. Therefore the term rapid prototyping is used frequently. If developed, it should be available much earlier than the actual product. A prototype should not be confused with a pilot. *Pilot projects* are normally done to gain experience with a new methodology, such as object-oriented design or a new programming language. A pilot project may or may not involve a prototype.

Modeling is a method to describe a system in a way that makes particular properties visible or allows some automated analysis. To use an economist's definition [Baum01]: 'A model is a representation of a theory or part of theory, often used to gain insight into cause and effect'. If we are unable to build a model, then our theory about how things relate or interact is inadequate. For an artifact still in the process of being created, the model depends on how we think the artifact should be. The quality of a model depends on how close it comes to reality and how well it explains the properties in question. A dynamic model of a system usually consists of a set of *states*, which are the values that the attributes of a system can take. During its execution, a program or system passes through a sequence of successive states.

The following related terms are used throughout this book. As stated before, a *project* is an organizational effort over a limited period of time, staffed by people and equipped with the other resources required to produce a certain result. For a development project, the result to be achieved is a *product*. In our case a product is a system, consisting of hardware, software, or both, to be used by people other than the developers. The term *process* is used here to designate a set of activities and methods used.

Another important set of terms is illustrated in Fig. 2-1. A *failure* is the inability of a product to perform its expected function, or of a project to achieve its expected results. Sometimes the word 'problem' is used instead. A *fault* is a deficiency in a product that causes a failure. If a fault or failure is a consequence of a human activity we call it an *error*. Most faults observed for software systems are errors, usually introduced during development or installation. Faults introduced during manufacturing may be human errors or mechanical failures (e.g. blank page in the documentation, unreadable electronic medium, etc.). In the hardware part of a system, faults can also be caused by unexpected power variations, temperature changes, water, dust, or

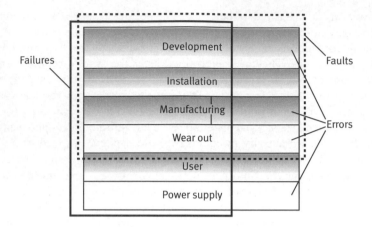

Fig. 2-1 Failures, faults, and errors

wear. To differentiate between errors in the product (code, device), and documentation errors, we shall use the term *defect*. Normally a defect requires an engineering change; in the case of software, a code correction or code fix. Until a fix is available, a temporary circumvention (or work-around) of the problem may be needed. A product failure can result from a fault, a user error, or a power supply outage. The same fault in a system can lead to multiple failures. Not all faults lead to failures: they exist, but remain undiscovered and cause no harm.

The *quality* of a product is usually defined as the degree to which it meets customer requirements. This view emphasizes one side of quality: the user's perspective. A more comprehensive view also includes the developer's or manufacturer's side.

View	Criterion	Definition
User	Availability	High degree of access
	Reliability	Low failure rate
	Efficiency	Economic resource consumption
	Installability	Easy and fast bring-up in user environment
	Usability	Well adapted to skills and preferences of user
	Robustness	Safe reaction to user errors and hardware failures
	Safety/Security	Low damage in case of negligent/malicious use
Developer	Testability	Good documentation and structure
	Maintainability	High readability and modifiability
	Portability	Low dependency on technical environment
	Localizability	Adaptable to national and regional requirements
	Reusability	High modularity and completeness

Fig. 2-2 Important software quality criteria

The quality of software products from a user's point of view can be
expressed as the fulfillment of several properties: availability, reliability, efficiency, installability, usability, robustness, and safety/security. In addition,
several criteria have to be added if a developer's interests are considered as
well. These criteria are testability, maintainability, localizability, portability,
and reusability. A short definition of each criterion is given in Fig. 2-2. Of
these properties, reliability is usually the most important and is often used
as a synonym for quality. In the case of software products, reliability (and
hence quality) is frequently expressed as number of errors or defects per
thousand lines of code (defects/KLOC). The problem is that this is a developer-oriented measure. A user-oriented measure for reliability is the number
of problems per user month. The relationship between these two measures
is complicated and depends on the actual usage of a system. System availability is a function of the number and the duration of interruptions. One
popular definition is:

Availability = MTTF/(MTTF + MTTR)

where MTTF = mean time to failure and MTTR = mean time to repair. The
unit used is usually percent (e.g. 99.9%). The inverse is down time, frequently expressed in hours per year.

The term *correctness*, which will be used later, denotes a subset of reliability, namely consistency with a formal specification. It is defined only if a
specification exists. If a user plans to use a software product as it is, i.e. he
or she does not have the intention to modify it, he or she should be concerned about the user-oriented criteria only. The intended use of a product
has to take into account typical handling mistakes. If safety and security are
issues, careless and malicious use have to be considered as well.

2.2 General observations

Requirements are supposed to define the 'What' and 'Why', rather than the
'How', of a system, i.e. it should state which functions should be there, but
not how they are provided. In practice, this separation cannot be strictly
maintained. Some requirements may directly prescribe certain design or
implementation aspects, such as compatibility with existing interfaces or language to be used for the implementation. In order to be able to define certain
requirements, some basic design decisions may have to be made first. Also,
developers may need an overall idea how certain functions can be implemented before they can accept them as meaningful requirements. As for all
development activities, one has to assess the consequences of each decision
for all consecutive steps. This occurs by mentally performing the next steps,
or if that is not sufficient, by actually advancing a part of it. Prototyping is
an example of that. As Davis [Davi90] put it, one person's 'What' is always
some other person's 'How', depending on the role he plays.

Requirements definition, prototyping, and modeling

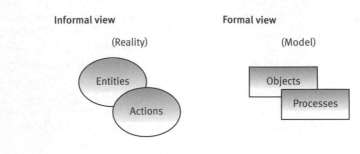

Fig. 2-3 Two world views

If the requirements are modeled, this amounts to a mapping of two different world views. The terms that may initially be used as part of an informal language have also to be mapped in terms of a formal language or system. As indicated in Fig. 2-3, entities in a colloquial language may become objects in an artificial model; actions may become procedures. Even if the same names are used on both sides, they no longer mean the same. One can only ensure that some basic properties that are relevant for the application are kept the same. Whatever approach is taken, this basic step remains. Any attempt to avoid it may increase the danger that misinterpretations will occur. The further the design of the target system evolves, the more the meaning of the terms diverges.

A system may be able to assume millions of different states. The states of a system can be modeled with the aid of finite state machines. The problem is how to structure the states in a meaningful way. A process model expresses which signals cause which state transitions. The model can be physical in nature (i.e mechanical, hydraulic, electrical, etc.) or symbolic (i.e. made up of words, graphs, or mathematical notation). In the case of physical models, the emphasis is on the understandability by humans; in the case of mathematical models, the focus is on the possibility of deriving certain information using computers. We may create models of existing or planned systems. If the system is complex, an abstraction is chosen that leaves out some aspects or properties. Examples are functional models, data models, or performance models. A model may not be executable. If it is, it requires an input that describes, rather than emulates the actual input; the output may be a description of the expected output or of other system properties. In a performance model it may be the amount of storage consumed by a data structure (given in bytes) or the time needed for a given task (expressed in seconds).

A complete specification has to be such that no legal state is excluded; nor does it allow that illegal states are considered legal. Of course, requirements definitions need to be 'good enough' only, not descriptive of all legal states. Agreement should be reached between all the stakeholders. Normally, requirements are a moving target. The reasons for changes may be technological advances, competitive products, regulatory constraints, external standards, marketing approaches, or financial conditions of the sponsoring company.

In an ideal development process, the entire requirements definition should be completed before design is started, in case an additional requirement changes the basic design structure. Since design and implementation may cost considerable amounts of money, one usually cannot afford to spend most of it before requirements are defined. On the other hand, it is an illusion to expect that perfect requirements can be formulated ahead of time. Both the developers and the users may need some feedback. They require a learning cycle. This is particularly important if dealing with a new application area, where developers and users have no prior experience.

When discussing the requirements process, we assume that customer and developer are not the same person; they may even belong to different organizations. The term customer is used to designate the person or group of persons who have a vested interest in the system. He or she is initiating and usually funding the development, and is the key stakeholder. However, he or she may not be the final user. As part of the requirements process he or she may ask representative users to contribute. Neither the customer nor the users have to be IT professionals, while the developer's side always consists of IT professionals. Directly interfacing with the customer may be people with limited technical knowledge – these could be sales people or system analysts.

An explicit requirements definition is less important if the target environment is familiar to the developer. End users who develop applications for their own use hardly spend time to gather requirements. Such efforts would in fact be counter-productive. However, if the project is outsourced and the time and money spent on it are critical, then careful requirements gathering and analysis are key. Systems developed merely for learning purposes or fun have requirements too, but they are not being considered here. The importance of a careful requirements definition clearly depends on the criticality of the system planned. There is a wide disparity between the criticality of a desktop game and that of a nuclear power station control system. Different types of products have different requirements, and they may change over time. In a public procurement situation, the requirements statement may be the basis on which bids are made.

In the case of products intended for a large user community, particularly for a consumer market, it is important to distinguish between the requirements of existing customers and those of non-customers. If the current customer base is small and specialized it may express requirements that make the expansion into new markets more difficult rather than easier. Many potential customers may not like a product because of properties that current customers love. The information obtainable from unsatisfied customers may contain similar clues.

2.3 Applicable laws and their theories

The laws quoted here mainly express warnings. They are based on the experience of some failed projects and the analysis of errors. This should not cloud the fact that the large majority of projects are successful.

2.3.1 Glass' law

The definition of requirements is usually the first step in a project. Robert Glass has investigated failed projects over several decades. The law that is quoted here is based on the conclusions of a recent book [Glas98].

> Requirement deficiences are the prime source of project failures. (L1)

Applicability Requirement deficiencies cause problems in many projects. The requirements may be determined incorrectly, or not enough attention given to their definition. Setting the goals correctly for any project is a demanding task. Although there are projects with well understood, specified, and stable requirements, more often this is not the case. More typical is the incomplete or erroneous requirements definition, especially if the definition is done by a third party for the customer and developer. But removing the requirements definition step is of course no solution to the difficulty.

Evidence The evidence provided by Glass for this law is essentially based on case studies. No controlled experiments were done. They would have been quite difficult. Of the projects that Glass has studied, three failed in his opinion because of requirements problems. All three achieved world-wide attention:

■ the baggage handling system for the Denver airport;
■ the welfare administration system for the state of Florida;
■ the air-traffic control system of the Federal Aviation Administration (FAA).

Glass' assessment is that the requirements were (1) far too many, (2) unstable due to late changes, (3) ambiguous, and (4) incomplete. In the case of Denver airport, the city of Denver had written the specifications for the baggage conveyer system without consulting its users – the airlines. In the recovery effort, three different baggage handling systems have been built, one each for the two major airlines, and a third for all others. The implementers of the Florida welfare system were told to reuse several million lines of code from an existing centralized system, although their requirements called for a distributed system. The FAA system was a long way from reaching its performance goals. The air-traffic controllers wanted to use the new 20" display units in the same fashion as they were using paper slips before. They (rightly) insisted on the same response times and the same low number of key strokes. Additional evidence supporting this law can be found in the studies by Curtis [Curt88] and Davis [Davi90]. Brooks [Broo87] alludes to the same when he says: 'The hardest part of building a software system is deciding precisely what to build. No other part of the conceptual work is so difficult, and is more difficult to rectify later'.

A recent field study on the requirements definition process is reported by Hofmann and Lehner [Hofm01]. The authors interviewed 15 teams in nine companies in the telecommunication and banking sector. The best results were obtained by those groups that had the 'right combination of knowledge, resources and process'. The knowledge aspect required getting the involvement of customers, consulting all sources, and assigning highly skilled people. Resources were sufficient if 15–30 percent of the project effort was spend on requirement definition. A successful process concentrated on prioritization, traceability and validation of requirements. Sometimes multiple cycles were required.

Theory The proper definition of requirements is a hard problem. The main reasons for this are differing needs of different user groups, natural conflicts of interest between participating persons or groups, and the difficulty of prioritization among conflicting requirements. Requirements definition is a process of learning and negotiation. Both the developers and users learn while implementing or using a system. The knowledge of every person involved is limited. People do not know everything and forget much of what they know over time. Sharing of knowledge does not occur by itself. These problems are inherent and will not go away as technology progresses.

2.3.2 Boehm's first law

While Glass looked at projects as a whole, earlier studies clearly hinted in the same direction. These studies were concerned with the analysis of errors made by the developers. When analyzing those errors, the first question is: 'Where in the development process was this error made?' This leads to an assignment of errors to individual phases or activities in the lifecycle. We quote here one of the most significant discoveries in this respect, attributed to Barry Boehm [Boeh75]. This law combines two observations that are closely related.

> Errors are most frequent during the requirements and design activities and are the more expensive the later they are removed. **(L2)**

Applicability Around 1974, several groups realized that the early phases, namely requirements definition and design are most heavily loaded with errors. Requirement errors are as numerous but more serious than design errors. If a developer does not know the domain, he or she can easily be misled. Nobody tells the developer that he or she is trying to solve the wrong problem until he or she interacts with customers or users again, which may be as late as installation. Design errors are found by the responsible developer, the developer of a related construct, or by a user who discovers the problem either accidentally or through a review process.

The cost incurred by an error is larger the later in the project cycle it is removed. It applies to all large system developments. The earlier an error is removed, the lower its cost. In other words, the lifetime of errors is the problem. Lifetime is the time between introduction or injection of an error and its removal. Since errors are unavoidable, provisions should be made to detect and remove them quickly. Put another way, if we know that we can catch errors early and completely, we can afford a higher number of errors in early stages of the project.

Evidence The evidence for this law is also based on case studies only. Most studies of software errors done before 1974, e.g. [Rube68], were concerned primarily with coding errors. About 1974, several studies became known that drastically changed this view. Boehm's paper refers to a study done at TRW in 1974 where 224 errors were analyzed. They were detected in a system consisting of about 100 KLOC. The main conclusion was that design errors outweigh coding errors, 64 percent versus 36 percent. Of the errors found during acceptance testing, the ratio was even 45:9. In that particular project, 54 percent of the errors were found no earlier than the acceptance test. It took twice as much time to diagnose and correct design errors versus coding errors.

At the same time as Boehm, an error analysis was done by one of the authors of this book [Endr75]. It will be discussed in more detail in Chapter 4. It also concluded that about 60–70 percent of all errors to be found in a project are either requirements or design errors. In the case of an operating system, this was not expected, because the application knowledge lay with the developers. A similar relationship in the number of design and implementation errors was observed in 1984 by Basili and Perricone [Basi84] for Fortran programs in an aerospace application where the design was done by people with good domain knowledge.

At about the same time various statistics appeared, showing that the cost of errors are the higher the longer they stay in a product. Although this observation has been attributed to many people, the first publication we know of that mentions it is from Peter Hiemann [Hiem74]. It is based on internal studies done at IBM between 1972–1974. Hiemann's characterization of the problem is reproduced in Fig. 2-4. In this figure, the assumption is made that the cost to remove errors at coding time is negligible. When the cost of inspections are considered the picture changes.

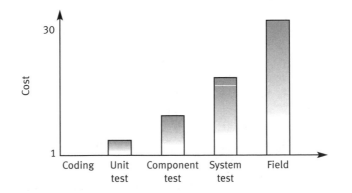

Fig. 2-4 Cost of problems per phase

Additional evidence supporting the second half of this law can be found in [Boeh76] and [Daly77]. An evaluation of several estimates is contained in [Boeh81]. It gives a comparison of earlier estimates from IBM, GE and TRW.

Theory Humans usually have problems if a multitude of situations need to be thought of at the same time. We tend to think of the main line only, and forget the special cases, the exceptions. Even if the human mind supports parallel processing, this does not mean that different units investigate in different directions. We possess no inherent means or mechanisms to explore a domain exhaustively (unless it can be represented visually). Errors of omission are therefore more frequent than misunderstandings. The costs for changes of a system grow as the development cycle proceeds. The reason is that subsequent investments are based on decisions made before. The number of people affected may grow from less than ten to several hundreds or thousands.

2.3.3 Boehm's second law

Prototyping is a well-known remedy against requirements errors. Although much has been written on this subject, we quote as a law the claims as derived from an empirical study by Boehm *et al.* [Boeh84a].

> Prototyping (significantly) reduces requirement and design errors, especially for user interfaces. (L3)

Applicability The usefulness of prototypes is hardly an issue. Prototypes of hardware systems are built frequently. One may use chips of a previous generation to build a new device or to explore some new architectural features. For most interactive systems, prototyping is appropriate. It has the advantage that it crosses the gap between description and implementation. As such it can communicate requirements better than a specification. A prototype may be helpful to educate the development team, spread confidence among users, and to convince the sponsor. Prototyping is a vehicle to facilitate participatory development; it reduces the possible tension between users and developers (the 'us versus them' syndrome). Depending on the type of questions to be answered, different types of prototypes may be constructed. In the case of software systems these types are:

■ *Demonstration prototype*: It may be used to help clarify some user requirements. It may demonstrate certain features that the user cannot imagine otherwise. It may impress the customer and win his or her confidence. The developer is not learning from the prototype, but gains other advantages, for example, a mock-up of the user interface or a 4GL implementation of a database query.

■ *Decision prototype*: It can be useful to help select the proper design among alternatives. It helps the designer evaluate decisions through a partial implementation. The prototype is created to answer a particular question. Its main benefit is a learning effect for the developers. They are done mainly during design, but may be useful also during construction.

■ *Educational prototype:* Its purpose is not to arrive at a specific design decision. It may make developers familiar with a new technology or may be used to help clarify some method or tool questions ahead of time, for example, the performance of a new version of a compiler. It may be applied during design, but mainly to prepare the implementation.

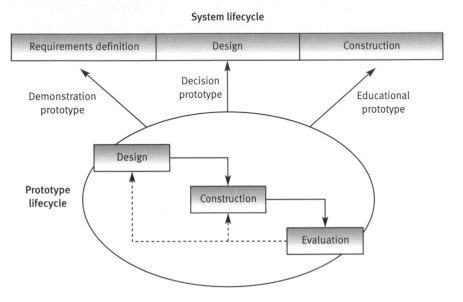

Fig. 2-5 Prototypes in the system lifecycle

As shown in Fig. 2-5, the different types have their use in different phases of a project. All three forms are normally throw-away prototypes. At least they should be, since they are not intended to become part of the final system. For software prototypes in particular, there is a high risk that prototypes are not being thrown away but used as part of the final product, which is in conflict with the goal to achieve a high product quality. Prototypes should normally go through a lifecycle of their own and be evaluated, i.e. tested, against the questions they were supposed to answer. Many are only constructed then forgotten. Prototyping typically has an iterative project cycle.

The law, as stated, puts the emphasis on the reduction of errors. As will be shown later, the reduction of errors entails cost reductions as well. The amount of reduction is not quantified, however. To be significant, at least 20–30 percent have to occur. This applies to all laws, even if the word 'significantly' is omitted. Changes in the range of 5–20 percent can be due to measurement or set-up differences, or can be caused by uncontrolled interferences.

Evidence The study by Boehm *et al.* [Boeh84a] is the first controlled experiment referred to in this book. However, it is not the earliest one. The study addresses the usefulness of prototypes for requirements definition. The experiments were conducted as part of a graduate course in software engineering and involved seven teams developing the same small system (2-4 KLOC). Four groups used a specification-driven approach, whilst the other three used a prototyping approach. The system to be developed was an interactive version of the COCOMO-I cost-estimating model. For the specification-driven approach both a requirements and a design specification were required. In the other approach, instead of the specifications an early prototype was required. Both had to provide a users' manual together with the running system. The same level of feedback was given to the specifications and to the prototype. In both cases, an acceptance test was performed, verifying functionality, robustness, ease of use, and ease of learning. The results of this experiment were as follows:

■ The prototype approach resulted in a somewhat smaller system (same overall function, fewer LOC).
■ The productivity was about the same in both cases (with larger varia-tions in the specifying approach).
■ The quality of the resulting systems were rated about equal. The proto-typing approach came out lower in terms of functionality and robustness, but higher in terms of ease of use and ease of learning.
■ There were no clear observations concerning maintainability.

Although this experiment was conducted in an academic environment, these conclusions are essentially in line with related experiences made in industry. The main advantage is better usability or user satisfaction. The motivational boost resulting from a prototype is a typical by-product for inexperienced teams. That the prototype approach shows more resistance to adding non-essential features is true only if the prototype code is the basis of the final product. As stated in the paper, the emphasis given to either specifications or prototypes should be based on a risk assessment. Specifications are not nec-essary for small, user-developed products; prototypes are not necessary if both the user interface and the overall design are given or well-understood.

Many reports exist on the successful use of prototypes. A report by Bernstein [Bern93] talks about a 40 percent reduction in effort because of it. The same developer gives a warning, however, about a well-known danger of prototyp-ing: 'Our customers loved it so much that we packaged it for sale'. This case is referred to as 'trap number 1' by the author. Not only customers may cause this to happen, but also the developer's management or the sales force. Prototypes can also be dangerous in the sense that they may mislead developers. A typical example is performance: a prototype handling only the normal cases fitted nicely into the allocated storage, but the fully-fledged system didn't.

Theory Prototypes give a view of the system in the way it will actually appear to the user. Contrary to other design representations it does not depend on a person's power of imagination to visualize it. It is a partial embodiment of the real system, not an abstraction. It may over-emphasize some details and thereby hide or distort the total view of the system. Prototypes need to be created for systems under development only, not for existing systems.

Comment Most developers are reluctant to throw prototypes away. The reason is that if the prototype was well done, people say, 'Why do we have to wait for the thing to be redone?' If it was poorly done, the project may not continue. In most engineering fields, the materials used to construct prototypes clearly differ from the final product. It is only in the case of software prototypes that managers can say, 'Why don't you add a few instructions and ship this to the customer?'

2.3.4 Davis' law

Modeling is used extensively to either represent an actual or a planned system. As stated before, models may be mechanical, hydraulic, electrical, graphic, or arithmetic in nature. This can be summarized in the following law, which is taken from an extensive study by Alan Davis [Davi90].

> The value of a model depends on the view taken, but none is best for all purposes. **(L4)**

Applicability Models are a very useful form to describe systems. This is true before, during, and after development of the system. Examples of models used in natural science are models describing the evolution of a star; the atom model; or the operation of a cell. They are first an intellectual concept, but can be transformed or expressed in a visible representation. In computing science, we may use models to study the static structure of the system's objects or components, the logical structure of the data used, or the dynamic structure of the interacting tasks and processes.

Model view	Elements considered	Practical notations	Mathematical equivalent
Data	Data structures, data relationships	Entity relationship diagram (ERD)	Heterogeneous algebra
Process	Processes, interconnections	Dataflow diagram (DFD)	Process graphs
State transition	Events, states	State diagram, including hierarchically structured state chart (Harel)	Finite state machine
Structure	Objects, classes, components	Class diagram, Component diagram	I/O functions
Behavior	Interfaces, message histories	Message sequence chart	Dataflow graphs

Fig. 2-6 Modeling views and notations

Fig. 2-6 gives an overview of the most frequently used models in software and systems engineering. In software development, at least two models are usually used, depending on which view of the system is more critical: it could be the process and data models; the data and state models; or all three. Thanks to the effort of the UML initiative [Rati97], the notations used for the different views have been largely standardized. Some effort has been made to develop mathematical foundations for the various models. The right-most column of the figure mentions the mathematical concept suggested for this purpose by Broy [Broy01]. With a proper mathematical foundation, it will be easier to determine where individual models overlap, if at all. It also allows the definition of some form of a refinement concept. With this, the relationship between different stages of a model can be expressed.

Whether modeling helps, and if so how much, depends on the situation. Models can normally be checked for consistency, but not executed. Like human models (which are also called mannequins), they frequently end up in beauty contests. Usually, models cannot be converted automatically into a prototype. They therefore have a life of their own and may grow or die. If they grow, the risk is high that all they will amount to is just another nice artifice to be admired. They distract from the real thing – the system. All that is needed are models that are 'good-enough' for the purpose in hand. If not countered, the development effort for a model can easily reach the same magnitude as that of the actual product. The advantage of a model is that it may answer questions that are difficult to obtain from the actual product, or it may do that before the product is available or in environments where the product cannot be used. Every program is a model of some real-world application.

Evidence The study that Davis did is a qualitative rather than quantitative analysis, and uses subjective rather than objective criteria. It is valuable, nevertheless. Davis selects three very different applications and tries to apply several different modeling approaches. The applications are of increasing difficulty as far as the problems to be solved are concerned. The applications are:

- Automating a book distribution company: including ordering, shipment, and accounting; possibly human resources, payroll, inventory, conveyor belts, and robots to move books.
- Automating the landing of a helicopter: ensuring a safe landing on one of 250 helipads within a large city, even in the case of zero visibility and an unconscious pilot.
- Transporting people from New York to Tokyo in 30 minutes: solutions to be considered include space shuttle, tunnel, bullet train, or digitizing and transmitting passengers (as in the movie *Star Trek*).

For all three applications, a problem analysis is done first, then the behavioral (functional) requirements are specified. In the first case, several different approaches can be used, i.e. an object-oriented analysis (OOA), a function-oriented analysis (DFD), or a state-oriented analysis. The conclusion is that all three methods lead to useful but different results. In fact, different aspects are emphasized by each approach. The second and third examples show that the contributions by the above techniques are small compared to the domain-specific questions that have to be investigated first. In the third example, it is unlikely that a solution can be found with today's technologies (a so-called 'hard problem'). The documentation, i.e. specification, step is only performed for the first two examples. The following techniques are applied: finite state machines, state charts (in the form proposed by Harel), a requirements engineering validation system (REVS), Petri nets, decision tables, a program design language (PDL), and two specification description languages (SDL, PAISLey). Davis finds that, like a skilled carpenter who builds a piece of furniture, one should use different tools and techniques for different types of job. Of course, the tools should co-operate in the sense that data entered once should not have to be re-entered again, and results produced by one tool should be understood by the other.

Davis' exercise showed that most of the available methods are more useful for the solution description than for the problem definition. The problem definition depends heavily on domain-specific knowledge. Although the first example appears technically trivial, a clear statement is needed to specify which of the above-mentioned functions are really to be provided. In the second example, the message is that computer scientists should not believe that they can assume responsibility for the correctness of a solution without relying on expertise from such fields as aeronautics, meteorology, and medicine. As the third example shows, computers may only play a small part in the solution, if at all. By taking an example that is clearly science fiction, Davis wants to warn his readers that science fiction aspects may be hidden in any requirement, even if it looks quite innocent. He concludes that the best this project could produce is a two-year feasibility study. We believe that saying 'No' even prior to such a feasibility study, would be the ethically correct attitude.

Theory A model of reality is an aid to explain our understanding. Models are descriptions of a system only. They are indirect views or abstractions, leaving out those things that are not considered important for the time being. Abstractions are useful for certain types of human understanding only. It is the conceptual knowledge that is enhanced. Not all users need this, want this or would even tolerate this. It may be asking too much of them. From the point of view of the system to be built, abstractions are a departure from reality, which, depending on the notation used, frequently deceive the observer. The movement of stars in a planetarium, or the orbits of electrons in an atomic model, have only a faint resemblance to reality. Nevertheless, such models often serve a useful purpose.

Comment A group of models not shown above may serve in performance investigations, describing the load distribution in a network or the timing of a transaction. They are usually dynamic models and may be executed. They can make timing relationships visible, either in slow motion or by time compression. A reference model may help in the communications among experts; it gives them a new language to express themselves. As Brooks [Broo75] has pointed out, if a model abstracts from the complexity of the system, it is abstracting the essence. In a software system, the repetition of identical parts is easily dealt with: they become common code or subroutines. The complexity of a software system results from the abundance of different parts. None can be ignored, however. Some may be lumped together to form subclasses, thus allowing us to factor out some properties. These subclasses can mentally be treated as units (called chunks later), so that we can get a better intellectual grasp of them.

2.3.5 Booch's first hypothesis

The most pervasive approach to modeling in recent years has been the object model. Its advantages have been eloquently presented by Grady Booch [Booc91]. Many variations of the object model have been introduced by other authors, e.g. Jacobson [Jaco92], Rumbaugh [Rumb91], Shlaer/Mellor [Shla88], and Wirfs-Brock [Wirf90]. With the following hypothesis we summarize the claims as made by Booch for the requirements activities.

Object model reduces communication problems between analysts and users. **(H1)**

Applicability The object model was first introduced into programming languages (Simula, Smalltalk, C++). Later it was applied to design and requirements analysis also. In the requirements and design phases it prescribes the way the system is divided into components or subsystems. It also postulates a specific form of interaction (message passing) among components. The arguments in favor of this approach are that (1) it appeals to the workings of the human cognition, (2) it facilitates the transition from requirements to design and implementation, (3) it treats data and processes simultaneously, and (4) it uses 'sound software engineering concepts', like abstraction, encapsulation, modularity, hierarchy, strong typing, and concurrency. While the values of the object model are hardly disputed for design and implementation, the situation is not as clear for the requirements definition activity. There is also some discussion whether concepts like inheritance and polymorphism should be used in the requirements phase. They may be looked at as techniques to aid the implementation.

Evidence In 1994, Capers Jones [Jone94] complained that there is a severe lack of quantitative data to support the claims of the object-oriented paradigm. There are more data now, but they are far from conclusive. A survey of the state of the art is given by Briand *et al.* [Bria99]. Of the empirical studies looking at object-oriented requirements definition, the study by Moynihan [Moyn96] stands out. It compares object-oriented analysis (Rumbaugh's method) with functional decomposition (following J. Martin).

The participants were 20 Irish business managers. The author asked them to comment on the two requirement definitions for the same hypothetical project (an IT solution for a health farm). His conclusion was that the functional model was easier to understand, more useful in detecting omissions and inconsistencies, provoked more comments and questions, gave a more holistic understanding of the business, and better helped to evaluate likely implementation benefits and priorities. This experiment was intended to emphasize the users' rather than the developers' perspective and did not look at potential cost savings in the subsequent phases, nor did it address the reuse aspect. Another weakness is the fact that the object-oriented analysis model was given in the form of a static object model only. Had a use-case model (as defined by Jacobson) been added, the result may have been different.

2.4 More on requirements definition

In this section, we will focus on several activities in more detail. We consider them as essential aspects of the requirements definition process. The discussion on prototyping and modeling will not be extended.

2.4.1 Vision statement

It is considered good practice to start the requirements process with a *vision statement*. This is a half or one-page document outlining the overall goals that should be achieved. It should be agreed to by everybody that may be affected by the new system, particularly by the highest level of management. For a small system, this may be all that is needed. The subsequent work has the purpose of filling in the necessary details. If in the process it turns out that the vision cannot be achieved, the vision statement should be revised and re-discussed.

2.4.2 Requirements elicitation and prioritization

Requirements have to be gathered from any source that can contribute. This process is often called *requirements elicitation* or requirements discovery. Contributions will come mainly from current or potential customers and users. If the funding does not come directly from customers, there may be other groups who have both interest and influence. In addition, third party experts, legal authorities, and standards bodies may have an input. However, the requirements of the expected users should get the highest priority. Therefore, one should understand who the users are, and what their skills, motivations and working environments are. They may not tell those things that are naturally part of their environment. It is important to make all requirements explicit by listing them.

After requirements have been identified, they should be prioritized. Three priority classes are usually enough: 'mandatory', 'essential', and 'nice to have'. Yourdon [Your97] who advocates a similar prioritization, calls the three categories 'must do', 'should do', and 'could do'. The prioritization

should be agreed to by all stakeholders. It is important to recognize that
requirements ranking high for a long-living product, may have lowest priority for a one-shot application. This is particularly obvious for several of the non-functional requirements, e.g. efficiency, maintainability, and portability.

2.4.3 Knowledge acquisition and management

In many cases, the requirements process depends on the discovery, clarification, and collection of problem-oriented knowledge. It is related to a specific application domain. Without this knowledge, we are not able to determine what functions the planned system should have, or whether it can be built at all. If the knowledge exists, people have to be motivated to make it available. This may be easy, if these people are the potential beneficiaries of the planned system. The traditional ways of collecting information are:

- *Interviews with individuals:* time-consuming; may cover small fraction of users only; allows two-way communication.
- *Questionnaires:* allow broad coverage, depending on return rate; essentially one-way communication only.
- *Meetings with groups:* good communication modus; positive motivational effect; immediate resolution of conflicts; limited degree of detail.
- *Surveys and studies:* necessary to understand detailed data and external trends; gives objective complement for other methods.

If the users are not supposed to know who is asking questions, so-called focus groups can be used. In this case, people may receive compensation for the time spent with the investigators. If novel solutions are sought, brainstorming is a popular method, where any wild idea coming to somebody's mind, will be recorded. As the knowledge collected has to be structured and organized, the selection or sorting out process will occur in a subsequent session. This is an application for database systems, sometimes referred to as knowledge bases.

2.4.4 Feasibility study or risk analysis

For a larger system, a feasibility study should be performed before the requirements are formally accepted. In this process, an answer to the following question for every item on the requirements list should be obtained: 'Can this requirement be met with the technology and the knowledge that is currently available?' This can be extended into a complete risk analysis. In this case, non-technical exposures will be addressed also. This may concern such questions as: 'Can this be developed or built in the time frame allocated?' 'Is the budget adequate?' and 'Are there competitive exposures?' To answer these questions, a form of partial design has to be done. Prototyping may also be considered.

2.4.5 Functional and non-functional requirements

Normally, the main emphasis is on functional requirements. In almost all cases, these have to be complemented by non-functional ones. Non-functional requirements are often tacit requirements, i.e. they are not explicitly specified. They may address such quality criteria as portability, reliability, efficiency, usability, testability, maintainability, and reusability. Their consideration may have a greater impact on the cost of the system than some of the functional requirements. They typically conflict with each other, and with the functional requirements. For this reason, the trade-off possibilities should be specified. As a case in point, the efficiency of a software solution usually conflicts with most of the other criteria. If efficiency is not specified, it will be neglected. No doubt the importance of this criterion has declined considerably during the last few decades because an easy remedy was often provided by spending more on hardware resources.

2.4.6 Safety and security requirements

A specific form of non-functional requirements concern the safety and the security of a system. *Safety* risks may cause harm to individual users, to groups, or to the public at large. Safety is of concern, particularly if computers control physical devices or plants, such as car brakes, planes, or nuclear power stations. Any malfunction of the computer may cause harm not through itself, but through the devices it controls. *Security* becomes an issue whenever valuable data are stored. These have to be protected against accidental misuse, as well as against attacks by malicious contenders. A well-known threat exists for networked systems because of viruses, Trojan horses, and worms. A special form are the so-called denial-of-service attacks. A network site may be flooded by millions of messages so that it may become incapable of performing its regular business. Almost every month new versions of these threats appear.

Some of the attacks occurring may be politically motivated. For some organizations it was a bitter lesson to learn that the large majority of their security violations originate from inside, i.e. from their own employees. Unfortunately, this area has become a playground, not only for criminals, but also for students and teenagers who like to misuse their intellectual energy to cause problems for business and society. The nature and priority of each of these threats has to be spelled out. Each one requires unique forms of protection and means of recovery after an attack. The recovery after a breakdown due to technical failure of the system is only a special case of this. Safety and security is an important example, where all requirements have to be recognized early, and the trade-off possibilities identified, before the design can start.

2.4.7 Detailed documentation of requirements

Well-managed projects often adhere to the principle that requirements only exist if they are documented. We refer to this document as the requirements specification. Only if the requirements are specified do we have a basis to compare the design against. The documentation can be at different levels of detail, depending on the intended readers. Frequently, large companies or government agencies have developed standard forms for requirements specifications, one example of which is the IEEE Guide to Software Requirements Specifications [IEEE84]. The borderline between requirements and design often is blurred. In such cases, it may be helpful to say that design information is given as an illustration only. Functional requirements can be expressed in unstructured text or in some formal notation. For the programming interface it may be a formal syntax notation; for the user interface it may be manual pages or screen images. For data and system structures, graphical diagrams are the favorite notation. Non-functional requirements are always expressed in text format.

Any notation used should keep the reading audience in mind. If the key reviewers and readers of the document have no computing science background, plain text and simple diagrams are the preferred medium. To describe the system for developers, it is customary to include a requirements model as discussed earlier. For modeling purposes, the UML notation [Rati97] seems to be favored above other graphical notations. This notation is currently supported by most CASE tools. The UML notation builds on the Object Modeling Technique (OMT) of Rumbaugh *et al.* [Rumb91], the Entity Relationship Diagrams (ERDs) as advocated by Peter Chen [Chen76], the state charts of Dave Harel [Hare88], and the Use Case notation of Jacobson [Jaco92]. The only older notation still in use is the Data Flow Diagrams (DFDs) of Tom DeMarco [DeMa78]. However, these individual notations will not be discussed here. Sometimes it is advocated that the requirements specification should make use of so-called formal notations. These will be discussed in Chapter 3.

2.4.8 Buy-in, validation and approval of requirements

The success of any development project depends primarily on the acceptance of the final product by the intended users. Unless we are talking about products that are acquired commercially off-the-shelf (so-called COTS systems) it is crucial that users are convinced that they had an influence on its generation. The best way to achieve this is through user participation. This joint effort always starts with the requirements definition. Users have to 'buy-in' on the requirements, i.e. consider them as theirs. If input to the requirements comes from multiple sources, conflicts have to be resolved. The resulting compromise should be validated again by asking for a detailed review and a formal approval by the users. In the case of COTS systems, people have to be found who represent the potential users. However, even if the highest level of user participation is achieved, this does not relieve the developer of any one of his or her responsibilities. For example, it remains his or her obligation to make sure that the originator knows what his or her requirement means to the project.

2.4.9 Requirements tracing and change control

For a large system, it may be necessary to make sure that no documented requirement is forgotten. In one particular case, an implementer felt obliged to demonstrate for every line of source code which requirement caused it to be there. This is hopefully an exception. Such a tracing of requirements to their origin may be very helpful for a thorough test coverage, but is difficult and laborious.

Requirements may change, during the life of a project, either prior to shipment or after. It is therefore necessary to establish a change control procedure for requirements. This procedure has to ensure that all parties concerned learn about the change when it is proposed, agree to its adoption, and follow up on all activities triggered by this change. This should apply equally when adding or removing code, performing regression tests, or making documentation changes.

2.5 Examples and study material

2.5.1 Text formatting requirements

To illustrate the types of errors occurring in software systems, we will use a small example program, originally published by Peter Naur [Naur69a]. Naur used it as an illustration of a formal and rigorous development process. It is a real toy example but large enough to make some important points. Because of the errors contained in it, this example has subsequently been used by several authors, particularly by Goodenough [Good75] and Myers [Myer78]. Its requirements specification consists of the following:

> *Given an input text consisting of words separated by blanks or carriage return (CR) characters. Transform the text into a line-by-line format where a line should start only where a blank or CR character was in the input text. Each output line should be as full as possible, and no line should have more than a given number (n) of characters.*
>
> *Peter Naur [Naur69a]*

A careful inspection of this text reveals the following potential problems for a person trying to design a solution. They can be classified as requirement errors:

r1: No condition specified for the normal end of the program.
r2: No information on the role of the CR character in the output file.
r3: No information on how to handle errors, e.g. words longer than n characters.
r4: Unspecified assumption on the sequence and non-changeability of words.
r5: No information on storage formats or medium of input and output.
r6: Open whether multiple consecutive blanks are allowed in the output.

In later chapters, the design and the implementation of this program will be given. For some of the above problems, arbitrary assumptions will be made by the developer in later phases.

2.5.2 Digital library requirements

Systems supporting digital libraries are well suited to illustrate data-intensive applications. The following example from [Endr00] is used to show how different model types can complement each other. The example uses a UML-like notation [Rati97]. Three models are shown. Together with the explanatory text, they convey a rough picture of what the library system is supposed to offer.

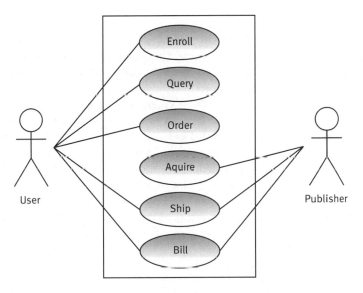

Fig. 2-7 Use case model

Use case model The use case model given in Fig. 2-7 describes what services are to be provided by the library system and with whom any external interaction takes place. There are two types of external actors: a user and a publisher. They may be interacting with the library through other systems rather than in person. It is assumed that the library provides six types of services, five of which interface with the users, and three with the publishers. Users are either the customers, or are representatives of a customer. Publisher is the generic name used for all suppliers of documents to the library.

Class model The class model shown in Fig. 2-8 is a static model showing the highest level of the object classes the library is dealing with. The library data and services is shown as a superclass with eight subclasses. The relationship is that of a specialization/generalization, and is expressed by an arrow point-

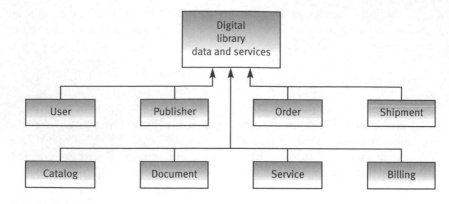

Fig. 2-8 Class model

ing from the subclass to the superclass. The classes are refined at lower levels. Each class has attributes and methods: the attributes identify the types of data elements belonging to this class; the methods are operations that can be performed. Attributes and methods are not shown in the diagram. The operations relate to the services shown in the use case diagram (Fig 2-7). Users are enrolled before they can query the catalog, which contains all documents that can be delivered. An order may be placed by any enrolled user, and may follow a query session or not. Queries and orders may address either documents or services. Documents comprise books, journals, audio and video recordings, and multimedia offerings, and may be held either on physical media or as electronic files. New documents or supplements of a subscription are acquired from a publisher. Shipments include mailings of physical media and making electronic media accessible. Some documents may be billed for, others may be free of charge. The same applies to the value-added services that are offered, for example, profiling, alerting, and professional search services.

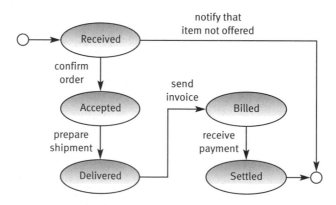

Fig. 2-9 State transition model

State transition model The state transition model given in Fig. 2-9 is an example of a dynamic model and shows the states that an order placed by a user can assume. The ellipses show the states in question, the arrows identify the operations that can change the state. An order received can be for a document or service that is not offered. In the dynamic model, documents and services are collectively referred to as items. Loaning of physical documents is not shown; they may be temporarily unavailable and may be reserved by the user. In the case of electronic documents, payments may occur before, after, or during delivery (pay-per-view). Settlements may occur in many different ways, including pre-payment, credit card or electronic cash. Cancellation of orders prior to or after delivery is not shown. This model will be used as the basis for a design in the next chapter.

Exercises

2-1   In which development situations is it important that requirements are defined? When is it unnecessary, or even detrimental?

2-2   How and from whom should requirements be elicited? How are they to be documented?

2-3   Why are requirement errors critical for the final product? What are the most frequent types of requirement errors?

2-4   What are non-functional requirements? How do they relate to functional requirements?

2-5   What is a prototype, and when is it useful? How does a prototype differ from a model?

2-6   Which modeling approach can help for which aspect of the requirements?

2-7   Why should requirements be validated and how can it be done? When should it be done?

2-8   Rewrite the requirements specification for the text formatting example so that all six errors are taken care of!

chapter 3

System design and specification

Every module is characterized by its knowledge of a design decision which it hides from all others. Its interface is chosen to reveal as little as possible about its inner workings.

D.L. Parnas [Parn72]

This chapter is about design. Design is technically the most demanding activity within the development cycle. We shall explain what is a good design and what is a good design process. We shall point out the difference between design and design documentation, and the relationship between architecture and structure.

3.1 Definitions and importance

Design is an activity that generates a proposed technical solution that demonstrably meets the requirements. In that process, we simulate (mentally or otherwise) what we want to make or do, before making or doing it. We iterate until we are confident that the design is adequate. The output of a design activity is a technical plan or blueprint of a system, not the system itself. It tells other technical people how to construct or build the system. The design effort typically has to give answers to the following questions:

- Which functions called for in the requirements document will be implemented, in view of the time, cost, and performance constraints given?
- How will these functions be invoked by the users, initially, and over time?
- How will the system be structured to allow the detailed design work and the implementation to proceed in parallel, and to ease extension and maintenance?
- How should each function be implemented, in terms of algorithms used, so that the performance, usability, security, and other goals are met?

The first two questions address external properties of the design, the last two are concerned with internal properties. Usually for each function more

than one solution is possible. Therefore, the one chosen has to be justified.
In a similar way to the requirements definition, a full design is usually only important for large and complex systems, and for systems that are being implemented by other people than the designers.

A *specification* is a document describing the properties of a system precisely. The term is used ambiguously in the literature to denote both the output of the requirements definition process and the results of the design process. Here it is used in the latter sense. A specification usually has two parts: the description of the external interface, and the description of the internal structure of the intended product. The two parts are frequently referred to as 'external specification' and 'internal specification', respectively. Both may be augmented by a design rationale, i.e. the justification of the design chosen. This information is very helpful for people who have to modify the design later.

3.2 General observations

Computing systems or software systems are artifacts. Artifacts are distinguished from natural phenomena in that they are usually based on a design. As a planned, purposeful endeavor, the design of an artifact is limited by the ability and foresight of the people making it and the circumstances of its creation. As Simon [Simo69] put it: 'Natural phenomena have an air of necessity; artificial phenomena have an air of contingency'. Design is at the core of most professions, whether medicine, law, business, architecture, or engineering. The members of these professions are not just called on to diagnose a problem; they usually have to devise a solution as well.

Design is the most challenging and most creative activity in software and systems engineering. Here it is where the knowledge of user requirements has to be translated into knowledge about computing systems. Good designs express a good match; poor designs a poor match. The knowledge about design has two aspects: properties and process. The design properties tell us what are good designs and for what reason. It is useful to distinguish between external and internal properties. The design process is concerned with how to perform a design task. Every student of computing science has to learn about design properties and processes. A document called the design specification must be produced as a result of the design process.

Except in student exercises, or in the case of reverse engineering, every design creates something unique – something that did not exist before. Reverse engineering is important if a product has to be manufactured whose design documents are lost or not accessible. Particular skills in this respect had developed in Eastern Europe before the fall of the Berlin wall. Either the external appearance or the internal structure may be new in a design, or both. If the externals remain the same, the new design is called re-engineering; it can occur for technical or business reasons. Some software systems are re-implemented in order to avoid legal problems, as was the case of the Unix operating system.

Design is easiest in the case of special purpose systems, i.e. systems where the functions and the user community can be clearly defined. A design is difficult if the requirements are conflicting or if the target system is a multi-purpose system to be used by a variety of different user groups. In that case the search for an optimum may be too cumbersome, but it may be possible to find a good compromise. In other words, designs have to be good enough for the purpose at hand. What goes beyond that is usually harmful; sometimes called 'gold plating'.

The task a designer is confronted with can usually be solved in many different ways. In a design contest for a new building, it is unlikely that two architects will come up with the same solution. The same applies in information and software systems design. It is this observation that is reflected in the remark quoted by Curtis [Curt88] about software design: 'In a design team of fifteen, two is a majority', i.e. if in a creative exercise two persons are of the same opinion, it is easy for them to dominate the rest. As for new buildings, it is not a good idea to have a software system designed by 15 architects. It is sometimes advisable, however, to have more than one solution put forward for evaluation.

The design process typically goes through a sequence of steps. Most important is the outside-in direction. The outside is the users view of the system; the inside is the manufacturer's or developer's (or modifier's) view. The detailed design of a computing system covers several dimensions, which are usually addressed in the following sequence: (1) network and hardware structure; (2) human interface; (3) data storage and retrieval aspects, and (4) processing programs. Since the design of programs ties together the other dimensions, it should occur at the end. Some programs that have neither a human interface nor rely on organized collections of data can be designed in isolation. The terms high-level and low-level are being used recursively for each of the four dimensions given above.

Design activities do not only occur prior to the first construction of a system, they also occur during evolution and maintenance. The main difference is that we do not start out from a clean sheet of paper. Many aspects have been fixed before. We have to understand which decisions that have been made have to be strictly adhered to, and which ones may be changed. This may make certain things easier, but it may make other things much more difficult.

The high-level design is commonly referred to as 'architecture'. The architecture is the external view, but also the long lasting structure. If conceived correctly, it survives generations of technology, i.e. implementations. The classical example is a watch. There are two external architectures: the analog version with number circle and hands; and the digital version with an illuminated numerical display. Watches with the same external specifications may be built either of mechanical or electronic parts. On the other hand, two watches from the same manufacturer may look quite different from outside but may largely use common parts inside.

There is no single best design for all systems, in the same way as there is no single best design for a house, room, or dress. Nevertheless, it is important to make use of standard architectures and common design styles as much as possible. A standard architecture allows sharing of components with other systems, or their reuse. This makes implementations less costly and more stable. Architectural considerations comprise both hardware and software; to ignore either one of them is a mistake. Even pure software products have to make sure that they do not contain dependencies on particular hardware features. They usually make assumptions regarding a particular hardware architecture or hardware configuration.

As outlined in the previous paragraph, the designer maps the application domain into the realm of computer solutions. For this, he or she applies knowledge that computer scientists have gained before. Such knowledge is reflected in the categorizations made. The last 50 years have produced many ways of categorizing software systems, although some are of historic interest only. We shall point only to two recent categorizations. Following Jones [Jone00], Fig. 3-1 lists 22 different application types.

1. Non-procedural (spreadsheet, query, generators, etc.)
2. Web applet
3. Batch application
4. Interactive application
5. Batch database application
6. Interactive database application
7. Pen-based application
8. Client–server application (two tier)
9. Client–server application (three tier)
10. Enterprise resource planning (ERP) application
11. Scientific or mathematical application
12. Systems or hardware control application
13. Communications or telecommunication application
14. Process control application
15. Embedded or real-time application
16. Trusted system with stringent security
17. Graphics, animation, or image-processing application
18. Robotic or manufacturing control application
19. Expert system with substantial knowledge acquisition
20. Artificial intelligence application
21. Neural net application
22. Hybrid program (multiple types)

Fig. 3-1 Types of software (according to Jones [Jone 00])

In a well-known treatise on the matter, Shaw and Garlan [Shaw96] classify systems according to their architectural structure, as follows: batch, interactive, real-time (sensor-based), embedded, distributed data or processes, data-centric, knowledge-based, peer-to-peer, and client–server. This can be regarded as a coarse-grained version of the classification made by Jones, where the term 'data-centric' stands for 'data base'; 'real-time' for 'process control'; and 'knowledge-based' for 'expert system'.

A concern for design decisions at this level is much more appropriate than worrying about how to draw boxes and arrows. However, since designs have to be understandable by humans, a common language is useful. Above all, designs are for humans, not for machines. As in the case of requirements definitions, developers often have to insist that it is better to spend more time on design rather than to start coding right away. As an example of this problem, Bill Gates of Microsoft has been quoted by Larry Constantine [Cons01] in saying that he does not believe in diagrams and does not want his programmers doing design. In the same context, Constantine suggested that certain people should use the title 'rapid code construction technician' on their business card, rather than software or systems engineer.

3.3 Applicable laws and their theories

Design is the area where practitioners really expect guidance from empirical studies. The laws cited here indeed reflect some deep and useful insights. They represent, in our opinion, the essence of what every software or systems designer needs to know and can learn. Some laws deal with the external properties of a design, and others with the internal structure and the process. Finally, a number of important claims are given which, at present, we consider to be hypotheses rather than laws.

3.3.1 Curtis' law

Bill Curtis *et al.* [Curt88, Curt90] studied the design process in several organizations, most extensively in the defense industry. Of the many results, the following one is picked as it best describes the essence of design. We have put this law first, because we want to emphasize that a design has, above all, to solve a problem in an application domain.

Good designs require deep application domain knowledge.	(L5)

Applicability Curtis' law applies to all types of system design. It applies to pure software projects as well as to hardware or combined hardware–software projects. Domain knowledge is that knowledge that is needed to solve problems in a certain application area. Application areas can be systems programming, or business systems, but also airplane construction, heat dissipation processes, chemical reactions, or human diseases. In systems programming, the domain knowledge may be compilers, operating systems, database management systems, networking, or others. Knowing how to program is not the same as being able to design a product. As indicated in Fig. 3-2, a designer maps application knowledge onto computational knowledge.

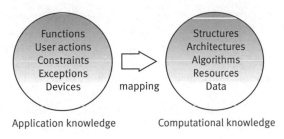

Fig. 3-2 Design expertise

The key problem with design is that it requires people to have knowledge in both of the above domains, otherwise knowledge in one of the two fields has to be acquired as part of the design process. We will ignore the case where a designer lacks knowledge in both fields (which occasionally may occur with students or novices). In the case where professional software or systems engineers are responsible for a design, it is normally the application knowledge that has to be acquired. It can also be the other way around, i.e. the domain expert acquires software or systems knowledge. Very often, software designers move from one application area to the next, in which case they have to learn new application knowledge with every project. There may also be projects where knowledge from one application domain may not suffice, i.e. interdisciplinary knowledge may be needed. Knowledge acquisition can occur in several ways: systematic training, interpersonal exchange, apprenticeship (mentor programs), or job rotation (learning while doing, or non-systematic training). Creating a design extends a person's knowledge, in the same way as doing an exercise in school does. It is usually more advantageous to spend time on gaining a better understanding of the problem (exploring the problem space) than to rush to a solution.

Evidence In his 1986 field study, Curtis [Curt88] interviewed developers and managers in 17 projects. The size of the products developed varied between 25 KLOC and one MLOC. The application domains were avionics, telephony, transaction processing, operating systems, and compilers. He looked at the processes involved at different levels of an organization. For this he used a layered model of an organization, starting with the individual, which is surrounded by embracing layers representing the team, the project, the company, and the business sector. His main findings were as follows:

- Application domain knowledge was thinly spread.
- In most cases, one or two people with the most knowledge took prime responsibility for the design.
- The same people communicated their vision and co-ordinated among all project members.
- Design meetings had the task of converting the design into a shared vision among all team members.

These observations certainly apply to many design situations. In another study [Curt90], Curtis observed that agreement on a design was reached fastest if the members of the design team had a similar background. In the case of diverse backgrounds, more time was needed. The design was challenged more thoroughly, and probably became better.

Theory Design can be understood as a special form of knowledge application. Not all knowledge is explicit, i.e. expressible in words. This part is also referred to as tacit knowledge. In a design situation, tacit knowledge also comes to bear if the designer possesses it. Tacit knowledge is acquired more often through experience than through training. This is particularly true for knowledge that crosses domains or maps one domain into another. Very often the capability to integrate knowledge from different areas is needed. Having the necessary knowledge is often seen as a primary problem for the design of large systems. As one system engineer in the above-mentioned study put it: 'Writing code isn't the problem, understanding the problem is the problem'. Having access to some knowledge, be it in books or in a database, does not mean that it is usable. It has to be active, i.e. useable in peoples' minds. Sufficient knowledge is needed to be able to correctly interpret the requirements definition, while good designers should be sensitive to unstated requirements. Since knowledge is spread unevenly, many system designs rely on rare experts, so-called gurus. They form the intellectual core of a project. In addition to knowledge skills, creativity and communication skills are required. Creativity is to do with the ability to generate associations among different pieces of knowledge. It also requires courage to try to combine things that have not been brought into connection before. Communication skills are called for if knowledge has to be acquired on the spot, be it from users or other experts.

Comment The designers are the communication focal points of a project; in that they have to educate the entire team. The team's learning phase, and possibly that of the designers as well, is usually buried within the design phase. It is an illusion that a design can be generated automatically from a requirements statement, except in a few simple cases.

3.3.2 Simon's law

All the following laws deal with the structure of the solution or the process used to find a solution. The first one is from the computer scientist and psychologist Herb Simon [Simo62], who has been referred to before.

Hierarchical structures reduce complexity.	(L6)

Applicability The definition of complexity used here is 'made up of a large number of parts that interact in a non-simple way'. By hierarchical we mean

that a system is partitioned in such a way that it consists of subsystems, each
of which is structured hierarchically until elementary components are
reached. When starting from the top, the subsystems comprising the system
form layers or levels, with the higher layers on top of lower layers. By structuring a complex system as a hierarchy of subsystems, complexity is reduced.
Simon's law is applicable to any complex system, whether natural or artificial. It is one of the few laws that are universally useful for structuring large
systems. Very often we tend to believe that non-hierarchical systems are
more flexible and scalable. An example is the Internet. Actually non-hierarchical systems usually require significantly greater efforts for their designs.

Evidence In this essay, Simon draws comparisons between natural and artificial
systems on how they deal with complexity. His observation from nature is that
hierarchically structured systems evolve more quickly than non-hierarchical
systems of similar size. Simon's definition of hierarchy is not concerned about
the nature of the relationship between subsystems (the term hierarchical is used
recursively). What is considered an elementary component depends on the
context; examples from nature are galaxies and stars, or molecules and atoms.
In social life, there are states, communities, and families. More in social than in
natural systems, a key determinant of a hierarchy is the frequency of interactions between the subsystems. Evolution obviously has a preference for
hierarchical systems, because they are more stable if interrupted.

That this is also true for artificial systems is illustrated by the difference
in the productivity of two watchmakers. One builds his product out of
subsystems, the other has to start from scratch after each interruption.
The one using subassemblies has a better chance of finishing the watch.
Simon finally concludes that many large systems are nearly decomposable
and contain high amounts of redundancy, meaning that identical substruc-
tures may occur repeatedly.

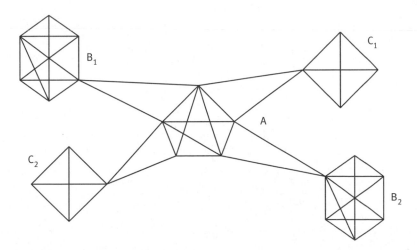

Fig. 3-3 Nearly decomposable structure

This is illustrated in Fig. 3-3. In this example, subsystems B_1 and B_2 are identical; so are subsystems C_1 and C_2. They communicate through subsystem A. Therefore, an alternate representation can be chosen to represent these properties graphically (Fig. 3-4). This figure happens to resemble what is known among computing scientists as a Bachman diagram. This is no coincidence, since the repetition of comparable elements occurs more often with data than with programs. The technique of making slightly different programs equal is called 'parameterizing', i.e. differences are factored out and passed to the routine as parameters.

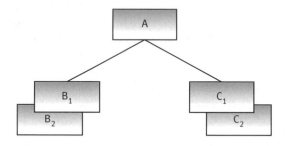

Fig. 3-4 Alternate representation

Theory Simon concedes that he does not know 'whether we understand the world because it is hierarchic or it appears hierarchic because those aspects of it which are not, elude our understanding and observation'. It is a chicken-and-egg problem for him. The complexity of a system is usually the result of its adaptation to the environment: it is the living environment that exposes a great variety of forms, and changes over time. As a result, more and more special cases have to be dealt with. The problem that is created by complexity is the description of the resulting structure. This is particularly true if different types of interactions exist.

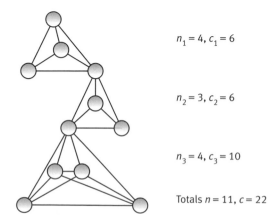

$n_1 = 4, c_1 = 6$

$n_2 = 3, c_2 = 6$

$n_3 = 4, c_3 = 10$

Totals $n = 11, c = 22$

Fig. 3-5 Connections in a hierarchical structure

As shown in Fig. 3-5, the number of interactions is reduced significantly in a hierarchical structure as compared to a non-hierarchical structure. In the hierarchical structure, 11 nodes are connected by 22 connections. This is considerably less than the number of connections that would be needed to connect the 11 nodes in the non-hierarchical case. In that case, $c = n \times (n-1)/2 = 11 \times 10/2 = 55$ connections would be required.

Comment In his paper at the 1974 IFIP congress, Parnas [Parn74] gives a precise definition of hierarchical structure, as follows: 'There exists a relation or predicate $R(x, y)$ between parts of the structure that define levels as follows:

- Level 0 is a set of parts such that there does not exist an x for any y such that $R(x, y)$, and
- Level i is a set of parts $x_i = (x_1, x_2, x_3, ..., x_n)$ such that (a) there exists a y on level $i-1$ such that $R(x_i, y)$ holds, and (b) if $R(x, z)$ then z is on level $i-1$ or lower.

Parnas also made the point that the term hierarchical structure is really undefined unless we specify precisely what relationship exists between the levels of the hierarchy. He offers the following examples: x contains y, x uses y, x has access to y, x gives work to y, x gives resources to y, and x uses resources of y. This clarification has certainly had the effect that hierarchical structures are being used in a more rational way.

3.3.3 Constantine's law

This well-known law is attributed to Larry Constantine. In the original publication by Stevens, Myers, and Constantine [Stev74], the authors state that the major ideas are the result of nearly ten years of research by Constantine. A comprehensive description can be found in a book by Myers [Myer75]. We state the law in the following way:

A structure is stable if cohesion is strong and coupling low.	(L7)

Applicability This law introduces two terms that have become base terms when talking about system structuring: *cohesion* (or binding) is the short term for intra-module communication; and *coupling* stands for inter-module interaction. Both terms can be related to Fig. 3-3. The subsystems B_1 and C_1 have a high degree of internal communication, meaning that they are cohesive units. Their communication with other parts of the system is less intensive, and their coupling is low compared to their cohesion. By applying this law, one other aspect of complexity is reduced. In this case, complexity is understood as the number and type of interconnections that exist between the parts of a structure. This allows the division of a system into pieces that can be implemented, fixed, and changed 'with minimal consideration of the effect on other pieces of the system'. The degree of coupling depends also on how complicated the connections are, whether they refer to the module itself or to something in it, and what is being sent or received over the connections. The fewer connections there are, and the simpler they are, the easier they can be understood. Often a distinction is made between export and import coupling. Cohesiveness may also have different characteristics, i.e. coincidental, logical, temporal, communicational, sequential, and functional. Functional cohesion is the highest and most natural, and should be striven for. The term 'stable' means that such a structure is less vulnerable to problems arising from normal incidents of programming life, i.e. to modifications due to design changes or maintenance. In other words, it is less error-prone. The application of the law lead to a design method that became known as 'composite' or 'structured' design. It is also one of the basic principles of object-oriented design.

Evidence The paper quoted above does not contain any empirical data. On the contrary, it contains the following disclaimer: 'This method has not been submitted to any formal IBM test. Potential users should evaluate its usefulness in their own environment prior to implementation'. Nevertheless, the law has been widely accepted since it relates to the experience of most practitioners.

Recently, several empirical studies have been conducted that were relevant to this law. Notably, Basili [Basi96a, Basi98a] Briand [Bria96, Bria98] and their colleagues have expanded and tested Constantine's law through controlled experiments conducted both with students and with professional developers. The studies were actually done in order to evaluate various proposals for code metrics. Metrics are used to describe different properties of a program or of a design. The most popular ones deal with product size (e.g. LOC) or product complexity. Metrics relevant to coupling and cohesion have been proposed by Chidamber and Kemerer [Chid94]. They are:

■ lack of cohesion in methods (LCOM)
■ coupling between object classes (CBO).

With these two metrics, cohesion and coupling have been redefined ('operationalized') so that they can be measured easily. LCOM counts the number of disjointed sets produced, by intersecting the sets of attributes used by all methods. CBO counts the number of pairs of classes that have methods or attributes in common.

In [Basi96b], the source code of programs in C++ (180 classes in eight systems) was analyzed. Several coupling and cohesion measures were put into correlation with the number of errors found during an internal test performed by independent testers. The hypotheses used, and their results, are summarized in Fig. 3-6. In the abbreviated text, the line $A \rightarrow B$ for each hypothesis should be read as follows: the more attribute A is present, the more attribute B can be expected.

Hypothesis tested	Correlation
Strong cohesion $\rightarrow$ few errors	Strong
High import coupling $\rightarrow$ more errors	Strong
High export coupling $\rightarrow$ more errors	Weak

Fig. 3-6 Evaluation of cohesion and coupling

Only the criteria expressing cohesion and coupling are considered here. The results on coupling even differentiate between import and export coupling. The investigation addressed many other metrics as well. However, errors eliminated through design or code inspections were not counted. Their number and severity was probably small compared to those errors found during testing.

Depending on the type of data evaluated, different correlation methods (Spearman, Pearson, multi-variance, or logistic) can be applied. In Fig. 3-6, the actual numerical values of the correlation coefficients are not given. We believe that the nature of the result is better expressed in words, and will do so for most results of empirical studies presented in this book. In the case of correlations, the following phrases are used for the values in parenthesis: 'very strong' (>0.9), 'strong' (0.7 to 0.9), 'moderate' (0.5 to <0.7), 'weak' (0.3 to <0.5), and 'little or no correlation' (<0.3).

Theory The idea of low coupling in Constantine's law is already present in the concept of nearly decomposable systems, as described by Simon. Localizing design ideas or functions in one place makes sure that they can be understood quickly and completely. Distributing them over several pages of program text is the same as burying them. If one has to look in a single place only, errors are avoided and changes are less error-prone.

3.3.4 Parnas' law

David Parnas, who has been mentioned before, has contributed many useful insights to our field. We will cite here what is known as the 'information hiding' or encapsulation principle [Parn72]:

> Only what is hidden can be changed without risk.   (L8)

Applicability This well-known law gives another important hint how systems can be structured, and it is a universal rule for modularization. It mainly talks about the implications for the developer. The Constantine and the Parnas laws are valid for any programming language, and are criteria of good design. The information hiding principle led to the development of the concept of abstract data types, and later became the basis of object-oriented design. Parnas' law can have a major effect on what documentation is needed or exchanged within a project. In the case of OS/360, the prevailing idea was that all design information has to be shared with all programmers. This resulted in a tremendous workload for all participants.

Evidence Parnas did not perform a controlled experiment but closely observed engineers at the Philips company in the course of their work. Parnas observed that modularization was important but poorly understood. In his paper [Parn72], he contrasted the conventional view of design with what he calls an unconventional view. The conventional view was only concerned with the size of each module and its interfaces. The size had to be small enough so that the module could be thoroughly understood and programmed independently. The interfaces had to be clearly specified. Parnas suggested that the modules be divide in such a way that they are largely independent of each other. Each module should be changeable without impact on the others. This requires that the implementation of one module does not depend on the implementation of the others. In other words, the implementation details should be hidden. The interface to each module should 'reveal as little as possible about its inner workings'. To come up with the proper structure, one has to list all difficult design decisions or the design decisions likely to change. Each module is then designed to hide such a decision from the others. Efficiency (i.e. short instruction path lengths) is no longer the only criterion for a good program construction.

Theory The reason why Parnas' law is considered a basic rule for system design comes from two aspects; the first is the recognition that design is a process extending over time. This is true for a one-shot product, but more so for one that evolves after its initial release. It is important to be able to defer things for later treatment without running the risk that this may percolate back and invalidate the work already done. The other aspect is that the exposure of people to knowledge costs time and energy. It is therefore advisable not to burden people with knowledge that they do not need. The traditional approach is to give all the design information to everyone on the project, or in other words: 'If in doubt, simply flood people with information'.

Comment As Brooks has stated in the second edition of his best-selling essay [Broo75], this is one of the major lessons that the industry has learned since the days of OS/360. Updating the specifications for OS/360, which were initially distributed in paper form, took about half an hour from every working day of a thousand programmers. One of the authors (Endres) was among them.

3.3.5 Denert's law

We cite the following law in order to fill an important gap regarding the structuring of systems. It also gives us an opportunity to recognize a German colleague [Dene91] for his contributions to software engineering.

Separation of concerns leads to standard architectures.　　　　(L9)

47

Applicability Denert's law is related to Parnas' law, but looks at the system from a higher level. It is not concerned with the relationship of individual modules, but of subsystems. It addresses design-in-the-large. It says that no module should be concerned with several things at the same time; i.e. application, presentation, communication, etc. For business systems, Denert postulated and successfully applied a three-layer architecture, the elements of which are shown in Fig. 3-7.

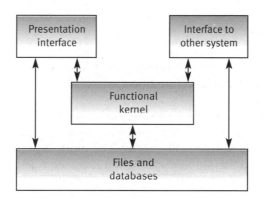

Fig. 3-7 Standard architecture of a business system

Fig. 3-7 shows a hierarchical structure with the relation 'x gives work to y' (in the sense of Parnas) between its layers. The lowest layer makes heaviest use of standard software components, e.g. database management systems. The functional kernel may make use of a transaction monitor. The presentation interface supports both interactive dialogs and batch processing. The interfaces between the layers are generic, meaning that they apply also in the case that a different product is chosen for a particular layer. The architecture as shown is not dependent on specific product types or suppliers.

Evidence This architecture has found wide application throughout the industry. As an example, many reservation or enterprise resource planning (ERP) systems follow this architecture. The three software levels may reside on the same processor or may be distributed. If distributed over two processors (two-tier hierarchy), the presentation interface is placed on a PC or workstation, and the function and data layers are on a host. In many cases, each layer resides on different processors (three-tier hierarchy). An extension of this architecture is called client–server architecture.

As shown in Fig. 3-8, not just the presentation interfaces but any program may invoke any other program to provide specific services. The different clients or servers may reside anywhere in a network of computers.

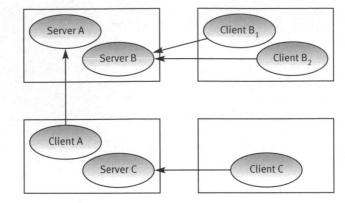

Fig. 3-8 Client–server architecture

Some of the interfaces are open, public standards, such as CORBA, DCOM, and Java Remote Method Invocation (RMI).

Theory Both examples are very illustrative of the concept of a standard architecture. The individual components are stable with respect to several types of changes that frequently occur. The most important property is its invariance with respect to hardware technology, be it in processors, storage devices or communication networks. Also, changes in standard software components, as well as potential changes in the application logic and the presentation format are strictly localized. An architecture of this type reduces the amount of unique code to be developed for each new application drastically. In addition, it protects the application code from changes in its environment. As a consequence, the system is scalable, i.e. can grow easily if the demand increases.

3.3.6 Fitts–Shneiderman law

An important area for the design of systems is the graphical user interface. As an example for this area, we will give one of the few empirically derived laws. The basic law was given by Fitts [Fitt54] in 1954, and was later extended by Shneiderman [Shne98].

> Screen pointing-time is a function of distance and width. **(L10)**

Applicability Fitts' law says that objects that are small and farther away are more difficult to point at than objects that are large and close. Fitts defined an index of difficulty as:

Index of difficulty = $\log_2(2D/W)$

with D as distance and W as width. From this follows the time to point as:

Time to point = $C_1 + C_2 \times$ Index of difficulty

where C_1 and C_2 are constants that depend on the device used. Interface design has a level that is different to its mere physical aspects. These are the cognitive aspects, which will be discussed under 'Gestalt' laws in Chapter 10. Interface design is crucial for the acceptance of a system by its users. The more users use a system only casually the more important it is that they cannot remember the idiosyncrasies of a system. The interface has to be 'natural', i.e. behave as the user expects, or the user has to be guided.

Evidence Ben Shneiderman is an author who has reported several empirical studies in this area. His experiments regarding Fitts' law yielded a pointing law consisting of three elements, time to initiate an action, time for gross movement and time for fine adjustment. Many empirical investigations have studied the influence of color. Colors direct the attention, e.g. red reminds us of fire. It is easy to overload an interface as far as colors are concerned. This then negates the mentioned advantages. Cognitive science is the basis of what Shneiderman calls the golden rules of interface design. These are also based on empirical evidence and are as follows:

- strive for consistency;
- enable frequent users to use shortcuts;
- offer informative feedback;
- design dialogs to yield closure;
- offer error prevention and simple error handling;
- permit easy reversal of actions;
- support internal locus of control;
- reduce short-term memory load.

Some of the terms used will occur throughout the book and need further explanation. A consistent approach tries to get along with a minimum set of different concepts. It is less of a surprise if a new situation occurs, after similar ones have been dealt with. Giving users feedback indicates that progress is being made. It creates a feeling of success. A dialog yields closure if some intended task will be completed rather than merely information collected. To be able to reverse any action is key to giving confidence. Otherwise the fear of damage may be overwhelming. The internal locus of control refers to the mental image that a user has of the system. A user believes that he or she is in control if he/she knows his/her position and destination. The last rule refers to the short-term memory. This is part of the human information processing capabilities and will be dealt with in Chapter 10.

Theory Our eyes are always focusing at an area of only a few degrees. To move away from this takes processing time, both for searching with the eyes and for positioning with the hand. To position a cursor (or any other pointer) on a small target, takes more time than positioning it on a large target.

3.3.7 Booch's second hypothesis

We have discussed the claims of object-oriented analysis under the heading Booch's first hypothesis in Chapter 2. We summarize the claims made for object-oriented design in the following hypothesis:

Object-oriented designs reduce errors and encourage reuse.	(H2)

Applicability The following specific claims are made for object-oriented design. The use cases and classes identified during the requirements process will be directly translatable into a design. There is no break in the modeling concept, no switch from one paradigm to another. In other design methods, a change of paradigms occurs when going from phase to phase. This made it difficult to keep the requirements model synchronized with the design model. Because objects encapsulate data formats, the precise data formats can be specified and modified at any time, even at runtime. For object-oriented design, more benefits are expected for the developer than for the user. Inheritance and polymorphism are two specific concepts that are considered as essential. As we will see below, they are the reason why we believe that the promises of the above hypothesis will only be partially met.

Hypothesis tested	Correlation
Deep inheritance → more errors	Very strong
Many descendants → more errors	Strong
Method overriding → more errors	Strong

Fig. 3-9 Evaluation of inheritance

Evidence To our knowledge, most empirical studies regarding object-oriented concepts looked at programs rather than at design documents. The studies of Basili [Basi96b] and Briand [Bria98], mentioned before, also contain an evaluation of specific concepts related to object-oriented design. They address the well-known problems associated with inheritance. As a result of correlation analysis, Fig. 3-9 shows that three aspects of inheritance are a potential source of problems. They should therefore be subject to special scrutiny during design inspections. In the programs studied, the depth of inheritance varied between 0–3, with an average of 1.32; the number of descendants (or children) amounted to 0–4, with an average of 0.23. Empirical investigation on how object-oriented design influences reusability will be discussed later.

3.3.8 Bauer–Zemanek hypothesis

For over 30 years, one specific hypothesis has occupied many people, mainly in academia. We credit it to Friedrich Ludwig Bauer [Baue82] and to

Heinz Zemanek [Zema68]. The question is how mathematical approaches can be used in the design of computing systems, and for software in particular.

> Formal methods significantly reduce design errors, or eliminate them early.   **(H3)**

Applicability The term 'formal methods' is used here to denote design methods that make use of mathematical concepts (like sets, relations) to generate and to document a design. According to Hall [Hall90], formal methods can cover the following activities:

- writing a specification;
- proving properties about the specification;
- constructing a program by mathematically manipulating the specification;
- verifying the program by mathematical arguments.

In this definition, it is left open whether 'specification' denotes a requirements or a design specification. Normally a design specification is assumed. Otherwise, the actual design process is bypassed or suppressed, namely selecting a specific solution out of a set of possible solutions. The transition from a design specification into a programming language is frequently achieved by a series of transformation steps, typically called refinement steps. The expected result is higher reliability of the product, because certain ambiguities and imprecision are eliminated at design time, that otherwise may only be found during implementation or test time.

Formal methods in design have a long tradition. The origins are clearly to be found in Europe. Both the Munich group of Bauer and the Vienna group of Zemanek made decisive contributions. Today, only two methods are serious contenders: VDM and Z. The Vienna Development Method (VDM) is an outgrowth of the work done by the IBM Vienna laboratory in the formal definition of programming languages. A system is defined by specifying the objects to be dealt with as sets, and the operations on them by means of pre- and post-conditions. The operations are then refined, i.e. designed, proving that the pre- and post-conditions still hold. A description of VDM can be found in [Jone90]. Z is a specification language originally developed by the Programming Research Group at Oxford University, UK (based on a proposal by J.R. Abrial). It uses a typed first order predicate calculus to describe the behavior of a system. A structuring mechanism called schemas provides a modularized description. One notation is documented in [Spiv89].

Formal specifications should be produced as a result of the original design work. In that case, they may become the official reference for the design. Other material, like text and diagrams, must also be produced, but it serves as auxiliary information only. It cannot be avoided because users demand a 'readable' specification in natural language, on which they base their evaluation. Formal specifications have sometimes been done as an afterthought based on some other design documentation. In both cases, conflicts between the two specifications may arise. Then a decision is needed, to determine what is binding. There might be reluctance to update both during the life of a project.

Evidence The empirical evidence on the benefits of formal methods in design is not conclusive yet. Hall [Hall90] gives an experience report based on a medium sized project (58 KLOC). The formal specification written in Z comprised 340 pages. It helped to improve the design and to remove some errors early. The product specified was a development tool (project and configuration management system), so the need did not arise to provide a user-oriented specification in natural language (at least not before the product was shipped).

Two other projects, both in the UK, are frequently cited. The one is the CICS re-specification performed by IBM Hursley in co-operation with the Programming Research Group at Oxford University [Haye85, Fent94]. In this effort, the external specification as documented in the application programmer's reference manual was redone using Z. During this process, a number of inconsistencies or missing details were found in the manual. They were resolved by studying the source code. Also, a part of the system was subsequently re-implemented. The claims are that the error density was reduced by 60 percent (probably compared to previous releases) and the cost savings were about US$5.5 million (perhaps as compared to the original implementation of the same system). The value of this experience is somewhat limited, because the project was essentially a re-documentation and re-engineering effort, completed over a 12-year (!) period. The formal specification was not used in the requirements process, nor in the design itself. It was an additional quality enhancement activity targeted at an existing system. The project received high recognition, including an award by the British Queen.

A very thorough analysis is reported by Pfleeger and Hatton [Pfle97]. The project produced a display system for the London Airtraffic Control Centre, comprising about 200 KLOC written in the C language. Essential parts of this system were specified either in VDM or with state diagrams. The analysis showed that the modules in those parts of the system that were specified formally had rather low complexity (in the sense of the McCabe metric) and loose coupling. The same modules demonstrated, prior to release, a slightly higher error density than the remainder of the system, and after release, a significantly lower error density. Fig. 3-10 shows the results.

Time	Error density	Formal	Informal
Prior to release	Changes per KLOC	19.6	21.0
	% modules changed	22	19
After release	Changes per KLOC	0.58	1.61
	% modules changed	0.12	0.27

Fig. 3-10 Results of formal methods

No information is available on the experience of the staff, be it with the application domain, the design method, the implementation language or the test methods. To train a sufficient number of developers and users in the formal methods was apparently no problem. Compared to other groups in industry, this project team seems to have relied on formal methods but did not make efficient use of inspections. This becomes clear from the fact that the bulk of the 3000 errors reported prior to release were removed very late in the development cycle, namely during system and acceptance testing (340 errors found in code reviews, 725 in unit test, and 2200 during system and acceptance test). An explanation for the thoroughness of the test effort may be that the project had been obliged contractually to achieve 100 percent code coverage.

One of the authors has reported on his experiences with formal design methods elsewhere [Endr93a]. In this case, the designer applied a formal design language to design a small change of an existing system. To aid the code understanding, a significant part of the old design (extracted from the existing code) was first translated into the new language. After hundreds of lines in the formal design language, the code change finally resulted in a few lines in the (old) implementation language.

Comments Even if the Bauer–Zemanek hypothesis were to be refuted, it would be hard to stop people from working in that direction, indeed some people with a mathematics background probably think they owe it to their professional reputation. The topic of formal methods is also related to the subject of higher-level programming concepts. If all that is needed for formal design specifications are sets and relations, the question that should be asked is: 'Why have they not been included in a very high-level programming language yet?' Years ago, this idea emerged from several authors who specified their designs in a language with high-level data structures (SETL, APL) first. They could 'execute' (i.e. interpret) the design in order to verify it. They had to translate it by hand afterwards into a standard programming language, however.

3.3.9 Gamma's hypothesis

During the last decade, software reuse has been heralded as a way to achieve both productivity and quality in software. Code, test cases, designs, and requirements can all be reused. The most popular form of design reuse is through patterns. Erich Gamma is one of four authors that made popular the idea of design patterns [Gamm95]. The claims made are summarized in the following hypothesis:

> Reusing designs through patterns yields faster and better maintenance.   (H4)

Applicability A design pattern is a schematic description of a possible solution to a design problem. It gives a template showing how elements of the solution (objects, classes) should be arranged. Gamma and his co-authors were influenced by ideas from mechanical engineering and building architecture. Notably, the architect Alexander had based his work on the idea of design patterns. The assumption is that experienced designers reuse successful elements of previous designs. The advocates make the following claims concerning patterns:

■ programmer productivity and program quality are improved;
■ the skills of novices are increased by allowing them to reuse proven concepts;
■ communication among designers is made easier;
■ it encourages the exchange of good design ideas;
■ the maintainability of programs is improved.

Patterns have found considerable interest, both in industry and academia: many other patterns have been published; journals and conferences have been initiated; and tools are being offered. The advantage of patterns over code reuse is in the crossing of language and operating system boundaries. Most examples given are related to OO concepts, however. Another way of reusing designs is through frameworks. Frameworks are a top-down approach to reuse. They provide a skeleton of an application where the details have to be filled in. They often come as a tree structure (of classes) where the branches can be reused, but some of the leaves have to be added. As a consequence, they are limited to a specific domain and application type. Design patterns are more general, although smaller.

Evidence Until recently the pattern community has only reported anecdotal evidence to support their claims. Two controlled experiments have recently been performed by Prechelt and Unger [Prec99], addressing the claim regarding maintenance benefits only. In both cases, only rather small programs (< 500 LOC) were used. In one test, conducted with students, comments had been added to the source text highlighting the fact that a specific pattern was used. The control group had to perform the same maintenance tasks for the same programs without the extra comments. The result was that the additional comments resulted in shorter maintenance time (time to understand the program and to make the fix on paper) and a larger percentage of correct solutions.

In another experiment, professionals from a German software house were asked to perform a maintenance task for several programs with and without patterns. Here the results were mixed. In those cases where the pattern yielded the cleaner solution the results were positive. Whenever the solution without pattern was simpler, the maintenance time was shorter. The results of both studies are summarized in Fig. 3-11.

Hypothesis tested	Correlation
Pattern documented as comments → fast maintenance	Strong
Pattern documented as comments → correct maintenance	Strong
Pattern used at all →easy maintenance	Weak

Fig. 3-11 Evaluation of patterns

Comment In a recent presentation, Gamma [Gamm01] mentioned that he had been reproached for looking backward, i.e. at existing design, rather than forward, i.e. at new visions. This criticism, if any, should be noted by all people who want to learn from others.

3.4 More on system design and specification

Many more questions regarding systems design are under discussion, and in the following section, we will address some of them. None of them have, to our knowledge, been subject to empirical studies so far.

3.4.1 Project goals and design criteria

From one project to the next, different project goals may have different importance. In many environments, the main concern is about project costs. The question 'Why does software cost so much?' is so prevalent in the industry that it has become the title of a best-selling book by Tom DeMarco [DeMa95]. This aspect is especially relevant to all environments where software is considered a necessary, but undesirable cost factor. This may be the case for a manufacturer of computer hardware, as well as for a car or airplane manufacturer, or an insurance company. It is mainly from this view that the discussion about developer productivity arises. In these situations, the best productivity can be achieved if new development is avoided completely or if it can be moved out to countries with lower labour costs. The cost gains achieved through development in India and Russia ('off-shore' development) cannot be matched by the best methods or tools.

Of course, there are many good reasons why one needs to develop software and why one has to do it in-house. Whenever software is considered to be an investment that may lead to returns comparable to, or even better than, other investments, the view changes. The cost is no longer the most critical item, because higher investments may lead to higher returns. The same is true if the software gives a competitive advantage to the business. The concern then shifts to the questions of skills availability, protection of intellectual assets, and the cycle time needed. Exceptional skills may be needed to be able to offer unique and new functions before the competition does. In a dynamic market, as exemplified by the Internet, time-to-market may decide whether a product becomes profitable or not. In such a case, cycle time is key; cost is secondary.

The same variations may affect the technical design criteria. The obsession with new function often leads to over-engineered solutions. They then suffer from a disease called 'featuritis'. Of course, the core function has to be there, but leaving out the frills that unduly destroy efficiency may be the crucial part of a design. If a function is offered, it has to perform according to the user's work speed. If it delays him, it will not be used. It is in this respect that the rapid progress in hardware technology increases the responsibilities of the software designer. The overriding goal of each design, however, should be to make the system reliable. There is no excuse for system breakdowns that are caused by design errors. This applies independently whether the respective parts will be implemented in hardware or software.

One property of design, that is normally not specified as a design criterion is its conceptual integrity. Brooks [Broo87] has described this property as follows: 'The product should appear to each user's mind as if it were designed by a single mind, although it may have been designed by many minds'.

3.4.2 Open architectures

As discussed in the context of Denert's law, large systems can only be developed effectively if they have a well-known, stable architecture. For a large company, this may be an internal or proprietary architecture. If the industry as a whole wants to have the same benefits, the architectures in question should be open. An architecture is open, if its specification is freely accessible. It may have initially been developed by a single person or a single company, and made public afterwards. Examples of this are programming languages, like PL/I and Java, operating systems like Unix, and text formats like Postscript and SGML. An open architecture can also be developed by a group of companies or a standards committee. Examples are CORBA and XML. An open architecture can be proprietary. In this case, the documentation is available, but changes can be made only by the originator.

Every developer is well advised to use open architectures. They give his or her product the largest possible market penetration and the longest business life. He or she then has the best chances to be able to share work with other developers or to reuse components developed by others. However, there are several risks that should be taken into account here also. An open architecture may undergo changes that are not under the developer's control and which cause additional work later to adapt to them. The open interface can also encourage a competitor to develop a replacement product or extensions to be added on top. This sometimes causes companies not to adhere to open interfaces, but rather to use internal, undocumented interfaces.

3.4.3 Design quality and iterative design

The quality of a design depends on how well it meets the requirements definition. It must not only meet the functional requirements, but also the non-functional requirements. Attempts to measure the quality of a design usually use only a single criterion: for example, measures of maintainability or reusability. In most cases such measurement attempts have been applied not to the design, but to the implementation.

When the quality of a design is judged, one should not only think of the quality of the proposed product. The intrinsic quality of a design is judged on how good the design describes the planned product for the customer and to the other developers. Have the architecture, the structure and the necessary implementation ground rules been specified in a way that it is easy to build a system that meets the requirements? In other words, an awful and useless product may be well designed, and vice versa.

If no requirements definition exists, iterative design may be helpful. It is not to be confused with prototyping, as described above. Iterative design produces a partial design, implements this part, then switches back to design mode again. This mode of operation was described in a famous quote by Andy Kinslow during the Garmisch software engineering conference [Naur69b]: 'We design until we can code, then code until we design'. He did not mean this to be a recommendation to be followed.

In every practical environment the question of when to stop designing arises. In other words, how detailed should a design be? A pragmatic answer can read as follows: 'A design should be detailed enough that the planning and cost estimating needed in order to proceed into the next phase can be done'. If a cost estimate is required for the entire project, including maintenance, the design has to cover the entire system and has to be detailed enough to serve as a base for all necessary estimates. The same is true if performance estimates are required. On the other hand, the volume of the design documentation should not exceed the level that can be digested by the intended readers. Applying Parnas' law, one should carefully evaluate which information is needed by whom and when. The final consideration should be to avoid too meticulous a design that restricts the intellectual contributions of the implementers. The construction of a system should remain an intellectual challenge for whoever is assigned to perform it.

3.4.4 Design of data structures and databases

The laws cited above all deal with the design of programs. The entire subject of data design has not yet been subject of empirical studies by the software engineering community. Data and data descriptions are an important part of any system. Frequently, both persist longer than programs, and the same data may be shared by many programs.

Data elements are the actual values the data assume. The description of a data element is often referred to as meta data. It gives meaning to an element. Because there are multiple elements with the same description, meta data are less numerous and change slower. Meta data are usually recorded in the form of a data dictionary. An installation may want to maintain one common data dictionary for all its applications. When we look at relationships between data elements, we talk of data structures. Primitive data structures are list, array, and file. Several files may be treated together in the form of a database. The three related fields of data structures, file organization, and database management have grown to become own branches of computing science, standing alongside software engineering. They have produced a considerable body of knowledge that every system designer can use. We will refer to some basic results in a later chapter. For all data-intensive systems it may be advisable to place the design of data into the center of the design effort. In this case, a data model with strong semantic relationships is useful. This role is usually played by the entity relationship model as introduced by Peter Chen [Chen76]. The object model, which has been referred to before, lumps together data elements and procedures.

3.4.5 Design for safety and security

Hardly any area has received more attention recently than the question of what technical means exist to improve a system's safety and security aspects. While the problem of safety is closely related to the question of reliability, security has a unique dimension. The higher the value of the information stored in a system, the more important is its protection. With the advent of distributed systems, particularly public networks, the number of technical options has grown significantly. Both servers and clients require adequate mechanisms and procedures. This starts with the proper policies for physical access, and involves the 'hardening' of systems (removing obvious risks and flaws), the authentication of users (usually via passwords), and the proper allocation of access rights for data and applications. It ends with the encryption of messages, and the detection of malicious use and intrusions (including viruses).

One frequently employed protection scheme is referred to as a *firewall*. It may be a separate computer or software package that screens all traffic between an external and an internal network, just as medieval cities protected themselves with a defensive wall. The access rights are simply split between user groups, i.e. citizens and non-citizens. More advanced approaches are required for applications like electronic commerce. Here different rights may have to be negotiated for each transaction type. More information on standard and advanced methods can be found in the Software Engineering Institute's CERT® documentation[1], which has been published by Allen [Alle01], and in Müller and Ranneberg's book [Müll99], respectively.

As a general remark, security is a typical example where software-only solutions are weaker than hardware-supported approaches. Therefore chip cards are used for authentication purposes, and special hardware implementations for encryption/decryption algorithms. Furthermore, the technical design can only provide the mechanisms needed for protection and detection. The policies and procedures that make use of them, have to be decided separately. They may have to change during a system's lifetime.

3.4.6 Technology impact on system design

As will be discussed later, the field of computing science is benefiting heavily from advances in technology. The most rapidly advancing technologies are those concerning semiconductor devices, magnetic storage media, and digital transmission. These three technologies are enjoying exponential growth, meaning that their key parameters double every two to three years.

Most systems are planned with a lifetime of one or two decades. As a consequence, no systems should be built in such a way that it cannot easily adjust to progress in technologies. The way to achieve this is to treat all devices as virtually unlimited, but optimize for their current geometrical and

---

[1] http://www.cert.org/security-improvement/

physical properties. If a device adheres to a proven architecture, the general framework for its use is given. From a practical user point of view, it is risky to rely on unproven technology. A new technology is less risky if it can be introduced through an existing architecture where, if there is a problem, a fallback to older technology is possible.

3.4.7 Documentation of design

The architecture of a system may be equally of interest to users and developers. The documentation should therefore address both audiences and consist mainly of text and drawings, augmented possibly with screen shots or syntax notations for a command interface (API). Traditionally, the external specification became the basis of the user manual. With the dominance of graphical user interfaces (GUI), such manuals have largely disappeared. In fact, they have migrated into the user dialogs and the help files. As discussed before, formal specifications are often an add-on to the external specification. They cannot serve as an external specification if the potential users of the system are not familiar with the notation.

The internal specifications mainly serve other developers or maintenance personnel. It can make use of any notation familiar to programmers. This may be a notation resembling a programming language (also referred to as pseudo-code) or any mathematical or graphic notation. The notations available under UML are normally sufficient to describe a design completely. However, prose is needed to explain the design rational. The comments in the source code, as used in the experiments of Prechelt and Unger, cannot be considered as genuine design documentation. They certainly describe the design, but as an afterthought to the implementation. This is very useful for maintenance purposes, particularly if no other design documentation exists.

3.4.8 CASE tools and design change control

With CASE tools, graphic representations of designs can be recorded, stored, updated and transmitted. Different vendors' tools differ in which diagram types they support. Most of them support entity relationship diagrams (ERD), dataflow diagrams (DFD), and state transition diagrams. The Rational tool set was the first to offer the Unified Modeling Language (UML). Some tools allow cross references between different diagram types. In some cases, the generation of code skeletons and backward linking between code fragments and design diagrams is provided.

CASE tools have frequently been oversold. They are usually only able to perform syntactic checks on the construction rules for diagrams. Their strength comes to bear if updates or small changes have to be made. This should motivate developers to keep designs current while changes occur during implementation time. No tool can generate design information that does not exist yet, nor can it detect flaws and gaps in the design.

3.4.9 Cognitive processes and group dynamics

The accomplishments discussed in this book are seldom achieved by individuals working in isolation. Of course, we cannot ignore the genius of an individual or his or her hard work. In practice, we will learn, again and again, that a single person's capabilities are limited. His or her span of comprehension or depth of knowledge may not suffice for the task at hand. Reducing the task so that it suits an individual is not a solution in every case. In some cases, but not in all, the way out is a team approach. In a team, one person's inadequacies may be compensated by other, differently qualified persons. On the other hand, the mutual stimulation may raise the level of output produced. Group dynamics is therefore a relevant topic, and not only for managers. It influences all activities, beginning with requirements definition, through design, verification, and installation.

Based on the studies referenced above, Curtis [Curt90] gives some valuable hints on the cognitive processes involved with design. He has observed that the individual designer oscillates between abstraction levels, jumps through discrete system states, and develops the problem and solution space simultaneously. The idea of a top-down design is an over-simplification, although it may be a good way to explain a design once it is completed. In a design group, the curve showing the agreement level reached follows an inverted 'U', i.e. it increases until the design is documented, but falls off again after the completion of the design specification.

Designers make extensive use of personal networks to obtain information they need. The more aware a designer is of his or her own limitations, the better he or she will be able to make use of other people. Other people are motivated to share their knowledge if they expect to gain in the process. One-way streets, where only one of the partners is getting ahead, are not popular. Putting the group's success above that of the individual members may help in some situations, but not always. Group members usually prefer fairness and justice over altruistic appeals.

3.4.10 User participation and growing of designers

The participation of users in the design process is an idea highly valued by some authors. It is often proclaimed as the Scandinavian approach. In our opinion, these authors confuse requirements definition with design. While the users' role for the definition of requirements is critical, no significant contributions can normally be expected during design. If the user is not a computing professional, he or she is neither capable nor interested in engaging him- or herself. No layperson will ever be asked to design a washing machine or a cooking stove, let alone a car or an airplane. That does not mean that they may not be able to contribute good ideas for the external appearance and the user interface. As with other commodities, a consumer who pays relies on experts for the quality of the product he or she gets. He or she may be willing to select among alternatives if they are presented in a convenient form. Prototyping is a good vehicle to do this. Most importantly, a designer cannot discharge his or her responsibilities to the user if the product does not satisfy all requirements.

It should be noted that the development of designers is a topic that is frequently neglected. The education given to professionals in our field often confuses coding and the drawing of diagrams with designing. Designing can best be learned by studying good designs or by watching other designers at work. From Brooks [Broo87] comes the plea that our industry should find ways to 'grow great designers'. Perhaps we can learn from architecture or industrial design in this respect.

3.5 Examples and study material

3.5.1 Text formatting design

In Fig. 3-12, the design of the text-formatting program is given as expressed by the author. The form chosen is that of pseudo-code. It highlights the control flow. The words starting with capital letters designate procedures; those with small letters are variables. The procedure BuffAdd places the incoming character into a buffer at the position given by the pointer buffpos (buffer position); LineAdd appends the content of the buffer to the output line at position linepos (line position). After each operation the respective pointers are incremented. The pointer buffpos is reset to 1 by procedure LineAdd; linepos is reset to 1 by StartLine. In this design document the following errors can be observed:

d1: Every output line will start with a blank character, unless it contains a word of length N.

d2: There will be two CR characters in the output line, if the word is N characters long.

d3: There will be two blanks or two CR characters in the output line, if the text starts with a blank or a CR character.

d4: The last word of the input will not be transmitted to the output, unless it is followed by either blank or CR.

```
Initialize;
Startline;
L: InCharacter;
    if separator
        then begin
                if spaceleft then LineAdd else StartLine;
                LineOut
                end
    else if buffFull then Alarm else BuffAdd;
    goto L;

Where: separator = blank or CR
        spaceleft = linepos + buffpos < N
        buffFull = buffpos = N
```

Fig. 3-12 Example in pseudo-code

Of the requirement errors mentioned in Chapter 2, three have been handled implicitly (r2, r4, and r5); errors r1, r3, and r6 still exist.

3.5.2 Digital library design

For the digital library system outlined in Chapter 2, a preliminary design is given. Four aspects of the system are described, namely the overall architecture, the network client, the network server, and the back-office system. The design is presented in a top-down fashion.

System architecture Fig. 3-13 gives an overview of the system architecture. It shows that the applications considered are split over two logically different systems, a network server and a back-office system. The applications on the net server can be accessed by local or remote users. Local users may be connected through a local network (LAN); remote users dial in via the Internet. The back office applications are normally only accessible for the library staff. Shipping and billing may be invoked automatically from a net application. Another important set of decisions reflected in this diagram concerns the interfaces used between subsystems and components. The net server is primarily accessed via the Hypertext Transfer Protocol (HTTP). This assures that local and remote users have the same interface. For the access to the data, three different interfaces are specified. For library documents stored in electronic form the preferred protocol is the Extensible Mark-up Language (XML), which can handle almost any data type, including multimedia databases (MM-DBs). For queries to the catalogs, the Structured Query Language (SQL) has been specified, which applies to relational databases (R-DBs) only. Certain other databases may require a

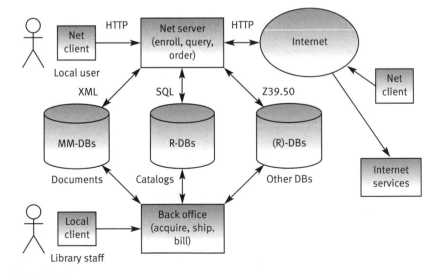

Fig. 3-13 System architecture

special interface that is explicitly defined for library applications (Z39.50). The library system will also provide certain portal functions, i.e. it provides access to relevant Internet services. Search engines are one such example.

Network client The network client as specified in Fig. 3-14 is that software function that has to be available on every PC or workstation to enable the network server of the library to be accessed. The important point of this specification is that only commercially available software components are used. Users do not require any library-specific code in order to use its services. A Web browser transfers files from a server, using the HTTP protocol. In addition, reader and display functions are needed for text, graphics, and images; depending on the type of material used, audio or video players should also be installed.

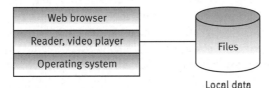

Local data

Fig. 3-14 Network client

Network Server The structure of a network server is shown in Fig. 3-15. Its key component is the Web server. It is the counterpart of a Web browser and understands the HTTP protocol. It sends files to the clients in any popular file format.

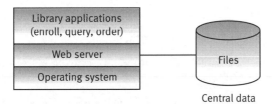

Central data

Fig. 3-15 Network server

Back-office system The back office system as shown in Fig. 3-16 is specified as a classical database/data communication (DB/DC) system. A DB/DC system is a combination of a database management system with a transaction monitor. It can reside on the same processor as the network server or may be a physically separate system. Several components that would be required for typical library systems are not shown. Examples include user administration, catalog management, document generation, accounting, and security facilities. The design given leaves most technology options open.

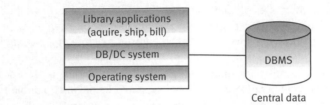

Fig. 3-16 Back-office system

Both data and programs can be centralized or distributed, and may reside on different media or use different languages or formats. For the network connection no assumptions are made on topology or technology. The same is true for all other hardware components. However, their performance, capacity, and reliability have to meet the requirements of the applications and the workload. A very important consideration is the scalability of the system, meaning that it should be able to grow, be it in capacity, perform-ance, or availability, without needing a change to its architecture.

3.5.3 Performance analysis

For a DB/DC system similar to the back-office system given above, a per-formance prediction is to be performed using, the simple model given in Fig. 3-17. This allows studying of the flow through the system of a transac-tion originating from a user. In this model, t_i $(i = 1–7)$ are the estimated service times of individual components of the system. The following values are given (corresponding to reasonable values of real systems):

t_1 = 300 msec: average delay for PC and LAN;

t_7 = 60 msec: average disk access time;

l_2, l_6 = 160k instructions: path-length in operating system for each service request;

l_3 = 200k instructions: path-length in DC system for each transaction;

l_4 = 40k instructions: path-length in the application program (installation unique);

l_5 = 400k instructions: path-length in DB system for each DB query;

g = 4 Mill. instructions per second (MIPS): processor speed of host computer;

k = 2: number of messages per transaction;

m = 3: number of DB calls per transaction;

n = 5: number of disk accesses per DB call.

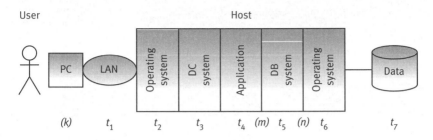

User   Host

Fig. 3-17 Performance model for DB/DC system

The values t_i ($i = 2$–6) can be calculated as

$$t_i = l_i / g$$

The response time (in seconds) for a transaction can be calculated using the following formula (no queuing is assumed):

$$T = k\,(t_1 + t_2 + t_3) + t_4 + m\,(t_5 + n\,(t_6 + t_7))$$

For the values given above, the estimated response time of a transaction is given by:

$$T = 2 \times (0.3 + 0.04 + 0.05) + 0.01 + 3 \times (0.1 + 5 \times (0.04 + 0.06)) =$$
$$= 0.79 + 3 \times (0.1 + 0.5) = 0.8 + 1.8 = 2.6 \text{ sec.}$$

This response time may be a problem since sub-second response times are normally required. The above model easily allows an investigation of alternate designs that might solve this problem. Of course, the easiest solution for the developers would be to propose a faster processor. Unless the processor was a singleton or already at the top of a family, the additional costs may be justified by the costs of the redesign alone. A processor upgrade is almost always justified, if the problem is discovered late, e.g. during installation time. Then a change of the implementation would not only considerably delay the introduction of the new system, it would also destabilize it.

The general message from this example is clear, however: the easiest compensation for software shortcomings is through better hardware. It also illustrates that the application-specific code in a DB/DC system is only a small part of the software functions invoked. The largest portion is standard systems software, i.e. commercial of-the-shelf software (COTS).

3.5.4 Metrics analysis

Many different proposals exist for software metrics. Obviously, not all metrics proposed measure different properties. In order to find out where this is the case, a correlation analysis can be performed. In Fig. 3-18, data are given for five different metrics collected in three different projects. The data originate from [Basi98a].

	Project A	Project B	Project C
Metric 1	1.41	1.19	1.69
Metric 2	1.50	1.50	1.52
Metric 3	0.11	0.16	0.16
Metric 4	30.4	37.2	8.04
Metric 5	5.02	4.63	5.34

Fig. 3-18 Comparative metrics data

Fig. 3-19 compares all five metrics in turn against each other. This is done by calculating the Pearson correlation coefficients (by means of a spreadsheet). The Pearson coefficient r is defined as

$$r = \text{Covariance}(X, Y)/(\text{Square Root}(\text{Variance}(X) \times \text{Variance}(Y)),$$

where $\text{Covariance}(X, Y) = \text{sum}((X - \bar{X})(Y - \bar{Y}))/n$, and $\text{Variance}(X) = \text{sum}((X - \bar{X})^2)/n$. ($\bar{X}$ designates average over X_1 through X_n).

	Metric 1	Metric 2	Metric 3	Metric 4	Metric 5
Metric 1	1	0.90	0.07	−0.97	0.99
Metric 2		1	0.50	−0.97	0.84
Metric 3			1	−0.29	−0.06
Metric 4				1	−0.94
Metric 5					1

Fig. 3-19 Pearson correlations of metrics data

Not counting the diagonal (with all 1s), we have three cases of strong correlation (>0.7), one moderate (0.5–0.7), and six weak (<0.5) ones. Five correlations are positive, and five negative. A positive coefficient indicates that the values of variable X vary in the same direction as those of variable Y. A negative coefficient indicates the values of variable X and variable Y vary in opposite directions. The conclusion to be drawn from this example is that metrics 1, 2 and 5 are most likely measuring the same property. Metric 4 is probably the inverse of the other three.

Exercises

3-1 How does the complexity of a system present itself to the developer? What can he or she do to control it?

3-2 Define the terms cohesion and coupling, and explain their importance for system design.

3-3 Why is information hiding or encapsulation important? How can it be achieved?

3-4 What benefits can be expected of standard architectures? What are open architectures?

3-5 Which aspects of object-oriented design should be carefully checked for errors?

3-6 What are design patterns, and why are they useful? How do they differ from frameworks?

3-7 Recalculate the transaction response time for the example in Section 3.5.3, assuming a processor of twice the speed. As an alternative, evaluate the response time effect if, instead of the processor, the disk device is replaced by a device with half the access time.

3-8 What does the term 'strong correlation' mean mathematically?

chapter 4

System construction and composition

The goto statement as it stands is just too primitive; it is too much an invitation to make a mess of one's program.

E.W. Dijkstra [Dijk68]

This chapter deals with the actual building of a system. We will state basic rules that apply to the construction of all types of systems, be they batch, interactive, distributed, or imbedded. Traditional and novel methods of producing quality products will also be considered.

4.1 Definitions and importance

Construction is a set of activities that converts a design into a running system. Construction is also referred to as 'implementation' and 'realization'. In the case of software systems, construction always involves the creation of source code, its compilation into executable modules, and the integration of these modules into a system. We use the term coding to denote the activity of transforming a design into the statements prescribed by the syntax of a programming language. Programming encompasses design, coding, verification, and test. If hardware is involved, the respective components may have to be build, procured, and installed.

The term *composition* is used if a system is being built primarily out of high-level components or building blocks. In the early days, every software system was built from scratch, i.e. one instruction was written after the other. The first application area that fostered sharing of existing routines among users was that of mathematical and statistical applications. Today, any application runs on a bed of common software functions. System software, for instance, supports all user applications in, for example, operating systems, database systems, and data communication systems. The applications that make use of these system programs can be custom-developed by users or their organizations, or can be a standard application, purchased from software vendors. A well known example of a standard application is a text-processing system, similar to the one used to enter, modify, and format this book. Ready-to-use business applications are not as widespread, but can be assembled or generated (customized) from the packages available. Enterprise Resource Planning (ERP) and Financial Systems are examples of off-the-shelf packaged software, the pieces of which can be mixed and matched.

Constructing a system is clearly an essential step if one wants to produce more than just paper documents (or paper tigers). The desire to produce something new and useful is what really motivates a developer. That desire may even induce novices and managers to skip or shortcut the preceding activities. Programming or coding is the most characteristic activity within the scope of system development, but it is also the most over-emphasized activity. Building a system is much more than just coding (which may be as little as a sixth of the total effort).

4.2 General observations

Software systems typically consist of multiple layers. This has turned out to be the easiest and safest way to achieve significant gains in productivity. Following Simon's law, layering allows the hiding of complexity. For a programmer, the peculiarities of a machine's architecture are no longer a concern if he or she can write the application in a simple high-level language such as Fortran or Pascal. The same is true for data storage and access, and particularly for network communication. The software offers abstractions for such basic concepts as device or file. Depending on the device type or the medium, different device drivers or file access methods are invoked.

Any application program may be written following different programming paradigms. A paradigm is a pattern or an example of something. The word also connotes the ideas of a mental picture and pattern of thought. Kuhn [Kuhn70] uses the word to mean the model that scientists hold about a particular area of knowledge. Using the term in this context compares software technology with science, in the sense that it proceeds from one paradigm to the next.

Fig. 4-1 gives a list of what Jones [Jone00] considers as different software paradigms. The procedural approach is only one of them. For certain types of applications a declarative, logical, functional, or rule-based approach may be equally useful; the declarative approach is the basis of most application generators. Even within the same programming paradigm, many languages compete with each other. Jones states that he has encountered about 600 programming languages in the installations he has investigated. It is very rare that, an installation gets along with a single language – usually, some three or four languages dominate within an installation. There is little language overlap between different installations, particularly between different branches or industries. A university installation may have not a single language in common with a banking system, and the same applies for most of the other tools, be it design, test, administration, or accounting. Many applications are written in multiple languages, or mix the object programs of components originally developed in different languages. In such a case, the respective languages have to adhere to a common call interface or the calls have to be translated into the proper format each time. This principle is used in a well-known open protocol, called Remote Procedure Call (RPC).

- Numeric, text or list oriented, recursive routines
- Batch, interactive, reactive (embedded) systems
- Procedural, declarative (4G) programs; deductive (logic) programs
- Object-oriented systems
- Functional (stateless) programs; finite state machines
- Loops with callback routines; monitors with transaction programs
- Neural networks
- Genetic algorithms

Fig. 4-1 Programming paradigms (according to Jones [Jone00])

In business applications, transactions play a prominent role. A transaction is invoked from a transaction monitor or data communication (DC) subsystem, using the services of the transaction monitor through a command or call interface.

For most languages, the *module* concept is the key structuring concept. The precise definition of a module varies by programming language. It may be a subroutine, a procedure, or a class. In some languages the term 'module' is used. A module (in a generic sense) is a vehicle to factor out repetitions, to facilitate parallel developments (separate name spaces), and to allow independent compilation. Above all, it is the main structuring aid, helping to make code readable. For large systems, a module is a rather low-level concept, however. Some systems have thousands of modules, particularly if they have more than a million source instructions or lines of code (MLOC). Most languages offer few constructs beyond the module level. These additional constructs are frequently defined outside the programming language, be it by the operating system, the transaction monitor, or the database system. For example, transactions, threads, and partitions.

A small system is distinguished from a large system mainly by the type of hardware used. From a software point of view, a small system usually requires the same set of functions than a large system, only they are used less intensively. A difference may show up in the size of the files and the databases, which is sometimes referred to as the 'small system paradox'. The client–server concept, as described before, is one way to make available to a small system functions that are only needed occasionally, for which permanent storage capacity cannot be dedicated. If the client only has a bare minimum of functions it is referred to as a 'thin client'.

The source code of a program is a complete entity, rather than a skeleton or torso, if it is interpretable according to the execution model of the language chosen, or it can be compiled into some machine code. The most important property of source code is, that it has to be readable by humans. The purpose of most of the rules discussed in this chapter is to ease the understanding of programs and to improve their utility for humans.

In spite of many declarations to the contrary, the real binding documentation of a software system is its source code. This is, of course, not the view of the user, but that of the developer and maintainer. A user has to be able to rely completely on the external specification, whether it has the form of a user manual or an online dialog. Whatever effort is made to keep the design documentation, i.e. the internal specification, synchronized with the source code, the developer or maintainer has no right to rely on it. It may help him or her enormously, it may show him or her what was intended, but that is all. Object code can be disregarded in this respect: compilers are fast enough today to recreate object code from source code when needed. In normal business life, there is no need to de-compile a program from object to source code, i.e. do reverse engineering. This is true for developers, maintainers, and users. Moreover, no user should be expected to ever have to compile a program or system he or she has not developed personally.

4.3 Applicable laws and their theories

4.3.1 DeRemer's law

The following law expresses an observation made by many practitioners in the late 1960s. It was formulated by DeRemer and Kron [DeRe75].

What applies to small systems does not apply to large ones.	(L11)

Applicability This law says that experiences made in a small, local environment cannot be transferred to a large, global environment. The experiences cannot be stretched: they do not scale up. Since it is easy to build small systems, it is a favorite utopia among managers to be able to build a large system with the help of a number of small teams. DeRemer's law also indicates the reason why technology transfer is difficult between academia and industry. Academic institutions are seldom in a position to develop large systems.

Evidence Although this law has not been validated empirically, it is widely accepted. DeRemer and Kron talk about programming-in-the-small and programming-in-the-large as two different disciplines. In their paper, they mainly talk about the need for different programming languages for the two disciplines. They call these two languages (1) programming languages, and (2) module interconnection languages (MILs). Their proposal however, has not caught on. Later authors have seen in the distinction more than just a language problem. Parnas [Parn72] describes the five-people/one-year project as the borderline between craftsmanship and industrialization. He suggest that software engineering should be defined as that part of our methodologies that apply to large projects. Brooks' experience report on the development of OS/360 [Broo75] also gives many hints in this direction. Every programmer believes he or she can program best if left to do it alone or in a small team. According to Brooks, the difference manifests itself in two directions: first going from a single program to a system; and secondly when going from a program to a product. Both come together in the case of a system product.

Theory To use Brooks' words, 'large projects suffer problems that are different in *kind* from those of small projects'. They usually result from the need to divide labor that is inherently difficult to divide. Nevertheless, if one wants to build large systems, one has to be in command of and apply the technology needed for that. Or as Jones [Jone00] puts it: 'One cannot build an ocean cruiser by planning to build 3000 rowing boats'.

4.3.2 Corbató's law

Over the entire history of programming, there have been constant discussions on the question which languages or notations are best. One of the most basic answers goes back to the Compatible Timesharing System (CTSS). The law in question is derived from an experience report by Fernando Corbató [Corb69] on the CTSS project.

> Productivity and reliability depend on the length of a program's text, independent of language level used. (L12)

Applicability At the time where this law was formulated it seemed to apply only to what were the high-level languages at that time, (e.g. Fortran, COBOL, Algol and PL/I). They were competing against low-level languages as represented by assembly languages. The law still applies today because it is independent of a specific language or language class. It is primarily the textual length of a program or specification that causes difficulty, both in creating and understanding it. The higher the language level, the higher the productivity and reliability. The price to be paid usually shows up at run-time, in the form of path-length increase, and memory consumption. The law is applicable to any document that has to be grasped in its entirety, with all details. For many documents cursory reading is sufficient, but this is not true for programs or data descriptions. Corbató's law works only if the shorter version of the text invokes higher conceptual constructs than the longer version.

The productivity gains mentioned in this context, of course, apply only to the activities following requirements definition and design. There is no reason why the time needed for requirements definition depends on the methods or tools used for the implementation. If a very high-level language is used, the design may have to skip over certain detailed aspects, such as storage layouts or code optimizations.

Evidence The time sharing system CTSS was a precursor of Multics and the first large system to be partially written in a high-level language. The language used was a dialect of PL/I. Corbató was the first author who observed that development effort and error frequency turned out to be roughly equivalent for a piece of code of given length, independent of the language used. His comparison was between Assembler and PL/I. What gives this law its deeper meaning is the fact that the functionality provided

by one line of PL/I code is three of four times that of Assembler code. The
success of PL/I for the development of both CTSS and Multics strongly
influenced the overall direction taken in systems programming from then
on. Some of the Multics developers later created the UNIX system, which
was also largely written in a high-level language.

Corbató's law has been proved many times in the last 30 years for several
third-generation languages (3GL). The most recent study in this respect was
performed by Prechelt [Prec00] with students at the University of Karlsruhe.
His comparison dealt with the following classes of languages: (1) non-script
languages, in particular C, C++, and Java; and (2) script languages, namely
Perl, Python, Rexx, and Tcl. The essential difference between those language classes is that the non-script languages are compiled but the script
languages are interpreted. For the same problem, about eight to ten programs were written per language, (to smooth the difference between
individuals) with a total of 80 programs. The result showed that the non-
script programs were about twice as long as the script programs and took
about twice the time to write. Also, reliability (inverse to number of errors)
was in favor of the script programs, but not as clearly. The price to be paid,
of course, was run time overhead and memory consumption. Incidentally,
the same relationship existed between Assembler and PL/I in 1968.

Several studies have shown that a similar relationship exists between 3GL
and fourth generation languages (4GL), also referred to as application generators. 4GL systems usually standardize classes of applications, such as database
query, file update, or report generation, in such a way that all necessary variations can be expressed by means of a few parameters. A study by Misra and
Jalics [Misr88] shows a size difference (in terms of source code lines) between
COBOL and dBase III Plus of a factor of greater than three, but only a development time gain of 15 percent. Other studies have claimed productivity gains
by factors of three to five. Corbató's law is also reflected in most estimating
formulas, such as in Boehm's COCOMO model. The law is also the reason
why certain software complexity measures (like Halstead, McCabe) can only
be used meaningfully if applied to modules of equal length.

Theory The explanation of this law relies on two aspects. By using a higher
set of constructs, we do not have to redo all the detailed decisions that are
required for the low-level building blocks. Even if we are proficient in doing
that, errors may occur. The second reason for this law comes from the peculiarities of human information processing. We are able to handle a limited
amount of information in our short-term memory only. The number of entities is restricted, but not the nature of the entities. These ideas will be
discussed further in Chapter 10 in the context of Miller's law.

4.3.3 Dijkstra—Mills—Wirth law

Besides the length of code, it is important to know which other properties are
significant. The new insight that was developed during the late 1960s and
early 1970s, concentrated on the logical structure of programs. Three of the

pioneers of this era were Edsger Dijkstra [Dijk69], Harlan Mills [Mill71], and Niklaus Wirth [Wirt71]. We therefore name the following law after them.

> Well-structured programs have fewer errors and are easier to maintain.   (L13)

Applicability A computer does not care how the code is structured. It executes anything as long as it is syntactically correct and functionally valid (i.e. 'executable'). Programs are normally used not only by computers, but also by humans, for whom, additional criteria have to be met. The most important criterion is called 'well-structuredness', which means being well-suited for a human reader. It has to be grasped easily, structured properly, and the purpose of each unit has to be clear and easy to remember. The format and structure have to help comprehension. Although Dijkstra [Dijk68] strongly advocated the avoidance of jumps (gotos), there are many other things that turn a program into unreadable text (or 'spaghetti code').

Evidence There was a recognition that higher structuring mechanisms or language constructs above procedure level were needed. Mills first applied these principles successfully in a commercial project for the New York Times. Since that time the idea of structured programming has been widely accepted throughout the industry. Early empirical evaluations of the structures and features used in programs are reported by Elshoff [Elsh76], Gannon [Gann77], and Dunsmore and Gannon [Duns80]. Dunsmore and Gannon studied programs written by students in several Pascal-like languages. They found that the percentage of global variables used, the total number of variables referenced, and the number of live variables per statement were contributors to errors. This is just another form of the same observation that was expressed by Dijkstra in his famous statement quoted in the chapter heading.

An experimental investigation of structured programming was made by Basili and Reiter [Basi81]. They define structured programming (called 'disciplined programming' by the authors) as top-down design, use of a program design language (PDL), design and code reading, and an organization as a chief-programmer team. The latter idea was promoted by Baker and Mills [Bake72]. An identical task was assigned to seven individual students and to two different groups (a test group and a control group) of six teams, consisting of three students each. The individuals and one group could work as they liked (called the ad-hoc method), the second group of teams followed the structured approach. The task consisted of the design, implementation, testing and debugging of a small system of about 1.2 KLOC, using a Pascal-like language. The development process was measured mainly by collecting data on the number of compile and test runs. The product was analyzed with respect to size, segmentation, and number and scope of variables. The claims tested and the results achieved are given in Fig. 4-2.

Hypothesis tested	Result
Structured method vs ad-hoc → higher efficiency	Confirmed
Structured method vs ad-hoc → lower cost	Confirmed
Structured team vs individuals → same quality	Partially confirmed
Structured team vs individuals → same efficiency	Moderately supported

Fig. 4-2 Evaluation of structured programming

The structured methods came out superior in terms of efficiency (cost per LOC) and total cost. The structured teams produced equally good results regarding the quality of the product (conceptual integrity of design, coherence of modules) as the individual programmers. The overhead costs for team co-ordination were usually offset.

A comprehensive study of the effects of higher language constructs was performed by one of the authors (Rombach) in 1985 [Romb87]. In a controlled experiment, 50 maintenance tasks were assigned to six test persons. There were two systems (a timesharing and a process control system), each one implemented in two languages (a Pascal derivative and a new language, called LADY). The characteristics of the systems that were tested are summarized in Fig. 4-3. The new language contained two important structuring elements, not present in the Pascal derivative, namely a set of processes (called teams), and the separation of the module interface specifications from module implementation. Each person had to apply the same 25 error corrections to two systems, one written in Pascal, the other in LADY. For the five hypotheses tested, the results of the experiment are given in Fig. 4-4.

Type of system	Language	KLOC
Time sharing	Pascal	10.7
Time sharing	LADY	15.2
Process control	Pascal	1.5
Process control	LADY	2.5

Fig. 4-3 Characteristics of systems tested

The measures used in Fig. 4-4 are defined as follows: maintenance effort is the staff time needed per task; comprehension is that portion of the maintenance effort needed to understand what has to be changed; locality is measured by the number of modules changed per task; modifiability is the actual correction effort, after the problem has been understood; and reusability is related to the portion of the system that is left unchanged. What gives the results of this experiment their external validity is the fact that the LADY versions of the systems were always larger (in KLOC) than the Pascal versions. Otherwise, Corbató's law would have applied. Only the results on the process control system seem to be influenced by this effect. The concern that the results could be skewed in favor of the new language (the Hawthorne effect) was addressed by the test set-up.

Hypothesis tested	Result
High language constructs → low maintenance effort	Confirmed
High language constructs → good comprehension	Confirmed
High language constructs → easy localization	Confirmed
High language constructs → easy modification	Partially confirmed
High language constructs → good reusability	Confirmed

Fig. 4-4 Evaluation of language constructs

A study comparable to the one just described was performed by Walker *et al.* [Walk99] with respect to a language (AspectJ) that contains structuring elements supporting aspect-oriented programming. In one case (synchronization construct) the new language was superior to the control language (Java). The time needed to debug and fix errors turned out to be shorter. In a second case (distribution construct), the new language required more time to make changes and resulted in more code to be written. Obviously, the second language construct is not conceptually clean. Users had to study its implementation in order to understand what needed to be done.

Theory In a well-structured text (whether literary, legal, scientific, reference, or software), logical concepts and ideas are localized. They are not spread over hundreds of pages. In the case of software, the execution of the program can easily be visualized by looking at the text. In a debugging system, where the interpreted source code is highlighted, the point of control moves sequentially down the text. It does not jump forward and backward in some erratic fashion. A well-structured text fosters comprehension speed and thoroughness. It is easy to imagine the opposite: a scrambled text that is not understandable at all.

4.3.4 Lanergan's law

A very important direction in software engineering is concerned with the standardization and reusability of software artifacts. The recent impetus for this movement goes back to the investigations done by Robert Lanergan and his colleagues at the Raytheon Corporation in Bedford, MA [Lane79, Lane84]. Their findings are expressed by the following law.

> The larger and more decentralized an organization, the more likely it is that it has reuse potential. **(L14)**

Applicability There are several possible technical directions that can be taken based on Lanergan's law. The most successful way has been the development of standard application packages. The so-called enterprise resource planning (ERP) packages are the best example. One of the companies taking that route was SAP, which has since become the largest software company in Europe, and third largest in the world. The second direction is to look for lower level functions, so-called components, that can be used to build applications. Examples are standard data structures, and GUI interfaces. The final direction taken is in-house reuse. This option only exists for companies with large and decentralized software development groups.

Evidence In the course of their six-year study, Lanergan and his colleagues looked at about 5000 COBOL programs. Their conclusion was that large portions of their business applications consisted of similar functions – in fact, all their programs could be described using six general functions: edit, sort, combine, explode, update, and report. After the introduction of standard routines for select, update, and report, they achieved about 60 percent of code reuse in their systems. Only about 40 percent of the code was unique to the applications. Many similar reports have been published since, for example [Neig84]. According to Jones [Jone00], all companies that employ more than 5000 programmers have a reuse program – examples being AT&T, Hewlett-Packard, and IBM. On the other hand, only 10 percent of those companies with less than 500 programmers have one. A startup company has little to share, as is also the case with competitors in general.

Theory The larger a company or an institution, the more likely it has program developments going on in separate areas. If all activities could have been strongly co-ordinated from the beginning, they would have been sequenced to avoid all redundancies. Since strict sequencing would create dependencies that cannot be managed, identifying components for reuse can reduce the redundant work. In this sense, reuse is a cure of an organizational problem. The cure may not be needed, if the problem does not exist.

4.3.5 McIlroy's law

Software reuse has become popular in industry and academia following an ITT workshop in 1983 lead by Ted Biggerstaff and Alan Perlis [Bigg91]. The underlying ideas can be found already in a visionary paper given by Doug McIlroy during the 1968 Garmisch conference on software engineering [Naur69b]. The promise of software reuse is conveyed by the following law.

> Software reuse reduces cycle time and increases productivity and quality. **(L15)**

Applicability McIlroy's vision was a software industry that would build products out of parts, as is done in other high-technology industries. For a given function, multiple parts could be selected from a supplier's catalog, with varying properties and different levels of trust. Software reuse, as it is understood today, can take on the form of generators, frameworks, and components. Component reuse has become the most frequent direction, and is often advertised as component-based development. For the component approach two modes are relevant: black-box or white-box reuse. In the case of black-box reuse, the source code is not essential; the user depends entirely on the interfaces as specified. If white-box reuse is pursued, the source code is studied and frequently modified. In this case, the reliability achieved by the component is lost. The advantage is that no dependence on the supplier exists and maintenance can be done in-house. As no market has developed yet for reusable components, software reuse is mainly concerned with reusing artifacts developed within the same company.

Reuse most often starts with code reuse. If the appropriate activities follow a disciplined approach, reuse can be considered for the following work products as well: requirement specifications, requirements models, design specifications, test cases, user documentation, screen layouts, cost estimates, and project plans.

Evidence One of the earliest groups adopting the component approach was lead by one of the authors (Endres). Between 1985 and 1990, a comprehensive set of black-box components were developed and introduced into various projects from all over the world. The Böblingen building blocks, comprising data and functional abstractions to be used in systems programming, were used in about 100 projects throughout IBM and became part of an external product (IBM classes). What convinced its users were their reliability and the efficiency of their implementation. The negotiations with users resulted in clear criteria that had to be met: the components had to be error-free, and the performance degradation compared to a hand implementation had to be less than 10 percent, as far as path-length was concerned, and less than 30 percent for the storage space required. Individual components were reused up to 20 times; the average was close to two. As a rule of thumb, if at least two projects used a component, the extra effort to make it reusable paid off. Reports on the Böblingen approach are given by Lenz [Lenz87] and Bauer [Baue93]. The HP experience is described by Griss [Gris93].

Clearly reuse is not a question of language, nor is it a technical question only. Fig. 4-5 summarizes the key technical problems encountered and some possible solutions. The last point, dependency on tools, addresses the question of which programming language to use.

Problem	Solution
Global variables and data structures	Data encapsulation
Incomplete functions	Generalized function
Poor parameterization	Full parameterization, generic parameters
Poor structuring, lack of cohesion	Good modularization, functional coherence
Insufficient documentation	Sufficient documentation
Dependence on environment, tools and history	Isolation from environments and tools

Fig. 4-5 Technical problems of reuse

Non-technical problems associated with software reuse may be just as important. They comprise: (1) an adequate requirements definition process (domain analysis) for the reusable components; (2) the development of consistent terminology and classification systems; (3) the establishment of a distribution and maintenance process for components; (4) library search mechanisms and tools; (5) the motivation of the developers; and (6) the motivation of users. While the motivation of developers is usually the easy part, the motivation of users is much more critical. If ways have been found to account for the extra effort required to make code reusable, developers love to make their code freely available to others. In fact one has to be quite selective, otherwise a reuse library can easily be inundated. Many developers like to dump their output across the fence, particularly if the library takes over the maintenance responsibility. Users have to overcome the not-invented-here effect, and have to learn to live with the risk involved in relying on other people's work. The content of a repository of reusable components should be determined more by what is needed and will be used, than by what happens to be available. It starts out with a small library, showing what is possible. Building up knowledge and trust is a recursive process. Software reuse is at the heart of a concept called software factory, which will be discussed later.

An experimental study addressing the key issues related with software reuse is reported by Basili [Basi96b]. In this experiment, students, in teams of three, developed eight small systems of between five to 14 KLOC. The components to be reused came from three well-known public domain libraries: (1) the OSF/Motif library of C++ classes for manipulating windows, dialogs, and menus; (2) the GNU library of C++ classes for the manipulation of strings, lists, and files; and (3) the C++ database library, with an implementation of multi-indexed B-trees. The errors counted were those found by independent testers during acceptance test. The hypotheses tested and the respective results are given in Fig. 4-6.

Hypothesis tested	Correlation
High reuse rate → few errors	Strong
High reuse rate → little rework	Strong
High reuse rate → high productivity	Strong

Fig. 4-6 Effect of software reuse rate

This experiment has several limitations: the systems being developed were rather small; the test process and coverage reached is not well defined; and any errors detected during design or code inspections were not counted. In addition, the absolute number of errors density, measured in defects per KLOC, is of interest, being 0.1 for the reused code, and 6.1 for the new code. What is surprising is not the range of the two numbers, but the fact that the reused code had such a high error density.

A very interesting empirical study regarding software reuse is reported by Zweben [Zweb95]. The goal was to investigate the differences between white-box and black-box reuse. A controlled experiment was used, involving two enhancement tasks and one modification task to be performed for existing Ada programs. Fourteen graduate students were the testers. The results are summarized in Fig. 4-7.

Hypothesis tested	Correlation
Black-box reuse → lower effort	Strong
Black-box reuse → high quality	Mixed

Fig. 4-7 Evaluation of software reuse modes

In this experiment, quality was equated with correctness. Black-box reuse showed higher quality only in one of three experiments. Although this experiment uses a rather small number of test persons, the results seem to be rather conservative. The industrial experience of the authors has confirmed that the quality argument is clearly in favor of black-box reuse.

We would also like to mention a study by Frakes [Frak94] that had the goal of evaluating search methods. This investigation is not directly relevant to the main claims of reuse, but deals with a technical question of interest for reuse. Assuming that a repository has more than a few hundred components, the search method may become critical. Four search methods that are widely used for library search were tested: (1) hierarchical classification; (2) faceted description; (3) attributes with values; and (4) keywords. The queries dealt with UNIX related components; the test persons were professionals in a software company with considerable programming experience (average about 12 years). Frakes observed no significant difference between the four methods in terms of recall and precision. Each method, however, retrieved a different set of components. The overlap was about 70 percent, meaning that each method found an additional 30 percent of components that the other methods had not found. The search time was shortest for the classification system; longest for the keyword search. Considering the overall costs, keyword search is superior, since no manual preparation of the data is needed. This is, by the way, consistent with the current practice on the Internet, where keyword searches have become dominant.

Theory Reuse will be technically successful only if components show low coupling and high cohesion, and if the details of the implementation are properly encapsulated. These are exactly the same properties that have been the basis of the Constantine, Parnas, and Dijkstra–Mills–Wirth laws cited above. Rather than writing new code, the highest productivity and quality gains are to be achieved by reusing well-tested code. The problems normally associated with development are reduced to a search problem. For a given task the right match has to be found. Reuse works only if there is a loosely coupled community that is not doing enough analysis to eliminate all similar functions beforehand and is close enough to be able to share code, i.e. trust each other.

To evaluate the business case for reuse a simple cost model can be used. It is based on the model published in [Endr88] and uses the following parameters:

C_d: cost of new development of a component;
C_g: cost of generalization, i.e. effort needed to make a component reusable;
C_a: cost of adaptation of a reusable component to using environment;
n: frequency of reuse, i.e. number of users of a component.

Using these variables, the cost of reuse for a component C_r is given by the formula:

$$C_r = C_g/n + C_a$$

This assumes that the cost for the original development has been absorbed by somebody else. A decision in favor of reuse within a project is economically justified if $C_r < C_d$ is true. Similarly, the productivity can compared with the base productivity, defined as:

$$P_0 = S/C_d$$

with S as size of product (e.g. expressed in KLOC). If, in addition, r is given as the rate of reuse (i.e. percentage of code originating from reusable components), then the productivity including reusable components is:

$$P_r = S/((1-r)C_d + rC_r) = (S/C_d)((1-r) + r / C_d)$$
$$= P_0/(1-r + rC_r/C_d).$$

In this formula, the ratio $k_r = C_r/C_d$ can be called the relative cost of reuse. Given $r = 0.4$ and $k_r = 0.3$ as an example, and using $P_0 = 1$, we obtain the following relative productivity:

$$P_r = 1/(1-0.4 + 0.4 \times 0.3) = 1/(0.6 + 0.12) = 1/0.71 = 1.39$$

In this example, the productivity has increased by 39 percent, assuming that reused code is counted as new code. There are other measures of productivity that do not take reused code into account, or at least not fully.

4.3.6 Conway's law

There is a relationship between the structure of the organization that builds a system and the structure of the system. This observation was first expressed by Melvin Conway [Conw68] and observed frequently since.

| A system reflects the organizational structure that built it. | (L16) |

Applicability Conway's observation was that organizations that build systems are constrained to produce systems which are copies of the communication structures of theses organizations. The organization chart reflects the first system design. Conway's example is the following: If a COBOL compiler is written by four people it will have four phases. A more general version (supposedly due to Cheatham) says: If n people are assigned to a project, it will produce $n-1$ modules (because one person will be the manager). Conway's law will apply unless the organization is willing to adjust to a structure that is more suited for the system. The communication between different project groups should follow the same interfaces as established for the system. Therefore one should organize the development team in such a way that it matches the system structure, and components should not be split among different groups. As the system structure may change as development proceeds, the organizational structure should change accordingly.

Evidence One of this book's authors (Endres) found many confirmations of Conway's law during his industrial career. One particular example was a project split between a group in the Netherlands and in Germany. The German data are given in [Endr75]. At the same time as the new functions were developed in Böblingen, a restructuring (a so-called clean-up) of the operating system nucleus was performed by the team in the Netherlands, which resulted in serious integration conflicts and caused considerable amounts of rework. After this experience, strict attendance to Conway's law was enforced by adopting a principle called module ownership.

A recent study investigating the applicability of Conway's law is reported by Hersleb and Grinter [Hers99]. They looked at a project in the telephony area that was split across two sites, one in the UK and one in Germany. Although the division of work followed the architectural lines of the system, the need for communication was still high, and integration problems were unavoidable. Interface specifications, thought to be 100 percent complete, were lacking essential details. Project plans would have to be 'over-engineered' if they were to solve all problems. The variability occurring during the project created unforeseen communication requirements. In spite of conference calls and e-mails, liaison assignments and on-site visits were needed.

Theory Conway's law is valid since system development is more a communication problem than a technical problem. It is more important to think about communication barriers and enablers than about tools that enhance the clerical or intellectual capabilities of the individual. This is also the reason it is listed here and not under management aspects.

The object-orientation paradigm is applicable to requirements definition, design and programming. The concept of object-oriented programming goes back to the languages Simula [Dahl67] and Smalltalk [Gold89]. The next hypothesis is therefore named after the designers of these two languages, Ole-Johan Dahl and Adele Goldberg.

> Object-oriented programming reduces errors and encourages reuse. (H5)

Applicability Simula 67 introduced classes and objects, mainly as a protection mechanism. They were intended to make programs more reliable by restricting the freedom of a programmer to associate any processing functions with any data type. This principle is referred to as strong typing and is available in most object-oriented languages to varying degrees. A notable exception is Smalltalk, which avoids strong typing in favor of late binding. All object-oriented languages support inheritance and polymorphism.

Evidence The studies referred to in Section 3.3.6 on Booch's second law regarding inheritance also apply here, because they were done with object-oriented programs. For the question of strong typing versus late binding a study by Prechelt and Tichy [Prec98] gives some hints. This was performed with 40 students and compared the effects of two different C compilers, one with and one without type checking. The subjects developed and tested small programs interfacing with a GUI library. The input to each compiler run was evaluated and the measurements taken included the time needed for the task, the number of errors made, and the number of runs needed until all errors were removed. As summarized in Fig. 4-8, all their hypotheses were supported by the results.

Hypothesis tested	Result
Type checking → better productivity	Supported
Type checking → reduced # of defects	Supported
Type checking → shorter defect lifetime	Supported

Fig. 4-8 Evaluation of type checking

The subjective impression expressed by the test persons was that type checking was helpful. Since code inspections are normally performed after the compile errors are eliminated, additional checks performed by a compiler let inspectors concentrate on other problem areas. The results of this study are consistent with the results achieved by Dunsmore and Gannon [Duns80] for the same questions.

Comment The results of tests performed for object-oriented programs are usually inconclusive if the measurements only span a single project. It may take at least two or three projects within the same organization before the benefits are seen.

4.3.8 Beck–Fowler hypothesis

One of the more recent software development paradigms is referred to as agile development, implying both rapidity and lightness. Two key proponents are Kent Beck [Beck99, Beck01] and Martin Fowler [Fowl01]. Its main emphasis is summarized by the following hypothesis.

> Agile programming methods reduce the impact of requirement changes. (H6)

Applicability As discussed in the context of Glass' law, the requirements process is a well-known source of problems. In certain environments, requirement changes are unavoidable. The only question is how to go about them. A development process that emphasizes careful requirements documentation and elaborate designs may not be best suited in such a situation. Rather than abandoning all forms of a systematic process entirely and adopting the 'code-and-fix' principle, some minimal and adaptable process is necessary. What is dubbed a 'heavyweight' process should be replaced by a 'lightweight' process.

Evidence Of the several new methodologies described in [Fowl01], Extreme Programming (XP) is certainly the best-known one. It relies on the following activities:

- Start the implementation with a basic design only and evolve the design as the project proceeds.
- Instead of producing lengthy documentation, foster face-to-face communication between developers and customers.
- Put a minimal system into production early and grow it later.
- Write test cases before programming starts and run tests for every development iteration.
- Integrate and test the whole system, if possible several times a day.
- Produce all software in pairs, i.e. two programmers to one screen.

Comments This approach has attracted significant attention. Clearly, this is incremental development in its purest form. It appeals to all programmers who consider documentation a nuisance, while for most novice programmers, anyway, coding is ranked higher than designing, since it gives assurance and satisfaction. There is no design notation around that is as stringent as source code: UML allows too many choices and it takes additional work to keep the design synchronized with the source code;

and XP emphasizes testing as the main and only verification method. Pair programming is only a weak substitute for inspections. If two persons work together day-in day-out, they become susceptible to the same errors. XP recommends an integration process similar to the one adopted some time ago by Microsoft [Cusu95] and many other companies. It certainly is ideal for a developer if he or she does not have to make any predictions or commitments, but has a customer who is very indulgent and willing to assume all risks. As Fowler states, XP is not applicable for every project, and especially not for fixed price contracts or projects involving more than 50 people.

4.3.9 Basili–Boehm COTS hypothesis

A set of ten hypotheses related to COTS-based software is given by Basili and Boehm [Basi01]. They are summarized in one hypothesis here.

COTS-based software does not eliminate the key development risks.   (H7)

Applicability Although the abbreviation COTS (Commercial Off-The-Shelf) is of recent origin, software has been offered commercially since the pioneering days. The first products were compilers, followed by utilities or applications of all kind. As indicated in the title and the introductory sections of this chapter, building systems using COTS packages is really the normal mode of system development. Most modern systems are built through composition rather than construction. Today, no software system is developed without using a platform comprised of an operating system and a file- or data-management system. Frequently, a transaction monitor, network management services, a user-interface package, and server and browser functions are involved. The degree of usage of these components varies somewhat between commercial and technical applications. Many technical applications, however, also make use of databases but research and education in software engineering are only gradually taking this into account.

Evidence There is no doubt in our mind that the hypothesis as formulated above is true. The question is merely what it implies in detail. Little empirical data are available on this subject, and are not normally to be found in any scholarly journal. Basili and Boehm [Basi01] have published the hypotheses listed in Fig. 4-9, in order to provoke more studies in this area. Although the original authors refrained from taking a position, we have added a first guess on what these studies might produce. Our judgment is given in the right-hand column.

No.	Hypothesis	Authors' guess
1	Over 90% of executed instructions are COTS code	True
2	More than half of features go unused	Likely
3	New release every 8–9 months; service for three releases only	True
4	Integration and post-deployment costs grow with square number of components	Likely
5	Post-deployment costs exceed development costs	Unlikely
6	Cost of glue code is three times cost of application code	True
7	License costs are significant	Varies
8	Assessment and tailoring varies with type of program	True
9	Personal skill and experience remain highest productivity factors	True
10	More schedule and cost overruns as for non-COTS-based systems	Unlikely

Fig. 4-9 Hypotheses for COTS-based systems

Comments The main use of COTS software is in the reduction of cycle time. Considering the relative expense of additional hardware, redundant functions are quite acceptable, although provision has to be made to ensure that they do not have to be learned by the users. The license costs for commercial software are normally no problem, with the exception of purchased software from development markets with a monopolistic structure. Competition clearly reduces software prices for COTS products. The schedule and cost risks can also be mitigated if the functions to be used are clearly delineated and if developers and users can gain experience with the corresponding interfaces early enough.

4.4 More on system construction and composition

There are a number of aspects that have not been addressed by the laws and hypotheses given above, which deserve more consideration.

4.4.1 Incremental development and integration

The construction or build plan for a system may call for a sequence of distinct steps, leading up to the final product. This should not be confused with prototyping, since each intermediate level is built with the same quality criteria that will apply to the final product and the intermediate levels are not typically thrown away (this should only happen if a total redesign is needed, or the project ends prematurely).

In the area of system integration, incremental methods clearly have advantages. Here there is a trade-off between (1) long integration cycles, with increased stability for the individual developers and high risks for the entire project, and (2) short integration cycles, with constant demands on each developer, but lower risks for the project. In the past, a trade-off was often made in favor of the individual developer, but today all major software developers have adopted processes with extremely short integration cycles. Daily builds, as practiced by Microsoft [Cusu95], are one such example.

4.4.2 Implementation languages

According to Jones [Jone00], around 600 different programming languages are in use today. Their frequency and use reflects both the history and the peculiarities of our field. Well-known criteria exist for the rational selection of an implementation language, and are listed in Fig. 4-10. Unfortunately, the actual decision can seldom be made independently for each project, since the decisions made for previous projects have a great influence, depending on where on the learning curve the team is, what tools have been paid for, and so on. Many language candidates fall short on such basic requirements as the support for decimal arithmetic, file management, and database access – one reason why many commercial users are still dependent on COBOL and PL/I.

Technical criteria	Non-technical criteria
Adequacy for problem domain	Compatibility with existing programs and data
Clarity, structure, self-documentation	Experience of users
Support of software engineering concepts	Demands of customer
Interface to system services and subsystems	License fee and conditions
Quality and performance of compilers	Quality of supplier support and service
Available development tools and libraries	Standardization
Portability, reusability	Future and strategic importance

Fig. 4-10 Criteria for language selection

PL/I was the attempt to unify the world of commercial and technical applications. For some time it became the most frequently used second language. If a COBOL programmer needed floating point, or a Fortran programmer more flexible data types and data structures, PL/I was their choice. On minicomputers, and later on microcomputers, Pascal, C, and Basic took its place. Today, C++ and Java are the dominant languages. Both are object-oriented languages; Java is a subset of C++ with special features that enable its execution in a distributed environment.

Programming languages are also a means for some vendors to differentiate their products from their competition. For a user, there is a risk, however, that he or she may become dependent on (be locked in by) a vendor, if he or she uses vendor-specific languages or features of a standard language that are vendor-specific.

4.4.3 Application generators

Application generators, also referred to as fourth generation languages (4GL), have achieved a clear role as productivity aid for professional programmers. They have not fulfilled, however, the expectation of those people who believed they could turn programming into a layperson's job, following the slogan 'Application Development Without Programmers', to quote the title of a book by Jim Martin [Mart81]. This class of languages usually follows the paradigm of declarative, rather than procedural programming. In a declarative language, the desired results are specified by means of high-level operations (like sum, average or largest value). In some cases, certain processing steps are implied, i.e. they are always invoked. In the case of the Report Program Generator (RPG), the dominant language for all small commercial IBM systems, this cycle implies the reading of one record per file, comparing so-called matching fields, performing a calculation, and printing the result.

Many languages are integrated closely with certain DB/DC or application systems. An example of the latter is ABAP/4 of SAP. The most successful type of application generators are so-called spreadsheets. They allow simple calculations to be performed for every row and column of a two-dimensional table. Spreadsheets turned PCs into a universal business tool. Modern spreadsheets have interfaces to database systems and graphics packages, and their output can be integrated into a text report, produced by means of a text system.

The disadvantage of 4GL languages is their lack of standardization, and hence their limited portability across suppliers. A notable exception in this respect is the Structured Query Language (SQL), which was originally developed for relational database systems by IBM, but has since been standardized and re-implemented for most other vendor products. With the exception of SQL, this entire class of languages is usually ignored by academia.

4.4.4 Visual programming languages

The subject of *visual languages* has been a research topic for about the last 20 years. The goal is to generate programs by means of two-dimensional graphical notations. These programs are either directly interpreted or translated into a conventional programming language. Some examples adhere to the procedural paradigm, i.e. the graphs describe operations that are to be sequentially executed. Of considerable interest are examples that realize a dataflow paradigm, or a functional paradigm. Some examples are mere decorations of CASE tools.

It is assumed that a multi-dimensional graphic representation of a program appeals better to the strengths of our visual system than a linear text. There is some hope that visual languages will enable children and non-experts to create simple programs by pointing at the respective building blocks, but so far this hope has not been fulfilled. Some successes can be found, however, in professional applications, for example, systems that support the selection and integration of components from a fixed repository, as in image processing.

Apart from visual languages in the sense described above, the attribute 'visual' is also used for development systems that support graphical user interfaces (GUI) and make extensive use of graphical manipulation facilities. As an example, Visual Basic is an implementation of Basic that makes use of a full screen editor, with drag-and-drop facilities, and a GUI package included in the generated code. Similar systems exist to aid in the construction of C++ or Java programs.

4.4.5 Programming by example

Even more far-reaching than for visual programming is the vision that is pursued by an approach to programming known as *Programming by Example* (PBE). The expectation is that computers could be taught in the same way as people are taught, i.e. by demonstration. As one author [Lieb00] puts it: 'This could break down the Berlin wall that has always separated programmers from users'.

In the case of numeric calculations, PBE is trivial if the number of cases to be handled is small (i.e. a few thousands only). Then all input–output pairs (or tuples) can be listed and stored in a table. The problem arises if cases are to be handled, that cannot be specified ahead of time. In such a case, the computer is expected to interpolate or extrapolate from the cases given. This may work if the range and type of input and output data can be strictly specified and the method of interpolation or extrapolation can be given.

The general expectation of people pursuing PBE is that they might find ways to automatically generalize from given input values. This may be possible in the case of graphical manipulations or robotic movements, where the total environment is clearly defined and the set of operations is limited. In some prototype systems, the system performs certain generalizations, based on heuristics, and the user is asked to confirm the results. To be able to perform correct generalizations for any given set of examples is clearly an unsolvable problem. The final point is that this approach to programming could eliminate testing, at least as we know it. The code is generated from the test cases, in such a way that it satisfies all test cases. Another form of testing would be required however, to verify that the generalizations were done correctly. Little thought has been given to that.

4.4.6 Software metrics

Many of the laws cited in this book either explicitly or implicitly refer to metrics. In the software engineering literature the term metric is used in the sense of measure. It is a mapping of empirical objects onto formal objects, usually rational numbers. Mathematically speaking, a metric is a function $m: X \to R$, with X as an arbitrary type and R as the set of (positive) rational numbers, where for all x in X:

$m(x)$ is defined,
$m(x) \geq 0$, and
$m(x_1 \cup x_2) \leq m(x_1) + m(x_2)$

Several hundred software metrics have been proposed, although not all of them are useful. Fig. 4-11 gives examples of some typical measures, most of which have been used in this book. The most basic measure is Lines of Code (LOC). Its precise definition and its relationship with the function point (FP) measure will be discussed in Chapter 9. In practical environments, tools are used to automatically derive size and structure measures (except for function points) as soon as source code exists. It is therefore relatively easy to obtain and to update these measures. If the same tools are used for comparison measurements, consistency of data is no problem either.

Category	Metric	Author/definition	Typical range
Size	Lines of code (LOC)	Many	50–20M
	Function points (FP)	Albrecht	5–500,000
Structure	Cyclomatic complexity	McCabe	3–50
	Fan-in/fan-out	Henry/Kafura	3–10
	Coupling between objects (CBO)	Chidamber/Kemerer	10–50
	Depth of inheritance tree (DIT)	Chidamber/Kemerer	0–20
	Lack of cohesion on methods (LCOM)	Chidamber/Kemerer	0–50
Quality	Error density	Defects/KLOC	0.1–50
	Field stability	Problems/user month	0.01–0.5
	Satisfied customers	Percent	50–95%
Process	Defect removal rate	Percent	30–90%
	Fixes in error	Percent	0.3–5%

Fig. 4-11 Examples of software metrics

The quality measures given in Fig. 4-11 are a refinement of the criteria listed in Fig. 2-1. The entity called 'defect' is a synonym for error, that may also designate fault or failure, particularly in cases where a distinction between the two is not obvious. The term 'problem' almost corresponds to failure. With the exception of function points, the metrics for size and structure have the great advantage that they can be derived easily and precisely from the source code. The data relating to the metrics for quality and process require a certain organizational effort if they are to be collected consistently. This effort is well justified because otherwise no basis exists for any systematic process improvements. Some readers may miss the Halstead measures. Based on our experience, however, they are not very useful.

4.4.7 Configuration management and version control

Configuration management is a process that assures that the physical pieces making up a system are properly identified and made available when needed. A configuration is a specific arrangement of components allowed for within the scope of the systems definition. For this purpose a system can be considered as a family of different configurations that can be derived from the specification. An example is a software system planned to support different, mutually exclusive, hardware device types. One configuration uses device driver A, another device driver B.

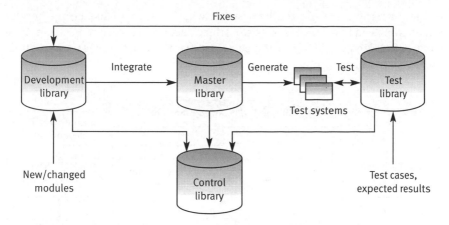

Fig. 4-12 Configuration management

A related but different concept is that of a version. Versions describe assemblies of components from a historical perspective. A version of a system combines those versions of the components that represent the same level of development. Fig. 4-12 illustrates the development process determined by configuration management aspects. New or changed modules are promoted from a private library (not shown) into a central development library. A module is only accepted after it fulfills certain criteria – it must at least compile without errors. From then on, every module is subject to formal change control. A changed module may only be accepted if a reason for the change is given, for example, the reference to a problem report in case of a corrected error. If a new version is built, all required modules have to be included. After potential conflicts have been resolved, the modules are integrated into a master library, which can be used to generate multiple configurations in order to perform testing. A configuration management process similar to the one described above is not only needed during development but also during maintenance. The reason for this is that normally three or four versions of a system have to be maintained simultaneously. Unfortunately, not all users can be induced to migrate to a new version as soon as it comes out.

A well-thought-out change control procedure may require additional steps. Usually a change proposal is made first. This is followed by an assessment of its impact (e.g. number of dependencies, cost) before it is approved. Configuration management makes use of a number of tools. The minimum is a development library with version control and access rights. Multiple versions of a component are normally stored in the form of one base version and modification chains (so-called deltas) from which the other versions can be derived. The backward delta approach is usually preferred.

4.4.8 Software factories

The term software factory, although a misnomer, was first used in General Electric by Bob Bemer to designate a highly organized facility for the development of software. At the heart of it was the idea to use computers to automate as many processes as possible. After a transitory use in a USA software company (SDC) in the early 1970s, the concept was successfully implemented in Japan.

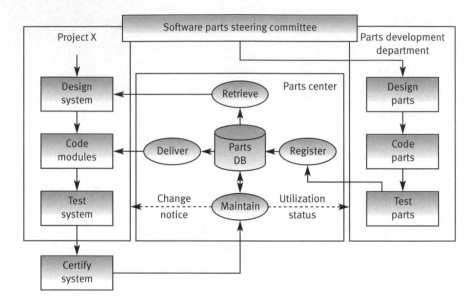

Fig. 4-13 Toshiba software factory

The environment established by Toshiba for its Fuchu site, shown in Fig. 4-13, has been in use since 1977. At that time the site had about 2,500 employees, which rose to about 8,000 by 1991. The site produced software for power supply stations and other control systems. As described by Matsumoto [Mats87], the organization centered around four strategies:

1. standardized development processes;
2. reuse of existing designs and code;
3. standardized and integrated tools;
4. training and career development for programmers.

A central department for the development of parts was funded separately. The term 'parts' is used to designate specifications, design, and code meeting predefined standards. In addition, programmers in development projects were asked to contribute parts to the central repository. Maintenance of parts is centralized and the using project is informed about changes. To motivate the user side, project managers had to agree on productivity targets that could only be met by making extensive use of existing parts. Developers would receive awards for parts they had registered if they achieved a high frequency of reuse.

Many other companies (including HP and IBM) have introduced reuse programs that are modeled on the Toshiba factory. Because of the progress in communication technologies, there is less need today to concentrate a large number of people in one location. Also, the rigid process associated with the term factory never became popular outside Japan. The fear was that it would strangle creativity and flexibility, which are both considered important for the American and European approach to developing software. The term 'manufacturing' found its place into the software vocabulary, designating the process leading to shrink-wrapped packages in sufficient quantities, after the actual development is completed.

4.4.9 Legacy applications

Software reuse as described above is concerned with reusing components, rather than entire systems. Existing applications, even if developed with older languages and methods, may be successful for several decades. They are then referred to as legacy applications. If for new applications a new system environment is required, the legacy application has to be integrated into that environment. For batch applications, the easiest way is to use separate hardware partitions that allow simulation of the old environment including the base functions provided by the operating system. Fig. 4-14 shows how legacy applications can be integrated into a Web application environment. The Web server is extended into an application platform. Special routines (Servlets) intercept all interactions with users and convert them into HTTP dialogs. On the client side, the browser is extended (via Applets) to interpret the interactions and convert them back into the format used before.

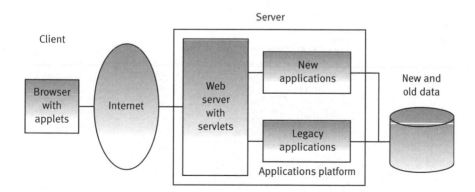

Fig. 4-14 Integrating legacy applications

4.5 Examples and study material

4.5.1 Text formatting implementation

Fig. 4-15 gives the text of a sample program as published by its author. It has been converted from Algol to Pascal. A careful analysis of this text reveals the following implementation errors or shortcomings:

c1: No input or output files are named; the system will assume whatever defaults or standards have been established.

c2: Without further explanation, the carriage return character (CR) is replaced by the line feed character (LF).

c3: The procedure Alarm is undefined.

c4: The variable k has not been declared.

c5: The text does not contain a single line of commentary.

In addition to the implementation errors introduced in this phase, three requirements errors (r1, r3, r6) and all four design errors are still present. It can safely be assumed that the program as published was never compiled nor executed. Although a rather small program, it has served many authors to explain several basic lessons on software development.

```
program textform;
const N = 30, BL = ' ', LF = char(10);
var buffer: array[1..N] of char, charact: char,
fill, bufpos: 0..N;
label 10;

fill := 0; bufpos := 0; write(LF)
10: read (charact);
    if (charact = BL) or (charact = LF)
        then begin
            if (fill + bufpos + 1) = < N
                then begin write(BL);
                            fill := fill + 1 end
                else begin write(LF);
                            fill := 0 end;
                for k := 1 to bufpos do
                  write(buffer[k]);
                  fill := fill + bufpos;
                  bufpos := 0 end
        else if bufpos = N
            then Alarm
            else begin bufpos := bufpos + 1;
                                buffer[bufpos] := charact end;
    goto 10
end.
```

Fig. 4-15 Program textform in Pascal

4.5.2 Program size variations

The purpose of this example is to illustrate the variability of size measurements. In Fig. 4-16, five different implementations are assumed for the printing of a single text line, consisting of two words ('Hello World'). The size of each implementation is given in terms of two measures, namely lines of code (LOC) of the source code, and storage bytes (Kbytes) used for the object code. On the left, the numbers are given for an implementation in a procedural language (C, C++), on the right are the respective numbers for implementations by means of a transaction processing (DB/DC) system or application framework. The implementation by means of an application generator (4GL) falls between these extremes. For this tiny program the overhead created by the more advanced modes of implementation is disproportionately high. For larger programs it hardly matters.

Implementation	C	C++	4GL	DB/DC	Framework
LOC	10	50	300	1,200	2,350
KBytes	0.2	0.4	1.5	5.3	9.5

Fig. 4-16 'Hello World' sizes

Fig. 4-17 shows for a given module the evolution of size and complexity over time. Size is measured again in lines of code (LOC), complexity is expressed as cyclomatic complexity, i.e. McCabes's metric. After the requirements definition and the design activities, both numbers are still estimates. After coding and test, both numbers can be measured. As the example demonstrates, the size has a tendency to increase, due to the fact that as the project progresses, more special cases are discovered that have to be handled. This trend can be reversed whenever optimization is attempted. The McCabe number can increase even if the size of a module is decreasing. This shows that both measures express independent properties.

Time	Requirements	High-level design	Low-level design	Coding	Unit test	System test
LOC	220	210	265	341	378	365
McCabe	15	15	15	18.5	19.3	28.4

Fig. 4-17 Growth of size and complexity over time

4.5.3 Metrics application

Fig. 4-18 gives example metric data for two projects. It lists eight structural metrics values that were derived manually from the specification of classes. The actual numbers are taken from a study by Sharble and Cohen [Shar93].

The same kind of numbers can automatically be derived from the source code (e.g. C++, Smalltalk, or other) by means of a metric tool. The first six belong to the Chidamber/Kemerer set referred to before. The exact definition of each metric is not important here, as, it can be found in the literature. The absolute values, as calculated by Sharble and Cohen, are contained in the two middle columns.

Metric	Abbr.	Range low	Range high	Project A [absolute]	Project B [absolute]	Project A [percent]	Project B [percent]
Weighted methods per class	WMC	0	120	130	71	108	59
Depth of inheritance tree	DIT	0	20	21	19	105	95
Number of children	NOC	0	20	19	13	95	65
Coupling between objects	CBO	10	50	42	20	80	25
Response for a class	RFC	50	250	293	127	121	38
Lack of cohesion in methods	LCOM	0	50	64	21	128	42
Violations of Demeter	VOD	0	100	64	44	64	44
Weighted attributes per class	WAC	0	50	40	0	80	0

Fig. 4-18 Metric data for two projects

In the two right-hand columns, the values have been normalized (to percent), using the range information given in the two left-hand range columns. Using these values, the Kiviat graph given in Fig. 4-19 can be drawn. The inner circle represents the lower boundary of the range, the outer circle the higher boundary. Some tools, for example, Logiscope, enable us to do this automatically. The range values chosen are somewhat arbitrary in this example. In practice, they should be selected based on actual experience. Their purpose is to make outliers visible. In this example, four measures (WMC, DIT, LCOM, and VOD) of Project A fall outside the expected range.

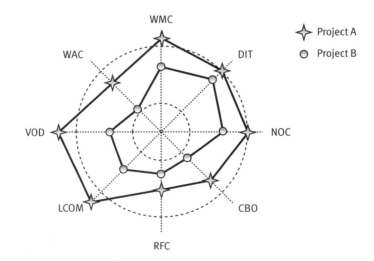

Fig. 4-19 Example of Kiviat graph

It may be of interest to note that Projects A and B developed the same system, using different methods (Wirfs–Brock versus Shlaer–Mellor). Following this example, we note that it is easy to derive many numbers, once the code is available and that some tools produce 50 to 200 different numbers. Single and absolute numbers have seldom illuminative power, nor is any single value either good or bad. The important thing to remember is that variations in numbers point to potential problems, providing an opportunity to ask questions, to look for reasons, and to improve our understanding.

Exercises

4-1   What is the difference between construction and composition in software development?

4-2   Explain the term paradigm in the context of programming.

4-3   What is a software module? Give examples for different languages.

4-4   What is the main advantages that can be expected from using high-level language constructs?

4-5   What are the circumstances for a successful software reuse program?

4-6   What is COTS software? What is the main advantage of its use?

4-7   Please name some technical and non-technical criteria for the selection of an implementation language.

4-8   What distinguishes an application generator from a procedural language? In what situations and in what respect is it superior?

4-9   Which of the software metrics listed in Fig. 4-11 are source code related? Which are not?

4-10 What constitutes a configuration? How does it differ from a version?

4-11 When is an application referred to as legacy application? What type of conflicts can arise between legacy and new applications?

chapter 5

Validation and static verification

We can conclude from experience that inspections increase productivity and improve final program quality.

M.E. Fagan [Faga76]

This chapter focuses on static approaches to system validation and verification. They do not rely on the execution of code or on the actual performance of system tasks, which will be described in the next chapter. We will show why these static methods are important and how they relate to other methods.

5.1 Definitions and importance

Validation is an activity that answers the question: 'Are we developing the correct system?' In a narrow sense, we are determining whether the design fulfills all requirements, assuming the requirements correctly describe what is intended or needed. Both functional and non-functional requirements have to be considered. *Verification* on the other hand answers the question: 'Are we developing the system correctly?' Or to put it differently, is the design an optimal solution for the requirements and is the implementation consistent with the design? The abbreviation V&V is frequently used for validation and verification. In the IEEE Glossary [IEEE90], a definition of both terms is given that is a little more restricted, but explains the essence nicely. Accordingly, validation evaluates a system or component to determine whether it satisfies specified requirements. Verification, on the other hand, evaluates a system or component to determine whether the products of a given development phase satisfy conditions imposed at the start of that phase. Here a phase-oriented process model is implied, where the goals for each phase are clearly specified at the beginning of each phase.

In contrary to the constructive methods of design and build, the methods applicable to V&V can be called *analytical methods*. V&V methods can be split into two large groups, namely static and dynamic methods. *Static analysis* means the respective document is read by humans, or perused by a computer, but not executed as a program. In the case of *dynamic analysis*, the program or the system is run (or executed) by means of a computer.

The key method for static V&V is *inspection*. We will use this term for any static analysis of requirements, designs, code, test cases, and project plans. Testing, which is a dynamic analysis method, is used only in the comparison of methods in this chapter. There are two approaches, black-box (or functional testing) and white-box (or structured testing), and both will be discussed in detail in the next chapter. For a definition of the terms failure, fault, and error, see Chapter 2.

Two terms used throughout this chapter are effectiveness and efficiency. *Effectiveness* measures the success rate of an activity. Many activities suffer from a variable number of non-successful results. The various error detection methods are examples of such activities. The more errors that are detected, the more effective a method is. *Efficiency* is result per effort spent. The effort is usually expressed as time in minutes or hours. While productivity measures the same attributes over an entire project, efficiency looks at a single activity.

A key challenge of system development is in meeting reasonably set quality targets. The pursuit of this goal distinguishes the work of professionals from that of amateurs or novices. To be able to take corrective actions early, the quality of the final product must be made visible during the design and construction periods. Clearly we cannot rely purely on the methods used for design and construction for this measurement, nor can we wait until the end of development to investigate quality. This analysis has to occur in parallel with development.

5.2 General observations

In the previous chapters, the emphasis was on methods of construction. We have discussed what it takes to make them more predictable and more effective, but errors are unavoidable for even the best such methods. It is better to prepare for them than to be caught totally by surprise. As a consequence of Boehm's first law, the cost of errors rises with their lifespan. It is therefore important to reduce the lifespan of errors, i.e. to remove the error as soon as possible after the time of commission.

In order to do this, the work products of all activities must be scrutinized. The key work products in question are requirement specifications, design specifications, and source code. Test plans, integration, and maintenance plans are important documents as well, but are not given the same level of attention. Analytical methods attempt to derive certain information from a work product, but which information is valuable depends on the questions asked. How the wanted information is obtained varies with the work product. The use of computers for this analysis has two key advantages: reliability and speed. Computer-performed analysis is therefore the normal case, and applies to all formalized work products, such as programs, data descriptions, design diagrams, etc. It is increasingly important also for natural language text. The spell-checker supporting the creation of this book is one example; another is a diagram checker within a CASE tool.

While an analysis normally checks whether a document has certain properties, the next step is to map a document from one representation into another. Depending on the type of mapping, we talk of conversions, transformations, compressions, formatting, etc. Well-known examples of this category are the formatting tools for text or print programs for a programming language. One particular important form of mapping is called measurement. In this case, a property is expressed by a numeric value, that may be simply a count of lines, words, or characters. Metrics are the sophisticated analysis of such measurements.

In many situations we need to compare two documents. The usual purpose is to find out about differences, such as the differences between two versions of a document. If one wants to determine how the content (or more precisely, the meaning of the statements) of one document relates to the content of another document, we are approaching what is called verification. Since automatic efforts in this direction have limitations, most verifications have to be done manually. Manual verifications are called inspections and, there are many approaches and different names used to designate this type of activity. Sometimes the names express levels of thoroughness, sometimes they are synonyms. In this context, inspections are rather well-planned, systematic activities as compared with reviews and walk-throughs. Reviews and walk-throughs have the same function, but are usually less rigorous.

For the quality criteria listed in Fig. 2-1, the following difference is important. While the user-oriented criteria, i.e. reliability, effectiveness, installability, usability, and robustness, can best be verified through testing, the developer-oriented criteria, i.e. testability, maintainability, localizability, portability, and reusability, have to rely almost entirely on inspections.

5.3 Applicable laws and their theories

The laws cited here represent very important achievements and form part of the basic knowledge for the professional work in our field.

5.3.1 Fagan's law

The most popular concept of inspections is referred to as Fagan inspections today. Michael Fagan [Faga76, Faga86] and his colleagues at IBM defined and introduced this concept first within IBM and later throughout the industry. The benefits of inspections are summarized by the following law.

Inspections significantly increase productivity, quality, and project stability.   (L17)

Applicability Inspections as defined by Fagan and his colleagues have the following key properties:

1. multiple reviewers receive the document or code to be inspected several days ahead of a scheduled inspection meeting;
2. the meeting between author and reviewers is lead by a moderator;
3. the reviewers raise issues while the moderator talks through sections of the document;
4. the moderator records the valid and unique issues; and
5. the moderator organizes the necessary actions together with the author.

Fagan introduced three types of inspection – design, code, and test inspections – and has given detailed guidelines for all three. The framework of Fagan's original study is given in Fig. 5-1. The different types of inspections are indicated with I_1 for design inspections, I_2 for code inspections, and I_3 for test inspections.

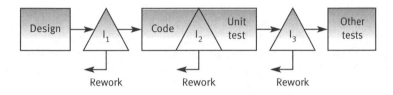

Fig. 5-1 Fagan inspections

Fagan's law applies to all developments that produce information or knowledge intensive products. It particularly applies if the required knowledge is not in the possession of a single person, but has to be collected from different persons or sources. Inspections are widely recognized as the most effective V&V method. They became a key ingredient in the Capability Maturity Model (CMM) of the Software Engineering Institute (SEI) in the USA. Nevertheless, its acceptance in industry is rather low and in academia even lower. As a colleague put it, it is difficult to explain to a mathematician or theoretical physicist why this can be the most effective quality assurance method, although it gets along 'without stochastic differential equations'.

Evidence Fagan's law was first substantiated with empirical data by Fagan himself. To determine the gains in productivity, he compared a process with inspections where rework was done early, with a process where all rework was done after testing. The overall productivity gain was 23 percent. Even more important than the productivity gains, were the gains in quality. While 82 percent of the errors were found during design and code inspections, the total number of errors found after seven months in the field was 38 percent lower than for the comparison product. Examples are given in [Faga86] of projects where between 50 and 93 percent of all errors occurring over the life of a product had been found through inspections.

One author's (Endres) experience with inspections dates back to about 1977. At that time, inspections became a prime method to improve the quality of code, be it for code under development or for code already shipped to customers. The inspections helped to reduce error densities by a factor of more than ten over a period of about ten years. The motivation of developers and managers, however, was not easy as first the fear that a new level of control was being introduced had to be overcome. A particular episode illustrates this point: when asking which programmers were in favor of inspections and which were against it, the answer was 'All programmers are against it, except A, B, and C. But those are exactly the people who do not need it'. Since these were the best programmers and rarely made any errors, there was no better argument to have all programmers do inspections. In this case, this argument was a winner; no further experiments and proofs were needed.

Empirical studies from other industrial environments are reported from, for example, Honeywell–Bull [Well93] and Hewlett-Packard [Grad94]. In the Honeywell–Bull report, a case is mentioned where code inspections were so effective that unit tests could have been skipped. Of 302 errors, 298 were found by means of inspections. It also mentions a case where a major design flaw was not detected in spite of 'successful' inspections, requiring the product to be put on hold. As a human activity, its success depends on the skill of the participants and the amount of time spent for the preparation. This is reflected in the HP version of the inspection process, which comprises the following steps:

- *Planning*: create inspection material.
- *Kickoff*: brief participants.
- *Preparation*: find items and issues to be addressed.
- *Logging*: log items and issues.
- *Cause/prevention*: determine causes and recommend prevention.
- *Rework*: verify and fix defects.
- *Follow-up*: document inspection experience.

In the HP case, with an average effectiveness of about 40 percent (assumed error removal rate across all inspections), the reduction in rework yielded a clear business case in favor of inspections. The cause/prevention step mentioned above will be discussed separately below.

A rational way to motivate an organization in favor of inspections is shown by Jalote and Haragopal [Jalo98] for an Indian software company. The resistance to inspections is explained by what they call the not-applicable-here (NAH) syndrome, which is quite common in our industry and means: 'Whatever works elsewhere will not work here, because our situation is unique'. A small experiment was conducted to convince the local developers in which the same modules underwent code inspections and unit test in parallel. The inspections revealed three times more errors than the unit test and the overlap of errors was small. The detailed numbers were: 54 errors found by inspections, 20 errors found by module test, and 12 duplicates. The effort per error was equal for inspections and unit test, namely 1.9 person-hours. Nevertheless, the fact that 42 errors were removed earlier than usual made a positive business argument. Under the assumption that these 42 errors would be caught during system test, the conclusion was that one hour spent on inspections saves 3–6 hours during system test.

Theory The validity of Fagan's law is a direct consequence of Boehm's first law described before. The high success rate of inspections is due to the high percentage of requirements and design errors. More than anything else, inspections are useful for breaking the vicious circle of misunderstood requirements. If the developer assumes that the requirements were stated correctly, he or she will not find requirement errors during design. Nor will he or she be able to look for those things in the code of which he or she was unaware when creating the design. The developer is in a closed loop, unless an independent thought process gets him or her out of it. A similar effect can occur if one looks at one's previous work after a vacation period of several weeks. Unfortunately, this method is too slow and does not scale.

Comments Removing errors early in the project cycle not only reduces their cost for the project, but also takes out risks that may cause poblems later. Besides their direct effect on quality, inspections have very important collateral benefits. They are an excellent means for education and skill transfer, and they provide for risk distribution within a team. If because of external events or an accident a developer should suddenly become unavailable, it is easier to find a back-up. Above all, inspections create awareness for quality that is not achievable by any other method.

5.3.2 Porter–Votta law

Adam Porter and Lawrence Votta [Port95, Port97a, Port97b] have studied the effectiveness of inspections under a number of conditions. A survey of their studies is given in [Port97c]. The main conclusion is summarized in the following law.

> Effectiveness of inspections is fairly independent of its organizational form. (L18)

Applicability This law explains why it is so difficult to improve on Fagan's basic idea. Fagan's law postulates that an independent thought process should be applied to recreate a work product. As discussed above, Fagan's original approach to inspections has been modified for different environments. The modifications are mainly concerned with the method of preparation and the role of the inspection meeting. Questions like the following were answered differently: 'Is the purpose of the inspection meeting to make decisions after the errors have been found or should errors be identified primarily at the meeting?' 'Should there be one meeting for a given set of modules or multiple meetings?'

Evidence The studies done by Porter and Votta involved students as well as professional developers. For the professionals, the study was done at Lucent Technologies, observing the work for a major release for its switching system (5ESS). The size of this system is about five MLOC. A total of 88 inspections were analyzed over a period of 18 months and the main results are given in Fig. 5-2.

Hypothesis tested	Result
Scenario-based approach → high detection rate	Confirmed
Physical meeting → high detection rate	Weak
Phased inspections → high detection rate	Weak
More than two persons → high detection rate	Wrong

Fig. 5-2 Evaluation of inspection approaches

In the case of requirements inspections, different scenarios were assigned to different inspectors. Scenarios in this case focused on different classes of errors rather than use cases. The inspections using scenarios were compared with ad-hoc inspections and inspections using a general checklist. The scenario-based inspections turned out to be superior because this way it is possible to avoid the gaps in the coverage and overlaps between inspectors. The inspection meetings as postulated by Fagan are expected to produce a synergy effect, i.e. bring errors to light that would otherwise not be detected. While this could not be confirmed, the number of false positives (issues raised that were not errors) can be reduced. If that is of no concern, the co-ordination of the different results can be done by a moderator over the network. Splitting up code inspections into multiple sequential sessions does not bring corresponding benefits. To the contrary, this may cause heavy delays because of scheduling problems. The final result is that inspections with one reviewer only are less effective than inspections with two reviewers, but four reviewers are not more effective than two.

Theory In order to detect errors, the mental processes leading to design or implementation decisions have to be redone independently. A single person can do this only to a very limited extent. It is key that this is performed by different minds because the biggest gain comes from the second person. Three or more are less efficient, producing a diminishing return only, unless they can perform their work under separate perspectives (as will be discussed below). The way in which this is organized and how information is collected and interchanged is secondary.

Comments The importance of a physical meeting has certainly been overemphasized. A meeting may be helpful, however, for people who are learning about inspections or who do not dare to express a criticism of a peer, unless backed by a group. It is a matter of education and experience, until reviewers learn that each problem or doubt can be valuable. The author has to learn not to ignore any comment, even if it appears extraneous at first glance. The Porter–Votta law is also consistent with recent findings of empirical psychologists [Krau00]. They have found that the benefits of brainstorming can be achieved without a meeting, provided that all ideas are evaluated. Even the number of different ideas being produced was higher, if individuals could work undisturbed, i.e. without a meeting.

The third important result on inspections can be attributed to Vic Basili [Basi96c, Shul00]. He also introduced the term 'perspective-based inspections'.

> Perspective-based inspections are (highly) effective and efficient.   (L19)

Applicability Under the Porter–Votta law a scenario-based approach for inspections was mentioned. It used known error situations to guide the reviewer. This idea was considerably extended by grouping scenarios into perspectives. A perspective is the view a certain stakeholder has on the system. Stakeholders are users, developers, testers, writers, and human factor specialists. The basic idea is to ask different reviewers to take on the role of different stakeholders and to perform the review from that angle. This way a better coverage is achieved and overlaps are avoided. As a consequence, the cost per error detected is lower.

Evidence The approach was originally validated at the Software Engineering Laboratory (SEL) of NASA in Maryland [Basi96c]. For this experiment, 12 professionals were asked to review two requirements documents (each of about 30 pages), using both their traditional and the perspective-based approach. One document required special domain knowledge (in aerodynamics), the other document described well-known business applications. The perspectives applied were user, developer, and tester. The experiment showed that there was a clear increase in effectiveness for the perspective-based approach. It was higher for the general purpose application than for the aerodynamics application.

Several efforts have since been undertaken to validate Basili's law in other environments. One very interesting, but rather small, experiment was conducted by Laitenberger and DeBaud [Lait97] at the Robert Bosch company in Stuttgart, Germany. Eleven professionals were asked to inspect three small C programs (<300 LOC each) from the perspective of an analyst, unit tester, and integration tester. The programs were unknown to the reviewers and had been seeded with about 15 errors each. The hypotheses tested and the results achieved are given in Fig. 5-3.

Hypothesis tested	Result
Type of perspective → detection rate	Analyst best
Physical meeting → detection rate	Small positive effect
Number of perspectives → overlap of detections	Little overlap
Domain/language experience → detection rate	Medium effect

Fig. 5-3 Evaluation of perspective-based inspections

This experiment gives raise to several comments. Of the three perspectives, the analyst was supposed to check the consistency between requirements specification and code. Since the traceability between requirements and design is an unsolved (or even unsolvable) problem, it is no surprise that the analyst perspective detected the highest number of defects. That this problem does not go away even in the case of object-oriented design is the conclusion of another study by Travassos *et al.* [Trav99]. The testers only look for the testability of the code that is provided, independently of whether it is consistent with either the design or the requirements. It is obvious that perspective-based inspections reduce the amount of overlap between different reviewers, something that is demonstrated in another study discussed below. The final point is that the successful contribution to an inspection is less dependent on the prior experience of the reviewer. In other words, a detailed guidance helps beginners to overcome their learning curve faster.

A third study in support of Basili's law was performed by Zhang, Basili and Shneiderman [Zhan99]. In this experiment, two existing Web interfaces were inspected for usability problems. One was a standard Web interface programmed in HTML, the second was a special application interface implemented in Java. The 24 professionals that participated were split into groups following one of the following three perspectives: novice user, expert user, or error handling. For each perspective an explicit set of questions had been generated to guide the review based on a usability model as described by Shneiderman's golden rules in Chapter 3. The results of this study are enlightening, not only with respect to Basili's law. The groups using guidelines found about 30 percent more usability problems than the control groups (without guidelines). The highest number of errors was reported for the error-handling perspective. For one of the two tasks, the overlap of problems between perspectives was as shown in Fig. 5-4. The authors observed that their usability inspections were considered to be very ineffective, and that the test participants were more interested in the usability problems themselves than in the methods used for their detection.

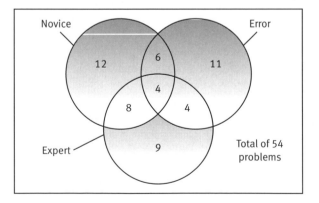

Fig. 5-4 Overlap of problems in GUI inspection

Theory This law rests on the fact that mental work is time consuming and, depending on the environment, may even be expensive. It makes sense to go about it economically. If not predisposed in a certain direction, even two independent minds may cover the same grounds. To avoid duplicate results, it is better to make sure that two persons working in the same area look at different angles. Any initial guidance or orientation also reduces the learning curve for beginners, and improves the repeatability of results.

5.3.4 Hetzel–Myers law

Although very effective, inspections are not the only verification method. A comparison of different V&V methods was first performed by William Hetzel [Hetz76]. It was publicized by Glen Myers [Myer78] through a well-known controlled experiment. The key result is quoted here.

> A combination of different V&V methods outperforms any single method alone. (L20)

Applicability The Hetzel–Myers law applies to inspections and black- and white-box testing. It says that the best results are obtained, not by focusing on a single method, but by using all three methods in combination. Contrary to what many people think, the three methods are not alternatives that compete with each other.

Evidence In his experiment, Myers gave a PL/I version of the Naur text formatting program to 59 experienced DP professionals (of whom 49 were programmers). The program contained a total of 15 errors known beforehand, but which were unknown to the test participants. The participants were divided in three groups: one was asked to do black-box tests; the other to perform white-box tests; and the third group was asked to do inspections only. The results showed that the three methods were more-or-less equally effective. The people time was highest in the case of inspections. Machine time, i.e. total cost, was not measured. These results are illustrated in Fig. 5-5.

	Black-box tests	White-box tests	Inspections	Two methods combined
Mean number of errors found	4.5	5.4	5.7	7.6
Variance of errors found	4.8	5.5	3.0	4.3
Median number of errors found	4.5	5.5	6	8
Range of errors found	1–7	2–9	3–9	5–10
Cumulative number of errors found	13	14	11	14
Man-minutes per error	37	29	75	75

Fig. 5-5 Results of Myers' experiment

Myers was surprised by the high variability of results among individuals, both in terms of number and type of errors found. From this he concluded that it is critical to determine which person is using which method. The most interesting conclusion was that the best result was obtained if he combined the results of the different groups. For this, Myers simulated additional experiments by pooling the results of individual methods. The right-hand column of Fig. 5-5 gives his data for combining black-box testing and inspections.

A similar study was performed by Basili and Selby about ten years later [Basi87]. The study was done at three locations, involving 74 persons, both students and professional programmers with different levels of experience. The programs used in the experiment were written in Fortran. The methods tested were code reading (a limited form of inspection), and black-box and white-box testing. The conclusions of the study were:

■ For professional programmers, code reading detected more errors than either black-box or white-box testing.
■ The three methods showed about the same results, even for students.
■ The types of errors found varied with the method used. Code reading detected more interface errors, while testing found more logic errors.

The Basili/Selby study was repeated by Kamsties and Lott [Kams95] in 1994 and again by Wood *et al* [Wood97] in 1997. Both experiments made use of a replication package originally developed by Kamsties and Lott. While both experiments essentially confirmed the previous results, they also produced additional information of interest.

Kamsties and Lott used three small C programs (<300 LOC) with between six and nine errors inroduced into each program. The test persons were students, in one group of 27 and another of 15. They extended the Basili/Selby experiment by adding a fault isolation step. Their main result was that the effectiveness (i.e. number of errors found) for the three methods was approximately the same. Fig. 5-6 shows those results that were new. The relative rankings of the methods, rather than the absolute values, are given. The 'time to reveal' is the time needed to discover that there was an error. The 'time to isolate' is the additional time needed to identify the piece of the source code that would have to be changed. The efficiency is the sum of both time intervals divided by the number of errors found.

Method used	Time to reveal	Time to isolate	Efficiency
White-box testing	Middle	Middle	Low
Black-box testing	Short	Long	High
Inspection	Long	Short	Middle

Fig. 5-6 Results of the Kamsties–Lott experiment

Another question investigated was which type of error would be detected by which method. Inspections found interface and data faults and were worst on type and class faults. No guidance was given how to inspect or how to test. Kamsties and Lott arrived at the same conclusions as Myers, namely that there are large individual differences, that the effectiveness of each methods is below 50 percent, and that best results are achieved by a combination of all three methods.

The results of Wood *et al.* are summarized in Fig. 5-7, which gives the percentage of errors detected for each of the three programs used. The first line is the best result of a single method (white-box testing). The second line is the calculated result of the worst pair of methods, while the last line shows the calculated result of a combination of all three methods. Wood *et al.* observed that the absolute effectiveness of each method is rather low and the variability among users is high, and the results very much depend on the nature of the program and its faults. Again, these observations agree exactly with Myers' observations 20 years ago.

Combination of methods	Program A	Program B	Program C
White-box testing only	48	53	73
Inspection, black-box testing	63	71	81
Inspection, black-box, white-box testing	76	83	90

Fig. 5-7 Results of Wood *et al.*'s experiment

Another study covering the same ground was published by Laitenberger [Lait98]. He applied inspection and testing in sequence to the same module. His conclusion was that defects that escaped the inspections were usually not found by a white-box test. He therefore suggests that inspections are combined with tests that are not mere coverage tests, e.g. boundary tests. Finally, the study by Jalote [Jalo98], mentioned above, confirms the fact that inspections can find a significant portion of errors that are not typically found in module tests. The consistent evidence established by a series of replicated experiments over more than 20 years, makes the Hetzel–Myers law one of the most firmly established laws in this book.

Theory Obviously different methods have their strength in different application areas. They address different criteria, and may have a different effect with different users, depending on their cognitive style. Some methods are related with each other in that they detect the same type of errors. It is important to know which methods are strong for which type of errors, and which methods complement each other. The best results are achieved if the methods applied are orthogonal, meaning that they work in different directions. This requires a good knowledge of the severity and frequency of error types. Errors made in different stages of development have different appearances and different causes.

Comment The work done by one of the authors [Endr75] on error classification may be helpful in this respect. More recently, similar work was carried out by Ram Chillarege [Chil92] and his colleagues, detailing the concept of orthogonal methods. This work will be discussed in Section 5.3.6.

5.3.5 Mills–Jones hypothesis

The following hypothesis was originally expressed by the late Harlan Mills [Mill83, Cobb90] and was made popular by Capers Jones [Jone96, Jone00]. Some people also called it the 'optimist's law'.

Quality entails productivity.	(H8)

Applicability Many people feel strongly that quality and productivity are positively correlated, in the sense that a concentration on quality from the beginning will entail productivity. Because poor quality results in a high percentage of rework, avoiding that may have a positive effect on productivity. By eliminating the causes of potential rework, quality and productivity may benefit simultaneously. This law is also a variation of Phil Crosby's adage that quality is free [Cros79].

Evidence Although substantiated in a field study by Card, McGarry, and Page [Card87], we still prefer to call this rule a hypothesis. Their data showed that reliability and productivity were positively correlated. They defined reliability as errors per lines of code, and productivity as LOC per person month. In this particular study, data from 22 projects were evaluated. All were different solutions to an aerospace application to be run on the same computer, and all were written in Fortran. The size of the project varied between three and 24 people years, delivering between 33 and 160 KLOC. Of the non-technology factors considered, only the application-specific experience of the development personnel showed a high correlation with both productivity and reliability. As a consequence, the following well-founded conclusions were drawn from the study: use experienced, capable personal, develop software as completely as possible before testing, read all code developed, document each phase of development, and conduct regular quality assurance reviews.

5.3.6 Mays' hypothesis

The next lesson is also still called a hypothesis. Intuitively, everybody concerned with quality issues thinks it to be true, although it is, however, extremely difficult to prove. It is named after Richard Mays of IBM.

Error prevention is better than error removal.	(H9)

Applicability Every error made causes some amount of rework, even if it is removed early. It is therefore a good idea to prevent errors from occurring. To do this, the causes of errors have to be identified and removed.

Evidence As an example of a defect prevention process, a process introduced in IBM development laboratories is given in Fig. 5-8. The respective process is documented in [Mays90].

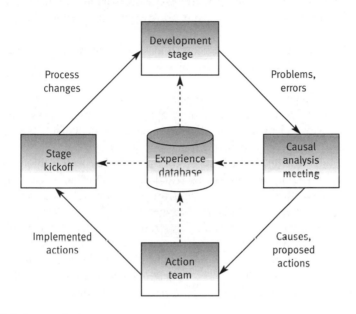

Fig. 5-8 Defect prevention process

A mini-postmortem is performed after each development stage. It culminates in the so-called causal analysis meeting during which specific problems and errors that occurred during the development stage are analyzed and their causes determined. The cause is an answer to the question, 'What was wrong in the current development process that caused this error?' This again leads to the question, 'What should be done differently in the development process to avoid this error from reoccurring?' From the resulting answers a number of proposed actions follow. Each proposal (or each related group of proposals) is evaluated by an action team, consisting of those people who are responsible for either the process or the tools. As soon as the action team has implemented the necessary changes, these are presented in the form of a stage kickoff meeting to those developers that may benefit from them. The problem and the available solutions are recorded in an experience database. The effect of this process on error rates has been studied for two products over a series of releases. A clear indication of its effect is not available since the observed reduction in error rates of the delivered products may be attributable to improvements in the error-removal process as well.

The same measurement problem exists for a more advanced form of this error prevention process, which also originated in IBM [Bill94]. This process was called the shuttle process by what was then the IBM Federal Systems Division, and was first applied to the space shuttle onboard software developed by IBM in Houston, TX. This process has the following steps:

1. Find the errors in the product and fix them.
2. Find the cause of the error (i.e. the process error) and eliminate it.
3. Fix other faults in the process that allowed the error to go through undetected.
4. Look for similar, as-yet-undetected, errors (both in the product and in the process) and eliminate them too.

The result of this process was that the detection and elimination of errors was shifted considerably up-front in the development process. To express this numerically: 85 percent of all errors were found before the code was integrated in the system (pre-built); whereas only about 7 percent were found through testing. We consider this ratio to be much more desirable than that achieved in the London air traffic system mentioned in Chapter 3.

The above-mentioned defect prevention process relies on a careful causal analysis of the defects observed. The danger exists that, in spite of significant efforts, each team will come up with a different nomenclature for problems and causes. To cope with this, and in order to ease both data collection and analysis, a general scheme has been devised within IBM for the classification of error data. It is referred to as *orthogonal defect classification* by Ram Chillarege and his co-authors [Chil92]. In this scheme, errors have five different attributes:

1. *Defect type*: nature of correction to be made.
2. *Missing or incorrect*: code to be added or changed.
3. *Trigger*: aspect surfacing error.
4. *Source*: stage in the process that caused error.
5. *Impact*: system property effected.

For each of these attributes, standard values are chosen from a given set of options, yielding mutually exclusive classes. The resulting classification is consistent between different development stages and uniform across products. By associating error types with development stages, conclusions can easily be drawn on the health of the current process. For example, if error types such as 'missing function' occur in late stages, then this would be reason to be alarmed. Such alarm would not be necessary if the error were a timing problem. The feedback produced this way can be used to improve the process while it is being executed.

5.3.7 Hoare's hypothesis

While inspections and testing have become the V&V methods that are most heavily used in practice, program proving has been received with the greatest expectations, both from researchers and from practitioners. Of all the approaches discussed, Hoare's method [Hoar69, Hoar72] is by far the most popular. Hoare's claims are reflected in the following hypothesis.

> Proving of programs solves the problems of correctness, documentation, and compatibility. **(H10)**

Applicability Inspections are people-intensive and people-dependent. Testing only covers particular cases of the input domain. Program proving has the promise that it can make statements with respect to the entire input domain of a program. For the purpose of program proving the term correctness has been given specific definitions, as follows:

- *Partial correctness*: the program produces correct output for those cases in which it terminates.
- *Total correctness*: the program terminates and produces correct output for all points in the input domain.

A proof of correctness compares the program text with a specification of the intended input–output relationship. For Hoare-type proofs this specification has the form of input and output assertions, also referred to as pre- and post-conditions. In his notation

$$P\{Q\}R$$

P is the assertion that has to be true before the program *Q* is initiated, and *R* is the assertion that will be true on its completion. For programs with loops, loop invariants are required additionally. The pre-condition *P* and the post-condition *R*, possibly augmented by loop invariants, can be considered as a complement to the specification or the specification itself. They can be closely associated with the code and serve as its documentation. If each module has an exact description of its input and output, this information can be used to check the compatibility between modules. We will not discuss the termination problem. Often the term verification is used for formal proofs only.

Evidence In the years up to around 1990, program proofs were mainly performed for small examples, typical examples being integer division, the factorial function, or the manipulation of data structures such as set insertion or array sorting. In the array sorting example provided by Hoare [Hoar71], the author's manual proof was only concerned with a partial property, i.e. that the elements in the output array were either equal or in ascending order. He did not consider it necessary to prove that the output was a permutation of the input values. Many automatic proving systems, so-called verifiers, have been built using Hoare's ideas. In addition to the minor and temporary problem that the machine time needed for a proof is quite extensive, there are many more general problems: it may be quite difficult to find assertions for programs that are more than toy examples; even if assertions are found, they have to be derived by an independent thought process – otherwise the danger exists that they contain the same misconceptions about the problem or the solution; finally, a typical proof may become much longer than the text of the program itself. The question then is, 'How does one verify the proof?' This problem was encountered by one of the first developers of a verifier, Eduard Marmier [Marm74] from ETH Zurich. He made the following observation: 'Either the proof was trivial, then I could do it by hand. If it was not trivial, and the machine took hours to find it, then I really felt insecure about its correctness.'

During the last decade, very powerful verifiers [Kauf97, Reif95] have been developed that allow proofs for programs comprising more than a few LOC. The most realistic approach is referred to as interactive proof generation. In this, an overall strategy for the proof is first developed by a human specialist using a computer-based logic system to administer specifications and code, to check type consistency, to derive verification conditions, and to prove individual lemmas. During the proof process additional axioms may be added to the logical base in order for the proof to proceed. Errors detected in the code or in the specification are corrected and the proof steps are repeated. Unchanged parts of the proof are reused. A realistic estimate of the human effort involved in an interactive proof can be derived from an example given in [Reif99]. As part of the EU-funded VSE project, about two person years (rather than two person days or weeks!) were spent on the proof of a single application consisting of seven KLOC with an accompanying formal specification of about 5000 lines. For safety-critical applications such an effort may be well justified. As a consequence of the Hetzel–Myers law given above, it should not be the only verification method used, however.

A proof can only ensure correctness relative to the specification, i.e. the assertions given. If a formal specification comprises 5000 lines or more it has to be considered as a development artifact in its own right. To assume that it is error-free is not realistic. Above all, there is no formal way to determine whether it is semantically correct. This can only be ascertained by applying an independent thought process, i.e. by performing an inspection. In a practical situation one may argue that the resources needed for an inspection of the formal specification could be more efficiently applied to an inspection of the source code. As for the Hoare example mentioned above, a verification condition may be imprecise, i.e. it does not exactly describe all values, but some properties of the intended function only. To perform a proof on this basis may be quite useful, but it should not be confused with a proof of correctness. Related to formal proofs are assertions that are added at critical points in a program to be checked at runtime. This can help to restrict a program so that it does not execute any path that may cause damage.

Comment Although significant efforts have been spent on the subject of formal proofs since Hoare's initial papers, the practical value of this work is still very limited. Even the official endorsement by some funding agencies, such as is the case in the UK, has not helped. This has had the same effect as

all internal software development. It certainly forced all arguments against
this approach into the open. Eventually the decision had to be rescinded.

5.4 More on validation and static verification

5.4.1 Formal analysis of code

The source code of any program can be viewed as a document in a formal
notation. As such it can be analyzed by computers. This analysis can be
very extensive – the limits depend on the type of language used. For all languages, a syntactic analysis is possible. It checks whether the program's text
fulfills certain criteria of well-formedness, the syntactic rules describing
which can be separated into context-free and context-dependent rules. For a
language of the Pascal type the following criteria have to be fulfilled if the
program text is compilable:

- all identifiers are declared;
- expressions, assignments, and parameters observe the respective type rules;
- indices of arrays and fields in a record are consistent with their declaration;
- a function name receives a value assignment.

While all compilers perform a syntax check, semantic checking is usually
optional. In the case of Pascal, its semantic rules define whether a program
is executable. Examples of semantic rules include the following:

- the program has at least one executable path;
- all results and intermediate results of arithmetic operations are repre-
  sentable on the machine that will execute the program;
- all variables used on the right side of assignments have obtained a value;
- index expressions do not exceed their defined range.

Usually this type of semantic error is not eliminated at compile time, but
rather is handled at run time by specifying assertions. More extensive
semantic checks as the ones described can be performed in languages that
support domain-dependent data elements and operations. The semantic
checks mentioned are a subset of what a formal verification system does.
They are easier for the user, however, since no dual specification is needed.
Any automatic analysis performed can assist inspections and considerably
reduce the needed human effort.

5.4.2 Static software visualization

To foster the understanding of a software system, the visualization of
selected properties is helpful. Visualization is understood as representation
in the form of two- or three-dimensional graphs, monochromatic or chro-

matic images, or videos. Visualization has become affordable because of high resolution display devices and appropriate software packages. The representation in audio form (sonification) is an additional possibility, but not important (yet) in this context. There are distinct advantages arising from this mode of communication, namely:

■ Exploitation of the full bandwidth of the human visual channel (which is larger than can be exploited by alphanumeric data).
■ Capability to perform associative pattern recognition.
■ Random access to different parts of the visual representation.
■ Reaction to the attractive stimulus of certain colors.

Software visualization methods can be split into static and dynamic visualization. *Static visualization* normally exhibits properties that can be derived without executing the software on a machine. The source code to be analyzed does not have to be executable.

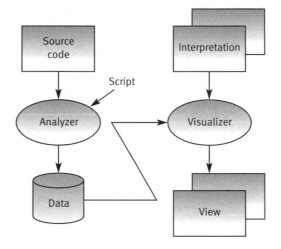

Fig. 5-9 Static software visualization

Fig. 5-9 gives the structure of a static visualization system. Logically, it consists of two parts: an analyzer and a visualizer. The analyzer extracts the desired information from the source code. Depending on the information, the source code may have to be parsed to discover its syntactic structure. The analyzer may be directed by means of a set of parameters, the so-called script. The visualizer extracts and presents this information according to a particular interpretation. For each interpretation (or model) a different view of the data is presented. The type of view chosen may be tree, network, floor map, perspective pyramid or cone, Kiviat chart, line graph, histogram, bar chart, pie chart, or other. Each of them may be two- or three-dimensional, and monochrome or color.

Examples for properties to be visualized are the static structure of the entire system or of each module, the size and structure metrics mentioned above, the relations between variable definitions and use, the use relations between modules, or the module change history. User interaction is restricted to setting the parameters of the analyzer and to the selection of views. Dynamic visualization will be discussed in the next chapter.

5.4.3 Model checking

Model checking is a promising formal method to support system verification. It produces a finite set of state spaces and state transitions of a program and evaluates them for liveness (reachability of path) and safety (deadlock freeness). The problem that the number of states may become extremely high (state explosion) is treated by special languages, representations (binary decision diagrams), and abstractions. Model checking has been applied so far mainly to hardware circuit designs (including processor chips) and communication protocols. It is expected that it can be very useful for non-ending programs, i.e. programs that are best described by their state transitions (deterministic finite automata). In a recent application [Clar94], Boolean functions with more than 10^{1000} states were handled. Given the appropriate tools, model checking requires less skill in logic than program proving.

5.5 Examples and study material

5.5.1 Formal specification

In 1979, an attempt made by Manfred Broy and colleagues [Broy80] to prove the correctness of the text-formatting program given in Fig. 4-15 turned out to be too difficult to achieve. A formal specification was developed, however, consisting of several interrelated recursive function definitions. Fig. 5-10 shows the headers only of four of the functions. The specification itself covered several pages. We shall skip the detailed logical formulas, since we believe that readers will not gain much from trying to understand them. Although the formal specification was developed with knowledge of the program's implementation, its structure deviates considerably from the program code. As an example, it implies three complete scans over the input file: one to check that no word is contained that is longer than N characters; then a run to eliminate all CRs and redundant blanks; and finally the conversion to the output format. No reasonable implementation would do that. That the recursive functions may have to be implemented as loops is a minor detail.

The positive outcome to this study was that choosing the proper data structure may be helpful to reduce the complexity of a problem and enable us to get a better understanding of the requirements. After the problem is understood correctly once, we may look for more efficient algorithms, and thus become able to solve this and similar problems with less effort and with fewer errors. Whether this goal has been achieved for the important area of text processing, may be doubted. Although nobody including the authors of this book can dispense with text processing systems these days, it has become quite fashionable to complain about the quality of the system one uses.

```
funct editor ≡ (string t: precond (t) string:
  that string S: norm(t) = norm(S) ≡ editcondition(S)

Where:

funct precond (string t) bool:
  m(first(t)) = NL ≡ V word w:  w in t→length(w) ≤ N
{describes the input, excludes words longer than N characters}

funct norm (string t) line
{eliminates all CR's and redundant blanks}

funct editcondition (string S) bool
{describes output condition that every line has CR at beginning,
is as full as possible, but less than N characters long}
```

Fig. 5-10 Fraction of a formal specification

5.5.2 Design inspection

In this example, some guidelines and an elementary checklist will be given for a design inspection. The application domain assumed is that of embedded systems in the automotive industry. Representative software functions in a car are the antilock braking system (ABS) and the electronic stability program (ESP).

After the requirements inspection, which is not addressed here, the design inspection is the key validation step. It will occur in stages, starting with the high-level design. Following this, different parts of the low-level design will be inspected in a single round of inspections. In the case of major problems, re-inspections may be scheduled. Design inspections will involve the originator of the software design in question, the corresponding hardware designer(s), the standards representative, one additional software designer, and a moderator. The last four persons will receive the material to be inspected, together with a checklist, either on paper or online. After one week, the moderator will determine whether a meeting is needed. If so, he or she will schedule the meeting.

Fig. 5-11 gives an example of a design inspection checklist, which may be updated for every project. Experiences from other projects may be included, or special considerations applicable to this project. After all the points raised by the inspectors have been discussed with the original designer and the moderator, the moderator will summarize the changes that have been agreed upon.

Design aspect	Sample questions
Traceability	Are all stated requirements addressed? How can they be traced?
Architectural compliance	Does design match with architectural framework established for automotive software?
Functionality	Are the algorithms that are proposed technically correct? Are all functions totally defined (for the domain specified)? Are the safety margins adequate? Are all special cases addressed?
Assumptions, limitations	Are the assumptions about the environment and the other modules correctly stated and verified? Are parameter ranges correctly specified?
Standards compliance	Are applicable industry standards properly addressed?
User interface	Is the user interaction reduced to essentials? Is interface presented in a standard manner?
Testability	Can all test cases be specified? Can functional and operational tests be planned?
Robustness	Are all exceptions and faults (user, engine) identified and their handling specified? Will software always restart automatically?
Performance	Are response times specified and correctly estimated? Is resource consumption (space, time) reasonable?
Readability	Are functions localized? Is coupling minimized? Are design patterns used where applicable?
Reusabilty	Is optimum use made of available components? Are components identified that will be reused elsewhere?
Documentation	Is design documented at enough detail? Is the design notation adequate and well-known within our organization?

Fig. 5-11 Design inspection checklist

5.5.3 Code inspection

This example complements the previous example with respect to code inspections: it assumes that a design inspection and the necessary follow-up actions have taken place. Code inspections will be scheduled for all modules after they have been compiled without errors. Not more than five modules will be inspected together. Participants in code inspections will be the owner of the module, together with one senior and one junior programmer, and a moderator. The junior programmer is assigned because of the training effect achieved. The last three persons receive online access to the source code with LOC and McCabe metrics provided by the code owner. A meeting is only scheduled in the event of conflicting recommendations. Fig. 5-12 gives an example of a checklist. The moderator ensures that agreed-to recommendations are documented in a traceable fashion and decides whether a re-inspection is needed.

Implementation aspect	Sample questions
Traceability	Is coding consistent with design? How can the consistency be traced? In case of differences, does the design documentation have to be changed?
Compatibility	Are all modules binary compatible with their environment? Are they re-entrant and linkable?
Embedding	Are all sensors and actuators correctly attached and controlled? Are all sensors and actuators reset for every restart?
Data types and formats	Are type and precision of all variables correct? Is double-precision float always sufficient? Are overflows and underflows handled properly?
Concurrency	Are all concurrent paths live (reachable) and safe (deadlock-free)? Can they be properly tested?
Initialization, termination	Are all fields properly initialized? Do all loops terminate? How is termination verified?
Data fields, buffers	Are all data fields and buffers protected against overruns?
Performance	Are path-lengths and storage requirements in-line with the estimates? In case of deviations, what is their impact?
Portability	Is the code platform-independent? Which environments need special treatment?
Maintainability	Is the code modularly structured and self-documenting?
Metrics	Are module sizes in the range of 300–700 LOC? Is the McCabe complexity < 20? If not, why?

Fig. 5-12 Code inspection checklist

5.5.4 Static visualization

The following three figures illustrate the use of a modern visualization techniques to gain information on the structure of a large system. This is a key method to assist program understanding. It can be used to aid inspections, and to ease maintenance and enhancements. Only the macroscopic views are given here, but the visualization system offers a zoom function to allow a closer look at the details. The application being visualized is a extension of the ET++ framework, called MET++ [Acke96]. The visualization tool was developed by Jörn Trilk [Tril98], who also provided the figures.[1]

Fig. 5-13 shows 30 (of 1550) classes of the system with their mutual static method-calls interrelationship. Approximatley 300 methods are involved. The classes have been arranged on the display by means of a clustering algorithm. The relative position of two classes is an indication of their affinity, in this case the static call frequency. All interconnections are drawn as equally thin lines. In Fig. 5-14 those classes that have been changed relative to the base system are highlighted, or in other words, the unchanged classes are 'ghosted'. Using this structuring technique, the complexity of the picture is reduced considerably but the context is not lost since it can be moved up into the foreground at any time.

---

[1] We gratefully acknowledge his permission to republish them.

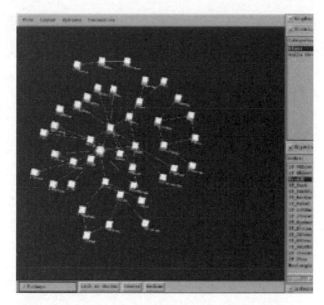

Fig. 5-13 Cluster with all classes

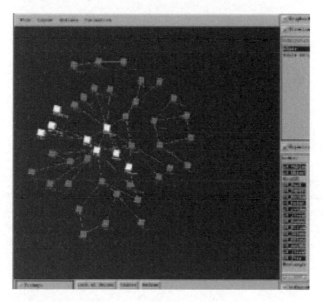

Fig. 5-14 Highlighting changed classes

Fig. 5-15 is an enhancement of part of the previous figure, with the unchanged (ghosted) classes eliminated. The picture now visualizes a dynamic property of the system. By varying the thickness of the connections, it shows the run-time frequency of interactions between the eight classes. The data have been produced by a profiling tool while executing the system, and are visualized afterwards by means of a static visualization tool.

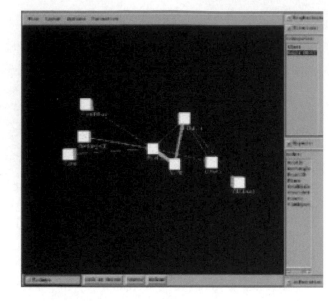

Fig. 5-15 Frequency of interactions

Exercises

5-1 Explain the difference between validation and verification. What is dynamic verification?

5-2 What are the reasons for the validity of Fagan's law? What are the essential parts of a Fagan-type inspection?

5-3 What are the essential results of Porter's and Votta's studies?

5-4 What is perspective-based reading and why is it of interest?

5-5 What lessons are expressed by the Hetzel–Myers law and why are they important?

5-6 How is correctness understood in the case of program proving and what are its limitations?

5-7 What are the advantages of a graphical versus a textual representation?

chapter 6

Testing or dynamic verification

Users don't observe errors or faults. They observe execution failures.
H. Mills [Cobb90]

This chapter is dedicated to the subject of testing. It distinguishes between functional verification and operational testing and shows how the different methods of testing are founded, whether through empirical study or theoretical investigation.

6.1 Definitions and importance

Testing is the key method used for the dynamic verification of a program or system. It does this by running a discrete set of test cases. The test cases are suitably selected from a finite, but very large, input domain.[1] During testing the actual behavior is compared with the intended or expected behavior. The emphasis of software testing is (to validate and) to verify the design and the initial construction. It is part of the development steps, not the manufacturing process. This is different to many other engineering products, where the emphasis is on testing the correct reproduction. Testing can also serve as a validation activity. It automatically has this effect, if satisfactory validation steps have not been taken before.

Debugging has the purpose of tracing a problem down to its source. It starts with the known failure, i.e. a suspected error, and ends when the piece of code is identified that needs to be changed in order to avoid the reoccurrence of the failure. To be effective, debugging requires a thorough understanding of the code. It is therefore usually performed by the code developer. The necessary code change is called a correction or fix.

Testing can be used to verify any one of the user-oriented quality criteria listed in Fig. 2-2. Typically, reliability testing has priority over all others and most effort is spent on it. *Reliability testing* is intended to verify that a pro-

---

[1] Although in mathematics we may deal frequently with infinite sets, this is never the case in computing. Even what are called real numbers in some languages are represented by a finite set of floating point numbers.

gram or system performs its intended function. The term function is used here both in the colloquial and in the mathematical sense. For most programs, *functional correctness* has three aspects: the program terminates; it produces the correct number of result items in the correct sequence; and the value of each item is correct. This definition does not apply, however, to non-terminating programs for which the sequence and the timing of events is key and no results are produced as such, for example, the kernel of an operating system or the input routine (message loop) of a graphic user interface. In such a case, the abstraction of a mathematical function as a relation of input and output values is not an adequate model for testing. The view of a state machine is more appropriate. This case will not be included in the following discussion unless stated explicitly.

Usability testing and performance measurements (efficiency testing) have received significant attention in most industrial environments. This has not always been the case for availability, installability, and robustness testing. Safety and security testing is an area whose importance has grown significantly over the last few years. All these tests have unique targets, follow different procedures, and require special test cases or setups. They will not be covered in the same detail here as reliability testing.

Test cases for reliability tests consist of input values and their expected output. The input values may be valid or invalid, i.e. lie within the specified input domain or not. If they are invalid, their purpose is to test robustness, i.e. to force error messages. These test cases are called diagnostic test cases, and may be accompanied by some handling instructions. 'Good' functional test cases are those that reveal functional errors in a system. For performance tests, workloads play the role of test cases; for usability tests we need task scripts. A *test suite* is a set of test cases intended for a specific test.

A *test strategy* defines the sequence in which test cases should be applied – in general, tests may proceed bottom-up or top-down. In the case of bottom-up testing, the individual modules of a system are tested first. What is called module or unit test occurs before the system test. To test modules outside of their system context, test drivers and module test cases are needed. A *test driver* (or test harness) simulates the environment that is needed in order to execute a module. In the case of top-down reliability testing, the main paths through a system are first tested, which may require that certain other paths are artificially circumvented. The coding necessary to enforce this is referred to as test stubs. Later, the test stubs are removed to reach and test individual modules.

Test methods for reliability testing can be divided into two major groups: black-box and white-box testing. *Black-box testing* is based on the product's specification only. Beyond that, it assumes nothing. The tester is 'blindfolded'. He has to assume the worst case, i.e. that all values of the calculated function are obtained by looking up a large table. Black-box testing is also referred to as specification-based or functional testing. A special case of black-box testing is statistical or random testing. It even ignores the specification and arbitrarily selects valid or in valid test cases. *White-box testing* assumes that the source code of the module or system to be tested is avail-

able, so that the tester can see how the specified function has been implemented, and select the test cases accordingly. The tester uses this additional
information on the test object to make his or her tests more efficient. White-
box testing is also called program-based testing or structured testing.

6.2 General observations

Testing is the development step that moves a system from the drawing board
(albeit an electronic one) into operation, placing the product close to its production environment. It usually begins in a controlled laboratory environment
and gradually moves out into the actual user environment. Testing is the
moment of truth for many developers: in all previous activities, assumptions
were made regarding the functions to be provided, the environment in which
the systems would operate, and about the skills and work habits of users;
during testing those assumptions are then 'put to the test'. Testing is a verification step executed before faults are known. Sometimes faults are detected,
sometimes not. Testing ends when a certain test coverage goal has been met. A
tester's concern about a fault is usually limited to identifying the test case
showing the failure. This distinguishes testing from debugging.

A famous quote that expresses some people's attitude is that of W. L. van
der Poel at the Garmisch conference [Naur69a]: 'If you develop programs
systematically, you can dispense with testing altogether'. Although this hope
is shared by everybody, it has unfortunately, never been achieved. In practice,
testing cannot be obviated by any other effort, be it a most careful design,
construction, or formal analysis. Elimination of testing from the development process just postpones the test with reality until the product moves into
production. Testing introduces the same degree of independence as described
for verification in the preceding chapter. In addition, test cases can be written
and applied by people who cannot perform other validations, because they
cannot read code or specifications. Testing puts the system or program in a
mockup of the intended operating environment, which helps to validate the
assumptions made about the environment, e.g. the compatibility with other
systems, and the skill level, work habits, and motivation of users.

As stated before, the correctness of a program must be understood with
respect to its intended function. Contrary to what happens in program proving, the intended function is normally not formally defined, and even if it is, it
is not the only yardstick. A specification is considered as the best possible textual definition of the intended function, but is usually only an incomplete
definition. It is not a revelation from above (*deus ex machina*), but a development product like any other. Many aspects relevant to correctness are only
implicitly defined. Examples are such requirements as no unintended side-
effects on other routines, no overflows or underflows of the arithmetic, no
rounding errors, etc. The user may not have been aware that these problems
can occur, and if so, he or she assumed that they would be handled 'properly'.
There may have been errors in the specification that were not detected in previous V&V steps. There may even be errors in the requirements definition

that did not show up before, meaning that the intended function has to be re-interpreted or adjusted. In this case, testing becomes part of system validation. Here the slogan 'better late than never' applies.

Testing is usually very expensive and labor-intensive, and in many projects it amounts to over half the development effort. Most developers resent testing because it can destroy the developer's self-confidence or illusions. Many projects suffer from the so-called 'last bug syndrome', which means that developers are willing to swear an oath that the last bug has 'just been found'. Usually this type of oath is broken instantly, particularly if tests are selected by people other than the developer. In the early years of our industry, testing was often delegated to newcomers or less skilled colleagues, but now it has become a professional activity in its own right. The test effort consists of the human time needed to determine the test conditions that need to be tested and to develop test cases for those conditions; the human and machine time required to execute the tests; and the human time needed to evaluate the test runs. Often not included is the time needed to correct the errors and validate the fixes. For large test efforts, the test phase is a project itself, requiring management of resources and the tracking of test progress.

The intellectual effort associated with testing is reflected in the selection of test cases. Their execution and evaluation, i.e. the comparison of actual with expected results, is a clerical effort and can be delegated to non-specialists. The test selection is determined by the test method chosen. Test cases for a black-box test can be contributed by non-programmers. For a white-box test, the test case developer has to be able to understand the code. We can compare white-box testing with tests in physics or chemistry. Here, we usually can see how big something is or what color it has, before we put it on a scale or measure its temperature. We combine data from different modes of observation to perform a test.

Exhaustive testing, i.e. executing a test case for every point in the input domain, is usually prohibitive. The main purpose of test planning is therefore to find that subset of test cases that is most effective. The effectiveness of testing can be expressed using the effort invested in testing in relation to the results achieved, specifically the number and type of errors detected. This is complemented by the assurance that certain types of errors do not exist. Testing has the goal to verify all functions of a system and to detect all errors down to a certain degree of severity. Certain errors may be detectable in a production environment only, because the cost to create all possible system configurations in a laboratory may be prohibitive, so it is therefore customary that a limited number of copies are shipped to customers who are willing to do additional testing (beta shipment).

The degree of severity of an error depends largely on the type of application. For most applications, errors affecting the main function are very critical, while typing errors in auxiliary messages are of low severity. A successful test gives a certain, but limited, degree of assurance with respect to the quality of the system. As stated before, the user-oriented criteria of system quality can best be addressed through testing. Besides reliability and robustness, this applies to efficiency, installability, and usability.

6.3.1 Sackman's first law

The two laws attributed to Sackman in this book are based on one of the earliest empirical studies conducted with programmers [Sack68]. The prime intention of this study was to prove the hypothesis that computers can be used to make the programmer's work more efficient. The result relevant for this chapter concerns online debugging versus offline debugging.

> Online debugging is more efficient than offline debugging. **(L21)**

Applicability This law can be considered as a commonplace today. When this study was published in 1968, however, there were raging discussions not only concerning the economics involved, but also regarding the potential negative influence on programmer attitudes and work products. Sackman's data clearly showed that the economics were in favor of online debugging, even at the low ratio of human costs versus machine cost effective then. The other arguments were only gradually settled. In a conference in 1971 organized by one of the authors (Endres) several participants took the position that online programming would be detrimental and should not be encouraged – it would produce a sloppy work style, enticing programmers to make fixes without careful consideration of their consequences. The resulting style was referred to as 'trial-and-error' programming. The turn-around times of half a day or more associated with batch runs for compilations and tests would force the programmer to invest more thinking into his or her code.

Evidence In Sackman's study two groups of programmers participated: group A consisted of 12 experienced programmers; and group B was made up of nine beginners. Each group had two different tasks to solve:

A1: Interpreting algebraic expressions (using the Bauer–Samelson push-down stack).
A2: Finding the only possible path through a 20×20 cell maze.
B1: Solving a cube puzzle (similar to the Rubic cube).
B2: Writing a sort routine.

The language to be used was a subset of Jovial. For the online environment, access was provided to a timesharing system developed by the System Development Corporation (SDC), which could be used through a teletype terminal at any time of the day. For the offline (or batch) environment, the turn-around time was arbitrarily fixed at two hours. This was better than what was achievable in many laboratories, but was long enough to be felt. Programming itself was done in offline mode. Debugging was defined as the time interval between the first compilation without major errors, and the time correct output was achieved.

Tasks	Offline	Online	Ratio		Offline	Online	Ratio
A1	50.2	34.5	0.69		907	1266	1.40
A2	12.3	4.0	0.32		191	229	1.20
B1	4.7	0.7	0.15		109	11	0.10
B2	13.6	9.2	0.67		875	290	0.33

Fig. 6-1 Offline versus online debugging

The results of the study are summarized in Fig. 6-1. For each task, the three left-hand columns give the average time (in person hours) needed by each participant for debugging; the right-hand columns gives the mean computer time (in CPU minutes) expended by each participant. Only group A uses more machine time for online debugging.

Theory The validity of this law is so obvious today that we were tempted not to mention it at all. We included it, however, as an example of where the essential parameters underlying the hypothesis have changed over time. In this case, it was the relation between human costs and machine costs. In 1968, depending on the system used, a CPU hour may have been accounted for with several thousand dollars and a programmer's time with less than US$50 per hour (in 1968 dollar values). Today, a PC with power in excess of a 1968 timesharing system can be purchased for a few $1000 (at today's prices). Online debugging is not only more effective than offline debugging, it allows the invoking of debugging tools interactively and causes no interruptions in the thought process, unless this is desired by the programmer. The temptation to fall into a 'code-and-fix' style of development is the greater the better the development environment is. It requires a conscious decision not to fall back into this style.

6.3.2 Dijkstra's law

The following law stated by Edsger Dijkstra [Dijk70] can be considered as the most famous law on testing.

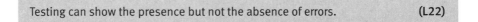

Testing can show the presence but not the absence of errors.   (L22)

Applicability This law asserts the most basic limitation of software testing. Unless an exhaustive test is performed, testing can not ensure that all errors have been found. Like most results derived from mathematical reasoning, it is negative in nature. While Dijkstra used this as an argument to concentrate on mathematical methods (formal specifications and proofs), testing has kept, and will keep, its unquestioned role in practice, at least for the foreseeable future. Dijkstra's law can never be used as an excuse not to test. This is the dilemma of most mathematical contributions to computing. It may, however, be a deterrent, suited to demotivate testers further. It may also have reduced the academic interest to study the scientific foundations of testing.

Evidence When quoted, the justification for Dijkstra's law usually comes from the reputation of its author. It is generally believed to be true. Since it is really mathematical in nature, collecting evidence does not help much. As in number theory, any mathematical law can be refuted only, but not confirmed by evidence. We will therefore present some arguments only (not a proof!) why we think that it is true.

Theory Two approaches can be taken to explain Dijkstra's law: one mathematical, the other practical. Mathematically speaking, programs are normally partial functions, i.e. they are defined for restricted domains only. As shown in Fig. 6-2 for a two-dimensional function, the delineation of the domains can be given by means of an arbitrarily complex function. In fact, many programs derive their meaning just from calculating these delineations. Moreover, the input domains need not be homogeneous (i.e. of the same type), continuous (i.e. without holes), or contiguous (i.e. without gaps). For instance, only distinct points of a sub-domain may be valid, e.g. all even or all odd numbers.

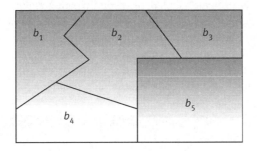

Fig. 6-2 Contiguous input domains (two-dimensional)

Theoretically, any program can be represented in the format given in Fig. 6-3. This is called the functional normal form for a program. This format was introduced by John McCarthy as early as 1962 [McCa62].

$$f(x, y) := b_1(x, y) \rightarrow e_1(x, y, f);$$
$$b_2(x, y) \rightarrow e_2(x, y, f);$$
$$.....$$
$$\underline{else} \rightarrow e_n(x, y, f)$$

Fig. 6-3 Functional normal form of a program

A two-dimensional function $f(x, y)$, is shown, defined over n sub-domains. The sub-domains are described by means of a predicate, $b_i(x, y)$. For each predicate another value $e_i(x, y, f)$ is calculated, where the term e_i is a path expression. Path expressions can be recursive expressions, i.e. containing a reference to $f(x, y)$. Normally, the sequence in which the predicates are written is important. In that case, the predicate <u>else</u> designates the remainder of some underlying 'catch-all' domain.

In the case of arithmetic calculations, the path expressions can normally be expressed as polynomials. They may even be higher functions, e.g. the Ackermann function, a case we shall ignore for the moment. If n test cases are used, this is akin to determining a polynomial based on n points. Unless the degree of the polynomial is given, there is an arbitrary set of functions that have n points in common. Fig. 6-4 illustrates this by showing a set of polynomials passing through two points. To be more precise, an infinite number of polynomials passes through those points, including those that have a higher degree. The latter oscillate at smaller intervals like the ones shown. It is also possible that the path expressions are quite trivial. It could consist merely of constants like `true` or `false`. Many query programs for databases have this form. Using this view of programs it becomes clear that testing is no more than searching for a needle in a haystack, unless more information is known about the types and families of functions involved. A method to convert entire Pascal programs into this form has been outlined by one of the authors [Endr77]. The purely functional view of programs is a helpful model to allow better understand testing, although practical programs will never be written in that form: for timing reasons, they will do repeated calculations only once; and for space reasons, they will share common expressions and routines whenever possible.

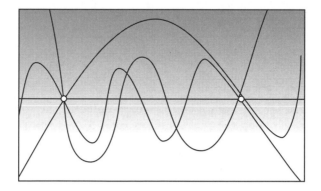

Fig. 6-4 A family of polynomials with two points in common.

The second approach is a pragmatic one. As stated before, if we look at the program as a black-box, the worst-case assumption is that all results are simply retrieved from a large table. We cannot assume that any connection or relationship exists between the individual values. Even if we know that it is not a table, program text may deviate from the specification in very unique ways; it even may contain a facility to mark all paths taken by test cases, and produce an invalid value in all other cases. This, by the way, is the methodology applied to obtain code coverage data. From both arguments it follows that black-box testing is very unsatisfactory indeed. In other words, Dijkstra's law is an excellent statement of the limitations of black-box testing.

6.3.3 Weinberg's law

Weinberg's work [Wein71], on which this law is based, dealt with psychological aspects of programming. The law quoted here, is the most revealing part of this work and became the basis for most approaches to quality assurance.

> A developer is unsuited to test his or her code.   (L23)

Applicability As soon as one accepts Weinberg's law, independent testing at some point becomes an imperative. In most situations the developer performs at least part of the unit test. An alternative is the clean-room approach, discussed later.

Evidence The point made by Weinberg's law is seen again and again in every project. Except for trivial cases, every programmer learns that immediately after he or she feels that the code is free of errors, a second person will discover errors.

Theory All explanations given for Fagan's law in Chapter 5 also apply here. Weinberg's arguments are based on the psychological theory that human beings always want to be honest with themselves. Therefore the developer is compromised, i.e. blindfolded, with respect to his or her mistakes. If he or she misunderstood the problem or implemented a wrong function he or she can only test what has been developed. The misunderstanding can only be removed by another person.

6.3.4 Pareto–Zipf-type laws

Pareto-type laws exist in many fields, and date back to the Italian economist and engineer Vilfredo Pareto (1848–1923). This law was first described in a publication in 1897 [Pare97]. Zipf's law[2] is from linguistic and postulates that many events (like the frequency of words in a language) have a logarithmic distribution.

---

[2] http://linkage.rockefeller.edu/wli/zipf/

Approximately 80 percent of defects come from 20 percent of modules.   (L24)

Applicability The economical example of Pareto's law at the time of its publication was that 80 percent of the income is obtained by 20 percent of the population. In more general terms it said that 80 percent of the desired outcomes are (often) derived from 20 percent of the activities. Contrary to other engineering fields, considerable care should be taken in software when assuming a statistical normal distribution. This is particularly true when dealing with software errors. It is simply wrong to assume that they are close to being evenly distributed over any one of the following populations: all programmers in a team; all activities in a project, all statements of a program, or all modules of a system. Wherever an author reported a distribution that was heavily skewed, we call this a Pareto-type law. As in economics, Pareto's law appears in several contexts.

Evidence The study done by one of the authors [Endr75] in 1974 was one of the first major studies of software errors published. The study analyzed about 740 problems of which about 430 were classified as software defects. The problems had been discovered during internal tests (component and system test) in about 500 modules of the DOS/VS operating system. The following types of problems were not considered to be software defects: machine errors, user errors, suggestions, duplicates and documentation errors. The conclusions of the study were:

1. More than half of the errors were requirements and design errors.
2. Approximately 80 percent of the errors were found in 20 percent of the modules.
3. Approximately 85 percent of the errors affected only a single module (not multiple modules).
4. The frequency of errors was higher for small modules than for large modules.
5. Changed code was more error-prone than new code.

It should be noted that several of the conclusions are consistent with some of the others laws cited, namely with Boehm's first law (see Chapter 2) and with the basic Basili–Möller law (see Chapter 8). Exactly the same findings were later reported by Myers [Myer79] and Möller [Moel85]. In Möller's case, the analysis was done for code developed by the Siemens corporation. Other examples related to software and systems are from Adams [Adam84] and Boehm [Boeh00a]. Adams states that 90 percent of system downtime comes from 10 percent of the system defects. Boehm reports about a case where 80 percent of the rework comes from 20 percent of the defects. A recent study that again confirmed this law was reported by Fenton [Fent00]. The data used originated from a telecommunications switching system and came from Ericsson in Sweden. In that case, 20 percent of the modules contained 60 percent of the errors.

Theory Pareto- or Zipf-type distributions have been observed again and again. We do not really know why they exist. Obviously, some distributions can be heavily skewed. In such a case, we should concentrate our efforts on the 'vital few, instead of the trivial many' [Fent00].

6.3.5 Gray–Serlin law

A testing area with a long tradition of well-engineered methods is perform-ance testing. In this field, modeling and measurement approaches complement each other, as do hardware and software-oriented approaches, and system-level and module-level activities. As a case in point, we would like to name a law after two proponents of standard system-level benchmarks – Jim Gray and Omri Serlin.

Performance testing benefits significantly from system-level benchmarks.   **(L25)**

Applicability Performance analysis has a number of goals: it should show bottlenecks and usage patterns, allow for the optimization of resources, and determine the competitiveness of a system. Competitive comparisons are usually based on price/performance, i.e. the ratio of price and performance. Performance is normally expressed in terms of throughput, which means work done per unit of time. Sometimes response time is the overriding crite-rion. Many possibilities exist to define the work done by a computer or its software. For the dominant commercial applications, transactions are a rep-resentative work unit.

As with other validations, performance analysis can be done at different stages of development. As part of the requirements definition, performance studies should determine which requirements are reasonable. As soon as a design or code is available, a static analysis can be done. The building of models can help to support design decisions. Most valuable, however, are measurements, which, as with reliability tests, are the encounter with real-ity. Performance measurement can be performed on a module as well as at the system level. The workloads, corresponding to the test cases in reliabil-ity tests, have to be different for different levels. Only a measurement for a specified workload and a specified configuration can say whether and how well requirements are met. If workloads are used to compare different sys-tems, they are referred to as benchmarks. Benchmarks can be internal or external to a company. In the latter case they can be used to compare com-peting systems. Performance evaluations are expensive in terms of skill and effort needed, and hence are usually carried out too late.

Evidence Following an initiative by Jim Gray and colleagues in 1985, the Transaction Processing Council (TPC) was founded in 1988 and led initially by Omri Serlin. This industry consortium was soon joined by some 30 other companies. Based on earlier work by Gray, the TPC developed a series of system-level benchmarks that were published by Gray [Gray91]. Initially, three different benchmarks were defined:

- *TPC-A*: a simple banking transaction, with screen input and output and several database accesses. The response time requirement is defined as 90 percent of transaction below two seconds. The configuration specifies ten terminals per transaction/sec (tps).
- *TPC-B*: a simplified version of TPC-A with lower permanent storage.
- *TPC-C*: an order entry application with a mix of interactive and batch transactions. It is roughly ten times as complex as TPC-A.

In the meantime, additional benchmarks have been defined, such as TPC-W for Web applications. Contrary to other benchmarks, the TPC benchmarks imply a specific computer configuration (storage capacity, number of terminals). As a consequence, these benchmarks allow price/performance comparisons. These can be expressed as dollars per transaction/sec ($/tps). The TPC workload is used for comparisons throughout the industry today. According to information provided by the Transaction Processing Council,[3] the price/performance range measured and published for TPC-A extends from 33 tps to 3692 tps, with costs of $25,500 and $4,873, respectively. A similar role is played by the SAP benchmarks used to measure the ERP application R/3 for different processors and database systems. The SPEC benchmark (Standard Performance Evaluation Corporation) is limited to the evaluation of processors. The acceptance of benchmarks is not equally spread in all areas, for example, the area of database systems is poorly developed [Jone00].

Theory Measurements are only meaningful if compared against a yardstick, which can be an earlier measurement or a competitive system. Application-level benchmarks make measurements more meaningful from a user's perspective, thus also helping the system developer. Competition and progress are stimulated if there is a clear yardstick to measure against.

6.3.6 Nielsen–Norman law

Besides performance, usability is the other requirement that receives high attention in many environments. One often hears excuses, however, that usability cannot be treated with the same rigor as functionality, reliability or performance. The fact that usability can be approached in an engineering fashion, is expressed by the following law named after two well-known pioneers in this field – Jacob Nielsen and Doug Norman.

Usability is quantifiable.   (L26)

Applicability Today most software products have a graphical user interface that determines mainly the external impression of the system (i.e. its look and feel). Whether a system is usable is not just a question of the external

---

[3] http://www.tpc.org/

interface. As stated in Fig. 2-1, usability is a measure of how well a system is adapted to the skills and the preferences of the intended users. As for all other design criteria, the attainment of this goal must be controlled during the entire design process. Early steps in this direction are usability inspections or walkthroughs, which can be based on the design specification or the code. The most important step is the usability test, which can be based on a prototype or based on the real system. Very often the main reason why a prototype is developed is to test it with potential users. As in the case of performance measurements, the proper execution of usability tests requires a certain amount of skill and effort. They are therefore often conducted too late, or not at all. Jacob Nielsen's book [Niel94] and a joint paper by Jacob Nielsen and Doug Norman [Niel00] explain in more detail why the neglect of usability efforts can become critical.

Evidence There are many ways to determine usability. The simplest form is to ask users to perform the intended tasks while developers are watching. This has been eye-opening for many developers, who have asked the users to stop and come back the next day, allowing them to change the system overnight. Usability tests can be more valuable if they are planned and setup in a consistent way such that they can be repeatable. This requires some well-defined tasks and equipment for the collection of data, which is usually achieved via a special usability laboratory. Extensive usability tests have been performed by several software developers, for example, IBM, Microsoft, and SAP. Typically, the following four items have been measured quantitatively:

- *Success rate:* number of given tasks performed without error and within time limit (measured in percent).
- *Time spend:* time needed by each test person to complete given task successfully (in min).
- *Error frequency:* number and type of errors made while solving a given task.
- *Help incidents:* number and type of additional information or tools requested.

As with performance data, these numbers have meaning only if they are put in relation to another set of numbers. These can come from a comparison to a reference product, be it a previous version of the same product or a competitive product. Also the difference between a first and a second session can be of interest, which is usually taken as an indication for the ease of learning. Besides these quantitative data, other information can easily be collected. Video recordings of the user actions can be very valuable particularly if the users have been asked to think aloud about what they are doing. Any subjective impressions should be documented as well.

Theory The usability of a system is quantifiable if we consider humans as part of the system. They have to be observed while performing certain tasks, which have to be meaningful and representative. The differences between humans can and should be factored out by either varying the tasks while the rest of the system is kept constant, or varying the system while the tasks are fixed. Besides the time needed for the task and success ratios, the attitudes and preferences expressed are valuable information as well.

Comment Measuring human attitudes and preferences is treated with disdain by many scientists. Computing, like most social sciences, can no longer do without it. To make these measurements meaningful, a number of criteria should be observed: first, the participants should be selected carefully to be representative of the user community, and should volunteer for the experiment; second, the groups should be large enough, so that the individual performance does not show through or influence the results too much; and finally, the test should be set up as a controlled experiment, meaning that the number of variables, independent and dependent, should be kept low.

6.3.7 Gutjahr's hypothesis

The following hypothesis regarding white-box (program-based) testing has been known intuitively for quite some time, but has been formulated only recently by Gutjahr [Gutj99].

Partition testing is more effective than random testing.	(H11)

Applicability Most authors that have published on software testing took the position that the poorest testing method is random testing. Random testing is the equivalent of unsystematic testing. Its advantage is that test cases can be generated mechanically, e.g. by using a random number generator. The problem of random testing is that it is normally very difficult to obtain the expected results. This is referred to as the oracle problem, to be discussed later. Partition testing is the term used to designate any method that breaks up the input domain into multiple sub-domains or partitions. In fact, all white-box testing methods do this.

Evidence Gutjahr's theoretical study tries to settle a controversy originally raised by Duran and Ntafos [Dura84] and Hamlet [Haml90]. These authors had developed simulation models showing that the probability to detect errors by random testing approaches or even exceeds the probability to detect errors by partition testing if the number of partitions is large. The analysis done by Gutjahr shows that partitions chosen based on the program's text are likely to invoke an identical processing of the input data from the corresponding sub-domain, i.e. the same path expression in the sense of Fig. 6-3. If at least one test case has been chosen per partition, every path expression has been covered at least once. This will not be the case, however, for randomly selected partitions.

Elaine Weyuker and her colleagues have studied different test approaches in detail [Weyu88], [Fran93]. From their results we present the following hypothesis regarding coverage criteria for white-box testing:

> The adequacy of a coverage criterion can only be intuitively defined.   (H12)

Applicability As stated before, white-box or program-based testing is the only approach where it is meaningful to look for some criteria to logically restrict the number of test cases to be run. Black-box or specification-based testing is needed to verify the consistency of specification and implementation. The most popular coverage criteria for white-box testing are listed in Fig. 6-5.

Criterion	Coverage to be achieved	Abbreviation
Statement	Every statement (or instruction) at least once	C_0
Branch	Every branch (or segment) at least once	C_1
Dataflow	Enough paths to cover data dependencies	C_d
Loop	Enough paths to achieve k loop iterations	C_k
Path	All paths	C_∞

Fig. 6-5 Test coverage criteria

Evidence The studies done by Weyuker and others have postulated that a relationship exists between the coverage criteria listed in Fig. 6-5. This relationship is as follows: a test suite T that satisfies criterion C also satisfies criterion C'. For the criteria C and C' this is a relationship, i.e. a partial order, whose essence can be described by words like 'covers', 'partitions', or 'subsumes'. The meanings of these words are as follows:

- *Covers:* the individual segments of the program's text are invoked in a similar way and to a similar degree.
- *Partitions:* the input domain of the program is split up in a similar fashion into disjointed sub-domains.
- *Subsumes:* the property includes the other property as a special case. It is more comprehensive.

Fig. 6-6 represents graphically the above relation in lattice form. In the figure, C_0 is the lowest criterion; C_1 subsumes C_0; C_d and C_k are higher than C_1, but not comparable among each other; and C_∞ is the top of the lattice. The most important point, however, is that the adequacy of a coverage criterion for the detection of errors cannot be stated formally. We assume intuitively that a higher criterion is more adequate than a lower one. Any explicit relationship between coverage and error detection would mean that we have a fixed distribution of errors over all statements or all paths, which is clearly not the case.

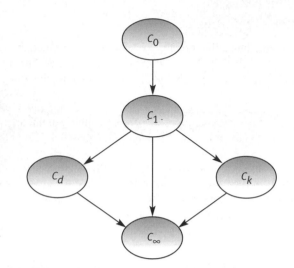

Fig. 6-6 Relationship of coverage criteria

For a specific type of dataflow coverage (all definition-use sub-paths), Weyuker [Weyu93] showed that about twice as many test cases are needed compared to a pure statement coverage (C_0). In general, for the definition of a test suite the actual number of test cases is secondary. A test suite satisfying the higher coverage criterion may consist of fewer test cases than the one satisfying the lower criterion. How a test suite is built may be influenced by other considerations.

6.3.9 Endres–Glatthaar hypothesis

After all the negative results on testing, we would like to add one very specific positive result that builds on the view of programs that has emerged so far. It is presented in order to explain an example given below.

> The test suite needed to verify an arithmetic path expression can be determined. **(H13)**

Applicability Path coverage can only be achieved in those cases where the number of paths can be determined. This is not possible, however, if the number of paths depends on input values. Many authors have suggested that at least one test case per path should be chosen. It is easy to show that this is not enough. One has only to imagine that instead of an assignment $z := x \times y$ the statement $z := x + y$ is encountered. A test case with the input values ($x := 2, y := 2$) will not reveal the error.

Evidence A paper by Endres and Glatthaar [Endr78] suggests how test cases can be found to test the correctness of arithmetic path expressions. As shown in Fig. 6-3, the path expression is a formula consisting of polynomial elements and recursive calls. If the degree of the polynomial and the number of recursive calls can be predetermined, test cases can be selected that determine the coefficients of the expression. The specific function within the class can be determined by a finite number of points. The predetermination of the degree (and the number of recursive calls) is the key point. This has to occur by means other than testing, e.g. through inspections.

As an example, a polynomial with one independent variable v and degree k can be expressed in the following way:

$$f(v) = a_k v^k + a_{k-1} v^{k-1} + \dots + a_1 v + a_0$$

An individual member of this class is determined if the coefficients a_0 through a_k are determined. By using $k+1$ value pairs $<v, f>$, we obtain $k+1$ linear equations that can be solved for the $k+1$ unknowns a_0 through a_k. Hence the number of test cases needed is $k+1$. If any k test cases are chosen arbitrarily, the fact that the determinant of the coefficients has to be different from zero leads to a condition for the $k+1^{th}$ test case. More details are given in an example below.

Comment The key problem to be addressed by any theory of testing is the delineation of sub-domains. This has been emphasized in several well-known papers by Goodenough and Gerhart [Good75], Howden [Howd76], and Weyuker [Weyu80].

6.3.10 Hamlet's hypothesis

We will conclude this section with a very practical hypothesis on reliability testing. Its wording is due to Richard Hamlet [Haml90].

> Suspicion based testing can be more effective than most other approaches. (H14)

Applicability Previous discussions have shown how difficult it is to derive 'good' test cases for either the black-box or the white-box tests. The purpose of test cases is to detect errors. Test runs that only satisfy some coverage goal and do not reveal errors are a waste of resources and should be avoided. Other criteria have to be added to make testing more effective. Hamlet's hypothesis certainly points in the right direction.

Evidence Following the suggestion by Hamlet, test cases should be written specifically to cover routines with the following properties:

- written by inexperienced programmers;
- a history of failures;
- failed in inspections and substantially modified late in the development cycle;
- late design change, introduced when most of the coding was complete;
- the designer or coder feels uneasy about it.

Practical evidence clearly confirms that the history of a module may be more often an indicator for trouble than its structure. Structure may have an effect, but this effect may be overwritten totally by history. The uneven distributions leading to the Pareto-type laws mentioned above, show that the skew is significant. In addition, the analysis of error frequencies, such as the one published by one of the authors [Endr75], can lead to more test criteria. Two error types that come to mind immediately are lack of variable initialization and boundary errors, i.e. calculations of ranges that are off by a value of one.

6.4 More on testing

In the literature and in practice, there are many methods and techniques for testing. We shall discuss a few that have not been adequately addressed earlier.

6.4.1 Compiler validation

Compilers are an example of popular software systems for which we have a high level of trust. One reason is that the input as well as the expected output are usually defined precisely. Another reason is that the theory, the methods, and the tools available for the construction of compilers are well advanced when compared with other applications. Last, but not least, formal procedures have been established for the validation of compilers.

The initiative for the establishment of a compiler validation process has been taken by government agencies for those programming languages that have relevance for government applications. Languages for which validation procedures exist are COBOL, Jovial, Pascal, and Ada. The goal is to demonstrate through testing that the compiler conforms to a standard definition of the language and its implementation. Sometimes not only the compiler but its entire execution environment are subject to validation. The test is executed under the auspices of a certification authority. The compiler validation process fosters the definition of reliable interfaces. It is highly desirable to extend this idea into other areas, such as text processing, databases, and cryptographic services.

6.4.2 Test planning and test case development

As testing requires considerable effort it has to be planned, otherwise the work needed is not done, done too late, or done inefficiently. Too often it is a mere afterthought. It is typical that when code is ready to be tested, no test cases are available or people available that are capable to run them. Sometimes project managers have the illusion that test cases are something one collects. However, test cases that happen to exist may be a useful complement to planned test cases, but cannot replace them. The effort needed to make them usable may be greater than the effort needed to develop new ones. Their only advantage is that they have been created without knowledge of the system's internals. This goal can also be achieved with new test cases if implemented strictly based on the specifications (the black-box approach).

Depending on the testing strategy, there may be a need for unit, integration, component and system test cases. There should be both small test cases and large test cases. Small test cases cover a single function only and do not require many prerequisite functions or other system resources. Large test cases should simultaneously exercise many functions. They are most useful for regression tests. Only regression tests can benefit from existing test cases, which may come from previous versions of the product, or from similar products.

Test case input can often be generated automatically. The biggest problem is normally to produce the expected output. This is referred to as the *oracle problem* (hoping that a mythical priestess will help). If the expected results are not available ahead of time the evaluation of the output may take excessive amounts of time or will be inaccurate. If the expected output cannot be developed, this is an indication that the design specification may lack detail. Even if the specifications are precise, however, the oracle problem may still remain. The very reason for having this program, may be that it is too difficult to calculate the results by hand. The oracle problem is less severe in the case of diagnostic test cases, which are intended to test the error detection and recovery facilities (robustness) of the system. As discussed before, some test cases should strictly rely on the specification (for black-box testing). Others will be developed with a coverage goal in mind (for white-box testing). Special attention needs to be given to stress tests.

6.4.3 Test support and automation

Testing is very stressful for humans. On the other hand, however, it is work that can be easily distributed among several people. These are two prerequisites that make automation desirable and important. Tools can be classified in test case generators (mentioned before), test drivers (or harnesses), capture/replay systems, assertion checkers, file comparators, and coverage analyzers.

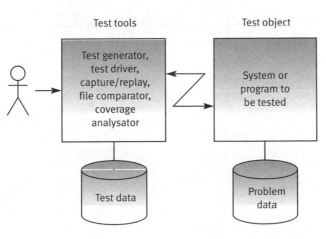

Fig. 6-7 Test automation

As indicated in Fig. 6-7, most of the test tools are usually hosted on a system different to the one being tested, although, test tools and test objects can reside on the same hardware system as well, provided they are properly separated. What is designated as test data can comprise actual test cases with expected results, or descriptive data from which test cases are generated, or test plans according to which test suites are selected. The test object may be equipped with probes or not, depending on the detailed level of feedback needed. If properly equipped with tools, all regression tests may be run fully unattended. Usability tests require different tools, e.g. video cameras. Performance tests make use of software or hardware monitors, among other tools.

6.4.4 Clean-room and other testing strategies

The first step towards a mature software organization is usually the establishment of an independent test department. This allows the development of test plans and test cases in parallel with the code. It also ensures that tests are controlled and repeatable. A trade-off is involved in the decision when the test department takes over. In most organizations the developers perform the unit test themselves. In these cases, the test department is only concerned with external test cases, i.e. test cases that can be developed based on the external specification. The test department runs tests, reports problems (failures), and verifies fixes. The developers debug their code and make fixes.

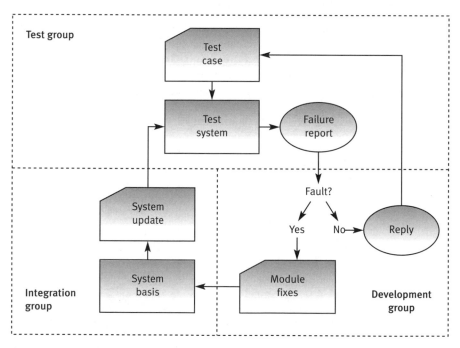

Fig. 6-8 Flow of information during test

Fig. 6-8 gives an example of a typical organizational setup during software testing. The communication between the test group and developers occurs by means of failure reports. The developer decides whether the failure is caused by a fault of the system, i.e. if there is an error in the code or in the documentation that has to be corrected. Test cases may fail because of test case errors or handling (setup) errors. The integration department integrates fixes and builds new test systems.

A much-publicized approach in this context is *clean-room development* as introduced by Harlan Mills [Mill87]. In this, developers are not supposed to test their own code: all testing, including unit testing, is done by independent testers. In some cases the clean-room approach became successful because it introduced independent testing for the first time.

6.4.5 Testing of object-oriented or real-time software

From the preceding discussions it should have become obvious that several system or software types require special attention with respect to testing. Examples are object-oriented and real-time systems.

For object-oriented programs, inheritance, polymorphism, and dynamic binding raise particular challenges. The static structure of the code may differ considerably from the dynamic structure. Testing cannot be based on the class structure only, be it concrete or abstract classes, but has to take into account the objects instantiated by the classes. Objects refer to other objects implicitly and use connections that only exist at run time. A state-based testing approach is required, which, as indicated in Fig. 6-9, is similar to functional testing, but has to be augmented by additional input and output [Turn93].

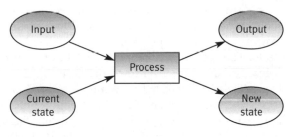

Fig. 6-9 State-based testing

Specific tests may have to be set up to cover so-called message-to-message paths. Methods inherited from higher classes have to be retested if reused in a different environment. Real-time systems are an example where it is totally inadequate to view programs as only mathematical functions that relate some input with some output data. The sequence and the timing of operations are the key properties to be verified.

6.4.6 Use of assertions and code-embedded test aids

The concept of assertions originated with program proving. It seems that an extremely useful application of assertions can be found in software testing. In this context, assertions are conditions or invariants placed at critical points in a program. They are evaluated every time the program reaches this point with the current state of the variables. If the assertions are not met, this fact is recorded or the program is interrupted. The use of assertions is an example of a defensive style of programming. It is always advisable to check the ranges of parameters when invoking a procedure, to test counters against overflow, floating point numbers against underflow, the validity of pointers, and the integrity of data. Such checks can be done in any language. Placing assertions has to be supported by the programming language used. Eiffel is a language that gains its strength from this feature.

Many other hooks or aids can be embedded into code during testing and debugging. This can be simple print commands to produce selective output of variables or intermediate results. It can be a whole set of probes inserted to monitor the execution of the system. Typically these tests aids are removed before the code is shipped to customers. Assertions may be left in the shipped code, as their time and space burden is usually negligible.

6.4.7 Dynamic software visualization

Contrary to static visualization, *dynamic visualization* requires that the program or system can be executed. For the purpose of data extraction either the source code is extended manually (annotated) or probes are inserted into the environment in which the object code is executed (instrumented). Fig. 6-10 gives an overview of a dynamic software visualization system.

The first step (compilation) may occur ahead of time, and may require the building of a running system, consisting of many modules. Many compilers have a debug mode which generates additional information (e.g. a symbol table) that may be used if the data to be visualized refers to source-code related objects. The term instrumentation implies that probes are set at the operating system or hardware level to record certain events. If this is not sufficient, the source code is extended (annotated) accordingly. During the execution, a script determines which events and data values are to be collected about the program or system under investigation. These records can either be displayed in real-time (animated) or visualized at any later point in time. For each animation or visualization the collected data may be interpreted in a certain fashion resulting in distinct views of the system.

Among the properties to be displayed are the dynamic structure of the system, the temporal relationships between events, the type and frequency of object and data accesses, the change of values or data structures over time, the resource consumption, and the user interaction. The visualization system itself can be disconnected, restarted, or put in slow-motion mode. Dynamic visualization is a very powerful method that can help to better understand the run-time behavior of a system. It is indispensable for the efficient debugging of object-oriented and parallel programs and systems.

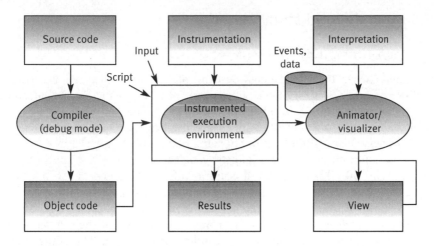

Fig. 6-10 Dynamic software visualization

6.4.8 Operational profile

Operational profile is the term introduced by John Musa [Musa93] to describe the probabilities with which functions of a system will be used after delivery to customers. Musa uses this primarily to make reliability projections for large telecommunication systems. If these data are available early enough they could be used to determine a test strategy. Unfortunately, so far only the telecommunications industry has good data on usage. Fig. 6-11 gives an example of an operational profile, it is corresponding to what Musa calls a functional profile. Other views could be organized by customer type, individual user profile, or environmental conditions.

Input Domain	Occurrence probability
b_1	0.42
b_2	0.21
b_3	0.12
b_4	0.07
b_5	0.18

Fig. 6-11 Operational profile

The input domains in this example are taken from Fig. 6-2, while the occurrence probabilities express how often the individual sub-domains will be invoked over a certain time period. The probabilities add up to 1.0. The time period is not spelled out, but could be a day, a year, one thousand CPU hours, or the life of the product.

6.5 Examples and study material

6.5.1 Text formatting unit test

As stated earlier, the text-processing example can be used to demonstrate a number of points. In Fig. 6-12, a small set of test cases is listed that could be run against the program given in the previous chapter. For sake of readability, the following special symbols are used to designate characters that are otherwise not printable, namely ^ for blank, and / for the line feed (or new line) character. The line length N of the output is assumed to be 3 (rather than 30). The right-hand column refers to the errors given before, explaining why the actual output deviates from the expected output.

It is assumed that the message 'alarm' is produced by the Alarm routine, and that the end-of-file indicator is properly generated for the output whenever the read routine encounters this indicator on input. The actual result corresponds to the expected result in none of the test cases, with the possible exception of 7. The 16 test cases given are certainly less than adequate to test this program. Both the statement and the branch coverage criteria (C_0, C_1) are reached, however. In addition, the example shows that the same error (fault) may cause several test cases to fail. In the reporting, each unsuccessful test case would be considered as a different problem (failure). On the other hand, the same test case may be affected by multiple errors.

Test case	Input	Expected output	Actual output	Causing error
1	^	/(no output)	/^	d1
2	^^	/(no output)	/^^	d1
3	a	/a	/(no output)	d4
4	a^	/a	/^a	d1
5	^a^	/a	/^^a	d3
6	^^^^^^	/(no output)	/^^^/^^	r6
7	aaaa	/'alarm'	/'alarm'	(correct)
8	aa^	/aa	/^aa	d1
9	aaa	/aaa	/(no output)	d4
10	aaa^	/aaa	//aaa	d2
11	^aaa^	/aaa	/^/aaa	d1,d3
12	a^^b^	/a^b	/^a^/b	d1,r6
13	^a^bb	/a/bb	/^^a	d1,d3,d4
14	a^bb	/a/bb	/^a	d1,d4
15	a^bbb	/a/bbb	/^a	d1,d4
16	a^^^b^	/a^b	/^a^/^b	d1,r6

Fig. 6-12 Unit test case suite ($N = 3$) with actual results

Although the above test cases can be used directly, they are really unit test cases. Their use can be simplified by providing a test driver that allows execution of all test cases in a single session.

6.5.2 Digital library system test

Based on the requirements model given in Figs 2-5–2-7, system-level test cases can be specified. Fig. 6-13 gives an overview of a potential test case suite for a system test. They are structured after the use cases in Fig. 2-5. Only key input parameters are mentioned, and certain alternative test cases are implicitly expressed in the expected results column. The results are mainly expressed in the form of actions to be executed next. In practice these actions will be given in the form of input parameters for a system transaction. This way the test cases can be executed individually or in sequence. In the latter case, they serve as integration test cases.

Test case	Use case	Parameter values	Expected results
1	Enroll	User: New	Check data; insert into user database
2		User: Known	Check data; update user database
3	Query	User: New	Suggest/perform enrollment
4		User: Known	Check and perform query
5	Order	User: New	Suggest/perform enrollment
6		User: Known	Confirm order if item offered, otherwise notify that item not offered
7		Item: On stock	Prepare shipment
8		Item: Not on stock	Acquire item from publisher
9	Acquire	Publisher: New	Obtain conditions
10		Publisher: Known	Request delivery; after receipt prepare catalog entry for this item
11	Ship	Item: Free-of-charge	Perform shipment
12		Item: Chargeable	Prepare billing; perform shipment
13	Bill	Customer: Prepaying	Deduct from account
14		Customer: Billable	Send invoice; receive payment

Fig. 6-13 System test case suite

The specification of this test case suite raises at least one question regarding the requirements model. It assumes that all users have to be enrolled before they can perform a query or place an order. This may be too restrictive. It is technically feasible to allow users to enroll while they perform a query or place an order. The two specifications are inconsistent in this respect and should be brought in line. It is not shown that items will probably not be shipped and billed individually, but rather collected into one package and one bill if shipped on the same day. Nor is a difference made for the delivery of documents and services. The assumption is that online access is provided in a similar fashion. The term shipment is still used in both cases.

6.5.3 Arithmetic test suite

The following is a simplified version of an example given in [Endr78]. The program to be tested is a function max(x, y) given by the following piece of Pascal code:

```
function max(x, y: integer): integer;
    begin if x>y then max := x else max := y end
```

In functional notation, this program would have the form:

$$f(x, y) = b_1 \rightarrow e_1, b_2 \rightarrow e_2 \text{ where}$$

$$b_1: x > y \quad \text{and} \quad e_1: x;$$
$$b_2: x \leq y, \qquad\quad e_2: y$$

As a test neighborhood we chose the class of polynomials with two variables of degree 1. This class can be represented by the following equation:

$$f(x, y) = a_3 \times x \times y \times a_2 \times x + a_1 \times y + a_0$$

To determine the coefficients a_0 through a_3, a total of four test cases are needed. We can characterize this set as follows:

$$TS = \{<x_i, y_i, f_i> \mid i = 1..4 \ \& \ D(x, y) \neq 0 \}$$

Here the suffixes are used to designate individual values from the range of the independent variables x and y, and the dependent variable f. The notation $D(x, y)$ is an abbreviation for the following determinant:

$$D(x, y) = \begin{vmatrix} x_1 * y_1 & x_1 & y_1 & 1 \\ x_2 * y_2 & x_2 & y_2 & 1 \\ x_3 * y_3 & x_3 & y_3 & 1 \\ x_4 * y_4 & x_4 & y_4 & 1 \end{vmatrix}$$

If we pick three of the four test cases at random, then the determinant $D(x, y)$ results in a condition that the fourth test case has to fulfill. As an example, we might choose the following values as the three first test cases:

$$\{<1, 1, 1>, <2, 2, 2>, <3, 3, 3>\}$$

The condition resulting from the determinant is

$$\begin{vmatrix} 1 & 1 & 1 & 1 \\ 4 & 2 & 2 & 1 \\ 9 & 3 & 3 & 1 \\ x_4 * y_4 & x_4 & y_4 & 1 \end{vmatrix} \neq 0$$

Solving the determinant leads to the inequality $x_4 \neq y_4$. Combining this with the path expressions b_i gives the conditions that the fourth test case for each path has to meet.

Exercises

6-1 Explain the difference between testing and debugging.

6-2 What is the content and purpose of a test plan?

6-3 What are the advantages of black-box versus white-box testing? What are the limitations of white-box testing?

6-4 What is the difference between a test driver and a test stub? When are they useful?

6-5 What is the practical implication of Dijkstra's law and why is it valid?

6-6 Which test coverage measure is more comprehensive: statement or path coverage? What does this relation imply?

6-7 What are performance benchmarks and why are they important?

6-8 How can usability be inspected and measured?

6-9 What is the purpose of compiler validation and how is it performed?

6-10 Correct the example program in Fig. 4-15 to obtain the expected test case results.

chapter 7

System manufacturing, distribution, and installation

Simple, elegant solutions are more effective, but they are much harder to find than complex ones.

N. Wirth [Wirt85]

This chapter covers briefly the activities at the end of each development project, i.e. manufacturing, distribution, and installation.

7.1 Definitions and importance

Manufacturing is the process that packages the outcome of the development process into a format suitable for distribution and generates multiple copies, if necessary. *Distribution* is a logistics process of shipping products from the developer location to the actual user. The intermediate step may be a distributor or distribution center on the developer's side, and a central support group on the user's side. Some authors also refer to this part of the product cycle as deployment or rollout, both terms still carrying somewhat of a military connotation. The *installation* process finally converts the deliverables into a usable application or system at the customer's site.

In order to move a software or system product from the controlled development environment to a genuine user's workplace it has to be manufactured, distributed, and installed. Software's unique advantages come to bear in these very processes. Only an installed product is a complete product, and only a complete product can produce the benefits expected or the revenues anticipated.

7.2 General observations

In many classical engineering fields, the steps following development were often treated as something trivial. Only when problems occurred did the attitude change. Engineers designing cars, appliances, or chips have learned that manufacturing aspects have to be taken into consideration in addition to development trade-offs. Today, an integrated view prevails, i.e. manufacturing engineers are usually involved early in the design process. The same lesson still needs to be learned in software and systems engineering. Very few textbooks on software or computer systems engineering give this subject a systematic treatment.

In the computer industry, hardware products have been able to considerably reduce their manufacturing costs over recent decades. Software manufacturing has always had comparatively low costs, so the concern has therefore been mainly on software development costs. Hardware development costs used to be low compared to the hardware manufacturing costs. The more hardware manufacturing costs fall, the higher the development costs appear in comparison.

System products need to be packaged to be shipped. Shipping may occur either as a pure hardware component (even including some microcode), as hardware with supporting software, or as pure software. After this basic decision, other decisions follow. As far as practicable, hardware components are assembled to be ready for use. The same is true if software is embedded, or supports a specific hardware device only. For embedded software, the end user may not even be aware that there is any software involved at all.

If software appears as a product in its own rights, it should be packaged such that it can be installed with multiple hardware devices or systems. The key determinants for a software product are its representation form and the medium. The main representation forms are source code and object code. Intermediate forms, like relocatable code, are less important today. Any electronic medium used to store data can also be used to store software. If software is shipped independently of hardware, the medium has to be removable.

Distribution solves the problem of getting a product from A to B when required and should take advantage of the users resources as little and as late ('just in time') as possible. To achieve this goal, a certain infrastructure is needed; distribution can occur prior to or after sale; the installation task should always be minimized; and ideally every product should be ready for use as delivered. This is not always achievable, or it may lead to considerable redundancies, i.e. things are delivered that are there already. For all these activities, Wirth's advice, as given in the chapter epigraph, applies.

7.3 Applicable laws and their theories

Instead of laws and hypotheses, this section offers some conjectures only. This is because the problems and issues addressed here have seldom been subject to systematic study.

7.3.1 Conjecture 1

The first activity to be concerned about in this context is software manufacturing. Its key problems are summarized by conjecture C1.

For COTS products, costs and risks of manufacturing can approach those of
development. (C1)

Applicability With the advent of software products for the mass market it
became obvious that software manufacturing can no longer be seen as an
insignificant activity. The question arises of how software products should be
packaged so that thousands of copies can be made reliably and cheaply. In
early times, when storage space and costs were overriding factors, a product
had to be offered with a high number of selectable features. As soon as the
number of copies to be produced grew, the number of features had to be
reduced. They were lumped together to make ordering and shipping easier.

Evidence In the period where software was mainly needed for mainframes,
a standard software package typically consisted of some reels of magnetic
tape, plus several manuals. For the mass products that are sold through
retail stores, the glossy shrink-wrapped paper box has become the typical
form of appearance, containing some diskettes or, more recently compact
disks (CDs) and, at most, one manual.

The experience of one of the authors (Endres) in this respect goes back to
1966 and 1967. Several months prior to the completion of system test we
had to convince IBM marketing to order several mainframes for their four
distribution centers in order to be able to handle the later distribution workload. We then sent them test data to check out their procedures and
programs. It turned out that our proposed packaging did not suit them at all.
We had intended to distribute a disk-resident operating system on a removable disk pack (which the customer would supply himself or order from the
software distribution center). To start the system generation tools supplied
on the disk, the customer would need a small deck of punched cards containing the Initial Program Load (IPL) program. We soon learned that
distributing five punched cards together with a disk pack to the expected
customer set would cost IBM around a million dollars. Fortunately, we convinced the hardware developers to add a new microcoded instruction to all
processors to perform IPL from disk.

A more recent case is documented in a Microsoft press release [Hoch00],
stating that the company had to increase its production facility seven-fold
and that it rented about 500 trucks to deliver several million copies of
Windows 95 within days to retail stores in the USA. Since a million copies
were sold during the first four days, this was clearly a good investment.

7.3.2 Conjecture 2

Software distribution is not only an issue concerning the supplier of standard products. Every author of a useful software routine wants to find ways
to make his code available to other users.

Distribution ends where the customer wants it to end.	(C2)

Applicability In many respects, software distribution can be considered as a precursor and test case of electronic commerce. A distribution center has to handle all activities described in Section 2.5.2 for digital libraries. A distribution service is mainly concerned with the receipt of orders, the control of the user's authorization, the delivery of the requested product, the billing, and the subsequent control of the license conditions (e.g. expiration date). Sometimes installation and maintenance support is also provided by the same organization.

Evidence Companies that develop software products are the originators for the distribution of software. They may have centralized their distribution activities or split them up by product type or by geographical regions. They may distribute their products to corporate users, private users, re-distributors, or retail shops. Today, most software developing companies accept orders through their homepage.

Many universities or state agencies have their own distribution centers. They may distribute products they have developed to external customers, or they may only handle the distributions within their own organization. An example of the first group is the UNIX distribution center (BSD) of the University of California at Berkeley; an example of the second is the Argonne National Laboratory or the Academic Software Cooperation (ASKnet) in Karlsruhe. Distribution centers serving large groups of internal users are usually justified by the price discounts obtainable for bulk orders. They also help individuals in negotiating conditions with suppliers or in clarifying legal issues. Some self-sufficient corporate users may by-pass distribution centers and order directly from suppliers or retail stores. As are libraries, software distribution centers are sometimes inundated by suppliers trying to find users for their mediocre products. A distribution center is well advised to attend to the needs of their customers rather than the selling wishes of suppliers.

7.3.3 Conjecture 3

A unique concern of the software industry is the ease and the existence of software piracy. The current estimate of the industry is that, worldwide, 37 percent of all licensed software products are used illegally [BSA00].

Prevention of software piracy by technical means is almost impossible.	(C3)

Applicability Software piracy is such a widespread phenomenon that it cannot be ignored. It is a problem not only in developing countries where the rate may be as high as 90 percent, but also in developed countries, including the USA. Our concern is not only about the revenue losses, but more about the attitude users take with respect to software. Users in this case are not only private persons and students, but also industrial corporations and government agencies.

Evidence Many attempts have been made to solve this problem by technical means. The following methods are ordered by increasing degree of protection achieved:

- *Object-code only:* the source code of a software product is only needed by those customers who want to change or maintain the package. The adaptation of the software to the hardware configuration can be done with object code as well.
- *Check for machine identification:* traditionally, many software packages were licensed for a specific CPU number. This situation can be assumed whenever software is pre-installed on a machine when delivered.
- *Check for software license number:* most large software packages have a license number assigned to them that is referred to in the license contract. It is not given to people who acquired the product without a contract.
- *Encoding and encryption:* software can be encoded or encrypted like any other data. The authorization of the user would require that a decryption key is transferred, unless a public key system is installed. Decryption is an additional step before the software can be used.
- *Watermarking:* watermarking is the method used to protect electronic media by placing certain information into the document itself (steganography). A watermark can be visible or invisible in the printed or displayed form of the document. It gives the original owner the possibility of proving his or her ownership in the case that a specific copy reappears.

Most of the technical methods to prevent piracy have not been overly successful. The supplier has to make a trade-off between the ease to obtain and use the product versus the degree of protection achieved. Usually organizational or business means are quite effective as a way out. Many suppliers split their products in to free and licensed parts or offer extended trial periods. Lowering the price or improving the support may also help.

7.3.4 Conjecture 4

A widespread technical concern of many software users is the problem of installability. We referred to it in Fig. 2-1 as an important quality criterion.

Installability must be designed in.	(C4)

Applicability Ease of installability has been a concern of the software industry from its beginning. The problem has gained importance as the usage of computers has extended from professional to non-professional users. If the installation process is not self-evident, it has to be verified as part of the development process. This can occur through inspections as well as tests.

Evidence For mainframe systems, the installation of software was typically performed by computer professionals. This task has since grown both in numbers and in complexity. Within IBM, a major breakthrough in this direction was achieved with a system called Small System Executive (SSX) developed and shipped by the Böblingen IBM laboratory in 1982 [Gatz83]. The major aspects are summarized in Fig. 7-1.

Although supporting what would be called a mainframe today (IBM 4300 processors), the SSX approach features several innovations that became the customary approach for the PC world about ten years later. The most important aspect was that the extremely error-prone activity of system generation could be eliminated entirely. This became possible because storage costs had fallen to a point that they could be traded against programmer time. The strict adherence to object-code, i.e. elimination of source code, simplified not only the installation task, but above all the maintenance process. The other major installation simplification was due to special hardware assistance, i.e. device sensing. This feature allows the operating system to determine which peripheral devices are directly (natively) attached to a processor and what its characteristics are.

Aspect	SSX solution	Previous solution
Distribution	Single magnetic tape	Multiple tapes or disk drives
Code format	Object code only	Partially source, partially object code
Generation	None	Several modules to be modified and compiled
Installation	4–5 hardware parameters to be specified	About 30 hardware and software options to be specified
Devices	Automatically sensed	To be specified individually
Applications	Installed by prompter	Manually selected and installed
Remote install	Unattended over network	Locally and by hand
Time needed	1–2 hours/system	4–8 hours/system

Fig. 7-1 Installation approach of SSX

Today, the installation of software products is still a major concern of users, mainly because of the number of different systems involved. For an industrial corporation or a research center it easily can involve some 10,000 systems. The most common ways to perform a software installation are:

- *At the plant or at a central location:* for most computers the operating system and some basic applications are pre-installed this way.
- *Locally by hand:* most user specific applications are installed on the local computer using some standard tools (e.g. Microsoft InstallShield).
- *Remotely over the network:* a representative of the support group may log-in locally to perform an installation or use some replication process to do it.

A very popular way to avoid the installation of multiple copies is to place all applications into a distributed file system, such as NFS. As discussed in [Gomb98], systems that rely heavily on graphical user interfaces (GUI) are usually more difficult to install remotely than those with a command interface. Other factors are the dependency on a particular operating system, the number of options to be considered and the total size (footprint).

7.4 More on system manufacturing, distribution, and installation

7.4.1 Software distribution methods and tools

Excellent distribution channels are key to the success of the software industry. The term channel refers to parties involved in the distribution process and to the business model implied. Typical channels are:

- developer to end user;
- developer to distributor to end user;
- developer to customer center to end user;
- developer to distributor to customer center to end user.

The coverage by distribution channels varies considerably between industrialized countries and developing countries. The technical aspects of distribution are largely determined by the medium used. The currently available distribution media are listed in Fig. 7-2.

Medium	Size	Properties
Diskette	2 MB	Limited capacity, modifiable
Magnetic tape	70 GB	Large capacity, sequential
CD-ROM	600 MB	Inexpensive, non-modifiable
DVD-ROM	17 GB	Excessive capacity
Network	Undetermined	Limited by transmission speed and costs

Fig. 7-2 Software distribution media

Considering the size of today's software products, CD-ROMs and networks are the preferred media. If network transmission times exceed 15 or 20 minutes, CD-ROMs may be more advantageous. They can also serve as backup copy and can easily carry the necessary documentation. There are several tools on the market to support the distribution of software within a local network. They must allow multiple versions of a program to exist. Software distribution tools may support a push or pull strategy: in push mode all nodes are kept at the same level, which has considerable advantages for problem determination and maintenance; in pull mode, the nodes have to explicitly request an update.

7.4.2 Software installation methods and tools

If not pre-installed prior to hardware delivery, software is typically installed by one of the methods listed in Fig. 7-3. Installation tools check the completeness of the material, resolve configuration conflicts, and register components in an inventory. In a large enterprise network, a medium-sized application (Netscape browser) could be successfully installed on 4,000 PCs in a single day [Luer98]. A distribution tool was extended by a small Perl script to handle configuration peculiarities.

Configuration	Installation method	Installation source
Single client or server	Local, hands-on	Original CD
Multiple servers	Local, hands-on	Replicated CD
High number of clients	Remote, unattended	File server, distribution tool
High number of servers	Remote, unattended	Scripts over network

Fig. 7-3 Software installation methods

7.4.3 User training and help services

The subject of user training is somewhat ambiguous. For the ideal system, no training should be required. Nor should there be any printed documentation. The functions should be what the user expects (and loves to have) and its use should be easy and self-explanatory. Since ideal systems are rare, it can be crucial to recognize what training is required. Not offering the appropriate training may reduce the acceptance of the product to zero. For planning a training package, the vendor has to be aware of the difference between available and needed skills of the potential users, and of their willingness to undergo a certain training effort. The user's willingness is determined by the ratio of expected benefit versus costs. Some costs may be successfully camouflaged by special forms of offerings, be it online or in a leisurely atmosphere. Also, independent consultants can motivate users to spend training costs that will result in revenue for them.

Most users expect, as a minimum, a help service, usually a phone number or e-mail address, to which questions can be directed. There are vendors who charge for such a service. If the phone service charges by the minute and does not provide technically qualified help, this is really a deterrent and will all but confirm to the user that he or she has made the correct product choice.

7.4.4 Customizing, localizing, and conversion

Whenever standard products are installed, the need may arise to adapt the product to the actual configuration or application requirements of the user – referred to as customizing. This may involve the setting of options and parameters, and the selection and loading of special modules. In former times, re-assembly or re-compilation of source code was considered a valid approach, but this is no longer the case. As an example, most ERP packages can be customized today by completing a set of tables. Choosing the correct values for theses tables may be quite a demanding task requiring professional assistance.

Localization describes the effort needed to adjust a standard software system to the requirements of the market in a particular country. It usually implies the translation of messages, help texts, and accompanying documents. In some cases, additional effort is needed for the handling of currency notations.

Very often, a new application uses existing data files. It may be appropriate to convert these data files from the format they were in to a format better suited for the new application. Standard tools can usually be used to perform this conversion. Conversion can also apply to databases if a different data model is required, such as relational instead of hierarchical. Whenever conversions are needed, it is important that they are planned carefully and executed completely in the time period allocated for them. To drag them along may give rise to awkward problems.

7.4.5 Applets and servlets

Whenever new modes of distribution are discussed, applets and servlets come up. Applets are small application programs embedded in a Web document. When downloaded, they can be activated by the browser residing on a Web client. Regular Java programs execute in their own window and have full access to the file system. They require the Java virtual machine as their interpreter. A servlet is a Java program that is executed on a server on request of a client, and which returns its result to the client. It can be expected that for all applications that are primarily used through the Internet, these forms of programs will play a key role.

7.5 Examples and study material

7.5.1 Manufacturing and distribution

As stated before, manufacturing and distribution costs for a software product can easily exceed its development costs. This example is intended to illustrate this conjecture. The base assumption is that 10,000 copies are to be produced by the vendor, to be installed by the same number of users. This number is typical for the mainframe world. In the case of PC software, several million copies may be sold. Fig. 7-4 gives data for six different distribution modes. All numbers are in thousand US$.

Distribution method	Fixed manufacturing costs	Variable manufacturing costs	Distribution medium	Distribution logistics	Total vendor costs	Installation	Costs: all users
Removable disk, books	100	2.0	1.00	0.50	35,100	2.0	20,000
Pre-installed disk, books	100	4.0	0.05	0.02	40,800	0.05	500
Magnetic tape only	40	0.5	0.10	0.05	6,540	2.5	25,000
Shrink-wrapped books, CD	80	0.3	0.05	0.02	3,780	0.5	5,000
CD only	40	0.1	0.005	0.005	1,140	1.0	10,000
Download	50			0.05	550	1.5	15,000

Fig. 7-4 Manufacturing and distribution options

Costs are identified as manufacturing, distribution, and installation costs. Manufacturing costs are split in fixed and variable costs. The fixed costs occur only once for a product, and may include the hardware and software needed for distribution centers, and the preparation and testing of the distribution material. Variable manufacturing costs are caused by every unit produced. Depending on the distribution mode, they may involve computer runs and clerical handling. Distribution costs are split into media and logistics costs. Logistics covers shipment, storage, and accounting. In the case of pre-installation, the software distribution costs are covered by the hardware distribution costs. Both manufacturing and distribution are considered as vendor costs. In some cases, the vendor may be able to bill these to the user. All user-related costs are subsumed under installation costs. This may include training, product customization, installation planning and execution, and security backup. Also the users' communication costs for downloading are included here.

As the example shows, there are many possibilities to shift costs between vendor and user. One case favored by users is pre-installation, which is applicable only in case of new hardware, however. Downloading takes away most vendor costs, which are partially compensated by the user. Whenever books are needed, the question who prints them is a typical shift of costs.

Exercises

7-1 Explain the difference between software and hardware manufacturing.

7-2 Which means or channels are available for software distribution?

7-3 What technical means exist to prevent illegal copying (piracy) of software?

7-4 Describe the effect on software installability of the following innovations: object-code only and device sensing.

7-5 What options are meaningful for the mass installation of client–server software?

chapter 8

System administration, evolution, and maintenance

The term evolution describes a process of progressive change in the attributes of entities. This may include improvement in some sense, adaptation to a changing environment, loss of not-required or undesired properties or the emergence of new ones.

M.M. Lehman [Lehm94]

This chapter deals with activities that occur once a system is complete. The activities explored in detail are administration, evolution, and maintenance. The relevant principles and ground rules are presented.

8.1 Definitions and importance

Administration is the activity that assures that a system is used properly. For many dedicated systems the end user is concerned about this personally. In other cases, specialists can be drawn upon to help. *Evolution* is the term used to designate the adaptation of installed systems to new requirements. By using this term from biology, we emphasize the fact that this activity is very important should a system survive over an extended period of time. *Maintenance* is the activity that is concerned with the elimination of failures. In the case of hardware, failures may be due to the physical deterioration of devices. In the software field, maintenance is mainly concerned with the removal or circumvention of faults, i.e. errors introduced during development. Many vendors make a distinction between service and maintenance support. A *service contract* may include consultation, information on fixes and updates as they become available, but with or without the actual fixes. Like with any complicated technical product, be it a car, a household appliance, or an airplane, its value heavily depends on the level of service provided.

After installation at a user's site, systems begin to perform useful work. They may or may not produce the benefits that had been expected. To improve the chances of doing so, systems have to be administered, evolved, and maintained. The lifecycle ends when the product is explicitly withdrawn.

8.2 General observations

When large mainframe computers were the norm, systems were all centrally administered. An economic or even orderly operation was not feasible otherwise. A computing center not only occupied special air-conditioned rooms, it also had a significant number of technical staff. Very often it was a separate organizational unit consisting of between five and 50 people. With distributed systems, the expectation arose that administrative tasks would disappear, i.e. if every employee had a computer of his or her own, he or she could do the administration personally. Maybe the central department could be off-loaded or even dissolved. In fact, the distribution of computers throughout an organization moved work from a specialist group out to many non-specialists. If their time is valuable, the question arises whether this solution is optimal. If the number of distributed systems reaches in the thousands, economies of scale will favor a centralized solution again, or at least a centralization of repetitive and time-consuming tasks.

The terms hardware and software came about when programs were considered a soft addition to impressive and solid computing systems. Today the relationship has reversed totally. One of the persons who predicted this very early was Barry Boehm. Fig. 8-1 is a modification of his graph from 1976 [Boeh76], which can still be found in many publications.

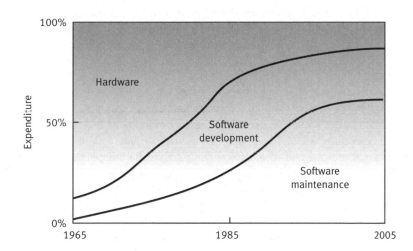

Fig. 8-1 Relative expenditure on hardware versus software

Fig. 8-1 shows the relative expenditures of organizations for hardware versus software. Boehm has drawn a similar graph, ending in 1985. Certainly, during the last decade, software maintenance costs have surpassed both software development costs and hardware costs for a typical commercial computer user. There are even some industries, such as mobile phones, where hardware is given away free if certain software business can be expected. The fact that software maintenance costs exceed software development costs indirectly points to the longevity of software. Boehm's assumption was that typically software is developed and maintained by the customer. It did not take into account that today more and more software can be purchased as commercial products (COTS). Therefore, the current situation concerning the two software cost factors somewhat depends on what is considered as maintenance cost. If it includes local administration and support, and the purchase of updates for existing products, the relationship still holds today.

It took both industry and academia quite some time to realize the true nature of software. It was at the Congress of the International Federation of Information Processing Societies (IFIP) in 1968 when the Russian computer scientist Adrei Ershov astounded the entire audience with the far-sighted statement: 'You better get used to the idea that OS/360 will still be around in the year 2000'. This was about three years after its first delivery. Today, the sixth or seventh generation of processors is being installed to run OS/360 or its derivatives. Similarly, several other operating systems developed more than 30 years ago are still significant revenue generators, e.g. UNIX and DOS/VSE. As the majority of all programmers in the world did not share Ershov's view, one result was what became known as the Year 2000 (Y2k) problem.

Both for customer-developed and for licensed products, an explicit decision has to be made concerning the type and duration of service provided. Although the technical life of a software product is not limited, the period for which service and maintenance support is offered may be limited. This is the subject of the service and maintenance strategy and will be discussed in more detail below.

There is usually a difference between the user's view and that of a service provider. The user first notices what we call an irregularity, which he may or may not report to a local service group. For the local service group, some reported irregularities can be solved by giving advice to the user, e.g. via a help desk. Others may need work on the part of the support group. If many users are affected, or critical applications are halted, this may put the support group into emergency mode. In some instances, the critical situation may have been caused by an apparent problem in a product of an external supplier. Only if a maintenance contract exists is an incident reported to a service provider. The service provider has the choice between supplying corrections only for the problem just reported by this customer (corrective maintenance), or may at this or any other occasion install fixes also for problems found at other installations (preventive maintenance). The number of events involved may be reduced by a factor of ten at each step.

All incidents that cannot be handled without specialist involvement will be counted as problems (failures). Software field service typically encounters two major problem types: duplicates and no-trouble-founds. A duplicate is a problem that has been reported before by some other installation, and a fix is available or in preparation. No-trouble-found (NTF) designates that the problem could not be reproduced by the service people. While the percentage

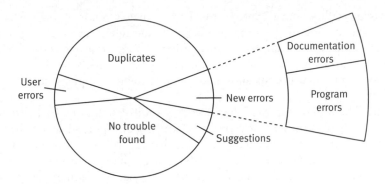

Fig. 8-2 Making a distinction between problems and errors

of duplicates depends on the service strategy, the number of NFTs is a function of the diagnostic tools provided. The three small groups, each with less than 10 percent, are suggestions, user errors, and new errors. The new errors typically consist of 25 percent documentation errors and 75 percent code errors. For both subgroups fixes have to be provided. Fig. 8-2 is based on historical data of IBM mainframe operating systems, analyzing some 400,000 problems.

8.3 Applicable laws and their theories

We will commence this section with three laws formulated and popularized by Manny Lehman [Lehm80], and quote them here verbatim. Lehman had originally defined five laws. We will combine the last three into one law.

8.3.1 Lehman's first law

The first law to be quoted expresses a fundamental observation about software and computing systems.

A system that is used will be changed.	(L27)

Applicability This law expresses a unique and essential property of software. It illuminates the Janus-faced character of software between a piece of machinery and an intellectual document. For many users, software is used as it is and never changed. Many small programs are written, used once, and then thrown away. The more typical situation, however, is that a software product is useful for some users over an extended period of time. Change is inevitable in that case. Change in the case of software normally means growth. The period of change varies with the type of software: a virus scan program will have to be updated three times a month; an Internet search engine may only need to be updated once per quarter; and for other types a yearly issue will be more appropriate. From a user's point of view, it is secondary which part of the program is being changed. Some changes may affect the data files or databases only, other changes may be code changes. As with legal reference documents, many software products can be seen only as a basic binder that is constantly being updated with supplements.

Evidence The initial empirical work on this subject was done by Lehman in co-operation with Les Belady [Bela76] during the period 1970 through 1975. They observed and analyzed the first 25 releases of OS/360, the mainline operating system of IBM at that time. The system grew from one to eight million LOC within a three to four year period. Similar growth patterns could be seen in other software systems as well, for example, DOS/VSE, MS Windows, UNIX, or the Netscape browser. Fig. 8-3 shows the growth curves for the three most important families of operating systems. The size numbers assume that, besides the kernel, some basic development tools are included as well.

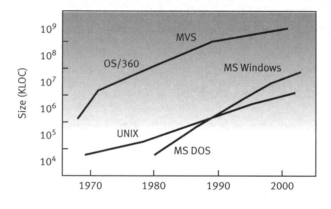

Fig. 8-3 The growth of operating systems

Fig. 8-3, which is based on a similar figure in [Denn84], shows the software systems associated with three types of hardware systems: mainframes, minicomputers, and microcomputers. Each one started by creating a new market below the other, then expanded by pushing the predecessor upward. In recent years, Windows and PCs are overtaking UNIX and workstations in size. The growth of MVS (the successor to OS/360) may have slowed down somewhat because most of the user related front-end functions have been off-loaded to PCs and workstations running MS Windows or OS/2.

Theory There are many reasons why software that is in use undergoes change. Some have to do with restrictions that may have been introduced initially. Some functions had lower priority and were left out. Once the initial applications were available that justified the introduction of the new systems, customers found other applications that were related and could be automated as well. From the vendor's point of view, there are opportunities to be exploited by expanding the system's usage into new market segments. There is a constant pressure to support new hardware, satisfy higher demands for security, and to achieve better throughput or response times. As Lehman [Lehm80] has put it: 'A large programming system models some part of reality. It either undergoes change or becomes less and less useful'. Two decades later, he stated the reasons for change more positively: 'The ultimate goal of functional growth is to increase stakeholder satisfaction' [Lehm01]. Being a non-physical system, a software system can change; it can be adapted to the changing environment.

We should not ignore the market forces that drive change. As an object that does not decay or dissolve, an existing software product has to be obliterated in order to be replaced. If a large portion of the potential buyers already use last year's version, the new version has to have a superior set of functions. No user wants to give up functions he or she is accustomed to. This forces the suppliers to constantly add features, since keeping the same set of functions may make it difficult to prove that the new solution is better. It is easier to distinguish a product from its competition by saying that it can do more than all the others. Under these circumstances, a user has to be quite brave to continue to use, for example, a ten-year old text processor.

8.3.2 Lehman's second law

The next law is almost as famous, but is more subject to controversy.

> An evolving system increases its complexity unless work is done to reduce it. **(L28)**

Applicability While the first law states the inevitability of growth, we now are looking at its effect. The ramifications of this law depend heavily on what is considered as complexity. For this reason we shall repeat the definition of complexity from Chapter 3 used in the context of Simon's law: 'made up from a large number of parts that interact in a non-simple way'. A system grows by adding functions and components, supporting more configurations, handling more special cases, and by accommodating different user styles, national languages, etc. With respect to its original design, the system degrades. It loses more and more of its original structure. In Lehman's words, 'The accumulation of gradual degradation ultimately leads to the point where the system can no longer be cost-effectively maintained and enhanced.'

In addition to functional maintenance a structural maintenance becomes necessary. This is referred to as clean-up or re-engineering, and amounts to a partial redesign. We will discuss this activity in more detail below. By the way, this kind of problem is not unique to a system in maintenance. It is a risk also with incremental development.

Evidence Lehman sees an analogy between his second law and the second law of thermodynamics. It says that in all energy exchanges, if no energy enters or leaves the system, the potential energy of the final state will always be less than that of the initial state. This is also commonly referred to as entropy. For software systems, Dvorak [Dvor94] talks about conceptual entropy. He applies this concept to class hierarchies in object-oriented programs. In a case study, he analyzed Smalltalk programs that underwent frequent changes. Additional subclasses were added, the existing classes were modified, and the hierarchy itself was restructured. Conceptual inconsistencies increased further down the hierarchy. This makes it difficult to use and modify. His conclusion was that: 'If left unchecked, the hierarchy can reach a state where it must be restructured.'

The above law is certainly true for the three families of operating systems referred to in Fig. 8-3. For all of them, major clean-ups and redesigns occurred at least once during every decade. In the case of the VSE operating system such a redesign had a major effect on maintenance costs. It reduced the number of fixes in error in half (from about 10 percent to under 5 percent). The latest re-implementation of the UNIX system is known today as LINUX.

Theory The rationale for this law can be found in [Lehm80]: 'If one tries to do the necessary changes to a system in a cost-effective way, this is what happens. If there are multiple objectives, one cannot fulfill all of them optimally.' In other words, one cannot redesign the system for every change. Since the process of system evolution normally extends over several years, some design ideas behind the original structure may get lost. They may simply have been forgotten. They must not always be explicitly sacrificed for other goals.

Comment Some people compare the evolution of software systems with evolution in nature. This is certainly an exaggeration, as in nature most systems seem to grow totally without a design. If one subscribes to Darwin's theory, the only design principle applied is survival of the fittest. All variations are accidental, i.e. caused by errors (or mutations) in DNA copying.

8.3.3 Lehman's third law

As stated before, we have combined three of Lehman's other laws into a single law, which we state in a somewhat generalized form.

System evolution is determined by a feedback process.	(L29)

Applicability The applicability of this law is not as strong and obvious as for the other two laws. The growth dynamics of a system depend highly on the business environment. The maintenance strategy is only one aspect.

Maintenance efforts may have a higher or lower priority than other considerations. For example, to remain in control of a newly emerging market, it may be extremely vital to bring out new functions soon. If the number of customers is still low, or their applications still not mission-critical, it would be wrong to concentrate on maintenance problems.

Lehman's fourth and fifth laws, which are not quoted here, are in our opinion special boundary conditions for this law. They postulate that the organizational work rate and the perceived complexity of the system remain constant. This seems to be true for a certain form of organizational setup only and cannot be generalized.

Evidence The evidence of this law was mainly drawn from OS/360. This system and its successor MVS were largely driven by hardware considerations. If new hardware was ready, software for it had to be shipped. Pure software functions and even software maintenance were postponed. In the early releases of OS/360, Lehman observed that releases with significant new functional content were normally followed by a release consisting primarily of maintenance. Completely different priorities existed for systems like Windows, R/3, or Unix. Here the tie-in with hardware vendors existed also, but had less influence over the software.

Theory In [Lehm80], Lehman tries to give the reasons himself why one should expect a feedback process with regular behavior. In his opinion, it is due to random input – the interplay of forces and 'multiple levels of arbitration, correction, smoothing and feedback'. This has the effect of 'economic and social brakes'. In our opinion, many systems have considerable degrees of freedom left. They can be adjusted to specific subsets of users or to changes in requirements quite easily. In our form, the law only points out that a developer is not entirely free in the way he or she can go about system evolution. He or she has created technical facts, raised expectations, and committed certain resources.

8.3.4 Basili–Möller law

The following law gives an important insight into software maintenance. We have named it after the two authors who independently published work on it, i.e. Vic Basili and Karl-Heinz Möller.

Smaller changes have a higher error density than large ones.	(L30)

Applicability The essential point of this law is that small changes to a module or a system are very critical. They usually have a higher density of errors per lines of changed or added code, than have larger changes. This law is not in conflict with the observation that error numbers are proportional to size, i.e. that larger systems have more errors than small systems.

Evidence The study that first brought out this law was performed by Basili and Perricone [Basi84]. The study was done in the NASA Software Engineering lab and was concerned with Fortran programs for aerospace applications. The study is based on 215 errors found during a three-year period of testing and maintenance. The distribution of errors was skewed with respect to the number of modules affected (Pareto's law!). Errors were found only in 96 of 370 modules (26 percent). The key data are given in Fig. 8-4. The results have caused considerable controversy, since they were regarded as counter-intuitive by many people. What astounded people most was the fact that the error-prone modules did not show more than average complexity. The other remarkable observation was that the error density (errors/KLOC) was clearly decreasing with module size.

Module size	Complexity: all modules	Complexity: error-prone modules	Errors per KLOC
50	6.0	6.2	65.0
100	19.6	17.9	33.0
150	27.5	28.1	24.6
200	56.7	52.7	13.4
› 200	77.5	60.0	9.7

Fig. 8-4 Error density and complexity sorted by module size

Evidence leading to this law was presented independently by Möller [Moel85] based on data for a Siemens operating system (BS/2000). The observation is also consistent with Selby's [Selb88] data from his study of software reuse. Selby observed that small changes create disproportionably high costs.

Theory The reason for this law is that small changes require the same amount of understanding of the old, surrounding code as do large changes. The relative costs of small changes, and their proneness to error are therefore higher. The exact amounts depend, of course, on how good the design is, and how well it is documented. If the system had been in use, the original structure may have deteriorated (following Lehman's second law). For larger changes, the knowledge required about the existing code is less in proportion to the added code.

8.3.5 McCabe's hypothesis

The following hypothesis is introduced to discuss the role of complexity metrics and their relation to error-prediction models. It is named after Thomas McCabe [McCa76].

Complexity metrics are good predictors of post-release reliability and
maintainability.   (H15)

Applicability Many developers and researchers are inclined to predict quality-
related properties from the structure of a module or system, be it static or
dynamic structure. The hope is that this would make a system more reliable by
changing its structure, or predict its quality without looking at its history.
Many software metrics have been proposed and tools developed to help in this
respect. The McCabe metric [McCa76] is the best known example.

Evidence The question addressed by empirical studies so far is the relationship
between complexity metrics and reliability. One such study was performed
under the supervision of one of the authors (Endres) in 1983. It is documented
in a thesis at the University of Karlsruhe and in an IBM technical report
[Niod83]. The study analyzed three products, totaling 324 modules from the
DOS/VSE operating system. They were consisting of about 105 KLOC and
were written in a high level language (PL/I dialect). Two groups of modules
were from products already in use with customers. One group was still in development. In the last case, the faults had either been detected by inspections or
internal tests. In each case the number of faults per module has been compared
with the size of the module and the McCabe number. The McCabe number was
derived mechanically from the source code of the modules. Somewhat as a surprise, the size measure correlated as well or better than the McCabe number
with the number of errors detected. Besides the McCabe metric, the Halstead
metric was also evaluated. It showed the same relationships.

The same conclusion can be drawn from the Basili and Perricone data
given in Fig. 8-4. A more recent and, very comprehensive study was published by Fenton and Ohlsson [Fent00]. They studied data from two releases
of an Ericsson telecommunication system. They came to the same conclusion
as the two other studies mentioned, namely that the McCabe metric is no
better predictor for post-release quality than is size (LOC). Another result of
this study is even more interesting: it says, 'there is no evidence to support
the hypothesis that the more errors are found during pre-release activities,
more faults will be found after release'. In fact, 93 percent of all pre-release
faults were found in modules which showed no errors after release.

Comment Before operational profiles were applied, software reliability projections were frequently made based simply on system size and system
structure information. Combined with data on the amount of errors
removed during testing, several authors developed reliability growth
models. The predictive power of theses models has turned out to be quite
good, although the approach contains severe theoretical flaws. As pointed
out before, it is wrong to assume anything approaching an equal distribution of errors across all modules of a system. The next assumption is
equally wrong, namely that if many errors are detected during testing this is

a sign of increased ('growing') reliability. Taken to the extreme, this means that if few errors have been introduced and found, the system is assumed to be unreliable. As Fenton [Fent99] pointed out, two flaws are not enough. Most of these models rely on an unknown relationship between faults and failures. Apparently, software reliability prediction is one of those areas where correlations are observed (and published) even when causal relationships do not exist.[1] In practice, complex modules are usually inspected and tested more carefully than non-complex modules. Complexity measures might be good predictors of maintainability, i.e. cost to do fixes. No studies of this hypothesis have been published yet.

Finally, we should mention that the IBM laboratory in Böblingen used McCabe measurements to great success in the case of software acquisitions. In one case, a vendor claimed that two successive releases of a product had not undergone any significant changes because the sizes of the modules had not changed. A short analysis producing McCabe numbers revealed, however, that many modules had undergone significant rewrites. This finding could be used to request additional regression testing from the vendor.

8.3.6 Wilde's hypothesis

Because of the current pre-occupation with object-oriented programs we want to focus separately on the property called maintainability. This has been triggered by a paper by Norman Wilde [Wild93] that stated the following hypothesis.

Object-oriented programs are difficult to maintain.	(H16)

Applicability The benefits of object-orientation have been sought in different areas where maintainability rates high. Depending on the use a program gets, its maintenance costs may reach the same magnitude as the development costs. Wilde's hypothesis, as well as some empirical investigations, raise doubt whether object-orientation has an advantage in this respect.

Evidence Wilde only uses extensive qualitative arguments. The purpose seems to be the justification of a maintenance tool. He argues that object-oriented programs are difficult to understand, because they typically consist of a large number of small methods that are difficult to relate. The other problem area is inheritance. An empirical study Daly *et al.* [Daly96] does not confirm this directly. In this experiment, two groups of students were asked to perform a maintenance task on a small program (< 400 LOC) in C++.

---

[1]In ordinary life, such a case is the correlation that exists between the population size of storks in a certain area and the birth rate of women. This correlation is supposed to support the hypothesis that babies are brought by storks.

One contained a three-level class hierarchy, the other one was flat, i.e. did not use inheritance. In a second experiment, a flat program was compared with a program containing a five-level inheritance hierarchy (deep inheritance). The time in minutes was measured until a correct change was made. Test and integration time are not counted. The results are given in Fig. 8-5.

Hypothesis tested	Result
Low vs no inheritance → maintenance time	Significant advantage for inheritance
Deep vs no inheritance → maintenance time	Small advantage for flat program

Fig. 8-5 Evaluation of maintenance costs

Here the hypotheses have a different form. They do not specify the expected direction of the results, i.e. whether the effect on maintenance will be positive or negative. For the correct interpretation of these results, the following information should be added. In the first experiment, the flat program was only slightly longer than the program with inheritance. In this case the existing class hierarchy could obviously be used as a template that guided the maintenance programmers. For the flat program, no such aid existed. In the second experiment, the flat program was about three times as large as the program with deep inheritance. The five-level hierarchy caused what the authors called 'conceptual entropy' (following Dvorak [Dvor94]), i.e. most programmers attempted several solutions before it became clear which class to specialize from.

An improved form of this experiment was conducted by Unger and Prechelt [Unge98]. Larger programs were used, and design information was given in graphical notation. The results showed that a program with a three-level hierarchy needed more time and generated more errors than a program with no inheritance, and a five-level program was worse than a three-level program.

8.3.7 Conjecture 5

Because the laws and hypotheses presented so far in this chapter deal mainly with evolution and maintenance, we shall add two conjectures. The first one addresses administration.

> The larger the system, the greater the administration effort that is needed. **(C5)**

Applicability We like to introduce this conjecture as a variant of Lehman's second law. We could call it a corollary. While Lehman's concern is the internal structure of a single application or component, similar observations can be made at the level of a system supporting several applications, or for a network of systems. Systems and networks, if used, will grow in unplanned ways. An administration effort involves adding or deleting components in a systematic fashion.

Evidence Administrative tasks are quite different depending on the size (and hence, the cost) of the systems involved. They also vary largely between organizations. An academic environment may have requirements quite different to those of a commercial or government installation. Following Halprin [Halp99], typical administrative tasks include the following:

- establishment of access rights and controls;
- provision of accounting methods and tools;
- management of problems, updates, and configuration changes;
- capacity planning and asset management;
- data security, archiving, and recovery;
- network management.

Some of the activities are primarily technical in nature, while others require a business or accounting background. The staff of a large mainframe computing center have to have both skills. One group of persons in a mainframe installation is concerned with the operation of the system, including replying to system messages, the mounting of tapes or disks, and the readying of printers. With distributed systems a similar task is performed in monitoring the network.

8.3.8 Conjecture 6

The next conjecture points out another basic experience of every system owner.

Any system can be tuned.	(C6)

Applicability While Lehman's first law views system change somewhat in a fatalistic way, there clearly is also a positive message involved that says that, if needed, any system can be improved. This is generally found to be true not only for one specific property, but only up to a certain point. Improvement of one property is easy if other properties allow it. To improve multiple properties at the same time is much more difficult. Changing a running system is counterbalanced by the observation that users are willing to adapt to a system's idiosyncrasies only if the benefits obtained are obvious. The other question is, is it worthwhile to change? Are the risks and costs in a proper relation to the benefits expected?

Evidence Of the many cases supporting this conjecture, the following experience is most vivid in one author's memory (Endres). To succeed in a certain bid situation, a limited number of benchmarks had to be run. In the first round, however, we came second because the path-length of certain transaction types were a problem. In the four weeks prior to the decisive showdown, we analyzed the particular transactions with all the available tools. We then moved all critical routines higher in the storage hierarchy, i.e. from disk to main memory, or even into microcode. In the 'best and final' run we outperformed the competition by a long way.

8.4 More on system administration, evolution, and maintenance

8.4.1 Security strategy and control

More than ever before, system administration has to focus specifically on security aspects. As suggested in Allen [Alle01], a security strategy has to address three time intervals, namely preparation, incident handling and follow-up. During the preparation phase, the policies have to be selected and the proper mechanisms and tools have to be installed. Each incident has to be handled in the following order: characterize the intrusion, inform all parties that need to be aware of it; collect all information on the intrusion, contain and eliminate the intrusion; and return to normal mode of operation. In the follow-up phase, the lessons learned should be analyzed and the protection mechanisms or policies should be improved, if possible.

As an additional measure of control, a security audit may have to be conducted from time to time. To check the adequacy of policies and mechanisms, and the capabilities of the people involved, an intrusion may be simulated.

8.4.2 Vendor strategies for service and maintenance

As indicated before, the value of a software product depends critically on the service available for it. From a supplier's view, the service associated with a product can considerably enhance its value. It may help users who bought the product to turn it from 'shelfware' into a useful tool. It establishes a relationship with the customers that easily can become a source of new business. Often service is a business in its own right and can generate revenue, be it for the supplier or a third party.

A service contract may cover advice and help only, and/or include the delivery and application of maintenance fixes. It may be free of charge or liable for costs. The duration of service can vary; it may cover an initial shake-out period only, the time up to the next release, or an arbitrarily set time period, e.g. four years after first shipment. The frequency with which updates are provided is another business decision. Typical options are once per month, once per quarter, or once per year. Determining arguments can be the amount of changes, their importance, and the user's effort to apply them.

Fig. 8-6 indicates the relationship of errors and product code in a multi-version product. In this case, version 2 reuses large portions of the code of version 1, and version 3 reuses code of versions 1 and 2. The customer shipment date of the version 1 corresponds to the y-axis, and the availability dates of versions 2 and 3 are indicated by means of dashed vertical lines. The upper part of the figure reflects the assumed distribution of the number of users with respect to this product. As users do not migrate from one version to the next instantaneously, but only gradually, maintenance support may have to be provided concurrently for all three versions. In the lower part, the error distribution over the three versions is shown. As an example, the errors E3 found by version 3 users may have been introduced during the development of version 1, 2, or 3. If quality analysis is attempted the data have to be collected such that a distinction can be made between the product where the error was found and the product causing the error. The time frame under consideration may be up to five to seven calendar years.

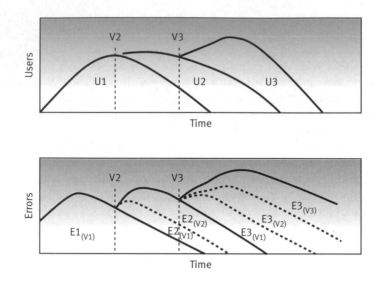

Fig. 8-6 Errors found in product versus caused by product

8.4.3 User strategies for service and maintenance

From a user's point of view, the main decision to be made boils down to the question whether one wants to be economically independent or enter into some long-term business relationship with a supplier or a third party. If skill and resources are no problem, a do-it-yourself approach may be appropriate. In that case, the source code of the system or component is needed, as well as the design documentation. Normally, business arguments will favor maintenance by the supplier or a trusted third party. Certainly, this approach takes into account the nature of software, as expressed by Lehman's first law.

Two questions regarding maintenance support have to be considered as risk management. At first, it should be determined whether the turn-around time of the service provider for problem fixes is satisfactory in view of the criticality of the application or the system for one's own business. This may require that an ability is created and maintained to develop certain types of fixes themselves. The other potential problem to be considered is the case that the service provider ceases business. For this eventuality, source code and design material should be accessible. The legal option most often taken for this is to place such material 'in escrow' with some safeguarding agency.

For software developed in-house, the normal approach is to perform the maintenance in-house as well. If the corresponding workload binds an excessive amount of resources and skills, outsourcing can be considered. This may result, however, in additional time delays and higher total costs.

One popular adage among users says, 'Never change a running system'. This reflects the experience that any update may introduce errors that did not exist before. For this reason, many users prefer corrective maintenance, meaning that they install only fixes for problems that occurred at their site. For the service provider this means that individual fixes have to be selectable. To achieve this, fixes are usually supplied in source code format. The user then goes through a lengthy, error-prone process of compilation for all components in question. For the vendor such a strategy means that all users will eventually run into all the problems that ever existed. The data shown in Fig. 8-2, are largely based on this approach. What are called 'duplicates' are problems rediscovered at installations different to the one where the first discovery occurred.

For this reason, some software vendors adopted a strategy of preventive maintenance. In the extreme case, this means that as soon as an error is discovered anywhere, it will be fixed everywhere. As a compromise, from time to time, users are asked whether they want to install maintenance updates, sometimes called refreshes.[2] Another approach, tried out with the SSX system mentioned before, was to install refreshes only at those installations that reported a problem. The category called 'duplicates' in Fig. 8-2 could be reduced significantly. As a prerequisite for this, the number of fixes in error had to be addressed and was practically eliminated. In order to be efficient, both for the service provider and the user, preventive service is typically applied based on object-code. Entire modules or components are replaced, ready to be used, without re-compilation. Several suppliers of Internet-related software successfully exercise a preventive maintenance strategy. They distribute and install refreshes over the Internet in rather short time intervals, e.g. once per month.

8.4.5 On-the-fly version updates

Many systems require a shut-down and restart after an update has been made. Since this can be a problem if uninterrupted service is offered, several approaches have been taken to perform software updates on a running system. At the simplest level, this means replacing entire modules or procedures that do not change the system kernel and whose interfaces with other modules are kept unchanged. A common approach to this uses dynamically linked libraries. Individual members of this library can be updated on an external medium up to the point in time where they are invoked. Sometimes special hardware features are used to assist. In highly available systems a stand-by processor may take over while the software is being updated. Several prototypes of such systems are described in [Sega93]. In many practical systems, changes of the system kernel occur, even in situations where it does not seem necessary.

---

[2] This term is used to differentiate from functional upgrades

Should kernel changes really become necessary, more demanding solutions are needed. In the most general case, the change has to occur while a module is running and the interfaces used by a routine have to be adjusted. This implies that in the moment of the update, the old state of the system has to be dynamically mapped into a new state. This can only occur at certain control points for which this mapping is defined. Finding these control points is a problem akin to dataflow analysis in compilers. For each such control point the life variables have to be determined and the appropriate state mappings have to be defined. A study of these problems is given in [Gupt96].

8.4.6 Re-engineering, re-development, and renovation

Re-engineering encompasses all activities whose goal it is to improve any or all of the developer-oriented quality criteria. As listed in Fig. 2-1, these are testability, maintainability, portability, localizability, and reusability. The user-oriented functions or criteria such as efficiency and usability are not considered as re-engineering. Since the external interfaces and functionality are kept, only the internal structure is changed. The system or component in question is brought onto a new technical base. Besides the structure, other elements of this technical base are the platform, the building blocks, the implementation language, and the language level used.

In contrast to re-development, re-engineering makes extensive use of existing material. This material may be manually or automatically converted. Re-development as well as re-engineering work is triggered as a reaction to Lehman's second law. In Lehman's terms, this is anti-regressive work [Lehm01], since it consumes effort without immediate visible stakeholder value. The investment has to be justified by expected future savings in development or maintenance costs. In the case of re-engineering the investment is expected to be lower than in the case of re-development.

Fig. 8-7 illustrates the software re-engineering process as propagated and used by Sneed [Snee87]. It shows four steps to be applied to source code, each of which can be supported by tools. The analysis step corresponds to the parsing and analysis step of a compiler. It decomposes programs and creates tables containing structural information and relationships. It may also derive certain software metrics. During the modularization step, monolithic programs may be split up into smaller components, observing certain interface or structuring rules (high coherence, low binding). The restructuring step may eliminate poor coding style at the module level. The final transformation step converts the intermediate results into the language notation used for the new system.

A special case of software modification is renovation. It improves the external appearance while keeping its function and technical base the same, for example, replacing an alphanumerical user interface with a graphical user interface (GUI). Very often re-engineering is combined with renovation, and both are combined with functional enhancements or performance improvements. It such a case, it may be easier to create a positive business case.

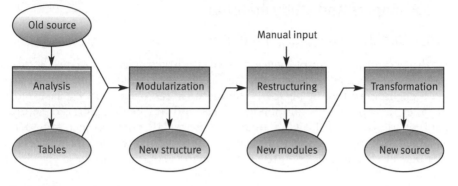

Fig. 8-7 The re-engineering process

8.4.7 Retirement and withdrawal

Software has the unique property that it does not decay or wear. As a consequence, there is no need to replace older parts, nor does a system ever die a natural death. Software systems only lose relevance. Should they disappear from an installation, they have to be removed explicitly. This may become desirable in order to save memory space on a computer, or to free up people and resources occupied for maintenance and service support.

For each individual user, the decision to drop an application may be rather easy, as is the effort required to un-install the corresponding programs and data. For an organization, looking inward, retiring an application or a software system is a removal of some service to some users, possibly effecting other organizations, and it has to be approached accordingly. For a purchased or licensed product, the termination may result in the cancellation of a service contract. If the product had been developed or maintained by the organization itself, it means dissolving the central maintenance group. For some products, this may only be the first step. Support by some local organization may continue for a while.

In the IBM tradition of software maintenance, a distinction was made between removal from the sales manual, withdrawal of central support, and cease of field support. Each step in the reclassification process was announced separately. Whatever steps are taken, the users have to be informed about the status change. They have to be told what to do in case of problems and where to migrate to. They should get advice how to perform the migration, should be provided with tools, should be offered help, and should have enough time to do it. In some cases, the announcement of withdrawal is considered by users as their last chance to report known problems and to request fixes.

8.5 Examples and study material

8.5.1 Quality tracking and prediction

In this example, a simple yet effective quality tracking and prediction method is illustrated. It is included in this chapter because it can be used to predict the maintenance effort. The method has been used over several decades in software development efforts and has been described before [Endr93a]. In the following figures, a waterfall-type project model is assumed. Six phases are assumed and designated using Roman numbers I through VI. The phases comprise the following activities, shown in Fig. 8-8.

I   Requirements definition
II Design, design inspection
III Construction, code inspections
IV Functional and operational testing
V Manufacturing, distribution, instillation
VI Maintenance

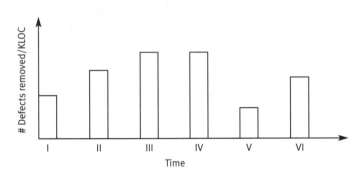

Fig. 8-8 Defect removal model

Fig. 8-8 is an illustration of the basic model used. It is a model expressing the number of defects removed per KLOC during the different phases. Although no scale is given on the ordinate, the example could be interpreted to represent about ten defects per KLOC for the two phases in the middle. Then this example would show that we assume that a total of about 45 defects per KLOC are inserted and removed over the life of this project.

This model encodes the specific experience of some organization with respect to error insertion and error removal. It is based on historic data gained for a certain application domain, a certain skill-level and a certain set of methods and tools. If a new project is started for the same domain, using people with the same skill level and following the same process, a similar result can be expected. Since every project is different, some changes in the assumptions usually have to be made. This may be reflected in the total number of defects, as well as in the distribution of the removals over the phases. In fact, this type of a model has been used for projects experiencing between 15 to 50 defects per KLOC over the life of a product. The number 50 was in vogue around 1975, the number 15 ten years later. The corresponding numbers for the post-development period (phase VI) were initially about ten, later less than one.

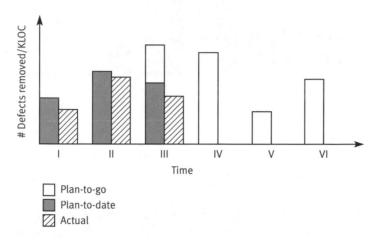

Fig. 8-9 In-process measurement

One of the big advantages of this model is that it can be used during the entire life of a project, and for several purposes. Fig. 8-9 shows its use for in-process measurements. It is a plot of the defect removal data at some point during phase III. Here two adjacent columns are used, with distinctive filling patterns. While the original plan (the plan-to-go) was represented by blank columns, for the portion of the plan that has been executed (the plan-to-date) the first column is tinted. In the example, phases I and II are completely done, phase III a little bit more than half. The second, hatched column gives the actual values. In the example, the actual values have been somewhat lower than the planned values. The questions triggered by this simple sketch are really useful. Typical questions are: 'Why is there a difference?' 'What is really different from what was expected?' 'Do we accept the deviations and their reasons?' and 'What can and will be done as a consequence?' The answer to the last question may result in a modification of the plan-to-go.

In Fig. 8-10, the data gained during development (i.e. phases I through V) are used to predict the residual errors. Residual defects are here defined as defects removed during the maintenance period (phase VI). Note that other definitions are not very practical. We can compare a prediction (plan-to-go) which was initially based on historic data from previous projects with the results achieved during the on-going project. Contrary to many other prediction models, we are not relying on the results of a single phase only, i.e. the test phase. In this example, the white cap on column III may mean that some planned code inspections did not take place. Testing may have been extended simply to compensate for the shortcomings in previous phases. It would therefore be wrong to assume less residual errors because more errors were found during testing than expected. Incidentally, to

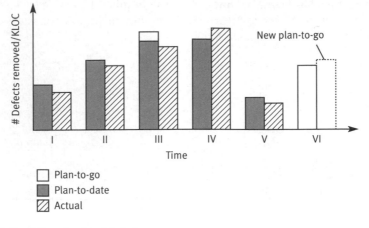

Fig. 8-10 Prediction of residual defects

assume that fewer errors are left the greater the number of errors that have been found is still a very weak assumption; it is better than the opposite, however. Data collected during the maintenance period can be used to recalibrate the model, and to reuse it for other projects. The most important benefit of this quality tracking method is that the quantitative effects of new methods and tools have to shown up in this model. It forces the empirical approach. Hype and hot air do not suffice.

8.5.2 Maintenance strategy

The maintenance strategy chosen can have a major effect on the post-shipment costs of a software product. This will be illustrated with this example. Another important message is that the bulk of the maintenance costs are not caused by the development of fixes, but by the field costs caused by incidents. The assumptions made for this example are listed in Fig. 8-11.

Assumptions	Year 1	Year 2	Year 3	Year 4
New users	1,000	4,000	3,000	2,000
New defects	80	60	40	30
Rediscovery rate	0.06	0.05	0.04	0.03
Total users	1,000	5,000	8,000	10,000

Fig. 8-11 Maintenance model assumptions

A four-year period is considered as the field life of a product. The acceptance of the product by new users has its peak in the second year. The number of residual errors to be detected totals 210, and peaks in the first year. As shown in Fig. 8-2, only a small fraction of the incidents are caused by newly detected problems. The majority are duplicates or 'no-trouble-founds' (NTFs). The assumption is made that in the normal case of corrective maintenance about ten times as many incidents occur as there are new defects. Based on this, a rediscovery rate is derived, which is highest for errors detected during the first year and decreases over time.

Incidents	Year 1	Year 2	Year 3	Year 4	Total
New defects Y1	80				80
Rediscoveries Y1	48	200	256	240	744
New defects Y2		60			60
Rediscoveries Y2		150	192	180	522
New defects Y3			40		40
Rediscoveries Y3			128	120	248
New defects Y4				30	30
Rediscoveries Y4				90	90
Total incidents	128	410	616	660	1814

Fig. 8-12 Corrective maintenance (base case)

The base case, as given in Fig. 8-12, assumes that error fixes are given only to those users who discovered a specific problem. As a consequence, all users may rediscover all defects. With the above figures, this leads to 1814 incidents. If we assume a cost of US$2000 per incident, this amounts to US$3.6 million for this product. Assuming 0.5 person-month per fix and a person-month at US$16,000, to produce the 210 fixes amounts to about US$1.7 million.

As the first alternative to be considered, shipments to new users are altered. After a certain period, new users will no longer receive the original product, but a product of higher quality, a so-called upgraded system. In our example, the assumption is made that such an upgraded system is produced once per year, including all fixes for errors found in the previous years. This leads to the numbers in Fig. 8-13. Rediscoveries can occur only at user sites that have received their shipment in previous years. In other words, the problems of year 1 (Y1) can be rediscovered only at 1000 sites, the problems of the second year (Y2) only at 5000 sites, etc. As a consequence, we see a decrease of field costs by more than 40 percent. We also have to add the costs for the production and distribution of the upgrades, however. In practice, the actual interval of upgrades will be determined by the frequency and severity of problems encountered in the field. It should be noted that the actual field cost will not go down if the manpower assigned to field support is kept constant. In that case, reducing the number of problems only has the effect of increasing the costs per problem.

Incidents	Year 1	Year 2	Year 3	Year 4	Total
New defects Y1	80				80
Rediscoveries Y1	48	40	32	24	144
New defects Y2		60			60
Rediscoveries Y2		150	120	90	360
New defects Y3			40		40
Rediscoveries Y3			128	96	224
New defects Y4				30	30
Rediscoveries Y4				90	90
Total incidents	128	250	320	330	1028

Fig. 8-13 Refreshing of distribution material

In the final case, as outlined in Fig. 8-14, we assume that once per year all users are forced or enticed to update their system. This is referred to as preventive maintenance. In the example case, it reduces field costs by another 40 percent. Companies pursuing this strategy may distribute maintenance updates as frequently as once per quarter. Preventive maintenance requires an excellent fix quality. If a significant number of fixes are in error, the users will not accept any preventive maintenance. In such a case, they will stay with the service level they have.

Incidents	Year 1	Year 2	Year 3	Year 4	Total
New defects Y1	80				80
Rediscoveries Y1	48				48
New defects Y2		60			60
Rediscoveries Y2		150			150
New defects Y3			40		40
Rediscoveries Y3			128		128
New defects Y4				30	30
Rediscoveries Y4				90	90
Total incidents	128	210	168	120	626

Fig. 8-14 Preventive maintenance

Exercises

8-1   What factors determine the technical and the economic life of a software product?

8-2   What are the dominant categories of reported user problems and why?

8-3   What can cause a software product to change over time?

8-4   Why does the complexity of a program increase during maintenance and what can be done about it?

8-5   What properties of object-oriented programs increase the maintenance effort and why?

8-6   Why is the complexity of a module (in the sense of McCabe) a poor predictor of its quality?

8-7   What are the advantages or disadvantages of doing maintenance in-house for purchased products? What particular risks have to be addressed?

8-8   Why is an on-the-fly installation of new software versions desirable? How can it be achieved?

chapter 9

Project management and business analysis

The software field is not a simple one and, if anything, it is getting more complex at a faster rate than we can put in order.

B. W. Boehm [Boeh79]

This chapter discusses two activities that permeate most projects from beginning to end: management and business analysis. Although considered as necessary evils by many technical people, we will show what issues they address and what results can be achieved.

9.1 Definitions and importance

The term *project management* is used here to designate the following activities: establishment of project plans and targets; selection and allocation of people; the definition of a development process; and the monitoring and control of the project progress. The establishment of project plans is referred to as planning. It requires estimation of effort and time, collectively called cost estimating. The allocation of people includes the definition of their role and their responsibilities.

Repeating a definition from Chapter 2, a *project* is an organizational effort over a limited period of time, staffed with people and equipped with the other required resources to produce a certain result. A *process* is the set of principles, methods, and tools used by a project. A development process defines which activities receive what emphasis, and how and in what sequence they are performed. Accordingly, different process models are used.

Business analysis comprises the estimating of the market potential, the determination of a product packaging and pricing approach (if applicable), the development of a business case, and the control of the return-on-investment. Besides revenue, customer satisfaction is an important indicator of product success.

In most projects, technical aspects are interrelated with management and business considerations. To be able to restrict oneself on the technical issues only, is really an exception and a luxury affordable only for some beginners or those in paradisical work environments. On the other hand, to be able to generate revenue from one's work is a source of recognition and satisfaction, eventually leading to economical independence.

9.2 General observations

We often encounter the attitude that software management is a necessary evil that disturbs a creative and mainly technical activity. It is seen as adding constraints that technical people do not like or do not need. Sometimes yardsticks are put up that may apply elsewhere. Creative people prefer to see their situation as unique, leading to the not-invented-here (NIH) syndrome. Some of them also sympathize with moderate forms of anarchism. In the software industry this phenomenon is typically prevalent in an environment of self-proclaimed cowboys. A very pragmatic view is to look at management not as some hostile group of people sitting on top of a project, but as an auxiliary function supporting a project from below. This view even produced some inverted organization diagrams.

The key activity associated with management is *project planning*. Planning does for a project what design does for a product: it identifies the goals, the success criteria, and the resources needed. In an ideal situation, the goals are obvious, the success criteria generous, and the resources to be used unlimited. Since such an environment is rare, any serious project needs a plan. The laissez-faire principle is inadequate. The questions here are 'How detailed and reliable is the plan?' and 'How is it generated?'

Cost estimating is a prerequisite to project planning. No planning is possible without estimating. Estimating the project effort is only possible if we understand the type of work to be done. Understanding usually progresses with the phases of a project: estimates are naturally very approximate at the beginning and should be improved over time. We should think carefully about which model to use and should not hope for simple models; we should rework estimates whenever better information is available. Following Boehm [Boeh00c], we can distinguish between seven estimating methods:

- *Algebraic models:* express relationships between independent and dependent variables by means of a formula.
- *Expert judgment:* ask people who are considered knowledgeable to express their opinion.
- *Analogy:* look for similar projects and use their actual data as a base.
- *Parkinson:* equate cost estimate to available resources.
- *Price-to-win:* equate cost estimate to price considered necessary to win the job.
- *Top-down:* derive costs from general properties of the resulting product.
- *Bottom-up:* estimate each individual activity separately or ask each participating subgroup to estimate its requirements and add up the result.

In practice, frequently more than one of these methods is used, mainly to validate the results achieved. Whatever method is used, it is important that the people responsible for the work agree with the estimate. This is the only way that a plan can be turned into commitments that people are willing to meet. The earlier in the project cycle an estimate is made, the lower is its accuracy. It is therefore customary to include a contingency factor into the planning. This may start as high as 30 percent and decrease while the project proceeds.

Algebraic cost estimating models usually rely on some notion of productivity. *Productivity* is to be understood as the amount of output per unit of investment. The question here is 'What is counted as output, and what investments are included?' As will be discussed in more detail below, the common measure of output for software projects is the size of the delivered system in terms of lines of source code (SLOC, or simply LOC). The investment is the labor cost spent. If the difference in manpower cost from country to country is to be excluded, only the effort (and not the cost) is considered. The effort is measured in person-time. For small projects (such as student assignments) it is person-hours or person-days, for large industrial projects it is usually person-months or person-years. When Brooks wrote his essay [Broo75], the expression man-year or man-month was more customary. A typical productivity measure (or metric) is thousand lines of code per person-year, abbreviated as KLOC/PY. The abbreviation PY stands for people-year or person-year.

Productivity numbers cannot be compared across organizations, unless unambiguous definitions of both elements, effort and LOC, are used. When counting effort, the degrees of freedom are as follows:

- which activities are counted, including requirements definition and maintenance;
- which people are counted, direct or indirect project members;
- which times are counted, productive and unproductive times.

The various LOC measures may also differ in several aspects. It should be clearly stated which of the following items are counted:

- only executable statements, or also declaratives;
- machine language (or assembler-equivalent), or high-level language;
- commentary and command language;
- physical lines or logical lines;
- newly developed, reused and changed code.

Depending on the way counting occurs, there may be differences by a factor of ten on each part. The most reasonable approach is to count only newly developed, logical lines, in a high-level language, excluding commentary, but including declarative and command language statements. Unless stated differently, this definition of LOC is used in this book.

Because of the wide variety of definitions, great care should be taken for comparisons between companies. Within a company and for comparisons between projects, a consistent definition has to be used. Two measures derived from LOC are essential in the definition of process or productivity measures. They are:

- *Changed Source Instruction (CSI):* Newly developed LOC + changed LOC + reused LOC – deleted LOC.
- *Shipped Source Instructions (SSI):* SSI of previous release + CSI of current release – changed LOC.

The LOC metric has the disadvantage that it depends on the design and the implementation chosen, including the implementation language. To solve this problem the measure *function points* (FP) has been proposed. In its initial definition by Albrecht [Albr79], five distinct functional elements of an application were counted (inputs, outputs, files, tables, and inquiries). These numbers were weighted and calibrated with historical data from 25 IBM projects to arrive at effort estimates. Later on, the definitions were generalized and calibrated with additional data. The problem with function points is that they cannot be directly measured. They can therefore not be used to plan the modification of an existing system. What makes their value even more questionable is the fact that FP measure size in a similar fashion as LOC does. This is demonstrated by the existence of tables that allow conversion from FP into LOC and vice versa, such as those published by Jones [Jone96]. According to this source, for typical third-generation languages, such as Ada, COBOL, and C, 1 FP corresponds roughly to 100 LOC. There are of course variations from language to language, particularly between Assembler and higher-level languages. Jones' table can also be found (as Table 2.4) in the COCOMO-II book [Boch00c], and has been incorporated into the COCOMO-II tool.

The skill to make good estimates can only be developed if actual data are collected with which to compare the estimates. To assure consistency of measurements, it may be advantageous to install an independent group to collect data across multiple projects. Process-related data should not be used for personal performance rating, however.

Another major management obligation is the choice of the right process model. There have been hundreds of different models proposed. They are usually variations of the waterfall model as first documented by Royce [Royc70] and the spiral model as proposed by Boehm [Boeh88]. We will discuss the essence of these two models below. As with any method, a process model cannot be introduced against resistance from below. The employees have to own the process.

Estimating the *market potential* of a product is really part of the requirements definition. If requirements are accepted this means that there are users who want this function. These users represent the potential market. Whether a market potential can be exploited depends on how motivated the users are, how well the actual products meet the requirement, and what alternate solutions exist. If a competitive product is already in the market and has satisfied the needs, a new product must be superior: it has to replace the existing product to gain users. Replacing an existing product creates additional costs for the user, which may have a major influence on his or her decision to move.

Pricing of a product requires the ability to estimate costs incurred in developing the product. It helps to determine a lower bound. For art and intellectual work, the value, and hence the price, is seldom determined by the effort that went into its creation. The value is what it is worth in the eyes of the viewer, collector, or user. A price is determined by considering the value for the user and the level established by the competition. Value-based pricing is usually only possible if the product or service is unique in the marketplace.

The slow growth in software development productivity frequently is seen as a problem, particularly in those environments where software is considered a burden rather than a business opportunity. If software is a business, the emphasis on productivity is secondary. It is certainly easier to double the revenue than to double productivity. Time to market may be more critical.

9.3 Applicable laws and their theories

9.3.1 Sackman's second law

This law is one of the oldest known in the industry. It dates back to a study done in 1966 by Sackman, Erikson, and Grant [Sack68] at the System Development Corporation (SDC).

Individual developer performance varies considerably.	(L31)

Applicability Although the purpose of Sackman's study was to prove the hypothesis that online programming is more productive than offline programming (Sackman's first law), the most surprising result of the study leads to this second law, which has achieved a much wider recognition than the first law. Without looking at the exact numbers, everyone knows that the variations between people are significant. In fact, they are much bigger than what can be achieved by a variation in methods. In spite of this, estimators have to make reliable predictions on the numbers, even before they know which programmers will be assigned to the project. A manager who is aware of this law will not attempt to force equal quotas on every member of the team. In fact, he or she will watch for the extremes at both ends, and will try to capitalize on the high performers, thus compensating for the low performers. It is an interesting question whether the use of tools smoothes the differences or not; many people believe that tools may increase the difference.

Evidence For this part of the study only the data for the group of 12 experienced programmers (group A in the study) were evaluated. The essence of Sackman's striking results is given in Fig. 9-1. The numbers given apply to the maze problem (A2). The study report does not provide the more detailed information that would be desirable, for example, whether the shorter program size correlates with the shorter coding times or not. The explanation of these findings leads Sackman into a discussion about the meaning of programmer skill. For beginners it is some general proficiency in problem solving and coding. Later on, the experience with the application domain, the tools, and methods prevails, so that a more diversified notion is needed. Sackman suggests the use of aptitude tests to detect the poor performers.

Activity	Best score	Poorest score	Ratio
Coding time (hours)	2	50	25
Debug time (hours)	1	26	26
CPU time (sec)	50	541	11
Program size (LOC)	651	3287	5
Run time (sec)	0.6	8.0	13

Fig. 9-1 Variability in programmer performance

Theory Programming is a key example of an intellectual activity. The intellectual capabilities of people vary. So do cognitive styles and work habits. The economic importance and the fact that first successes can be obtained easily, attract many people that have difficulties with more demanding problems into this field. Beside the basic skills, knowledge about many application domains has to exist or has to be acquired. Certainly, specialization can help.

Comment The statistical quality of this part of the data has been questioned [Prec01b]. Besides the small sample size (12 programmers) it is considered inappropriate to express variability by giving the extremes only. A better approach would have been to form quartiles and to take the median of the lowest and highest quartile. In addition, the data include variations caused by the use of Assembler (by three programmers) versus a high-level language (by nine programmers), as well as the use of a timesharing system (by six programmers) for debugging instead of a batch computer (by six programmers). If those programmers using the same methods are compared, the ratio in debug time is 14 : 1. If the medians of the lowest and highest quartiles were used, the ratio becomes 7 : 1. Even after this adjustment of the data, the variability is still significant. It is surprising that no similar study has been done during the last 35 years. Obviously, nobody expects that the numbers will change dramatically.

9.3.2 Nelson–Jones law

The following law combines work done as early as 1964 by Edward Nelson of the System Development Corporation [Nels66] with very recent observations by Capers Jones [Jone00].

A multitude of factors influence developer productivity.	**(L32)**

Applicability Both authors, whose work was carried out more than 30 years apart, emphasize the fact that productivity of software developers is really determined by a host of factors. Reducing this number to some ten or 15 parameters is certainly a major simplification. Together with Sackman's second law quoted above, the Nelson–Jones law characterizes the environment in which project managers work.

Evidence Nelson's study [Nels66] was based on data from 169 projects, covering both aerospace and commercial applications. Correlation analysis was done between about 100 factors and their effect on human effort, machine time needed, and schedule. The conclusion was that software productivity at least correlates with 15 factors. The factors chosen appear somewhat arbitrary today. The linear cost estimating model developed by Nelson proved to be of little use. Jones' experience [Jone00] is based on consulting work done for about 600 companies all over the world. Jones started his work within IBM about 1975, was with ITT from 1978 to 1985, and founded a company called Software Productivity Research (SPR) afterwards. Jones has written 11 books on software assessments and benchmarking. He claims that about 250 factors influence the work of programmers and thus the outcome of a project.

1. New development
2. Enhancement (new functions added to existing software)
3. Mandatory change (update for new statutes or regulations)
4. Maintenance (defect repairs to existing software)
5. Performance updates (revisions needed to improve throughput)
6. Conversion or adaptation (migration to new platform)
7. Nationalization (migration to new national language)
8. Re-engineering (re-implementing a legacy application)
9. Mass update (modifications for Euro or Y2K)
10. Hybrid (concurrent repairs and functional updates)

Fig. 9-2 Nature of projects

1. Subroutine of sub-element of program
2. Module of a program
3. Reusable module or object
4. Disposable prototype
5. Evolutionary prototype
6. Stand-alone program
7. Component of a system
8. Release of a system
9. New system or application
10. Compound system (multiple linked systems)

Fig. 9-3 Scope of projects

Looking at the different project environments and the different types of software to be written, Jones distinguishes between project nature (Fig. 9-2), project scope (Fig. 9-3), and project class (Fig. 9-4).

1. Personal application for private use
2. Personal application to be shared by others
3. Academic program developed in academic environment
4. Internal application to be installed at one location
5. Internal application to be accessed via an intranet or timesharing
6. Internal application to be installed at many locations
7. Internal application developed by contract personnel
8. Internal application developed using military standards
9. External application, to be freeware or shareware
10. External application to be placed on the World Wide Web
11. External application leased to users
12. External application embedded in hardware
13. External application bundled with hardware
14. External application marketed commercially
15. External application developed under outsource contract
16. External application developed under government contract
17. External application developed under military contract

Fig. 9-4 Class of projects

Considering, in addition, the 22 software types (as listed in Fig. 3-1), Jones arrives at a number for the multitude of variations. By multiplying 10 × 10 × 17 × 22, he obtained 37,400 different forms of software projects.

Theory Software and system development reflect the diversity of our social activities. There is no hope to reduce it unless we give up parts of our economic or social liberty. This reflects the basic difference between social and natural science. Social systems usually have a history, as do biological systems. This history is the main reason for a multitude of forms (and species) and the complexity of structures. It is only in some parts of inorganic nature that more simple structures can be discovered.

9.3.3 Boehm's third law

With this law we would like to give credit to Barry Boehm for his outstanding contributions to software cost estimating. Two books [Boeh81, Boeh00c] and several publications document his work in this area. A short overview is given in [Boeh84b].

Development effort is a (non-linear) function of product size.	(L33)

Applicability The law as formulated expresses the essence of a class of cost-estimating models, particularly those developed by Boehm. This class of estimating models requires that a size estimate be done first. In other words, they turn a cost estimate into a size estimate.

Evidence Software cost estimating has a long tradition. Any organization concerned with software development from the late 1950s was confronted with this problem. Brooks [Broo75] referred to work published during the early 1960s by Aron [Aron70], Corbató, Nelson, Portman, and Wolverton [Wolv74]. Later, the algebraic models of Putnam and Doty and their respective tools received wide acceptance.

Difficulty	Representative system	LOC/PY
Difficult	Control program	500 – 700
Medium	Compiler	1000 – 1700
Easy	Application program	2000 – 4000

Fig. 9-5 Productivity rules-of-thumb

Fig. 9-5 lists what could be considered as the industry's rule of thumb up to the time where more detailed models became available. As with Aron's estimating rule [Aron70], it uses three levels depending on the difficulty of the code in question. Other people made a distinction between high, medium, and low interaction. It is customary to equate these levels with the types of systems given in the figure.

A major empirical study looking at a wealth of data, was that of Walston and Felix [Wals77]. Their study focused specifically on the effect of different development methods in one particular environment (the federal business of IBM). It showed that the methods in question (top-down design, structured programming, chief programmer team) all had a positive effect, but always in the range 1.3–2. The following factors had an influence ranging from 3–7, however:

- amount of old code;
- experience of developers with the problem;
- experience of developers with the tools;
- proximity of customer.

In the course of his work, Boehm analyzed data from multiple sources and reviewed most of the software cost estimating approaches used in the industry. Boehm elaborated on algebraic models and produced a very detailed model, called the Constructive Cost Model, abbreviated as COCOMO. The original model published in 1981 has undergone a major revision recently. The COCOMO-I model [Boeh81] was based on data from 63 projects, representing business, scientific, systems, real time, and support software. The essence of the model is expressed in two exponential formulas of the form:

$$E = c \times S^g \text{ and } T = 2.5 \times E^h$$

where E = effort (in people-months), S = size (in KLOC), T = elapsed time (in months), and c, g and h are constants. The constant c can be modified with 15 so called effort multipliers. They express product, computer, personnel and project attributes. The constants g and h assume one of three values depending on the development mode. The modes and their values are: organic ($g = 1.05$, $h = 0.38$), semidetached ($g = 1.12$, $h = 0.35$) and embedded ($g = 1.20$, $h = 0.32$). From the fact that $g > 1$ it follows that in the case of large projects their effort grows more than linearly. In other words, a 'dis-economy' of scale is assumed. The COCOMO-I model can only be used if a size estimate (LOC) is available, meaning that reliable LOC estimates can only be done after the design is complete.

With COCOMO-II [Boeh00c], a wider applicability has been attempted. The structure of the formulas remains essentially the same, but the adjustments have changed considerably. The model was calibrated using data from 161 projects. The data have been augmented by expert opinions. Two different sets of adjustments are given: one to be used in the requirements phase or early in the design phase, the other one after design is completed. The latter is called the post-architecture model, for which five scale factors and 17 effort multipliers have been defined. The scale factors are precedentedness (meaning: 'degree of novelty'), development flexibility, risk resolution, team cohesion and process maturity. The exponent g in the effort equation above is now a function of the scale factors and may turn out to be smaller than 1. The effort multipliers express product, platform, personnel and project attributes. For the early design model, it is assumed that the size of the product is given in terms of function points rather than in lines of code (LOC). In this case, the conversion rules from function points to lines of code, developed by Jones [Jone96] are to be applied.

Theory Many people argue that we should not measure intellectual work by the size of its output. What is measured here is not the quality but the effort. The effort, even in the case of a genius, is reflected in the time needed. This certainly applied to the writing of this book. Size has a close relation to functionality. Complexity (Simon, McCabe) correlates better with size than with anything else, assuming a common higher-level language. In practice, nobody throws in arbitrary code just to improve productivity. Many of the non-coding activities depend on size.

Comment The success of this class of cost estimating models is limited by the fact that size estimates are difficult. Whether done in terms of FP or LOC, it does not make a real difference. To do them correctly, a design is needed and a decision made as to what is reused, bought as ready-to-use (COTS) from outside, or newly developed. As the design evolves, the size estimates have to be updated. Even if this is done, not every project manager is willing to correct his or her cost estimate. He or she simply hopes that a sudden increase in productivity will bail him/her out.

9.3.4 DeMarco–Glass law

With the next law, based on the work of Tom DeMarco and Robert Glass [DeMa82, Glas98, Glas01], we shall highlight the most common problem associated with cost estimates.

> Most cost estimates tend to be too low. **(L34)**

Applicability Estimates are usually needed and performed at the beginning of the lifecycle. In extreme situations, it may happen before the requirements definition, i.e. before the problem is fully understood. Estimates can reasonably only be done after the design phase, when it is determined how the problem at hand will be solved. During the design activity we decide whether everything will be developed from scratch or whether large parts can be reused from previous projects or from COTS. Even if an estimate is performed after a design is available, it may soon be out of date. Not only may the design change, but we may learn more about how to implement the given design.

Evidence In his study of runaway projects Glass [Glas98] defines a runaway project as one exceeding its cost estimate by more than 30 percent. Whether the number of runaway projects has increased or decreased recently is an open question. Apparently, schedule overruns are more frequent than cost overruns. In [Glas01] many reasons are listed which explain why cost estimates are not met: they are too optimistic; performed too early; done by marketing or the customer rather than by the developer; not adjusted as the project proceeds, or not taken seriously at all. Often projects are conducted without clear responsibility for project performance. Some projects have been seen as quite a success by the developers, although the estimates were not met.

Theory It is more likely that an estimator forgets work items than adding unnecessary work. Frequently, not all efforts are considered ahead of time, for example, the amount of rework. Or as Humphrey [Hump97b] puts it: 'There are always surprises, and all surprises involve more work.' A professionally done estimate therefore includes contingencies. Contingencies are always positive. They should be higher the earlier in the life cycle an estimate is made.

Comment If the contingency of the cost estimate is included in project plans, it will be used up. The same is true if the initial estimate is too high. This is frequently referred to as the Parkinson effect. If an organization exists, it tends to keep itself busy. DeMarco [DeMa82] suggests that estimates should be done by professional estimators only as they would have pride in the precision of their estimates. If done by a designer or project manager, the accuracy of an estimate is only one problem among others.

9.3.5 Humphrey's law

With the following law we recognize the essential contributions made to our industry and profession by Watts Humphrey [Hump89, Hump96, Hump97a]. The work discussed here had its roots largely in IBM, but was extended and made popular after Humphrey's retirement from IBM.

Mature processes and personal discipline enhance planning, increase productivity, and reduce errors. **(L35)**

Applicability The work that has lead to this law is known under two different names: the Capability Maturity Model (CMM) and the Personal Software Process (PSP). Humphrey found a unique environment that helped him to institutionalize and publicize his ideas. This is the Software Engineering Institute (SEI) at Carnegie Mellon University in Pittsburgh. CMM and PSP are closely related. PSP has recently been extended to the Team Software Process (TSP).

Because of Humphrey's work, our profession has an excellent understanding of what a disciplined and mature process is all about. There have been other attempts that were not oriented as much towards software, such as ISO 9000, which defines minimal criteria that a quality system has to meet for companies designing or supplying products. An effort funded by the European Community, called Bootstrap, has extended the CMM concept and applied it to European companies. As shown in Fig. 9-6, CMM defines five levels of maturity. Each of the boxes in the figure lists what is called the key process areas (KPA) that have to be addressed if this level has to be reached. The SEI conducts CMM appraisals according to a detailed questionnaire, and has trained and qualified people all over the world independently to perform the CMM assessment leading to an equivalent appraisal. The rapid acceptance of CMM within the USA was certainly promoted by the fact that the US Department of Defense evaluates many of its vendors based on the CMM scheme.

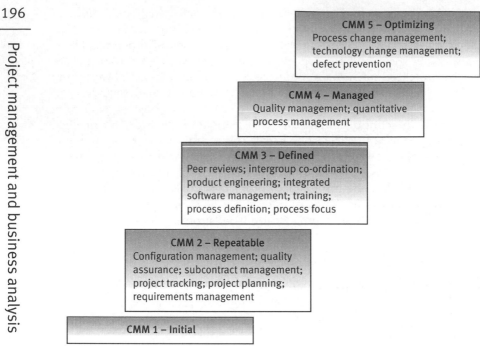

Fig. 9-6 Capability maturity model (CMM)

While the CMM assessment is a scheme to be used by companies that are interested in improving their software development and software acquisition processes, PSP is a vehicle that can be used by individual developers to advance their professional skills. As shown in Fig. 9-7, the personal process matures through four phases. The PSP is a bottom-up complement to the

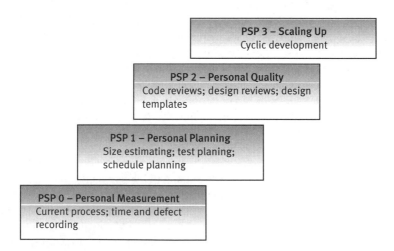

Fig. 9-7 Personal software process (PSP)

CMM, that addresses a subset of the key process areas, and emphasizes the personal responsibilities for schedule commitments and the quality of work products. It starts out by creating awareness for the process being used and demonstrates how to collect data about one's own performance as a software developer. Using this as a base, one's own work can be planned more systematically. The key message is that project plans are nothing but aggregations of personal plans. The third step is an emphasis on quality, where the focus is on design and code defects. This step relies on the concept that design has to reach a certain level of completeness before coding starts. The final phase introduces an iterative development cycle where requirements are refined and the design evolves through the aid of prototypes.

Evidence The CMM has been subject to many empirical studies. As an example, we will discuss the data published by Diaz and Sligo [Diaz97] of Motorola. Fig. 9-8 summarizes their data from 13 organizations, comprising about 350 software developers. It reflects a period of four years (1988–1992) and 34 different projects. During this time period, 104 CMM assessments took place, moving some organizations up to CMM 5. For the performance of the project groups, three criteria are given, i.e. defects/KLOC, cycle time, and productivity. For each, a short explanation is provided.

Maturity level	Number of projects	Defects/KLOC	Cycle time (X factor)	Productivity
CMM 1	3	n/a	1.0	n/a
CMM 2	9	4.4	3.2	1.0
CMM 3	5	2.1	2.7	0.8
CMM 4	8	1.0	5.0	2.3
CMM 5	9	0.6	7.8	2.8

Fig. 9-8 CMM-related project performance (at Motorola)

As defects, only those errors are counted that escaped detection in the phase they were introduced. Instead of a high-level language-based KLOC metric, the paper uses Assembler-Equivalent KLOC (AE-KLOC), where 1 KLOC = 5 AE-KLOC. Cycle time reduction is expressed as a positive factor. If the base project needed 30 calendar months, and the compared project only three months, this is an improvement by a factor of ten. Productivity is also given as a relative number only. In this case it was discovered that productivity slightly decreased when going from CMM 2 to CMM 3. At the same time cycle time increased. The reason is that additional effort, such as peer reviews, was introduced that was not spent before.

First empirical data on PSP are contained in the paper by Humphrey [Hump96]. He reports that 104 students or engineers that took the training program were able to reduce the errors found during development by 58 percent, and those found during testing by 72 percent. For the small program exercises completed during the course, productivity expressed in LOC/hour improved by 20 percent (comparing programs written at the beginning with programs written towards the end of the course). More data are contained in the paper by Ferguson *et al.* [Ferg97]. The data published originate from three companies that had completed PSP training. Fig. 9-9 shows the data from one of the three companies (Advanced Information Services). The projects were rather small (between one and three programmers only). Given are the planned-versus-actual schedule mismatch and the total number of the defects discovered during acceptance test and after delivery.

Staff	Project	Delivery: planned/actual	Acceptable test defects	Usage defects
Non-PSP	C	2/5	11	1
	D	10/19	6	14
	G	2/2	0	3
PSP	B	7/5	1	0
	E	6/6	0	0
	F	2/2	0	0

Fig. 9-9 PSP-related project data (at AIS)

Finally, some data from the study by Prechelt and Unger [Prec01a] in a university environment should be mentioned. They compared the performance of 29 students who had completed PSP training with that of 19 students in a control group. The PSP students achieved a higher degree of reliability for the programs they wrote, which was attributable mainly to fewer diagnostic errors because their programs provided for better error checking. They also estimated their productivity more accurately than the others, but not the program size and effort. The productivity as measured in LOC/hour was higher than that of the control group, as they typically wrote larger programs for the same task within the time allocated for their work.

Theory The philosophy behind Humphrey's law is that good quality and high productivity are worthwhile and can largely be achieved through organizational and personal discipline. The way to approach this is through detailed and reliable planning. Improvements will not be obtained as a single shot, but as part of a gradual process. The individual, as well as the organization, learns best from analyzing his or her own performance.

Comment Not all organizations have the resources and the time to apply all CMM required process elements. For different products, the quality level required may be different. The CMM approach has been criticized for focusing too much on the organizational side and not enough on technical aspects. It could be applied successfully to a low technology process as well, for example, assembler language coding. Based on Humphrey's and other work, many forms of quality improvement programs (QIP) have been established in industry.

9.3.6 Brooks' law

This is probably the best-known law in software engineering. It was stated by Fred Brooks [Broo75] in exactly the following words.

> Adding manpower to a late project makes it later. **(L36)**

Applicability The law says that, in a software project, people and months, i.e. effort and duration, are not simply interchangeable. This applies to all types of multi-person projects where knowledge level gained is essential. The effect is smaller if the additional people join early in the project. The only safe way out is to reduce the scope of the project, i.e. defer part of the functions of the system being developed. In his book on death march projects, Yourdon [Your97] calls this solution 'triage', i.e. sifting by prioritizing.

Evidence Brooks' statement is based on his experience as development manager of OS/360. As stated by Brooks in the Anniversary Edition of his book, the law was validated by two studies: one is by Abdel-Hamid and Madnick [Abde91], the other by Stutzke [Stut94]. They are not presented here. Brooks' law is also reflected in Boehm's COCOMO model, where project duration is a non-linear function of effort.

Theory Brooks gives three reasons why the law is valid: training, re-partitioning, and additional communication cost. The training that has to be given to the new people diverts current team members from their original task. The re-partitioning of work has a disruptive effect. The amount of communication needed raises roughly with the square of the number of members. Another reason is that certain types of activities tend to be sequenced, such as requirements definition, design, and system integration. They cannot be shortened, nor can they be overlapped. The maximum number of people to be productive in a project depends on the number of independent subtasks that can be executed in parallel. This is highest if the need for communication is low or non-existent, such as in picking apples or similar manual tasks. Co-ordination effort reduces productive work: many programmers consider meetings a waste of time.

9.3.7 Baumol's disease

The computing industry, like several other industries, has two kinds of offerings: products and services. The next law, formulated by William J. Baumol [Baum01, Peng98], addresses their relationship. The principle, also known as Baumol's disease, represents a valuable economic insight.

> Products replace services through productivity gains. **(L37)**

Applicability In an economy that is low in capital, the majority of people live from services, e.g. catching fish or raising agricultural products. If capital is available, a high portion of the goods traded are produced mechanically. As long as the level of automation is rather low, a significant industrial work force is needed to supplement the machines. As the industry progresses to a higher degree of automation, it reduces the required work force. Now many more people move into services again, but into entirely different services than before. In a high-technology field, the product and service business are complementary. Many complex products need service to be useful. This is true of cars, airplanes, nuclear reactors, etc. Service may comprise selection, evaluation, configuration, installation, deployment, operating, tuning, maintenance, and recovery.

Evidence Baumol's famous example is the Mozart string quartet. In 1793, the year it was composed, to perform a Mozart quartet, required four persons, four stringed instruments, and about 30 minutes. To produce a Mozart quartet today requires precisely the same effort, time, people, and materials. Only turning the live performance into a product allowed its industrialization. The shellac record or the CD version achieved prices that opened up markets not accessible to a live performance.

Services need not be provided by the developer (or, as in the case of the Mozart quartet, the composer himself.) The skill to perform a meaningful service can be acquired by other organizations or individuals as well. In the software industry, some developers were stronger than others at motivating third parties to provide services for their products. Two examples are SAP and Microsoft. The acceptance of their products in the market relies to a large extent on the fact that they are important sources of income for many consulting and service companies throughout the world. Companies that are not financially equipped to do product development, for example, two to three person start-ups, can provide services economically. Service companies are therefore willing to operate at lower margins than most developers.

Also in the software field, a service may easily be turned into a product. It is typical for the industry that products evolve in a direction that reduces the support service needed. The major growth of the software industry during the last decade has only been possible by making the installation and maintenance of products easier. This way the industry can gain customers that are not able to pay the extra service costs or develop the appropriate skills in-house. Turning a service into a product, or reducing service by enhancing the product, also opens markets in less-developed countries where a local service is not offered. In highly developed countries, the scarcity of skilled resources also pulls away people from services into product development. The more business that is done over the Internet, the more services can and will be turned into products. In spite of this, there are people who are creating new service markets by giving away products for which they gained access without major investments of their own. This is referred to as the open source business model and will be discussed in Section 9.4.8.

Theory Baumol's principle reflects the fact that productivity gains can normally not be achieved for services. In a capital intensive economy, investments can be made to develop and build products. They can be manufactured and distributed at lower cost and can replace services. Because productivity in the service jobs tends to lag behind productivity in manufacturing, the cost of services ends up rising constantly over time. If the nominal wages remain equal across the two sectors, the lower productivity growth will show up as a relatively faster growth of prices. Baumol calls this handicap a disease.

9.3.8 Boehm's hypothesis

With this hypothesis we will address another area of Boehm's work [Boeh88, Boeh89a, Boeh89b, Boeh91]. It is a key aspect of software and systems management.

Project risks can be resolved or mitigated by addressing them early. **(H17)**

Applicability Even the most careful planning of a project cannot exclude all risks. A project risk is the probability of failure. Risks can be considered as potential future exposures that are accepted to gain advantages that would not be achievable otherwise. Risks may exists from the beginning, or develop during the course of the project. Projects without risks are either boring or not worth doing. Some risks are generic, some are project-specific.

Fig. 9-10 gives the top-ten list of generic software project risks as identified by Boehm [Boeh88]. For these risks, every software manager should be constantly on guard. In addition, he/she should watch out for risks due to his specific situation and constraints. As Tom Gilb [Gilb88] put it: 'If you do not attack risks, they will attack you.' Project risks have to be distinguished from product risks. Even if a project was executed as planned, the product may possess risk potential. There may be a risk for the individual user, its owner,

1. Personal shortfalls
2. Unrealistic schedules and budgets
3. Developing the wrong software functions
4. Developing the wrong user interfaces
5. Gold plating
6. Continuing stream of requirements changes
7. Shortfalls in externally furnished components
8. Shortfalls in externally performed tasks
9. Real-time performance shortfalls
10. Straining computer-science capabilities

Fig. 9-10 Top ten software project risks

or the public at large. The latter risks are being discussed by Neumann in a regular contribution to the ACM Software Engineering Notes.

Evidence Boehm has made several proposals to address this aspect of project management. In [Boeh89a] and [Boeh91] he proposes to make risk management an integral part of project management. He suggests the identification of risks once a month and, if necessary, that action should be taken to manage them. Managing risks means assessment and control. As part of the assessment, the risk exposure should be quantified. Boehm defines the risk exposure or impact as the product of probability of failure times the amount of damage, as follows:

$$R = P_f \times D_f$$

Risks can be mitigated, resolved or transferred to somebody else. The latter is possible only, if the other party is capable and willing to accept the additional responsibility. Whatever actions are taken, they need time and resources. Unless they have been planned as a part of a buffer, they will have an impact on the project.

The well-known spiral model [Boeh88] is an example of a risk-driven process model. It contains other process models (e.g. the waterfall model) as a special case. The waterfall model relies heavily on firm requirements and a thorough design step. Otherwise the implementation work cannot be handled as a closed entity and farmed out to multiple groups working in parallel. It requires elaborate documents and phase completion criteria, which, as we have seen before, is difficult to achieve for certain types of projects. In the spiral model, before entering into a waterfall-like process, one or more iterations should be performed to address specific risks. Each spiral ends with a new risk assessment. Unless this is done, and the appropriate consequences are drawn, the spiral model may deteriorate to a code-and-fix process. If the funding of the project comes from somebody else, this party has to be closely involved and agree with the risk assessments. Unless he/she agrees that all major risks are not due to the project team itself, we cannot expect this party to tolerate additional costs and schedule delays.

Finally, with 'Theory W', Boehm [Boeh89b] tries to take away the negative image of risk management. The goal of this management principle is to make every stakeholder of a project a winner. He suggests they constantly look out for win–win conditions, meaning situations where more than one project partner can gain. Win–lose situations should be avoided or managed as risks. It is important to establish reasonable expectations among all stakeholders. Unquestionably, the set of observations leading to these proposals is shared by many people in the industry. The evidence provided by Boehm is typically based on single projects only. Other authors have not followed this example. It is for this reason, that we have called the underlying assumption a hypothesis, rather than a law.

Although the key issues are addressed by the laws and hypotheses quoted, we will extend the discussion by giving some further details.

9.4.1 Project plans and commitments

While the result of design work is documented in a design specification, the result of project planning finds its expression in a project plan. As long as both exist only in somebody's head, their value is marginal. A project plan normally addresses at least the following topics:

- goals and scope of project;
- overall schedules;
- organization and responsibilities;
- detailed plans for major activities (sub-plans);
- resource requirements;
- status meetings and reports planned;
- dependencies, open questions.

A project plan is primarily a means of communication between the parties responsible for the project. During its development it constitutes a proposal for negotiation. As soon as it is accepted, it becomes a commitment on which people can rely. Commitments are necessary between project members if parallel work is considered. Commitments are frequently made towards external partners, be it the customer or the marketing organization. Projects that can live without commitments, i.e. where nobody else is really interested, are not worth pursuing. Exceptions are training exercises, which, as shown under Humphrey's law above, can be used to test our ability to meet commitments.

The accuracy of a plan has to be a function of the criticality of the project. If the risk of failure is high, more careful planning is necessary. Using Boehm's definition above, if either the probability of failure or the damage are low, little effort should be spent on planning. The project plan is a means for the project owner to manage risks. Its establishment should not detract from other project activities. Plans are normally internal documents only, and not deliverables. It is important that a plan be a 'living' document, i.e. updated and refined as needed. As an example, detailed plans should be established 'just in time'. If an activity is performed during phase n of a project, the corresponding plan should be ready at the end of phase $n-1$.

Plans can only address those things that we understand and know will happen. By laying out plans for this portion of the immediate future, we are better able to react to unpredictable events. A plan is not a program that will execute automatically, i.e. without human intervention. It is not a prediction that we have to work on to ensure that it becomes true. Nor is it an achievement to brag about, or a reason to lull oneself into complacency. The best plan cannot serve as an excuse for poor project management, nor for deficiencies of the project outcome.

9.4.2 Project and process models

As part of a project plan, a project or process model should be selected. Not to do this, would be a major management error. In any case, a model should be chosen that best suits the project. There exist a large variety of options: we will not discuss them in detail. Project models are either a derivative of the sequential (waterfall) approach or of the iterative (spiral) approach. Very often, they have elements of both.

A process model is the level below. It prescribes how the individual activities in a project are to be approached. A very elaborate process model might define entry and exit criteria for each activity, specify which organizational groups are involved, and prescribe which methods and tools should be used, etc. As with a project model, it should be tailored to the needs of the project. It is the vehicle by which experience can be transferred from one project to the other, or from one group to the other. For most organizations, the adaptation of project and process models, is the key means for becoming a learning organization. The formal adoption of certain models (like SEI-CMM or ISO 9000) can be considered as a high level commitment of a company to quality targets and business ethics.

9.4.3 People assignment and skill management

Project members should be selected based on skill and motivation. For college and university graduates their skill level can only partially be deducted from the school's curriculum and the grades achieved. Since the emphasis in most curricula is more on analytical and technical skills than on constructive and human skills, special attention has to be given to these aspects during an interview. Those with professional experience may have gained with respect to non-technical skills, but may have adopted certain working styles or habits, which may be advantageous or may cause difficulties within a project team.

A project team ideally consists of complementing skills. Such a team can produce better results than if people are totally equal and exchangeable. It may be advantageous, if different technical and psychological roles can be assumed: technical roles are database designer, network specialist, user interface, or performance expert; psychological roles are pusher, motivator, or arbitrator. Specialization can occur best if people are allowed to do the same type of work repeatedly, which is more likely to be possible in large organizations than in small ones. Doing the same work over and over again may conflict with other goals, i.e. broadening our experience and skill, which is where job rotation may come in. A project's success strongly depends on the motivation of its team. Personal motivation is determined by how well a project's goal matches individual goals. Professionals are not only interested in the money they earn, but also in the skills they gain, the satisfaction of creation they experience, and the recognition they receive. For professionals, salary is frequently a 'hygiene' factor, meaning that it has to be in line with what is customary.

Every project is a learning opportunity, and this is true both for individual learning and organizational learning. While the basic professional training is an individual's responsibility, an organization can help an individual to keep abreast of technical developments during his or her career, a topic that will be discussed further in the next chapter. Professional training should not be confused with project training. For project training, the needs of the project have priority over those of the individual; the training must fill immediate gaps and must do this in the shortest possible time. The subjects to be learned may be the methods and tools used for coding and testing, the content of the requirements, the principles and contents of the design, etc. Learning by doing is often used as a fallback if other possibilities do not exist. It may be the riskiest method, however.

9.4.4 Work environment and tools

It was recognized long ago that the physical and social work environments directly influence developer productivity. Only a few instances are known where the physical environment was created specifically with the requirements of software developers in mind. A well-known positive example is the Santa Teresa laboratory of IBM, which was built for some 2000 programmers and opened in 1977. Its architectural philosophy and design process were documented in a paper by McCue [McCu78]. The planning of the building was preceded by a study showing that programmers in this organization spend 30 percent of their time working alone, 50 percent in small groups and the remainder in large groups, traveling, etc. As a consequence, the building is constructed as a campus-like cluster, with a monastic touch, embedded in a garden landscape. It provides privacy through single person offices, with small meeting rooms in close proximity. Other advantages its occupants praised were the automatic forwarding of phone calls to a secretary, and a reference library close by.

That these principles have not been commonly accepted in the industry is proven by the success of a book by DeMarco and Lister [DeMa87] a decade later. For this book the authors had collected data showing the effect on productivity of such factors as floor space per programmer, noise level of the office, and number of interruptions by phone calls or by other people. Besides postulating the proper physical environment, this book is also an excellent source regarding the social environment suitable for software developers. Even many traditional companies (where Dilbert-like managers are the exception) have great difficulties in creating the correct social environment for intellectual work. As DeMarco and Lister point out, there are hundreds of ways to influence productivity, and most of them are non-technical; besides, overemphasizing productivity is the best way to loose it.

More recently, a major shift in work environments was frequently associated with terms like 'old' and 'new' economy. Since the new economy heavily relies on intellectual work, some start-ups experimented with new physical and social environments. Many of them offered flat organizations, loosely coupled groups, very flexible working hours, remote workplaces and, of course, economic participation through stock options. After the new economy has lost its credibility, we hope that any good ideas will move over to economically more persistent companies.

Development tools are certainly helpful, but they are only part of the story. While the other considerations apply consistently, tools change frequently over time. In McCue's example the programmers needed considerable storage space for listings and punched cards, and good elevator connections to the central computing center to deliver or pick up print outs several times a day. In some development laboratories, this technology period was followed by a time where most programmers needed more than one terminal in their office (one for designing and coding, and one for testing), until such time as all terminals could be replaced by powerful workstations or PCs.

Incidentally, McCue's building project mentioned above followed a cyclic design process iterating through requirements definition, high-level (conceptual) design and low-level design. It was plagued with conflicting requirements, sought user participation, and used prototyping at various levels, including testing furniture mock-ups under working conditions.

9.4.5 Software pricing and business case

Software (and many hardware components) are knowledge products. As such they are comparable to lectures, books, musical recordings, and films. For all these products the development costs are high and the replication costs low. Therefore the same pricing models apply:

- *Target groups:* prices are established separately for different user groups according to their price sensitivity, for example, private and corporate users.
- *Time delays:* early buyers who usually have a higher demand pay more than late comers. The price of the old version is lowered after a new version is out.
- *Versioning:* for the same product, different functional or performance levels are offered at different prices.
- *Personalizing:* the product is part of an enhanced or tailored offering, possibly together with some local service.
- *Bundling:* the product is sold only as part of a package consisting of multiple products. Limits to this are usually set by law.
- *Negotiating:* the price is freely negotiated between seller and buyer. Customers who buy large quantities expect special discounts. The extreme case is an auction.

The following options are specific for software: the vendor differentiates between initial purchase price and upgrade price or may give away certain teaser products, for example, development tools. Products may be sold through different marketing channels. The most important ones are direct marketing through own agents or online ordering, and indirect marketing through independent agents or retail stores.

A business case is usually done on a per product basis. Sometimes it may be extended to a family of products. For COTS products, it may be done for one market segment only, or for multiple markets. Accordingly, different revenue and cost figures apply. The revenue is an aggregate of the forecasts for the different channels and pricing models. For internal systems, instead of revenue the benefits are calculated either as savings or as additional revenue made in the traditional business segment. For a COTS system, the costs include development, distribution, maintenance, and marketing costs. For an internal system, the costs comprise development, installation, conversion, operation, and maintenance. A product is profitable if the ratio

Profit = (Revenue – Cost)/Cost

exceeds the profitability target. This ratio is also called return on investment (ROI), where investment corresponds to the costs incurred. A profitability target should be higher than the current interests of a bank account. A key factor affecting revenue and costs is the assumed life of the product, which depends strongly on the point in time when a replacement product is expected, be it from the vendor itself or from a competitor.

An important aspect of a business case is cash flow, which is concerned not only whether a return on investment occurs, but when. For projects with similar profitability ratios, their break-even points may differ considerably. Fig. 9-11 shows one way to illustrate the financial history of a project. As long as a product is under development, the monthly costs create a negative cash flow. This starts to change after shipment or delivery of the product. Depending on the speed and the degree of acceptance in the market or within the own company, revenues or savings will gradually turn the cash flow into a positive figure. The point in time where this happens is called the break-even point. A time-scale for this is not given in the figure, because the time frame shown may range over three to seven years. The earlier the break-even point is reached, however, the better for a project. We may even accept lower profit rates if the return comes early.

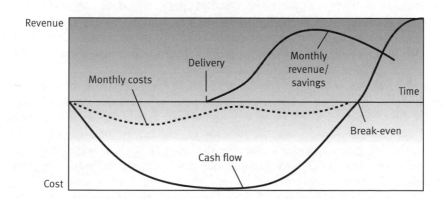

Fig. 9-11 Financial history of a project

9.4.6 Product packaging and licensing

While computer hardware did have the character of a commercial product from the beginning, this was not the case for software. For quite a while, many people were against such an idea. This is reflected in the opinion nicely expressed by one of the participants of the 1968 Garmisch conference on Software Engineering [Naur69b]: 'Software belongs to the world of ideas, like music and mathematics, and should be treated accordingly'. The change came about gradually after IBM decided in 1969 to offer some of its software as separately priced products. In the case of IBM, it took about 15 years until all new software was unbundled, i.e. priced separately from hardware.

Software pricing has an influence on how software products are packaged. The first requirement is that each product should be self-contained, i.e. all dependencies it has on other products should be well-justified. A product has to be big enough to justify not only the separate distribution, but also the transaction costs (billing, accounting). The number of separately priced features has to be low. On the other hand, a product cannot be too big: it has to be handled and paid for by its intended user.

Software licenses can take on many forms. Usually, they only give the right for a non-exclusive use. In this case, the vendor retains the ownership of the software and all other rights. Most common license models permit installation on one computer only, or on multiple computers used by the same person. Simultaneous use by several persons is either not allowed or handled separately. Other rights that a user may have, depending on the license model, is the right to make a backup copy, to transfer the software from one machine to another, or to sell the license to another user. The right to do modifications is normally not given.

The license also specifies what type of on-going support (telephone, on-site) is given, and at what price. The same applies to error corrections and functional upgrades. A somewhat controversial subject is the question of warranty. A warranty may say that the software will perform according to documentation (i.e. according to specification) as far as 'best practices' allow. The exclusion of responsibility for consequential damages and the guarantee that other people's intellectual property rights are not infringed are normal business. Users should be alerted of the license conditions through a visible copy of the license that can be inspected at the time of purchase. For products downloaded in the network, an online message that requires an 'I agree' reply is sufficient.

Fig. 9-12 shows some typical software license types. The price may further vary by the nature of the contracting organization, be it business, academic, charity, or government. Fees may be collected as monthly license fees or as a once-only charge. Monthly license fees are typical for mainframe software, once-only charges are dominant in the PC market (shrink-wrapped software). In the case of once-only charges, functional upgrades are usually paid for separately. Unfortunately, users do not install upgrades as frequently or as fast as many vendors would like. Periods of three to five years are common for office-type software. For this reason, recently, one vendor wanted to replace his 'perpetual' licenses with subscription-type licenses valid for several years only, but including free updates. The move was not well-received. More details on software licensing can be found in a typical reseller's homepage, for example, from Softmart.[1]

License type	Pricing condition	Typical customer
Single end user	No discount	Private user
Variable volume	Staged discount without forecast	Small and medium organization
Forecasted volume	Staged discount based on 2–3 year forecast	Medium or large organization with variable suppliers
Enterprise	Fixed discount	Medium or large organization with firm supplier relationship

Fig. 9-12 Software license types

9.4.7 Intellectual property rights

The term intellectual property rights usually denotes copyright, trademark, and patent law. All three areas are relevant for software and system products. The developers and users have to be concerned about two aspects, namely avoiding infringements of other people's rights and gaining protection for the products being developed.

Copyright, originally intended to protect literary work, protects the particular expression chosen by the author, be it in writing, drawing, or musical composition. In the case of software, it protects the textual expression of a program in a particular programming language. It does not protect the ideas leading to this expression, or the algorithms chosen for a solution. The great advantage of copyright protection is that it becomes effective for any document at the moment of its publication, independent of whether it has been registered with some agency. To register a document with the US copyright office (or its equivalent in other countries) only improves the evidence in case of legal quarrel.

Both trademarks and patents have to be applied for and are only granted after examination. In the case of the USA, this responsibility lies with the US Patent and Trademark Office. In Europe, the European Patent Office (EPO) can issue patents that are valid in all its signatory states. Since its existence, the EPO has granted some 200,000 software patents. In spite of this, there is still a discussion about the patentability of software-related inventions, particularly in Europe. Early software patents, issued during the 1950 decade, had to be disguised as hardware inventions in order to be granted. The clarification, that has since been achieved in Europe allows software-related inventions to be patented if the invention solves a technical problem. Saving costs is not considered a technical problem, but saving storage space, time, and energy is. In the USA, this point is treated more liberally. Any invention

---

[1] http://www.softmart.com/licenseguide/

that is new, useful, and non-obvious can be patented. A good source of information on the status of the relevant legislation is the Intellectual Property Law Server.[2] The specific questions concerning software are discussed in several papers by Pamela Samuelson and others, for example, [Davi96, Samu01].

Many discussions on this subject, particularly those regarding software patents, are really strange. Some people seem to ignore that everyone can give away as much of their intellectual property as they want to, provided other people are interested. On the other hand, people who want to use their invention to make a business from it should not be hindered from doing so. If an inventor is not able or not interested to exploit the invention through products, he or she is well advised to find licensees. A well-known example where this is happening are the patents on MP3 encoding, which are owned by the Fraunhofer research center in Erlangen, Germany. The license fees obtained for the corresponding patents are sufficient to fund the group's future work in this area. To argue that all software-related patents are trivial is simply untrue, and if applicable in a specific case, should be taken up individually in the courts, rather than in the trade journals.

9.4.8 The open source model

The open source model is a combination of a unique development approach, a software license model and a business model. Well-known products following this model are GNU, Linux and Apache. GNU (the acronym stands for 'Gnu is not Unix') was a project started in 1984 by Richard Stallman. It has created a C compiler and a text editor (Emacs). Linux is a UNIX kernel, originally developed by Linus Thorvalds of Helsinki University, while Apache is a Web server. The open source model is documented in several books by Eric Raimond [Raim00], and an overview is given by Wu and Lin [Wu01]. A current source of information is the homepage of the Open Source Initiative.[3]

The open source development cycle starts out by announcing an interest to develop a software product. Typically, this happens over the Internet. If enough volunteers are found, a work plan is agreed upon. Requirements definition and overall design is frequently handled by the initiator. He or she publishes the design specification and collects comments from the other project partners. A configuration management plan and version control system are agreed upon, so that code development can be done remotely. A first integration level of the product is built early with minimal functionality. After that, gradual enhancements are build in short intervals. Unit testing is assumed to be done by the original contributor. System testing is done by all developers, sometimes following an agreed test plan.

The software license model is usually a derivative of the GNU license model or the Berkeley Software Distribution's (BSD) UNIX license model. The main difference between the two models is the way derivative work can

---

[2] http://www.intelproplaw.com/
[3] http://www.opensource.org/

be used. The GNU model requires that all derivative work has to follow the GNU model, i.e. the code has to remain open so that it can be modified by any subsequent user. The BSD license model requires that proper credits are given, but the derivative work can be used as desired.

Several business models are in use: for GNU, Stallman had founded a tax-free charity to collect donations; and most Linux distributors claim that they can get along with a nominal charge for the code and cover their expenses by offering service to the users. Some hardware vendors, like IBM and Sun, see a potential in the open source model, as it gives them additional options in those software areas where they are dependent on other vendors, like Microsoft. It also provides a vehicle to distribute certain teaser products to users who cannot or do not want to buy regular commercial products.

The open source model has some appeal for people in the academic community. It allows developers to contribute small pieces at their own speed, and let other people worry about integration and commercialization. This is similar to publishing. The main limitation of the open source model is that it works only for selected types of software. The contributors have to have an interest as users. This is the case for certain operating systems and many development tools. The UNIX environment has always had that appeal and some Internet services also qualify. There is little chance at present for normal major business applications, for example, an ERP system, to be developed using this model. Several projects proposed simply have had to wait years for volunteers. There has always been talk that, for certain security problems, fixes were available for an open source system faster than for a proprietary system. Experience shows that it is certainly easier for somebody to propose a fix than making sure that it works with the entire system, particularly with the coming release.

9.4.9 Total cost of system ownership

Generally, users of IT products are well advised not to take the procurement price as the only decision factor. Other aspects, besides quality, are the expected lifespan, the cost of usage, and the degree of dependency, all of which can be lumped together in what is called the cost of ownership. The degree of dependency can have many aspects, the first of which is the ability to do without the product once it has been introduced. If the business can no longer function without it, the dependency is absolute. Many efforts are taken to protect the system from malfunction or misuse and all provisions necessary for problem determination, recovery, security, and safety have to be accounted for under this aspect. The second consideration concerns the ease and certainty to obtain service from the vendor, be it help, fixes, or updates. Without proper service, the product may have to be depreciated within a short period of time. The final consideration is what are the chances to obtain assistance from other users or to find people that are knowledgeable in using the product? This is much easier for a product that has a significant presence in the market than for a very rare and unprecedented product.

9.5 Examples and study material

9.5.1 Cost estimating (bottom-up approach)

The example given in Fig. 9-13 is a development estimate using a simple spreadsheet. It shows the number of persons needed by activity by month, relative to the project start. It is assumed that the estimate for each activity is provided by the experts responsible for it, which in some cases may represent a negotiated agreement. Depending on the business ground rules, a distinction may be necessary between direct and indirect costs. Only direct costs may be charged against a product, while indirect costs are part of the overhead that may be allocated at a fixed rate to all products.

Activity/ Month	M1	M2	M3	M4	M5	M6	M7	M8	M9	M10	M11	M12	M13	M14	Sum
Requirement	3	3	1												7
Prototyping			2	1											3
Design			1	4	4	3									12
Testcase dev.					1	1	2								4
Coding							5	5	5	5					20
Test tools								2							2
Unit test									2	3	4	4	1		14
Perf. analysis						1		1			1	1			4
Integr. + system test												1	4	4	9
Documentation							1				2	2	2	2	9
Manuf. + distrib.						1		1			1		1	2	6
Total direct	3	3	3	5	5	6	8	8	8	8	8	8	8	8	90
Marketing interface	1	1	1									1		1	5
Financial analysis						1					1		1		3
Management		1		1	1	1	1	1	1	1	1	1	1	1	12
Grand total	4	5	4	6	6	8	9	9	9	9	10	10	10	10	110

Fig. 9-13 Development effort estimate

The strength of this approach is that it explicitly shows which activities are assumed and when. Additional activities can easily be added, and others can be shortened, moved, or deleted. The semi-graphical representation of the estimate exhibits visibly the essentials of the project schedule, points out dependencies, and emphasizes the different skills required. To calculate the costs, the effort has to be multiplied by the manpower cost rate ($/person month), and has to be augmented by the costs for equipment, travel, and software licenses. If we assume US$16,000 per person-month, the direct costs for this project will amount to US$1.44 million.

In the next example, an algebraic model is used to perform the estimate, specifically the COCOMO-II model [Boeh00c]. It starts out with a size estimate, using the function point (FP) metric. The input values and the appropriate transformations are given in Fig. 9-14.

Function type	Low	Average	High	Subtotal
Internal logical files	1	1	1	32
External interface files	2	2	1	34
External inputs	7	3	0	33
External outputs	2	4	4	56
External inquiries	0	2	0	8
Total unadjusted FPs				163
Equivalent LOC in C				20864

Fig. 9-14 Size estimate using function points

The columns headed with Low, Average, and High list the input values for the number of function types with low, average, and high complexity. Using standard weighting for the various function types, the numbers in these three columns are converted into 'unadjusted' function points, and shown in the right-hand column. For this example they add up to 163 FPs. Assuming that the programming language chosen is C, 1 FP corresponds to 128 LOC, following the conversion table of Jones. This yields a product size of about 21 KLOC. For the scale factors affecting the exponent of the COCOMO formula, we assumed nominal values throughout, which gives an exponent slightly larger than 1. To determine the effort multipliers, the seven cost drivers of the Early Design model are used. Fig. 9-15 gives the ratings that have been chosen for the example. Multiplying the seven factors in the right-most column gives an Effort Adjustment Factor (EAF) of 1.15 for this example.

Cost drivers	Abbreviation	Rating	Multiplier
Product reliability and complexity	RCPX	Nominal	1.00
Reusability	RUSE	High	1.07
Platform difficulty	PDIF	High	1.29
Personnel capability	PERS	High	0.83
Personnel experience	PREX	Nominal	1.00
Facilities	FCIL	Nominal	1.00
Required development schedule	SCED	Nominal	1.00

Fig. 9-15 Effort multipliers

With these parameters, COCOMO-II produces the effort and schedule estimates as given in Fig. 9-16. Three levels of estimate are given: optimistic, most likely and pessimistic. Besides effort and schedule (really project duration), the productivity is calculated (in LOC/person month), as well as the average number of people needed. Not shown in this example, are the conversion of effort to cost, and the risk analysis, which are also provided for by the COCOMO-II tool. It is important to consider that these estimates cover only the effort from design through integration. The efforts for requirements definition, acceptance test, or maintenance are not included.

Estimate level	Effort (PM)	Schedule (M)	Productivity (LOC/PM)	Staff (P)
Optimistic	63.7	13.8	327.3	4.6
Most likely	95.1	15.6	219.3	6.1
Pessimistic	142.7	17.8	146.2	8.0

Fig. 9-16 Resulting effort and schedule estimates

Based on different project models, the COCOMO-II tool can also perform an allocation of the calculated estimates to individual activities or phases. Fig. 9-17 gives an example of an allocation for a waterfall-type project model. It has built-in assumptions for the percentage of effort or schedule needed for each phase. Although the above effort estimate was done for the activities starting with design, the allocation also calculates data for the planning and requirements activities. In Fig. 9-17, the corresponding values are placed in parentheses.

This example clearly illustrates the advantages of an algebraic model: it is easy to change the parameters, or to recalibrate the model with new data. The COCOMO model, in its current form, allows so many degrees of freedom that it can be easily adjusted to any environment. It can be used at different points in a project to recalculate the estimates as soon as better data are available. There are two points, however, that we should point out to an enthusiastic user of this tool: first, the user should be careful in distinguishing between when the model is wrong or when the plan is wrong; second, he or she should not be lulled into a false sense of security by the three-decimal-digit precision of the print-outs, or by the multitude of pages with numbers produced from a few pieces of actual input.

Activity/phase	Effort (%)	Effort (PM)	Schedule (%)	Schedule (M)	Staff (P)
Plans and requirements	(7.0)	(6.7)	(19.1)	(3.0)	(2.2)
Product design	17.0	16.2	25.5	4.0	4.1
Programming	59.4	56.5	49.9	7.8	7.3
Detailed design	25.5	24.2	–	–	–
Code and unit test	33.9	32.3			–
Integration and test	23.6	22.5	24.6	3.8	5.8

Fig. 9-17 Allocation to activities

Many, if not most, software development projects are conducted in a business environment. The costs incurred have to be recovered from revenues. In this example, we will therefore start out with an estimate of the market potential. With a given set of functions, a price level, and an assumed marketing plan, a certain level of market penetration may be reached. Such an estimate as done by a marketing expert is called a sales forecast, and an example for a software product is shown in Fig. 9-18. It partitions the market in three sections, i.e. end users, enterprises, and dealers. A different price can be achieved by the vendor for each sector. The forecast in Fig. 9-18 predicts the number of licenses sold (as once-only charges) over a four-year period.

Customer type	Price ($)	Year 1	Year 2	Year 3	Year 4
End users	200	1,000	5,000	4,000	2,000
Enterprises	500	300	1,000	2,000	700
Dealers	100	1,000	3,000	5,000	4,000

Fig. 9-18 Software sales forecast

Using the forecasted quantities, the gross revenue can be calculated. Fig. 9-19 gives the corresponding numbers in the first row. To calculate net revenue the gross revenue has been adjusted by the costs associated with actual sales. Three cost types are shown, i.e. manufacturing/distribution, marketing, and maintenance costs. It is important to consider that a large portion of these costs will also occur, if the sales targets are not met. The last line of Fig. 9-19 gives the net revenue (in US$ million), after the sales related costs are deducted. A net revenue of US$1.9 million corresponds to a gross revenue of US$5.7 million.

Revenue and cost	Year 1	Year 2	Year 3	Year 4	Total
Gross revenue	0.45	1.8	2.3	1.15	5.7
Manufacturing/distribution	0.2	0.4	0.3	0.2	1.1
Marketing	0.5	0.6	0.4	0.2	1.7
Maintenance	0.2	0.4	0.3	0.1	1.0
Net revenue	−0.45	0.4	1.3	0.65	1.9

Fig. 9-19 Revenues and sales related costs

We will calculate the allowable development cost for this business case in the next step. This may seem like putting the cart before the horse, but is often the most realistic approach. To simplify the calculation, we do not discount the revenue numbers over time, but assume a reasonable profit margin. We can then calculate the allowable development cost from the following formula:

Allowable cost = Revenue/(1 + Profit)

If we assume a profit margin of 20 percent, we obtain the allowable development costs as 1.9/1.2 = US$1.6 million. For typical software products, this number may indeed be lower than the marketing or even the distribution costs. As a final point, we consider the cash-flow of this product. For this we assume that the development costs are all spent in a period of 12–14 months, called year 0, prior to the first year of sales. This leads to the numbers given in Fig. 9-20. This part of the example is an illustration of Fig. 9-11 above. The numbers used represent US$ million.

Cash-flow	Year 0	Year 1	Year 2	Year 3	Year 4
Annual	−1.6	−0.45	0.4	1.3	0.65
Cumulative	−1.6	−2.05	−1.65	−0.35	+0.3

Fig. 9-20 Cash-flow analysis

The figure shows that investments have to be made, i.e. financial credits are needed, over a four-year period. The break-even point of the project lies in year 4 of the sales period. From this point of view, the project is not very attractive, and it may therefore have difficulties to compete for money with other proposed investments that have a better cash-flow, i.e. an earlier break-even point.

9.5.4 Project tracking

While the challenges of estimating are largely technical in nature, the problems with project tracking are predominantly psychological, i.e. people do not want to be supervised. If appropriate checkpoints have been established, the tracking of schedules is trivial. To rely exclusively on schedule tracking is not sufficient, however. If a schedule is not kept to, many things have already gone awry. In this example we therefore present two ideas that are helpful in gaining information on a project's progress, independent of established schedules. In the first part of this example, we will rely on information that is generated routinely.

		Last month			Year-to-date	
	Plan	Actual	Percent	Plan	Actual	Percent
Labor	60	61.5	102.5	360	362.5	100.6
Overtime	1	2.5	250.0	6	10.3	171.6
Computing center	10	8.7	87.0	60	47.2	78.6
Travel	3	2.8	93.3	18	19.8	110.0
Phone, mail	2	3.2	160.0	12	13.0	108.3
Subcontract	6	9.4	156.6	36	39.6	110.0
Total	82	88.1	107.4	492	492.4	100.0

Fig. 9-21 Project cost accounting

Fig. 9-21 is an excerpt from a standard cost accounting report. The units are thousand dollars. The left part shows data for the last month (say June), the right portion brings the year-to-date status. The middle of the year is assumed. With respect to both the monthly and the cumulative totals we seem to be perfectly in line with expectations. Two of the individual cost items, however, reveal alarming information for the project manager: overtime[4] is excessive; and the utilization of machines is below plan, which means that, whatever the phase we are actually in, we have less material ready for machine processing than expected. Of course, the manager will know whether it is the code development, unit test, or system test that is running late.

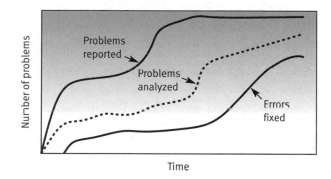

Fig. 9-22 Tracking of test progress

The next part is an argument in favor of graphical representations. Fig. 9-22 shows one specific view of the test progress. It plots the number of problems reported versus the number of problems analyzed and the number of errors fixed. In this case, at the beginning of the test, which was performed by an independent test group, the developers were flooded with problem reports. The reports receded for a while, and then increased again. The real problem is the middle curve, which indicates an enormous backlog. As long as problems are not analyzed, it is unclear whether the problems reported are test case errors, handling problems, documentation problems, or errors in the code. In addition, the fixing rate is rather low. This data can be indicative of a project situation in which the developers are still developing new code and not yet ready to scan problems; the errors reported are all very difficult to fix, because they are caused by weaknesses in the design. Making information available to everyone for their own interpretation and scrutiny may obviate the need to ask embarrassing questions; if there is a major problem in the project, everyone can see where it is and why.

---

[4] This example assumes that programmers are paid for overtime. This may not be true in some environments.

Exercises

9-1   Describe the tasks of project management. Which tasks can be ignored in the open source model?

9-2   What is measured by the LOC metric? What variations can exist regarding its definition?

9-3   Explain the advantages and disadvantages of the function point metric.

9-4   What are the strengths and the limitations of the COCOMO model? How can the size of a software product be estimated?

9-5   What is considered to be a mature development process and why is its definition useful? How do the key process areas (KPA) relate to the capability maturity model (CMM)?

9-6   What are the reasons for Brooks' law? What solutions are available to solve the schedule problem?

9-7   What are typical project risks and how can they be mitigated?

9-8   Why are people skill and motivation important for a project? What can a project manager do about it?

9-9   How is the profitability of a product defined? What are minimal profitability targets?

9-10 Describe some of the license and business concepts associated with the open source model.

9-11 Explain what is meant by 'total cost of system ownership'.

chapter 10

User skills, motivation, and satisfaction

The best engineers or scientists don't work for a company, a university or a laboratory; they really work for themselves.

W.S. Humphrey [Hump97b]

This chapter discusses the issues and experiences relevant to the assessment of human skills, motivation, and satisfaction. We will heavily draw on work done outside the field of computer science. The results usually originate in psychology and sociology.

10.1 Definitions and importance

In this chapter (as in the IT industry), the term *user* designates any person that may come in contact with computers. In contrast, a *customer* is the person or organization that has the financial responsibility for the acquisition of computer-related products and services. In the private sector of the economy, user and customer are the same person. In business, education, and administration the functions are normally separated. The assumption is that users are both professionals and non-professionals. Professionals include computer scientists, and systems and software engineers.

Skill is a combination of knowledge and capability. To use a computer, both are needed. The knowledge consists of a model of what the computer does and how it does it. The capabilities depend on the type of interaction needed. They may require the processing of information and the command of mechanical chores, like typing or pointing. Information may be presented to the user in visual or acoustical form. The user reacts with tactile or, less frequently, with acoustic signals. There is a relationship between information and knowledge that permeates the discussion. It is indicative of the role that information systems can play in this context. *Motivation* is the inclination a person has towards some activity or idea. *Satisfaction* is a measure expressing how well a user likes a product or service.

The topics discussed in this chapter are extremely relevant to our field. Computers and software are, among other things, cognitive tools. In addition to such functions as data acquisition and machine control, they are used to increase the effectiveness of both clerical and knowledge workers. They augment human skills and change the ways humans work. Software and systems engineers, therefore, need a much greater knowledge of human sensory and cognitive capabilities, and of mental limitations and motivational aspects, than do most other engineers or scientists. Of concern are not just the physiological and cognitive aspects of human–computer interaction: it is the relation between humans and computers, in general, and their effects on our lives and on society that has to be considered. This may help us to understand some attitudes and to assess the impact on people and organizations.

10.2 General observations

An information-processing system consists of people, procedures, data, software, and hardware. Only the last four are subject to engineering design. Unless adapted to the people they support, they cannot fulfill their purpose. There are common properties that are shared by most people. Of these, the human information-processing capabilities are most relevant.

While in the past computer access was a privilege for certain parts of society, it now penetrates all layers and realms. This is certainly the case in all developed countries, while developing countries are following this trend with a certain delay (of maybe five to seven years). It is worth looking at the potential users of computers in distinct groups. A first grouping can be made based on age:

- *Children of pre-school age*: their use of computers is limited to game playing.
- *Children of elementary and secondary school age*: increasingly, elementary and secondary schools offer access to computing facilities. While game playing may be allowed for motivational reasons, the real intent is to spread computer literacy. This comprises typing, searching and communicating, as well as receiving some basic instructions and performing simple exercises.
- *Students*: it can be assumed that in almost all branches of academic education, computers play a key role. They are used for advanced forms of instruction, to facilitate literature search, and to perform exercises, particularly those involving large amounts of text processing (term papers), data transformations, and calculations.
- *Adults, for private use*: the typical home computer is used for correspondence (e.g. e-mail and letters) and for simple accounting applications (spreadsheets).
- *Adults, for business use*: this is the largest and most influential group and will be discussed in more detail below.

The largest group of computer users are adult people in business. According to some industry estimates, 80 percent of the workforce will be

computer users soon. It makes sense to break down this user group into
the following subgroups:

- *Computer professionals*: with about 1–2 percent of the workforce, this
  subgroup has a very unique relationship to computers. It is the vehicle to
  provide their service, which may include software development, database, network and system administration, and computer and software
  selection, installation, and tuning.
- *Other technical professionals and industrial workers*: engineers and professionals from many fields use computers to do technical design, to
  procure parts and equipment, and to perform cost analysis and budget
  planning. In most major industries the work of production workers is
  supported in detail by computers, for example, in car manufacturing. In
  some cases it may even be substituted by computer-controlled robots.
- *Business professionals and clerical people*: most businesses, even the
  smallest ones, rely heavily on computers. The main applications are
  accounting, ordering, inventory control, and billing. With the advent of
  ERP systems, these applications have become more and more integrated.
  Recently, e commerce has changed them again.
- *Doctors, lawyers, architects, journalists, and similar professionals*: all these
  professions have the need to store reference data (e.g. addresses, prescrip-
  tions, and case histories), do accounting and perform correspondence.
- *Public administrators, policemen, etc.*: Local and state governments
  store vast amounts of data to perform their duties. This may relate to
  car licenses, real estate and people registration, or to tax collection and
  social administration.
- *Instructors, consultants*: the role of the computer as an aid in teaching is
  constantly progressing. It started out with the preparation of course
  material, and is now expanding into their delivery.
- *Research scientists*: here the use of computers is most varied. In many
  branches of science it has become a new and indispensable means of conducting research. Many experiments are complemented by simulation
  models of processes in nature and society. Computers have also taken on a
  new role in the traditional task of publishing scientific papers and results.

Not all users mentioned above are also purchasers of a system. The decision
to buy may be taken by somebody else on behalf of the actual users. The
user's needs and desires determine which systems have a value in the
market. The overall acceptance is limited by the skills and the motivation of
users. Since the potential range of users is so broad, some aspect of general
human physiology and psychology come to bear.

Computers are information-processing devices. As such they are an
important resource for every professional. *Information* can be used to store
or transmit knowledge, but not all information is knowledge: we can be
flooded with information without gaining knowledge. Humans have the
capability to process information, which implies the reception, storage, and
retrieval of information. There are unique properties and limitations to

human information processing. Because computers are used to process information this concept is central to computer science. The most commonly used definition is that information is any message that can be interpreted. A message may have any form that can be observed by our senses or their extensions, such as electrical meters or X-ray devices. A message is interpretable if we can associate its components with components of a set (e.g. an alphabet) we know already. If a message is not interpretable we consider it as noise (in the case of audible messages) or as blur and jumble (in the case of visual messages).

Knowledge is a set of models we (or other humans) have about objects and their relationships that we consider true in the sense that they correctly describe the world in and around us. Our knowledge comprises things that exist in reality as well as abstract concepts. It is developed by condensation and confirmation of observations and experiences, and held constant despite frequent challenges. Knowledge can be represented through information, which can be used to store things that are not knowledge. Examples of this can be found in art, entertainment, and advertisement data. Not all knowledge is stored as information. We call this tacit or implicit knowledge, which may be acquired by observing or imitating some other person. A large portion of the skills a person or a company has may be tacit knowledge. It is not recorded in handbooks and cannot be stored in computers. It can be transferred only through personal interaction (e.g. an apprenticeship). Knowledge has to be complemented by the ability to use it. This requires capabilities that can only be acquired through practice or exercises.

Human *motivation* is an essential aspect if we want to understand human behavior. Motivational research tries to identify the forces that influence people when making decisions. People can be motivated or coerced to pursue certain goals. Not all goals are of equal importance, and they may also change over time. When discussing the motivation as it affects the attitude towards computers, a distinction has to be made between professional and non-professional users. Professional users use computers if they help them to achieve their professional goals. As pointed out by Humphrey [Hump97b], professionals are people who employ specialist knowledge and are concerned with the most efficient way to solve a task. They want to do important work that advances them professionally. As implied in the chapter epigraph, they may judge their work environment on how much it helps in this respect. They perform best and are most productive for their employers whenever there is a close match between company and personal goals.

Computers can be extremely helpful for a professional, as long as they can be used as an unobtrusive tool. They can enhance the attractiveness of a workplace by offering an important resource as well as an additional communication facility. Non-professionals may have a completely different attitude towards computers: they may look at computers as yet another annoyance of the work environment; or even as a threat of control or a means of de-skilling. Children and young adults who first encounter computers through games, may have an entirely different experience again. This may influence their later attitude, both as a professional or as a non-professional. In any case, satisfaction is highly dependent on a user's motivation. It raises or lowers the level at which products or services are considered enjoyable, useful, acceptable, or frustrating.

Computers may not only influence the attitude of individuals, but of groups as well. Humans may act differently if alone or in a group. Groups follow unique laws, depending on their constituents and their purpose. Some answers to this spectrum of questions can be found in studies of group dynamics.

10.3 Applicable laws and their theories

The rules cited here are the ones considered most important for computing science and are a selection from a multitude of results. They are only partially based on empirical studies, but all reflect deep and useful insights.

10.3.1 Kupfmüller's law

Karl Kupfmüller has published some basic data on the capacity of human senses and cognition [Kupf71]. We have condensed his observations into the following law.

> Humans receive most information through the visual system and store it in a spatially organized memory. **(L38)**

Applicability Since the aim of computer usage is to support human information processing we should understand what the human capabilities and limitations are. It is of key importance to consider that not all senses are involved equally. The predominance of the visual system explains why signs, pictures, posters, books and screens play such a role in daily life, both in business and culture. Of course, audio information is useful as a complementary channel, for example, in schools, army drill, or traffic, and may even be very enjoyable emotionally, as in the case of music. The importance of the spatial or visual memory varies between people.

Evidence The essence of Kupfmüller's data are represented in Fig. 10-1. The total signal rate is estimated to be 100 Mbit/s on the sending side, and about 10 Mbit/s on the receiving side. The sending side is divided according to the portion of the body from which they originate. More than half of the signals emanate from the trunk (including legs), the hands, and the face. This part of our communication is also called body language, and we are usually able to recognize it without being explicitly trained. It is very common across cultures. The voice, i.e. the speech muscles, are only a small part of this (23 percent). The receiving side is divided according to the senses involved. The visual system is responsible for by far the largest part of our communication

(87 percent). Hearing is responsible for only 10 percent, although this has probably been changed by the invention of the mobile telephone. The other senses include taste, smell, and touch, but also the sensations of heat, cold, and pain. They collectively receive 3 percent of the signals.

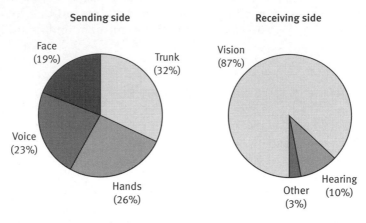

Fig. 10-1 Human signal sending and receiving

Our vision system has two other remarkable properties. It is very strong in recognizing patterns (e.g. faces), and it can discern millions of shades of color. As we will see in the next section, all our senses work in close co-operation with the brain. There is a discussion among scientists whether the things that we observe really exist in the way we observe them. One example is colors: many people argue that colors do not exist in the real world, but only in the human mind. In order to make sense of our observations, our senses (watch the dual meaning of the word) have constantly to make hypotheses about the world. Without it, all we hear is noise, and all we see is blur and jumble. The second part of the above law is not directly due to Kupfmüller. It says that we are able to find things most easily if they are arranged in a spatial manner. This applies to books on the shelf as well as to dishes in a kitchen.

Theory The eye is the most elaborate of the human organs. Each eye has about 100 million receptors and is closely connected to the brain by about 1 million nerve fibers. As a comparison, the ear has only about 1500 receptors and 1000 nerve lines. The origins of spatial memory are not well understood yet. Its strength varies among individuals.

10.3.2 Gestalt laws

There is a group of laws derived from experimental psychology that are usually referred to by the German word 'Gestalt' (pattern). Gestalt psychology was founded by Max Wertheimer [Wert23]. The gestalt laws, looked at as an entity, express the following observation about human perception.

Humans tend to structure what they see to form cohesive patterns. (L39)

225

Applicable laws and their theories

Applicability Five gestalt laws usually are quoted. In abbreviated form they are:

- *Proximity*: we tend to group things together that are close together in space.
- *Similarity*: we tend to group things together that are similar.
- *Continuation*: we tend to perceive things in good form.
- *Closure*: we tend to make our experience as complete as possible.
- *Figure and ground*: we tend to organize our perceptions by distinguishing between a figure and a background.

The gestalt laws apply to all forms of human perception. They influence what we see or hear. Sometimes we add information that is not there. As Wertheimer put it, we are seeing an effect of the whole event, not contained in the sum of the parts. If we have interpreted a picture once in a certain way we have difficulties in seeing it differently. The gestalt laws are obviously not restricted to perception although this is the area in which they were first discovered and have been studied most thoroughly: they also seem to apply to human memory. When remembering things, we straighten out odd lines or add meaning that may not have been there originally. We often learn not only the literal things in front of us, but the relations between them.

Evidence In this case, evidence can be presented directly. When looking at Fig. 10-2 we add lines and see shapes that are not there. Psychologists have many more examples. In a well-known experiment using cards, a black four of hearts is mixed with correctly printed cards. In a short exposure to the cards, about 90 percent of test persons recognize the incorrectly printed card as either the four of hearts or four of spades. Of course, the ratio decreases as the exposure time increases.

Fig. 10-2 Law of continuation

Theory Our perception is not independent of our cognition. In other words, we cannot avoid thinking while we are seeing. Our memory interferes with what we are seeing. We are built to experience the structured whole as well as the individual sensations. And not only do we have the ability to do so, we have a strong tendency to do so. Humans are innately driven to experience things in as good a pattern (gestalt) as possible. 'Good' can mean many things, such as regular, orderly, simple, or symmetric. A possible physiological explanation is that there are more nerve lines from the rest of the brain to the vision center of our cortex than from the retina.

10.3.3 Miller's law

The following law, made popular by the psychologist George Miller [Mill56], is quoted frequently in the computing science literature.

Short-term memory is limited to 7± 2 chunks of information.	(L40)

Applicability When trying to understand human information processing, the component following the sensory system is the human memory. Its properties have to be considered when designing systems to support human work. It is Miller's law that led to the last of Shneiderman's golden rules of interface design, mentioned in Chapter 3. It says: 'Reduce short-term memory load'. It is also behind Corbató's law in Chapter 4.

Evidence Human memory is usually described as consisting of three distinct parts (according to the Atkinson–Shiffrin model). They are the sensory memory, the short-term memory, and the long-term memory. The sensory memory is like a buffer and is associated with each sense, for example, the iconic memory with vision and the echoic memory with hearing. The number quoted in the law is true for short-term memory, which is the working memory. The number given by Miller is 7 ± 2, unless 'chunked' and interrupted by something else. The short-term memory can hold single items for about 1–3 minutes. The storage duration drops rapidly in the range of 10 to 30 seconds for multiple items. The long-term memory is virtually unlimited in size. The duration of its storage may be up to a lifetime.

The number quoted by Miller is based on work done by the German psychologist Ebbinghaus more than 100 years ago [Ebbi85] who investigated the remembering of individual words. Miller's contribution consists in the definition of 'chunks'. Miller determined that, instead of words, more complex pieces of information can be remembered, a process referred to as chunking. A *chunk* is a cluster of semantic entities that can be treated as a unit. The individual components must have some relationship that puts them into a cluster. Technically speaking, chunking is a form of recoding, an adjustment of the representation. It draws on prior knowledge stored in long-term memory [Ashc89]. The deeper the understanding of the relationship between the units, the larger the number of units in a chunk.

The level of education also determines which items are chunked. While for an adult European the string 'Salt Lake 2002' or 'London fog' may be single chunks, it is not the case for a child who is just learning to read. This point is illustrated by an experiment with a chess board as reported by Simon

[Simo74]. There is a game in progress with about 25 pieces on the board. Test persons are asked to look at the board for a few seconds and then to reproduce the positions of all pieces from memory. Usually novices can only place five to six positions, but chess experts can reproduce the entire board in most cases. This is the case only if the board positions are actual games. If the pieces are placed at random, the experts do not perform any better than novices.

According to Simon, the number of chunks should be 5 ± 2 instead. Whether Miller's or Simon's number is correct is not as important as the fact that the short-term memory is severely limited. Since the long-term memory is practically unlimited, many extraordinary achievements come about when people use it in cases where ordinary people have to rely on their short-term memory. This was the technique used by an arithmetic genius on German TV who could multiply ten-digit numbers without paper and pencil.

Theory Some authors believe that short-term and long-term memory are distinct systems. This has been confirmed by medical cases in which part of the long-term memory has been lost, but the short-term memory is unaffected. Recent investigations indicate that there may be no physiological difference between the two. The different behavior may be the result of a different organization of content only. The bottleneck that clearly exists for short-term memory may also be the result of a limitation in processing capacity [Ashc89].

Comment Short-term memory seems to be equipped with some 'general purpose' storage facility, while for long-term storage the neural 'wiring' (i.e. connection of neurons) is permanently altered by the information. While the long-term memory has a semantic and associative structure, the short-term memory seems to be of syntactic nature. As we will see when we discuss learning, the human memory stores data and 'programs'. We can store knowledge about the world as well as skills to perform certain activities, such as walking, knitting, or tree climbing.

10.3.4 Krause's law

The next law also comes from experimental psychology and was published by the German psychologist Werner Krause {Krau00}.

Multimodal information is easier to remember than single mode.	(L41)

Applicability There is considerable discussion among educators as well as among computer scientists as to the value of multiple media. Krause's law is the best argument for using multimedia in education.

Evidence What Krause calls a mode of information is similar to what computer scientists call a medium. Different modes are, for example, text, drawing, image, and voice. In the course of his empirical studies Krause found that highly talented people are not only building simpler structures of the things to remember, but are storing information in multiple modes. If possible, the same concept is associated with a picture, a melody, or a movement. Most ordinary people learn better if reading is combined with their own kinetic movement of writing or illustrating a text. An important restriction is that the alternate representation of what we hear or see is not a mere replication of the other representation. Reading a text is aided less by listening to the exact wording than by augmenting it with related images or sounds. In the same way, if we have to learn a certain manual procedure (e.g. changing gears in a car) it can help to verbalize it. Similar evidence was provided as early as 1971 by studies focusing on visual imagery, notably by Paivio [Ashc89].

Theory Krause believes that if we read a text that is illustrated by an image, they are stored as different entities, and their relationship is stored also. The method of information storage used is different for different media. In the case of different media, multiple copies of the same semantic entity will be stored. This points to the fact that long-term memory is organized by semantic concepts and not by syntactic similarities.

10.3.5 Librarian's law

The following law addresses the field of knowledge management and retrieval, which is of increasing importance for individuals, organizations, and society. The wording of this law has been influenced by a book by Nina Degele [Dege00].

> The more knowledge that is available, the more effort has to be spent on the processes to use it.　　　　　　　　　　　　　　　　**(L42)**

Applicability Economy and society are more and more dependent on the generation and rapid dissemination of knowledge. For this purpose, industries such as chemistry, pharmacology, and transportation have to process huge amounts of information. The same is true in fields such as medicine, biology, or social administration. With this law we want to emphasize the fact that, besides the knowledge itself, an ever increasing level of skill is needed to get at this knowledge.

Evidence Knowledge management has been recognized as a problem by many organizations. Because the essential new knowledge can no longer be found in printed books, the traditional library cannot be called upon to help. Neither does all new knowledge originate from those institutions that publish in public journals and books, nor is the knowledge always presentable in text format. An example are the results of the various human genome projects. The information describing one particular human chromosome (chromosome 22) with 33.4 million base pairs, would fill 500,000 pages of paper. Searching and evaluating this can only be handled by means of networked computers.

Theory To solve the knowledge management problem through further specialization is only feasible for knowledge that is unrelated. In many areas, progress is possible only if we combine existing knowledge. The obvious answer is knowledge about knowledge, known as 'meta-knowledge'.

10.3.6 Apprentice's law

We have to distinguish knowledge management from learning. Learning concerns the individual. Of the many laws applicable in this area, we use one in a form given by Doug Norman [Norm93].

> It takes 5000 hours to turn a novice into an expert. **(L43)**

Applicability To make human knowledge effective, it has to be applied by individuals. As long as it sits on paper or in a machine it is unproductive. It has to be moved to a person's head. Different people have different capabilities to learn: the speed, the thoroughness, and the amount vary. An expert in a field not only possesses a certain amount of knowledge, he or she is also able to decide in what manner it should be applied.

Evidence The 5000 hours quoted above amount to two to three years, which is the typical duration of an apprenticeship or a study. Becoming an expert means acquiring a body of knowledge and the skills related to it. The knowledge in all fields of science and technology does not consists of thousands of individual pieces that can be picked up selectively. It usually consists of deep structures and multiple layers that build on each other. Skill differs from knowledge in that we are able to apply it intelligently. Knowing how to ride a bicycle or play tennis does not mean that we can do it. It takes practice. The same is true for playing a piano, flying an airplane, or performing surgery. It is certainly possible to retrain a person from one specialty to another, maybe from musician to programmer, or from dentist to lawyer, but it can happen only once or twice per lifetime.

Theory There are definite time constants to learning. We learn by receiving the same stimulus repeatedly. Physiologically, learning means connecting neurons by the forming of electrical or chemical synapses within the brain.

10.3.7 Maslow–Herzberg law

The next law originates from general motivational psychology. It helps in understanding human requirements. We name it after two authors, Abraham Maslow [Masl54] and Frederick Herzberg [Herz66] who developed related models from their observations.

> Human needs and desires are strictly prioritized. **(L44)**

Applicability We often have the impression that human needs and desires are unlimited and unstructured. While the first may be true, the latter is not the case. It is Maslow's accomplishment to have shown that human needs and desires are indeed well structured. Their motivational relevance was clarified by Herzberg.

Evidence Maslow identified five ascending levels of human needs that should be fulfilled in sequence. Fig. 10-3 shows what has become known as Maslow's pyramid [Masl54]. At the lowest level of the hierarchy we have the basic needs for air, food, health, and shelter. They have to be satisfied before we are concerned about the higher levels. At the next level we find the need for safety and security. We often forget this, until we are reminded by some natural catastrophe (e.g. earthquake, storm) or social conflict (e.g. war, terrorism). Once they feel secure, most people want to be socially accepted as part of a family, a sports team, or a community. At a still higher level we want to be recognized as a valuable person or as an expert on some topic. At the highest level we then must meet our own goals and standards. Another popular term for this is self-realization. This is the level of motivation most important for professionals. Managers of technical people are well-advised to seek this motivation level for their people. It is important to note that a person (or group) is not progressing from the bottom to the top of the hierarchy, but that we are constantly shifting levels. These needs are a driving force motivating behavior and general attitude.

Herzberg [Herz66] took Maslow's ideas a step further by listing a larger set of needs and then grouping these needs as either making people primarily satisfied or dissatisfied. The first group he called motivator factors, the second group hygiene factors. As an example, the level of salary paid he considered to be a hygiene factor only. It only motivates weakly and for a short period of time, but if it is not considered as being adequate, it de-motivates people heavily. Again, it is important for a manager of professionals to know which attributes of a job are motivators, and which are hygiene factors only.

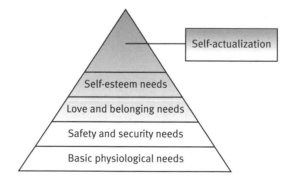

Fig. 10-3 Maslow's pyramid

Theory The reason for this law can probably be found in the history of evolution. We can assume that human needs evolved in accordance with the human species, particularly as determined by the development of the brain. As for all other species, the first needs were those for food, air, water, and an adequate temperature. Safety became a concern when man started to live among hostile neighbors or beasts that might hunt them. Social needs arose while living in the family or in the tribe. The individual's spiritual ambitions could only rise after there was a mind realizing itself as a self-reflecting human being.

10.3.8 McGregor's hypothesis

With the next rule we will state a widly known organizational principle. It is named after the MIT management scientist Douglas McGregor [McGr60].

Motivation requires integration and participation.	(H18)

Applicability While the Maslow–Herzberg law is useful in understanding the relationship of needs and motivation, McGregor's law points out a specific course of action. It is particularly applicable to professionals.

Evidence In his book [McGr60], McGregor contrasted two types of management. He purposely gave them the vague names 'type X' and 'type Y'. Each type adheres to a different theory of management, called theory X and Y, respectively. As Fig. 10-4 shows, type X managers believe that the workforce is not interested in the work itself, but only in the monetary income that is provided through it. Therefore workers must be driven. It is often compared with Taylorism. Type Y managers believe that the employees want to be involved and should therefore participate in all decision making. The manager's job is to create the proper environment and to establish the general direction.

Theory X	Theory Y
Humans dislike work	Expending physical or mental effort is natural
People must be coerced, directed, and controlled	People will exercise self-direction and self-control if committed; commitment is a function of rewards associated with achievements
People avoid taking on responsibilities, want security	People not only accept, but seek responsibility
	Imagination, ingenuity and creativity are widely distributed
	In modern industrial life, intellectual potential of the average human is only partially utilized

Fig. 10-4 McGregor's theories X and Y

Theory Y is, of course, what McGregor recommends. In his opinion, the higher motivation that results, leads to a 'greater realization of both individual and organizational goals'. A climate of trust between employees and management is seen as a prerequisite for an effective organization. To be more effective is another expression for improved productivity. McGregor saw substantial evidence for his principle, but reported a few case studies only. The views described under theory X and Y are really two extremes on a graduated scale, and not all people match either extreme. Management, therefore, has to take both views into account. Since we are not aware of any systematic studies verifying McGregor's assumptions, we prefer to call this a hypothesis.

Comment One reason we quote this hypothesis is that it puts Boehm's Theory W in the context of other management theories. What applies to employees, also applies to customers and users. This is the basic attitude leading to the Scandinavian style of participative development.

10.3.9 Hawthorne effect

The next subject is a well-known result from group dynamics, which is based on the work of the industrial psychologist Elton Mayo [Pars74]. For reasons given below, however, we classify this effect as a hypothesis.

Group behavior depends on the level of attention given.	(H19)

Applicability The Hawthorne effect is quoted here because it applies to the introduction of any new tool or method. It is the general rule saying that increased organizational attention has an inherently positive effect. All new methods, tools, work conditions, or even managerial changes will, at least on a short-term basis, result in improvements in the workers output. So if one only needs performance to improve for a few weeks, one can really implement any sort of plan. For any empirical investigation, there exists the risk that any small improvement that is being observed may have to be discarded. Either the improvement has to exceed a certain limit (e.g. 30 percent), or reasons have to be found why the Hawthorne effect does not apply.

Evidence The Hawthorne effect was demonstrated in a research project conducted from 1927 to 1932 at the Hawthorne Plant of the Western Electric Company in Cicero, Illinois. The series of experiments, first led by Mayo, started out by examining the physical and environmental influences of the workplace, such as brightness of lights, and humidity, and later moved into the psychological aspects, such as breaks, group pressure, working hours, and managerial leadership. The major finding of the study was that, almost regardless of the experimental manipulation employed, the production of the workers seemed to improve. One reasonable conclusion is that the workers were pleased to receive attention from the researchers who expressed an interest in them.

There has been a discussion whether the Hawthorne effect also applies in the case of knowledge workers. In a workshop discussion reported by Fenton

[Fent93], this point was strongly disputed. It is our experience that it fully applies in software and system development, as long as the rate of changes does not overstress the employees. Many productivity studies on new tools or methods did not prove anything more than the Hawthorne effect.

Comment Three other conclusions have been drawn from the Hawthorne studies: the aptitudes of individuals are imperfect predictors of job performance; the informal organization and work-group norms affect productivity; and, lastly, the workplace is a social system. These three assumptions have since become part of the model or the theory of an industrial workplace.

10.3.10 Marketer's hypothesis

To introduce the subject of user satisfaction we start out with a well-known hypothesis. We cannot attribute it to any specific author.

> One unsatisfied customer can hurt more than two satisfied customers can help. **(H20)**

Applicability With the orientation of modern industry towards customers it is worthwhile to have statistical data showing how certain marketing efforts pay off. The quoted hypothesis is one such example.

Evidence The following are some numbers that are quoted frequently in this respect: it costs five times as much to recruit a new customer than to keep an old customer; one dissatisfied customer tells seven to 20 people about his or her experience; one satisfied customer only tells three to five; and only 4 percent of the dissatisfied customers complain, the rest switch supplier without complaining. We have seen these numbers cited in several places. We find them plausible, but are not aware of any study to support them.

10.4 More on user skills, motivation, and satisfaction

Assessing user skills and motivation is a task that computing professionals are confronted with during several activities. The most obvious ones are requirements definition, user interface design, and system administration.

10.4.1 Conducting user studies

Trying to systematically collect data about users is akin to doing field studies in the social sciences. The most popular methods are interviews, questionnaires, and conferences. Interviews have the advantage that they can provide for two-way communication: the persons being interviewed do not only answer the questions that have been thought of in advance; and the questioning may lead to additional questions or new problems.

Interviews can be done by telephone or in person. Their cost depends on the approach taken, the number of people interviewed and the amount of time spent for each interview.

Questionnaires are less expensive and can therefore cover a larger population. The questions asked can be very detailed. Their disadvantage is the time delays encountered for the answer and the risk that the return rate may be low. It is essentially a one-way communication, apart from any free comments that may be entered. The time delay can be shortened by using the Internet instead of the mail. Conferences can provide immediate feedback. They may even lead to a resolution of conflicts if one fraction of participants adopts the arguments of others. It is not necessarily the majority whose view prevails. These three methods may be complemented by tests and observations. One very important group of methods is controlled experiments. They will be discussed in Chapter 12.

10.4.2 Special abilities and attitudes

Designers of computers and software are well advised to take users with disabilities into account. They can make accommodations for users who have poor vision or are blind, as well as for users with hearing or mobility impairments. For blind people, special hardware like keyboards with Braille characters on them, or a voice input, may be needed.

A unique problem of computers is the behavior it provokes among certain types of mainly young people, usually referred to as hackers. They are not usually criminals, but they have a strong desire to show off their intellectual capabilities. They typically do that by penetrating into other peoples' systems. Their favorite targets are large companies and government agencies. They force companies to establish walls around themselves (called firewalls). Several of the attacks by viruses, Trojan horses, and worms that have threatened the Internet and caused millions of dollars in damages were originated by people who had no intent to gain an economic benefit for themselves.

It should be no surprise that computers are also used as a vehicle for committing crime – any area where monetary gains can be expected is a candidate for criminal misconduct – this includes theft and bribery, but may involve drug and weapon business, prostitution, and pornography. Some of the same methods that help against hackers also help here.

10.4.3 Customer feedback and satisfaction

Customers are people or organizations who have acquired a product. They have paid for it once. This does not necessarily mean that they use the product and that they are satisfied with it. Both questions are important because their answer determines whether these customers buy again from the same supplier. As stated under the marketer's hypothesis above, it is advantageous to do business again with an existing customer.

Feedback is therefore needed from individual customers as well as from groups of customers. Some customers may prefer to remain anonymous.

Many industrial companies conduct regular satisfaction surveys. The same methods can be used as discussed before, i.e. interview, questionnaire and conference. Such a survey may be performed by the supplier him or herself (stating his or her identity) or by a third party (with the name of the supplier not being revealed). If surveys are repeatedly performed, such as once per quarter, this may help to expose trends or show the effect of new versions or enhanced products. For the feedback obtained it is helpful if each product is positioned relative to its competition. The individual customer who gave information to a supplier expects a reaction. If this cannot be done, it may be better not to bother asking questions. This is the heart of customer relations management.

Fig. 10-5 lists the software quality attributes that are measured in the quarterly customer satisfaction surveys of IBM and Hewlett-Packard [Kan95].

The final point to be made is that it is not enough to talk only to customers. It is important to know why potential customers or users are not buying or using the product. A customer will only concede reluctantly that he or she bought the wrong product.

IBM	Hewlett-Packard
Capability	Functionality
Usability	Usability
Performance	Reliability
Reliability	Performance
Installability	Serviceability
Maintainability	
Documentation	
Availability	

Fig. 10-5 Software quality attributes measured

10.4.4 Social opportunities and risks

The spread of computers can have a positive effect on the spread of knowledge and education. The reason is that it can ease and accelerate the distribution of information. As stated before, information is only a carrier of knowledge. Whether computers have a greater learning effect than other media mainly depends on the content that is provided. As for all media, knowledge content has to compete against the other contents. The track record is everything but encouraging. All existing information media are heavily used to distract or overload people with entertainment and advertisement. An additional problem that exists today is that for computers 'content providers' are considered highly paid specialists, while for paper, radio, and TV the respective skills are acquired as part of a basic education. These specialists can be compared to medieval monks who were then the experts for copying books.

Many people believe that computers, and particularly the Internet, may have a greater influence on society as a whole than previous analog media, such as books and films, or electronic media, such as radio and TV, had. This is probably an exaggeration. What can be expected is that it may take less time for computers to achieve the same penetration that books, radio, or TV have achieved. Another difference is that the information flow by means of the Internet is not necessarily one-way, as is the case for the other media. Most people are more interested in the information they receive than in what they can send out. Therefore, in developing countries radio and TV usually have a much higher penetration than the telephone. Since the Internet will soon be accessible from mobile phones (or from computers little more expensive than a mobile phone or pocket radio) computers cannot be more guilty of creating a 'digital divide' among mankind than pocket radios are. The digital divide is supposed to have split mankind into haves and have-nots.

Another social risk that is often quoted is the fear that networked computers may be used to infringe people's privacy rights. While the capabilities to do that not much exceed those of mobile phones, it is worth keeping an eye on. Particularly in times of war or terrorist activity, a good balance has to be found between the needs for security and individual privacy.

10.5 Examples and study material

10.5.1 Professional development and career planning

The skill or competency of a professional is his or her key asset. How well it matches the requirements of current and future tasks, and how it relates to other professionals, determines not only their reputation, but also their bargaining power in the market. As stated before, skill comprises knowledge and capability. Knowledge has to be accompanied by the capability to apply it. Capabilities deteriorate if not used. Career-long skill development is crucial for all professionals, particularly with respect to computer competency. On the other hand, computers can assist all professionals in this respect. This example presents an outline for an individual skill development plan. It should be the result of a joint assessment of the professional and his or her manager. As stated before, professional development differs from project training. The needs are determined by the individual's long range requirements. The goal is to make the workforce better qualified not just for current but for future tasks.

Fig. 10-6 summarizes the result of a skill requirements assessment. Such an assessment may have to be conducted once per year. The report first lists the goals for the skill development. The middle column gives a number of detailed subjects where there is a gap between required (or desired) and available skills. The last column indicates the relative priority of each subject.

Goal	Subject	Priority
Understand business strategy	New business potential	3
	Customer relationship management (CRM)	2
Understand technology	Client–server networking	1
	Object-oriented databases (OODB)	2
	Image storage and retrieval	1
Improve project management and	Cost estimating	1
team building skills	Business analysis	3
	Counseling and coaching	2
Increase development efficiency	Inspection process	1
and quality	Component-based development	3
Assure system availability and security	Firewall products	2
	Encryption methods	2
Develop information retrieval skills	Digital libraries	3

Fig. 10-6 Prioritization of skill requirements

As a response to this assessment, Fig. 10-7 gives the agreed-to plan. In the example, only subjects of priority 1 and 2 are addressed. For each subject the training resource is given that will be used to enhance or build up the skill. Depending on the subject, different resources will be used. In one case (image processing), no plan is established due to a lack of available resources. The item may lead to an update of the plan or may be carried over into the next year. The right-hand column gives the planned timing. This is chosen considering both the resource availability and the job or project schedules. Both the professional and his or her manager should invest their best efforts to determine the requirements and identify the available resources, and then agree on a schedule that is realistic. Unless this work is done, the plan is worthless.

Priority	Subject	Training resource	Timing
1	Client–server networking	Professional society course	3Q
1	Image storage and retrieval	(open)	
1	Cost estimating	Inhouse via job rotation	Summer
1	Inspection process	Consultant class (on-site)	1Q
2	CRM products	Industry fair (with follow-up contact to vendors)	March
2	OODB products	Internal self-study group (with pilot installations)	2H
2	Counseling and coaching	External training course	June
2	Firewall products	Online course (Internet)	Fall
2	Encryption methods	Purchased book	ASAP

Fig. 10-7 Individual development plan

While the development plans given above usually address a short-term period of one or two years only, long-term aspects are part of career planning. Every career is unique. Nevertheless, it is helpful if some guidance can be provided. This purpose is fulfilled by publishing so-called model careers or career roadmaps. Fig. 10-8 is an example of a technical career roadmap. It is tailored after similar roadmaps in use within IBM and published by Humphrey [Hump97b]. The boxes in the middle name some of the stages achievable as part of a technical career. The position titles are examples only. They may vary from company to company, or from industry to industry.

What is shown is referred to as the dual-ladder principle. The two branches in the upper part represent both high-level management and high-level professional positions. Fluctuations between the two branches are possible. One aspect of the dual-ladder principle is that salaries are comparable for positions at the same level on both sides of the ladder. The number of years given designates the typical professional age necessary to reach the position. This is a rule of thumb, but deviations are possible. The dotted boxes on each side mention some broadening activities or assignments that may support the career path chosen. Included are on-site as well as off-site training, and rotational assignments. They are representative for a large technically-oriented company. A laboratory is understood as a development or research establishment, comprising more than a thousand mainly technical employees. A system manager has both development and marketing responsibilities for a major line of products. This can be hardware, software, or both.

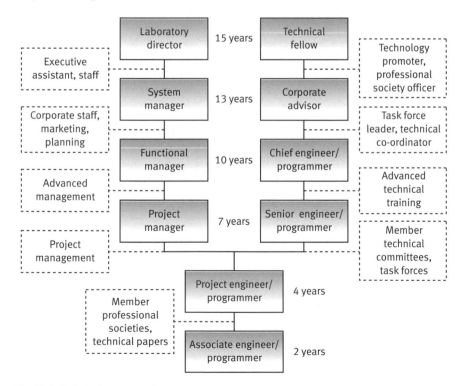

Fig. 10-8 Technical career roadmap

10.5.2 Customer satisfaction survey

Customer surveys are a well-known means to obtain feedback of a product's performance. The example here highlights some of the methods used by IBM during the period between 1985 and 1995. Similar examples have been presented by Kan [Kan95]. Software products were tracked with respect to eight different quality criteria:

- *Capability*: adequacy of functions provided.
- *Usability*: ease of learning and use.
- *Performance*: response time and throughput.
- *Reliability*: stability and freeness of defects.
- *Installability*: ease of installation and upgrade.
- *Maintainability*: skill and effort for application of fixes
- *Documentation*: adequacy and quality of printable information.
- *Availability*: mean-time between failures.

When filling out the survey questionnaire, the customer could judge the above criteria on a five-point Lickert scale: Very satisfied, Satisfied, Neutral, Dissatisfied, Very dissatisfied. In addition to the individual criteria, the overall satisfaction was asked for. In the subsequent evaluations, key emphasis was given to the negative results. Therefore the charts given in Figs 10-9–10-11 only show the percentage of dissatisfied customers. The various columns only differentiate between neutral and dissatisfied customers. (In the charts, dissatisfied includes very dissatisfied!) For space reasons, only six of the eight above criteria are shown.

Fig. 10-9 gives a comparison between three different releases of the same product. The adjacent columns represent the different releases. These releases have probably been measured at about the same time in their life cycle, like six months after shipment. The individual criteria do not differ

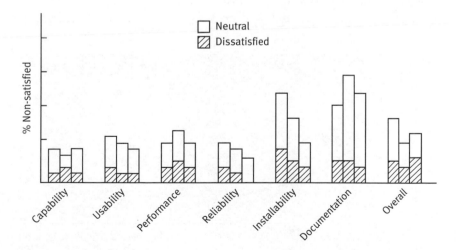

Fig. 10-9 Release comparison by criteria

very much. Obviously, some progress has been made with respect to reliability and installabiltiy. All other criteria, particularly the documentation, have not improved in the customers' opinion.

Fig. 10-10 shows a similar evaluation, but for different products. Adjacent columns represent three different products now. The survey could have included products of a competitor. In such a case, the survey has been performed as a 'blind' survey by an independent consultant. In a blind survey, the customer is not told who is getting the results. The numbers in this chart vary over a much larger range, and show differences in unrelated places.

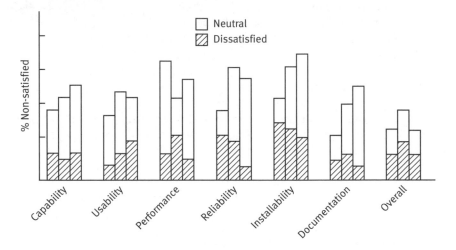

Fig. 10-10 Product comparison by criteria

Fig. 10-11 shows a comparison of two products over a four-year time period. Measurements have been made twice a year. The quantity plotted is overall satisfaction. The ups and downs of the curves can only be understood by looking at the detailed criteria. If the two products compete

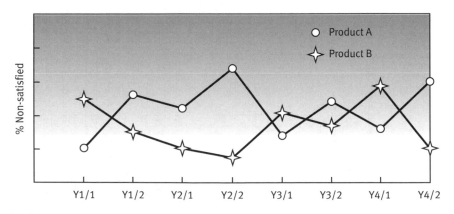

Fig. 10-11 Product comparison over time

against each other, one product may loose its attractiveness, even if it is technically unchanged. If product A raises the bar, users of product B will become dissatisfied. Other factors, like marketing, support structure, or even the visibility of the vendor as a company, can have an influence on the perceived quality of a product. A constant focus is required.

Exercises

10-1 Explain the difference between information and knowledge.

10-2 How can we express the information processing capacities of the human senses? What are the unique strengths of the vision system?

10-3 What are the key properties of human memory? What are some of the consequences for system design?

10-4 Why are multiple media advantageous in learning?

10-5 What does Maslow's pyramid describe? What is the difference between a motivator and a hygiene factor, according to Herzberg?

10-6 What is the Hawthorne effect? Why is it important?

10-7 What is a professional development plan? How does it differ from project training?

10-8 Why is it useful to obtain feedback from non-customers?

chapter 11

Technology, architecture, and industry capabilities

Software architecture involves the description of elements from which systems are built, interactions among those elements, patterns that guide their composition, and constraints on these patterns.

M. Shaw [Shaw96]

This chapter gives some basic information that may be helpful for an assessment of technology, architecture, and industry capabilities. We will discuss the most important laws that determine this field, and give advice how to make use of them in the planning of systems or for the development of an information systems strategy.

11.1 Definitions and importance

Technology is the set of scientific discoveries and engineering inventions, and the methods and tools derived from it, that form the basis of a technical field. A technical field is generally characterized as low or high technology, depending on the relative sophistication of the technology used and its penetration with technology. Information technology (IT) is considered to be a high-technology field, and comprises computer hardware, communication equipment and software. IT provides the components and tools to build products and systems. In contrast, some fields may not advance technically (or may only advance slowly). These are called low-technology fields.

The *architecture* of a computing system expresses what it does, how it does it, and how it appears from outside. The term architecture is used in two respects: first, it designates the external appearance and high-level structure of any system; and second, in a more general sense, it designates a framework in which systems are embedded or through which components of a system interact. Many architectures are first defined by means of a *reference model*, which usually describes high-level concepts and terminology, without fixing interfaces. A *standard architecture* is the set of interfaces formally adopted by some industry consortium or standards body. Products are based on a technology, and adhere to an architecture. In many cases, an architecture is established or made popular through products.

The term *industry* is used to designate the supply side of the market. *Markets* are the places (not only in a geographical sense) where supply and demand meet. Markets exchange products and services. A market evolves whenever consumers have difficulties in producing the goods and services for themselves. There have to be specialists that can do it better, or partners that are able and willing to deliver at lower cost. Consumers must have buying power from sources where they are suppliers.

When the term market is used we frequently imply that this market has properties of an ideal free market, i.e. open to every supplier, transparent for the purchaser, and prices are freely negotiable. All markets deviate from the ideal in one or the other aspect. A technology or architecture has market relevance as soon as the industry is able to supply products and services based on it in a reliable fashion. The demand side of the market was discussed in the previous chapter in the context of user desires and potential. The importance of this aspect is quite different depending on the part of the world considered. What seems easy and obvious in a mature market is not that way in an emerging market, for example, China or Russia.

To assess the state of technology or the capabilities of an industry is a responsibility of technical professionals in all fields. The same is true for computing professionals. They may be called upon to do this independently of particular projects. As an example, many organizations require what is called an information systems (IS) strategy. It ties together the business goals with a technology and industry assessment. This responsibility is not discharged in a once-only event, but remains a constant challenge. Unfortunately, the methods and tools to perform an assessment of technologies, architectures, and supplier capabilities are seldom dealt with in the computing science literature. They are often the subject and carefully protected know-how of specialized industry consultants.

11.2 General observations

Technology is the arena in which individuals, companies, and national economies compete. Technology advances arise from a variety of factors, a key one being competition. It may not advance in those areas, where there is no competition. We frequently tend to underestimate the progress of technology. In certain areas, technology seems to advance almost at its own volition. Architecture evolves slower than technology. In our field, technology changes every five to seven years, hardware architectures usually are in vogue for ten to 15 years.

As stated before, information systems consist of hardware, software, data, procedures, and people. The work of people is mainly regulated by procedures (also called orgware), which is frequently where the resistance to change lies. Contrary to what the term software suggests, data and programs are the durable part of a system. Computer hardware changes in rather short intervals. A hardware generation usually lasts from 18 months to maybe five years. For communications hardware, it may take somewhat longer. Both adapt to existing applications and software structures. A software architecture only changes over decades, not years. In that sense, software permanently limps behind hardware.

Architectural knowledge is a set of structural ideas and concepts that help to build complex information systems. It normally consists of empirically derived rules of what works or does not work in fitting together the components of a system. An architect knows how to translate user expectations and requirements into system functions. Small systems or components have a simpler architecture than large systems. Beneath the architecture is the system's structure. It realizes the architecture. A structure is chosen based on whichever elements or components are available to achieve the architectural purpose.

While a system's structure is dependent on technology, architecture may or may not be. There can be different structures implementing the same architecture, or different technologies supporting the same structure. We talk of re-engineering whenever the technology (and maybe the structure) of a system are changed without altering its function and appearance. While architectural knowledge is conveyed mainly through the products of (great) architects, technology is transferred by a set of tools that a professional in the field applies to solve any given problem. Both are important. Architecture is often undervalued. In computer science, it is more important than in some other fields that are not as much concerned about creating new artifacts. In the case of computing systems, the same engineers are often responsible for both architecture and structure.

In the information technology (IT) market, products and services are offered and are competing. For various reasons, the market can not be considered as a totally free market. One key constraint is the so-called switching costs, i.e. the internal cost involved in moving from one set of products to another. If years ago a decision was made in favor of one vendor, this vendor has the advantage that his products benefit from the investments made by the user. Unless the other vendors takes specific actions to be architecturally compatible (plug-compatible), the user may encounter high costs for converting programs and data, and even larger costs for converting to new procedures.

11.3 Applicable laws and their theories

The laws cited in this section are among the most fundamental laws of our industry. They are about hardware and about software. The hardware laws are usually better known than their software counterparts. This reflects that they are older and probably more subject to systematic investigations.

11.3.1 Moore's law

This law is due to Gordon Moore, the former chairman of Intel. The law dates back to a publication in 1965 [Moor65].

> The price/performance of processors is halved every 18 months. **(L45)**

Applicability Originally Moore predicted doubling of the number of transistors on a chip every two years. This corresponds to a factor of 32 in ten years and a factor of 1000 in 20 years. This has indeed happened over the last 25 years. The most general form of the law is the form given above. Moore's law is by far the best known technology law in our field. It applies to all semiconductor products, i.e. processors and storage chips. It is predicted to be valid for another two to three decades. The industry has several options to exploit the advancements in chip density. Lowering the price or increasing the performance. Both options are reflected when we talk of improved price/performance.

Without doubt, Moore's law has been the driving force for our entire industry. It has made applications possible that could otherwise not have been thought of. The growth in both processing power and storage capacity has had tremendous influence on the development of software technology and business. Without it, software would have to suffer severe limitations, be it in terms of function or usability. The spread and importance of programmed devices would just be a fraction of today's. Moore's law is responsible for the fact that computing equipment is outdating faster than most other industrial products. When designing a system it is very important to correctly identify those components for which Moore's law is applicable. It is equally important to keep an eye on those components where it does not apply, for example, mechanical parts. They may become the real performance bottlenecks or cost drivers. One very important consequence of Moore's law is that one should not start a software project that provides a performance improvement less than that coming from the advances in hardware during the project's lifetime.

CPU Name	Year of introduction	Transistors/chip × 1000
4004	1971	2.3
8008	1974	6
8086	1978	29
286	1982	134
386	1985	275
486	1989	1,200
Pentium (P5)	1993	3,100
Pentium Pro (P6)	1995	5,500
Merced (P7)	1998	14,000

Fig. 11-1 The Intel family of processors

Evidence Evidence for Moore's law abounds. The most often quoted example is the Intel family of processors. Fig. 11-1 lists the best known products of this family. The figure shows the year of introduction into the market and the number of transistors per chip. It should be noted that the size of the chip has increased slightly. The same information is plotted with a logarithmic abscissa in Fig. 11-2. It shows that for the period from 1970 to 1990 the density doubles every two years. Starting in 1991 it doubles only every 2.5 years.

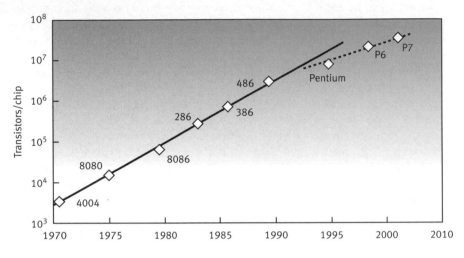

Fig. 11-2 Moore's law for Intel processors

Theory Only part of the reasons for Moore's law come from physics. A higher density of circuits means shorter connections; shorter connections mean higher speed; shorter connections also mean less power; less power means less heat dissipation; less heat means less cooling. Smaller chip floor space and less cooling both mean lower costs. This is an amazing coincidence that cannot be found elsewhere in industrial applications of physics, i.e. more performance for lower cost. The other part comes from economics. Moore's law works only because lower prices or higher performance trigger new demands. In other words, the market has to be either cost-sensitive or function-hungry and has to expand if the price/performance declines. This has happened so far. To achieve the technology advances requires significant investments. The fixed costs associated with development and manufacturing increase with every generation. The variable costs become an ever smaller part of the equation. As an example, if the next generation of chips will be at one-fourth of the manufacturing costs of the current generation, but the costs for the development and for the plant that that produces is four times higher than for the generation before, it has to achieve at least 16 times the output. A saturation of the market may occur, or investors may run out of money, before the physical limits have been reached. The really amazing conclusion that Moore draws himself today [Moor97] is the following: 'The fact that the industry has accepted Moore's law as its guideline turned it into the competitive industry that we know'.

Comment Many people believe that Moore's law may be repealed by 2010–2020, mainly because of problems in lithography for lines thinner than the wavelength of light. There are people who feel that it may be of advantage at least for some users (e.g. schools) if Moore's law finally came to an end and they would prefer that an investment in a PC would last for about 10–12 years, comparable to that for desks and other furniture. Lately, the industry has been focusing on what is called physical gate length. It is the space between two key components on the transistor. In the most advanced chip designs, this space has shrunk to just 90 nanometers which is equivalent to about 360 atoms laid end to end. Along this line, Diffie [Diff01] comes to the conclusion that Moore's law is really about the size of computing elements. The smallest elements in physics (today) are strings. They are 10^{228} times smaller than the smallest features on today's chips. After electronic computers, he envisages quantum computers, and finally string computers.

In early years, another technology law received attention. That was Grosch's law. It postulated economies of scale for larger systems versus smaller systems. Today many people think that Grosch's law is no longer valid due to the tremendous progress of microprocessors. Other people think that it still applies if one takes into account the true costs of small systems, namely those costs that have been moved from the purchase to the use of the systems. As a consequence of this view, many large corporations are moving masses of distributed servers back to a central system again.

11.3.2 Hoagland's law

The next law we cite is credited to Albert Hoagland of IBM San José, California. He was one of the initial developers of IBM disk files in 1955 to 1960 [Pugh91]. We will quote the law in the form given by Gray and Reuter [Gray93].

> The capacity of magnetic devices increases by a factor of ten every decade. **(L46)**

Applicability Next to processing power, storage capacity is a determining characteristic of computing systems. Magnetic media in the form of disks and tapes have become the most important long-term storage devices. This is due to the fact that it is a non-volatile technology, meaning that the contents are preserved if power is switched off. Hoagland had predicted a remarkable increase in the area density of magnetic storage devices, starting with a capacity of 10 Mbit per square inch in 1970. His prediction amounts to an increase of 25 percent to 30 percent per year, or a doubling every three years. For the decade starting with the year 2000, this would mean 10 Gbit per square inch. As a consequence of the higher area density, disk storage comes in ever increasing units of capacity. This is true, although the form factor of devices has decreased (from 11 to 3.5 inches in diameter).

Evidence Today's magnetic disk technology brings 35 GB (about 300 Gbit) on a device with a diameter of 3.5 inches. This is the storage technology available for a notebook-type PC. Obviously, Hoagland's law has been exceeded. According to Schechter and Ross [Sche01], IBM has achieved a 60 percent increase per year in area density since 1991. This was mainly due to improvements in the sensitivity of read heads. This trend is reflected by the unbroken line in Fig. 11-3. The dashed curve shows the typical prices paid by users. As an example, from 1990 to 2000 the prices dropped from about $100 to about $3 per Gigabit. How far the current technology can be extended is a subject for discussion. Some authors predict at least one more decade. Optical storage has developed in a different direction. It provides low cost storage and serves as a removable medium. Its current representatives are compact disk (CD) and digital versatile disk (DVD). The progress of magnetic recording depends on the fact that head and medium are in a fixed assembly, a technique used for the first time by the so-called Winchester disks.

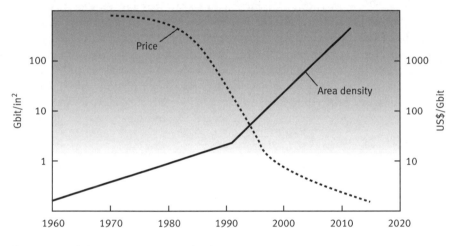

Fig. 11-3 Trends in magnetic storage technology

Theory The tremendous progress in the magnetic disk recording technology was achieved over the last 40 years by a combination of improvement actions, namely by reducing the size of the read/write heads, by reducing the space between tracks and between bits within a track, by positioning the head closer to the surface, and by increasing the sensitivity of the read heads. Further improvements are expected from thermal-assisted recording and perpendicular rather than longitudinal magnetization. Since the storage market is very competitive, we can assume that advances in technology will be passed on to users as price reductions.

Comment In the long run, storage devices are envisioned reaching millions of gigabits per square inch, namely by rearranging single atoms. The technologies to do that have been demonstrated using either the atomic force

microscope (AFM) or the scanning tunneling microscope (STM). Using the
AFM approach, the Zurich research laboratory of IBM has plans to store 1
Tbit (about 125 GB) of data on a 1.4 inch-square surface [Sche01].

11.3.3 Cooper's law

Of similar importance to the growth in processing power and storage
capacity is the development of communication capacity. We therefore also
quote one law from this area. The growth in communication capacity can
be characterized by the growth in bandwidth. It is a major design factor.
This law has been known for quite some time; the wording chosen here was
provided by Cooper [Coop01].

Wireless bandwidth doubles every 2.5 years. **(L47)**

Applicability Bandwidth is the key parameter in telecommunications. It is
usually expressed in bits per second. The most frequently used abbreviations
are Kbit/s, Mbit/s and Gbit/s designating Kilobits, Megabits or Gigabits per
second, respectively. It is the interplay of Moore's law, Hoagland's law, and
Cooper's law that determine which system structures are feasible and economical. If processing is ahead, it is better to compute locally and to distribute
data in compressed format. If communications is ahead, one can reduce the
amount of computing and send uncompressed data from one point in a network to the other. When storage is cheap, redundant copies can be stored. It is
Cooper's law that makes many applications possible which otherwise would
not make sense. Examples are the transmission of music and video.

Evidence Cooper's law is not based on a thorough empirical analysis. He
simply claims that this law has been valid for 105 years, i.e. since Marconi's
invention of wireless telegraphy in 1896, and will be valid for the next 100
years, leading us to forms of personal communication that we are unaware
of today. It will allow an awareness of events anywhere on earth, not only by
hearing and vision, but also through the senses of touch, smell, and taste.

Theory Cooper's law is less determined by advances in technology than are
Moore's or Hoagland's law. New technologies have entered the telecommunication field in several waves. The most important one was the introduction of
optical fibers. Additional bandwidth is being created mainly by a better
exploitation of an existing medium. An example is copper wires. They have
been around for decades and were used in the Kbit/s range. Only recently have
they been extended to transmit in the Mbit/s and even in the Gbit/s range.

Comment Optical wire-based transmissions are usually a magnitude ahead.
Here single-line transmissions in the range of 5–10 Tbit/s are being demonstrated by various vendors, for example, Alcatel and Siemens. Transmission
technologies typically share single lines for multiple bands. Methods to

achieve this are time division, frequency division and most recently wavelength division multiplexing.

11.3.4 Morris–Ferguson law

This law is described in a landmark paper by Morris and Ferguson [Morr93]. The authors refer to it as the Silicon Valley business model.

Architecture wins over technology.	**(L48)**

Applicability One of the key questions of our industry is how architecture and technology relate to each other. Typically, any software or system product does not exist in isolation. It is a building block in a total system or in a network of systems. At the same time, it forms the basis on which other products are built. Technologies can make new applications feasible or lower their entry costs.

Evidence After a study of the computer industry, Morris and Ferguson drew the conclusions that good products are not enough. It is the architecture that matters. Most successful are proprietary, but open architectures. In this case, the architecture is accessible to everybody, but the owner has the advantage that he can provide products implementing the architecture first. He can also have the better implementations. With an accepted general purpose architecture, special purpose solutions can be absorbed and low end systems can swallow high end systems. The best known example is the PC. It also applies to diskette and CD formats, text and image formats, operating systems, programming languages, spreadsheets, and user interfaces.

Theory The theory behind this law comes from economy. An innovative company usually establishes a new market with a proprietary architecture. 'Proprietary' here means that the architecture is developed and controlled by one company. Only if that architecture is openly specified will it be adopted. Not specifying an architecture, i.e. keeping it secret, only makes sense for a company that already dominates a market. In any case, users are afraid to be locked in. In the case of an open architecture, several companies and technologies can and will compete. The innovator has the best chance to be the first and the best exploiter of the architecture. If he does not lead, he will loose the market. Only those companies will win, for which the respective products lie within their core competency. They will be able to introduce new technologies into a given architecture faster than others.

11.3.5 Metcalfe's law

Robert Metcalfe defined this law in his Ph.D. thesis [Metc73] at Harvard university. It has since been widely quoted.

The value of a network increases with the square of its users.	(L49)

Applicability This law says that communication networks are subject to a unique phenomenon. It works first as a barrier, and later as an accelerator. A communication device or network is of little value as long as there is nobody or only a few partners to communicate with. This changes after a critical mass has been reached. The more partners there are, the more every device or connection gains in value. From the tipping point on, the growth is exponential or faster than linear.

Metcalfe's law applies to all two-way communication products, like telephone and fax. It does not apply to the radio, walkman, and TV, which up to now were one-way communication products. It applies to most software products, however. Because each software product implements an architecture or interface, its usefulness increases if that architecture finds acceptance. Typical examples are text and image formats and the corresponding processing software. If a software product cannot exchange data with other programs, other qualities do not count.

Evidence Plenty of evidence can be found for Metcalfe's law throughout the industry. The law applied to the Ethernet first, a local area network, and to the Internet, an interconnection of local networks, afterwards. The time needed to reach critical mass varied with the different technologies. The telephone needed about 30 years, the Internet about 20 years (1972–1992). Metcalfe used his law himself to argue for common network standards. For software products and architectures a critical boundary is a market penetration of about 20 percent. If this market share cannot be reached quickly, it may be better to forget the product. Depending on the product type, the market may be a national market or the world market.

Theory The root of Metcalfe's law is certainly in economics. A communication product obtains its value for the user not from its consumption, but from its use. It requires that there are other people who use the equivalent product as a means for communication. If there are n users, each user has potentially $n-1$ partners to communicate with. Considering all users in the network, there are $n \times (n-1)$ possible one-way interconnections. Even if we count connections between the same partners as two-way connections only once, there are still $n \times (n-1)/2$ connections, which mathematically is an expression in the order of n^2.

Comment In a recent interview [Metc96], Metcalfe expressed his concern that the Internet may loose its strength if it becomes divided among many private networks whose users do not communicate with users of other networks.

11.3.6 Shaw–Garlan hypothesis

The following hypothesis gives credit to the work of Mary Shaw and David Garlan [Shaw96].

> A sound architecture significantly reduces development and maintenance costs. **(H21)**

Applicability Architectures are usually the result of an explicit design effort. As shown in the case of Denert's law in Chapter 3, a certain architecture may be the answer to one specific concern. Given different environments and applications, different architectures may be feasible. Not all of them are equally sound or appropriate. At different levels of a given system, different architectures may be applicable. Examples are the user interface, the database or the communication network. Thinking in terms of architectural styles allows the designer to recognize the different paradigms, and to determine what is the best architecture for a given purpose. In a case of an existing system, any deviation from its architectural style may have disastrous effects. The success of software reusability largely depends on whether the modules in question are consistent with respect to the architectural framework they support. Fluency with different architectural concepts allows the designer to make better choices.

Evidence In the cited book, Shaw and Garlan not only define different architectural styles but give a number of examples also. They also postulate generally applicable architecture description concepts and languages. The evidence, supporting the above hypothesis, is mainly presented by means of case studies. Whether experiments can be designed and conducted, in order to clarify questions in this area, is doubtful. The costs are usually prohibitive. Due to the importance of the subject, more systematic studies are needed, however.

11.3.7 Bayer's hypothesis

As an example of a technical achievement in data management we quote the following insight which is due to Rudolf Bayer [Baye72].

> In spite of disk capacity increases, data access can be kept efficient. **(H22)**

Applicability Hardly any system is being built that does not have the need to access data efficiently. Active data usually reside on disk. All disk devices have a rather low access time, but a high data rate. With the larger capacity of devices, the geometric limitations of its access mechanism have not changed. As a consequence, the time to scan the entire disk has increased by a factor of ten since 1969. For a dynamically changing file with frequent insertions or deletions, the problem arises to keep the access time within reasonable bounds. For data structures in main storage, balanced trees (like the AVL-tree) provide the optimal solution in this case. The path-length or time needed for retrieval or insertion/deletion is proportional to the logarithm of the number of elements (log n). This is a theoretically proven lower bound.

To take the properties of disk devices into account, a data structure, called B-tree, was introduced by Bayer. It provides access times near the theoretical optimum, as given by balanced trees. Bayer's original intention was to apply the concept to index structures. Indexes are directories (often consisting of multiple levels) pointing to the data in a file. Fig. 11-4 gives an example of a B-tree. The boxes represent contiguous disk blocks (also called pages). They contain between k and $2k$ index entries (in the figure, $k = 2$), except for the root. Within a block, the entries are sorted. New entries are inserted at the leaves (the bottom of the figure). If they do not fit, the leaves are split and a new node is created, containing links to both the leaves. The tree grows from bottom to top. During deletion, the tree is shrunk whenever a leaf has less than k entries.

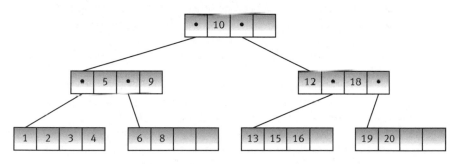

Fig. 11-4 Example of B-tree

Evidence The B-tree has become the basis of the widely used data access method VSAM and the database product DB2 of IBM. VSAM uses the B-tree concept not only for indexes, but also for the data itself. The data segments of a file start out with a given amount of free space. If this is taken up, the data segments are split in a similar way as the indexes. As shown by Keehn and Lacy [Keeh74], VSAM has excellent access properties, both for sequential and random access. For all main frame operating systems of IBM, VSAM was well accepted by the customers and has replaced all other access methods within a short period of time. Investigations concerning the access behavior of System R, a precursor of DB2, have been published by Blasgen and Eswaran [Blas77]. It shows that the number of accesses to secondary storage has been minimized. Another major advantage of an access method implementing the B-tree concept is that both data and indexes are very stable, i.e. they are seldom restructured or rewritten. This contributes to the integrity and recoverability of the data.

11.3.8 Codd's hypothesis

One of the best-known achievements of software technology is associated with the concept of databases. The following rule is quoted, to introduce Ed Codd's [Codd70] contributions.

Databases can be independent of devices and applications.	(H23)

Applicability Apart from the physical access of data, most systems are concerned with the logical organization of data as well. This is the realm of databases, a crucial part of software and systems engineering. Database technology allows the organization and storage of data in a way that is largely independent of how they are used in a particular application and what appears to be necessary due to the geometry of a device. This principle is most consistently and effectively realized by means of Codd's relational data model.

Evidence Codd's relational model, as first presented in [Codd70], stores all data in tables. This way the data become independent of ordering, indexes and access path. Since its initial publication, the ideas have been refined through the work of many authors, including Codd himself. A relational system is defined today as a system supporting the following properties and criteria [Codd82]:

- All information is represented by values in tables. Only the values count, not their location within the table, meaning that the left-to-right ordering of the columns and the top-to-bottom ordering of rows is irrelevant.
- These values can be manipulated by means of relational operations, such as select, project, and join, and set operations, such as union, intersection, and difference. These operations transform tables into tables.
- Additional integrity constraints, called entity integrity and referential integrity, ensure that all values can be manipulated with the above operations.

Implementations of the relational model dominate the market of database management systems (DBMS) today. Due to the progress in processing power and special optimization techniques developed for this model, the performance of relational systems is no longer a problem. Structured Query Language (SQL) was standardized as the language to retrieve data from relational database management systems. It has found wide acceptance throughout the industry. Recently, the concept of a relational DBMS has been extended to handle non-scalar data elements. This class of systems is referred to as object-relational systems.

11.3.9 Engelbart's hypothesis

Human–computer interaction is an area where considerable knowledge has been developed over the last decades. Doug Englbart's [Enge68] name can be associated with the following fundamental insight.

Conceptual integrity is the result of a consistent mental model.	(H24)

Applicability Quoting Brooks [Broo87] again, a product should present a coherent impression to a single user's mind, even if designed by many minds. The mental model is the image the designer has in his mind. This determines the image that a user has of the system. Conceptual integrity denotes that property of a system that makes a homogeneous impression. It is a perfect whole for its user. One way to do this is through metaphors.

Evidence Hardly any concept has changed the external appearance of software systems more than the WIMP interface (windows, icons, mouse, pull-down menu). They were originally invented by Engelbart and his colleagues at the Xerox Palo Alto Research Center. During the mid-1960s they implemented a natural language system (NLS) that pioneered the mouse, windows, and hypertext. The same group later developed the Xerox Star, the first commercial system with an all-points-addressable display offering the desktop metaphor, using symbolic icons and multiple, non-overlapping windows. Later these ideas were extended, first by Apple's systems (Lisa, Macintosh), and then by IBM's OS/2 and Microsoft Windows. The fact that all graphical user interfaces (GUI) today 'look and feel' quite similar is due to this common heritage. The concepts developed by Engelbart and his group have been extremely convincing.

Most attempts to come up with similarly useful metaphors as the desktop have failed. This points to a general limitation of metaphors. They may be very useful at the beginning, like the coach metaphor was in the history of automobiles. As soon as additional functions are added, they are either a hindrance or have to be abandoned.

11.4 More on technology, architecture, and industry capabilities

Some additional aspects are helpful when assessing technology and architecture status and trends. They all come to bear when a professional is called upon to propose an information systems strategy for his or her organization.

11.4.1 Technology assessment and prediction

We have stated before that technology advances quickly. This is only true in general. If we look at different technologies, we see that the speed can be quite different for different technologies or different application areas. The reason is that the effort and the motivation to move technology may vary considerably. If we look at the rate of acceptance, most technologies follow a similar lifecycle, which is usually described by an S-shaped curve, such as the one given in Fig. 11-5.

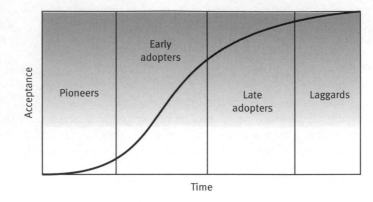

Fig. 11-5 Technology lifecycle

The time represented may comprise a period between three and ten years. Acceptance usually starts with pioneers, reaches 20–50 percent with early adopters, and ends with laggards. Another view is to talk of emerging, mature, and aging technologies. In some cases, we refer to one technology lifecycle as a generation. Generations follow each other at shorter or longer intervals. The time to introduce a new technology is very often a function of the learning curve, i.e. how difficult it is to make users familiar with it. Some fields can or will stay at low levels of technology, others strive for and adopt a high level. We have already distinguished between high technology and low technology fields at the beginning of this Chapter. They may coexist next to each other. A high technology usually requires large teams of specialists with scientific knowledge, uses complex processes, demands a high capital investment for equipment or tools, and can be transferred with considerable effort only. A low technology can be mastered by small groups of low-trained persons, uses simple processes, demands little capital, and has a short learning and transfer period. High technology is usually the prerogative of advanced economies. Developing countries often have to compete using low technology.

Technology predictions are as risky as any other prediction. They can only be made if the driving forces are understood. The technology laws quoted in this chapter are such predictions. All of them were made for existing technologies. To predict totally new technologies is much harder. Glaring failures abound.

11.4.2 Management of technology and innovation

The economic life of a product is usually very short. Technically it may last for 10 or 15 years, but after two to three years it may be challenged by new technologies. In a global market, product leadership can be maintained only through technology leadership. A company that can introduce new technology and new products in a timely fashion is not forced to compete on a price basis.

To develop new technologies or attractive products requires innovation. Innovation depends on creative people and a climate that fosters new ideas. The organizations most successful in this respect, surpass others by providing good internal and external communication, and by concentrating on core competencies. Above all, new ideas have to be recognized as such and their feasibility investigated. After that, they can be called inventions and treated accordingly. To achieve this level, appropriate funding may have to be given and bureaucratic hurdles removed. Whenever inventions are to be exploited commercially, patenting is helpful. This applies to software as well as hardware related inventions.

Not all new technologies need to be developed in-house. Companies can buy or trade technologies. In this case, we have to know who the players are with which it is worthwhile to negotiate. Any technology transfer requires a match of interests between the giving and taking side. The giving side has to be willing to share its knowledge and has to know who is interested in it. The taking side has to recognize a gap and must be motivated to close it. A technology gap can be closed by training, by hiring or transfer of people with the desired knowledge, but also through co-operation, acquisition or licensing.

With respect to technology management, a company can pursue different strategies. Fig. 11-6 lists four different strategies. For each of them, different strengths are needed, both in research and development (R&D) and in marketing.

Strategy type	Development strength	Marketing strength
Innovator	Daring in new technologies	Raises demand, creates markets
Fast follower	Quick technology transfer	Expands markets, differentiates
Mass producer	Optimizes quality and cost	Minimizes sales and service cost
Niche dweller	Exploits applications	Excels in customer service

Fig. 11-6 Technology management strategies

11.4.3 Some emerging technologies and applications

As stated before, a professional cannot dodge his or her responsibility to make assessments regarding emerging technologies. No speculations are allowed – this would be rated as science fiction. Rather the best professional judgment should be applied. In this sense, we shall list a number of technologies or applications that, in our opinion, are likely to achieve market relevance during the next five to seven years.

■ *Portable terabyte RAM*: magnetic or semiconductor random access memory (RAM) technology will advance enough to provide storage capacities in the range of 10^{12} bytes. Such a device will be able to store all our books or our favorite music or movies, and can be carried everywhere.

■ *Terabyte ROM under US$1*: the optical or other read-only memory technologies will provide a medium the size of today's digital versatile disks (DVD) with a capacity of about 10^{12} bytes. For the amount of text or image data, it will be cheaper than paper and will be given away. It will become the main carrier for audio or video recordings.

■ *Network bandwidth of several Gbits/s*: networks with this bandwidth are in the experimental stage today. This bandwidth will allow us to hear music with high fidelity, see videos without significant compression, and to reload the portable terabyte RAM frequently.

■ *GFLOPS processor power*: a processor power of a billion floating point operations per second is about a thousand times more powerful than today's PC (Pentium 4). In a laboratory or office environment, it will allow us to perform extensive data conversions, visualizations, virtual reality applications, and other calculations.

■ *Throw-away computers*: computers will no longer be recognizable as such. They will be sewed into clothes or bags, inserted in furniture or garden equipment, glued to food packs, etc. They will record all kinds of data and send out messages. They will be thrown away with their carrier.

■ *4B read devices*: digital displays are still quite bulky. In the future they will become flat like cardboard or paper. They will finally allow us to read computer-generated print pages (e.g. newspapers, or books) while in the bath, in bed, on the beach, or on a bus. These devices will compete with smaller displays for less demanding applications, such as mobile phones.

■ *Electronic paper*: several laboratories are experimenting with a medium that looks like paper and carries electronically changeable or erasable information. Every dot is realized by a small partially colored sphere whose side is turned under electronic control.

■ *Flexible voice recognition*: today's voice recognition software requires pauses between words and a special training session. More advanced systems will recognize fluent speech and adjust automatically to the voice of a speaker.

■ *On-the-fly natural language translation*: based on the recognition of fluent speech the translation into a foreign language will occur with a delay of only a few seconds. The output may not be perfect, but is useful.

■ *Biometric pattern recognition*: apart from the voice, finger-print, head contour and retina form are biometric patterns that can be useful to identify a person.

■ *Medical monitoring*: for certain patients, a device implanted or carried close to the body will transmit medical data (e.g. temperature, blood pressure, etc.) to a doctor or hospital at given intervals.

■ *Personal diary*: the storage capacity described above, will be sufficient to record everything we hear or see during the day.

■ *Location sensitive computing*: combining computers with global positioning devices will allow us to transmit information as needed or desired at specific locations. This may be information about facilities or persons in the neighborhood, but also traffic advice and weather data.

■ *Artificial sensory organs*: Advances in neuro-physiology will allow the connection of electronic devices to our nerve system. These devices can function as a substitute for, or complement, the human eye, ear, nose, or skin.

This list represents a realistic forecast, because all the technologies exist today – at least in a laboratory stage. When and how they will reach production depends on diverse factors. Some may simply not make it in the given timeframe, since its promoter may make a false start, either by selecting a technically risky approach, by expecting too high a margin, or by choosing the wrong customer set.

11.4.4 Assessing industry capabilities

Whenever a decision is made whether to develop a system or to buy it from outside, an industry assessment is involved. The same is true in the case of services when the decision is between an in-house solution and outsourcing.

The IT industry is generally structured as hardware vendors, software vendors and service companies. There are overlaps in the form, that some hardware vendors also offer software, or that software vendors also supply service. A rational decision usually has to start with the application in question. If the decision has been made for the application, for example, an ERP application, this triggers other software decisions. The application may be offered for certain operating system platforms only, or may require certain DBMS products. From the operating system and the database follows which hardware is eligible. No hardware vendor is strong for all product or device types. Mixing software components or hardware devices from different vendors is possible only, if they are compatible with an overall architecture.

Since any decision of this kind has an effect over several decades, many factors should be considered besides compatibility and price. The type of service provided can be as critical as the geographic proximity and the long-term financial viability. While these criteria apply to any industry, the companies in the IT industry should be evaluated on their ability to define and promulgate relevant industry architectures. Nothing will lead to more wasted investments than building on architectures that will not survive.

To contract with an independent service company is advisable when the problem to be solved is only a temporary one, or if the skill required is not useful for the business. In all other cases, it may be better to acquire or develop the skill in-house. Involving a consultant can be helpful if an objective evaluation of competing vendor offerings can otherwise not be achieved. To rely on outside resources, particularly from developing countries, to achieve lower costs is often an illusion. Lower salaries do not always translate into lower cost per product or unit of service.

11.4.5 Developing an information systems strategy

Many computer scientists are confronted with the task of developing an information systems strategy for their organization or company. This demands all the knowledge presented in this book, and more. The professional knowledge has to be combined with the knowledge about the business goals, the priorities and the possibilities of their own organization. The joint development of an information systems strategy is an excellent opportunity for IS people to communicate with the rest of their company, particularly with upper management.

The establishment of a strategy requires an assessment regarding technologies, architectures and industry capabilities. It relates them to the needs of the business and puts them into a framework. Strategies are always iterative developments. They require a continued updating. A strategy usually covers a five to ten-year period; shorter periods are considered as tactical or operational periods. In some cases, the actual decision does not need to be made at the strategic level at all. A decision at the tactical level is sufficient.

Several options are worth considering. If most computer applications are not critical for the business, a reactive strategy may suffice. In this case, only those applications should be considered for automation, where their manual execution produces higher costs or higher risks. For application areas where fast and technically advanced solutions are key, an aggressive strategy may be chosen. The risks should be well identified and controlled. In order to be able to react fast, when needed, no area should be allowed to fall totally behind.

The strategy chosen may vary from business area to business area, depending on the competitive situation. If a strategy has been developed, it should be executed. To spend the effort first, and then put it away on the shelf, does more harm than not developing a strategy at all. This will result in a major loss of credibility for the entire management team. An illustration of an information systems strategy is given as an example below.

11.5 Examples and study material

11.5.1 Information systems strategy

The example gives a strategy for a financial institution, such as a bank. It is based on a strategy proposal developed by Dewal and Schnichels [Dewa00]. The strategy is outlined in the form of three tables. They split the entire strategy into three parts: business, technology, and process. Each table identifies a number of aspects important for each sub-strategy. The real content of the strategy is given in the column entitled 'Options chosen or considered'. The right-hand column gives an indication of how long the strategic decision is supposed to be binding. In the case of a short planning cycle, this part of the strategy may have to be reviewed every two to three years. A long-term binding decision may be valid for up to ten years. This is a judgment, too, and may have to be revised.

Fig. 11-7 summarizes the business part of the strategy. Apart from the last aspect, the figures originate directly from the referenced publication. Of course, in other situations, other points may be taken into consideration. In Fig. 11-8, the technical part of the strategy is given. This is where the professional knowledge and judgment of systems and software engineers are required.

Strategy aspect	Options chosen or considered	Planning cycle
Multiple sales channels	Support of home-banking, mobile phones, branch offices, and point-of-sales; others can be added easily	Medium
Accelerated processing	Generate and protect revenue by shortening business processes and reducing cancellation rate	Medium
New business potential	Ease definition of new finance products; react quickly to competitive pressure	Short
Customization	Taylor function set and interfaces to individual customer needs	Medium
Flexible operation	Allow variations and extensions in a timely fashion	Medium
Credit risk assessment	Provide comprehensive support for credit decisions	Short
Investment policy	15% return-on-investment, project break-even after 3 years	Long

Fig. 11-7 Business strategy

Strategy aspect	Options chosen or considered	Planning cycle
Processing	Optimize between centralized and distributed processing power (multi-tier); driven by application demands and architecture constraints	Medium
Storage	Provide adequate capacity, including backup and buffer (20%); fixed and removable	Medium
Networking	Assure sufficient bandwidth for non-image applications, local and remote, wired and wireless; build up pilot for image applications	Short
Display, print	Accommodate new handheld devices, pluggable into running applications	Short
Voice, image	Gain further experience; test pilot applications; introduce successful ones	Short
System availability	Total allowable outage of central systems < 6h/year	Long
Data management	Extend use of relational databases, add improved recovery and data mining facility	Medium
Transaction processing	Enhance availability and throughput; move to component-based products	Medium
Text processing and document management	Win more users for text systems and electronic mail (90% of employees); evaluate and install state-of-art document management products	Short
Security, recovery	Reduce intrusions into central systems (by 50% in 2 years), introduce password protection for all remote computing devices; provide auto-restart for central systems and network	Medium
Other	Evaluate workflow products and mobile agents	Short

Fig. 11-8 Technology and architecture strategy

Finally, Fig. 11-9 addresses the process part of the strategy. This area is undoubtedly the domain of systems and software engineers. The material in this section builds on the two previous parts, of course.

Strategy aspect	Options chosen or considered	Planning cycle
Procurement, outsourcing	Buy if standard product can be reliably and economically obtained; build if important unique function required; use outsourcing to fill temporary capacity gaps (not skill gaps!)	Long
Development methods, tools	Cycle time and quality have highest priority; productivity and costs should be industry average; use empirically evaluated methods and tools only	Short
Integration, migration	Every application will adhere to the overall architecture; stepwise migration to new architecture and applications	Medium
Evolution, maintenance	Keep all applications up-to-date with respect to legal requirements; negotiate functional enhancements with users; perform maintenance in-house for all self-developed code	Medium
Administration, operation	Optimize service and support for all applications and devices used throughout the company; assure smooth and safe operation of central facilities	Medium
Human resources	Identify skill needs of IS department for implementation of this strategy semi-annually; provide training in-house; new hires only to complement skills	Medium
Organization	Establish line responsibilities in accordance with this strategy; use project organization as base, cost center as exception	Long
Risk management	Identify project risks early; assign responsibilities	Long

Fig. 11-9 Development and operations strategy

Exercises

11-1 What are the key properties of a free market? In what respect does the IT market deviate from it?

11-2 What effect did Moore's law have on the IT industry? What physical limitations may affect its validity?

11-3 Why does Metcalfe's law apply to many software products?

11-4 What is the relationship between architecture and technology in our industry?

11-5 Explain the implications of Bayer's and Codd's hypotheses for system design.

11-6 Describe the different strategies that can be employed for technology management.

11-7 What factors should be considered when selecting hardware vendors, software vendors, or service companies?

11-8 What constitutes an information system strategy? What are the main options?

chapter 12

Measurements, experiments, and empirical research

Experimentation in software engineering is necessary but difficult. Common wisdom, intuition, speculation, and proofs of concept are not reliable sources of credible knowledge.

V.R. Basili [Basi99]

The empirical approach to science relies on measurements and empirical studies. This chapter presents some general rules and guidelines for conducting empirical studies in software and systems engineering.

12.1 Definitions and importance

Measurements are observations done carefully. Rather than relying on our senses, we often use special equipment such as measuring-rods or stop-watches. We take special care to achieve precision, reliability, and objectivity. Measurements are used to identify new phenomena (exploratory measurements), test hypothesized phenomena, or guide engineering in the application of models. Every measurement requires a scale or metric.

As stated in the introduction, empirical investigations rely on three methods: experiments, case studies, and surveys [Basi86, Zelk98, Juri01]. In this section, all experiments are taken to be *controlled experiments*, which are intentional studies conducted in a specially prepared environment, and based on some hypothesis [Prec01b]. They are sometimes referred to as 'in vitro' studies, meaning that they are conducted isolated from a living organism where the test object is artificially maintained, such as in a test tube. All influences, that are not considered variables to be measured are excluded or kept constant. The hypothesis is either verified or falsified by the controlled experiment. In addition, a clear distinction is made between independent and dependent variables of the hypothesis at hand. Independent variables are the input parameters, as set for a given experiment; the dependent variables are the output parameters, which assume certain values dependent on the input parameters.

Case studies (or quasi-experiments) are empirical studies conducted in a field environment, and based on some hypothesis. They are also referred to as 'in vivo' studies, meaning that they are conducted within the living organism. They are superimposed on some real project and less stringent in terms of variable control than controlled experiments. The challenge is to collect measurements without interfering with the project at hand. Owing to the fact that many hidden project variables may influence the measured dependent variables, the importance of qualitative analysis techniques is increased. The broadest and least detailed empirical study is a *survey*. Surveys are empirical studies aimed at acquiring data from people via questionnaires or interviews. Surveys can be conducted 'a posteriori', i.e. data can be collected based on peoples' experience and recollection. Very often surveys are also used to formulate a hypothesis to be followed up by controlled experiments and/or case studies. They require sound methods for data collection to avoid biases, data validation to ensure data accuracy and analysis. Survey methodologies have their origin in social and cognitive sciences.

Empirical Research is research based on the scientific paradigm of observation, reflection, and experimentation as a vehicle for the advancement of knowledge. Observations gather data on some object of study, reflections analyze the data to understand them and, if necessary, modify the object of study, and experimentations observe and determine the effects of this change. Empirical research is important to science and engineering, although there are basic differences in the approaches used in both. Empirical research is guided by the needs of the professional community, particularly those of practitioners, as well as the interests of the researchers themselves. Comprehensive introductions to this subject can be found in [Wohl00] and [Juri01].

12.2 General observations

Usually several measurements of the same phenomenon are taken by different observers to protect against measurement errors, the key sources of which are subjective metrics and scales; perceived pressure of empirical situations (known as the Hawthorne effect); inappropriate metrics and scales; inconsistent ties between metrics and objects of study; and unclear motivation by missing explicit ties between metrics and measurement goals or hypotheses. If, as in geodesy, there is an accepted theory as to the source of errors, multiple measurements are needed in order to deal with the first two sources of measurement errors. The differences in measurements are then settled using a special adjustment calculus (e.g. the least squares method). The latter three sources of measurement errors can only be dealt with by applying sound empirical methodology 'a priori', i.e. from the beginning.

The empirical paradigm is used in all sciences, ranging from social sciences to natural sciences and engineering sciences. The differences stem from the differences in these fields. For example, in natural sciences (e.g., astronomy) the real world exists and cannot be modified, so the emphasis is on observation and reflection. In engineering, the real world can be changed, therefore, initial observation and understanding is followed by the changing of methods. This may entail the creation of new models, the formulation of a new hypothesis, and re-testing.

Since computing has aspects of both science and engineering, it is important to distinguish the approaches used in both fields to discover new knowledge. Some aspects of this difference are illustrated in Fig. 12-1. In science (shown on the left side), a theory may come first. It predicts certain observations. Based on an operational version of this theory, certain hypotheses or models can be devised, which can be tested, either through observations as in astronomy, through experiments as in physics, or by proofs as in mathematics. If the result of this test is in line with the theory, the theory is accepted; otherwise the experimental setup or the proof procedure may be changed. If this does not help, the theory is either modified or rejected.

On the engineering side (right half of Fig. 12-1), there is usually a goal or target. There is a problem to be solved. This problem can be solved by developing an artifact, be it in hardware or software, or by fixing a deficit of an existing artifact. The target is pursued using a certain set of methods or processes. To be able to measure success or failure, a metric has to be defined. Measurements will indicate how close we got to the target. If the methods that were selected did not get us closer to the target, the method is changed, or other methods are tried. If the methods solved the problem, they become part of the repertoire. Quite frequently the target is raised. We then want to solve the next largest problem, or attempt a more perfect and less costly solution.

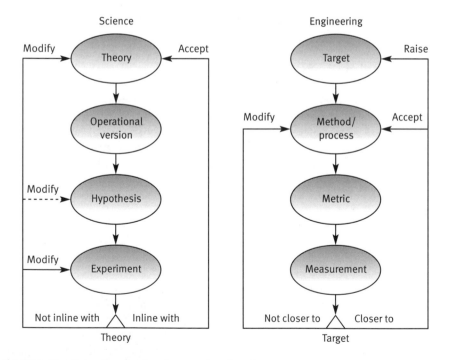

Fig. 12-1 Knowledge discovery in science and engineering

12.3 Applicable laws and their theories

In this chapter we will present one law and one hypothesis only, and a number of conjectures. Most rules cited here are not based on quantitative measurements, but solely on expert experience.

12.3.1 Bayes' theorem

This is a well-known theorem in probability theory, from the work of the eighteenth century mathematician Thomas Bayes, that allows us to calculate the probability of a hypothesis, based on both observations and prior knowledge. This concept was later generalized and made popular by Pierre-Simon Laplace, the French mathematician.

> The probability that a hypothesis is true increases the more unlikely the new event is that confirms this hypothesis. **(L50)**

Applicability Bayes' theorem is usually given by the following formula [Chal99]:

$$P(h|e) = P(h) \times P(e|h)/P(e)$$

In this formula h is a hypothesis, and e is an event, $P(h|e)$ is the (posterior) probability of a hypothesis h considering a new event e. $P(h)$ is the prior probability. It represents the prior knowledge. $P(e|h)$ is the probability of e occurring under h. $P(e)$ is the probability of e occurring at all, independent of any hypothesis. The term $P(e|h)/P(e)$ is often referred to as the likelihood factor (LF).

An application of Bayes' theorem can be found in the derivation of the COCOMO II model [Boeh00c]. In the case where the sampling data from 161 projects show a high variability (or low precision), data from expert interviews are used as prior knowledge. By combining the two data sets using Bayesian regression, the total precision increases. Bayes' theorem can be used to calculate the incremental reliability gain for a hypothesis by adding additional measurements.

Evidence Bayes' theorem is used in many empirical investigations. For example, in medicine it allows us to estimate the probability that the right medicine was prescribed, by observing what happened to the patients. If one in ten patients who are wrongly prescribed recovers, and one in two patients who are correctly prescribed recovers, Bayes' theorem makes it five times more likely that the right medicine was prescribed.

Theory The theorem represents an induction principle. It combines new data with old information. It is valid wherever the past shows up in the future, or the larger environment in the small environment, and vice versa. A new theory is more likely to be true the lower the probability that it can be explained with existing data or with data that are valid for other theories as well. Or inversly, the best theory is that which requires unique data for its verification, i.e. data that cannot be explained by other theories.

12.3.2 Basili–Rombach hypothesis

The following hypothesis has received wide acceptance, both in academia and in industry and it has been put forth in a series of publications [Basi88, Basi94a].

Measurements require both goals and models. (H25)

Applicability The hypothesis implies that metrics and measurements have no value by themselves. They need to be motivated by goals and questions. If an organization wants to take measurements in a meaningful way, it must proceed in a top-down rather than a bottom-up fashion: it must first specify the goals for itself or for its projects; then it must trace down these goals by means of questions to the data that define these goals operationally (operational model); finally, the data have to be interpreted in a certain technical framework (metric). This goal-question-metric (GQM) paradigm is a hierarchical structure, starting from goals, then leading to questions, and finally moving to metrics. The refinement of measurement goals into metrics requires (possibly implicit) models of the artifact to be measured or the quality aspect to be measured.

Evidence In the 1960s and 1970s measurement of software received a bad reputation: lots of data had been collected in companies without having a positive effect on project performance. The reason was that the data had been collected according to ease of collection rather than need. The result were large numbers of unused data cemeteries. In the 1980s, the idea of focusing on the goal of measurement ('What?') before addressing the necessary metrics ('How?') permeated the software development community. This reflected the fact that software had become an important asset that needed to be treated professionally. One facet of this move to professionalism was the relating of business goals to software (process) improvement goals, which in turn were related to software measurement goals. The GQM approach to measurement [Basi88, Basi94a] has since become one of the most referred to and widely used approaches to sound measurement. Since measurement programs in industry have been established and serve as drivers for maturation of the software development process, it is considered by some authors as one of the most influential 'inventions' in the software development domain over the past 20 years.

12.3.3 Conjecture 7

The majority of the methods used in software and systems engineering depend on people for their execution. This leads to the following conjecture.

| Human-based methods can only be studied empirically. | (C7) |

Applicability This conjecture suggests that the majority of software development methods cannot be investigated any way other than empirically. Human-based methods (e.g., designing, inspecting) include human judgment and depend on human factors such as motivation and experience. Therefore, the results of applying such methods depend on these factors. As the result is not deterministic, empirical studies are needed to understand and control these factors. One cannot determine analytically the effects of an inspection method. The effects of an inspection method depend on a multiplicity of independent factors such as application domain, experience of people, notation of document to be inspected, etc.

Evidence The most important evidence is the large gap between research and practice in software development. Many promising development methods have been proposed. Few of these have been tried out in practice, even fewer have been sustained in practice despite project pressure. One of several reasons is the inability of researchers to present practitioners with realistic judgments as to the strengths and weaknesses of candidate methods and their potential to solve problems existing in the industrial environment at hand. This is the result of either a lack of empirical evidence regarding new methods at all ('What is it good for?') and/or lack of context relevance ('Does it work for my project?'). Understanding the impact of context variables is the major challenge of empirical studies in the software domain. In order to adapt existing empirical evidence to specific characteristics of an industrial environment, practitioners need to be able to (partially) replicate published empirical studies. An example where this has been done are inspections [Lott96]. For researchers to advance the scientific body of knowledge, they need to perform families of empirical studies across different contexts [Basi99].

12.3.4 Conjecture 8

To gradually evolve the methods used by an organization, a process improvement plan is necessary. Improvements require feedback regarding their effectiveness.

| Process improvements require action-based feedback. | (C8) |

Applicability Only if an individual is convinced (by data) that the new process works for him or her will he or she adhere to it. As was suggested by conjecture C7, different applications of a method will lead to different results. That means that without action-based feedback there is no repeatability of methods, which in turn means no repeatability of results. No repeatability of results means no return on investment in process improvements. Very often this is caused by the fact that improvements are not sustained. All engineering disciplines accept the fact that teaching a new method is not sufficient for successful application. In addition, engineers require time to practice the new method in the context of a specific application domain. Only such offline experiences, without project pressure, allow re-adjustment of old mental problem-solving models. The development of a complex software system is certainly an engineering task. Wide-spread ignorance of action-based training and feedback have led to many unsuccessful method transfers from research into practice.

Evidence There are many stories about non-sustained process changes. Who does not know the cases of 'not-lived' methods, e.g., object-oriented programs that reveal the developer's history as a Fortran or COBOL programmer, or inspection methods that are more or less faked because of project pressure. In all these cases, methods cannot produce the expected benefits and cannot therefore be sustained. This problem of sustaining desired process changes at the (human-based) software engineering level has been experienced in many industrial improvement programs. Successful examples are reported by several institutions (e.g. [Romb02]).

12.3.5 Conjecture 9

Action-based feedback for individuals and learning of the entire organization requires empirical studies. Both controlled experiments and case studies have to be combined.

> Learning is best accelerated by a combination of controlled experiments and case studies. **(C9)**

Applicability In the same way that physicists learn from observing planets, software developers learn from observing software developments. The observation of software developments takes place in the real world (*in vivo*) via case studies superimposed on real projects. The weaknesses of case studies includes their intrusion on time-critical projects and their lack of providing cause–effect insights. Therefore, a smart combination of controlled experiments to study new methods or investigate specific cause–effect relationships of already applied methods, and case studies to scale-up experimental results to realistic complexity, project characteristics, and project pressure, is essential. Researchers prefer case studies to identify

real-world hypotheses or scale-up experimental results, but rely on controlled experiments to demonstrate cause–effect relationships. Practitioners
view case studies as the preferred way of testing applicability of new methods in their project domain. Controlled experiments are typically not
performed in industry.

Evidence A well-known example of a smart combination of controlled
experiments and case studies is the introduction of Cleanroom software
development into NASA [Selb87]. Controlled experiments in the university
environment were used to overcome the 'factoid' that testing is a more effective defect detection mechanism than human-based inspections. It was
demonstrated that rigorous inspections based on a stepwise abstraction
analysis procedure outscore any testing approach. Only after this was
demonstrated by a student experiment and repeated by practitioners, were
the developers open to Cleanroom software development. Cleanroom software development which clearly separates the creation of software and
testing, has become a successful development practice, as demonstrated by a
series of case studies. It is obvious, especially if one compares the Cleanroom
experience with the fate of other formal development approaches, that
Cleanroom would have never been accepted by practitioners without the
sequence of controlled experiments and case studies. Other evidence exists
from many industrial success stories of development methods transferred
after experimental pre-evaluation.

Comment As stated before, the conclusions drawn by Basili *et al.* [Basi92]
at the NASA Software Engineering Laboratory (SEL) are not easily transferable to other environments. They are biased to a particular context because
effects of the Cleanroom approach were compared with the results of a
process where all testing was done by the developers. Most development
organizations take the step from the archaic (pre-Weinberg) process to the
establishment of independent test groups first. They may evaluate the
Cleanroom approach based on the higher quality level already achieved. In
that case, its benefits may not be as clearly visible.

12.3.6 Conjecture 10

Measurements are being taken from actually performed developments. A true
model of the actually performed process is required to start measurement.

Measurements are always based on actually used models rather than on desired ones. **(C10)**

Applicability Development models are being used to instrument software
developments, i.e. to provide a framework for measurements. Very often,
the development model used is rather prescriptive, but does not agree with

the actually performed development process. Such inconsistencies result in complications during data collection as well as in irritations regarding resulting improvement suggestions. In general, it can be said that the executed software development process is not captured yet, and needs to be captured descriptively by interviewing developers involved.

Evidence Many measurement programs in industry are terminated because of a lack of valid data and/or lack of use of data to manage projects better or trigger process improvements. One cardinal mistake, besides the lack of goal orientation (see hypothesis H25 above), is the reference to the wrong process. Typically, general project models are used instead of the live process models from which developers can collect data. Developers recognize the discrepancy easily and fake data collection. This marks the end of any measurement program.

12.3.7 Conjecture 11

When considering the transfer and reuse of empirical results in a new environment, two questions arise:

1. Do they apply to this environment?
2. What are the risks of reusing these results?

In order to allow potential reusers an intelligent judgment, empirical results have to be packaged, i.e. completely documented.

> Empirical results are transferable only if abstracted and packaged with context.(C11)

Applicability Effective reuse of empirical results requires the abstraction of models from the actual data. Information has to be translated into knowledge. This knowledge has to be packaged with its context. The context necessary from a scientific point of view includes all information necessary to (at least theoretically) repeat the empirical study. This enables testing and thereby inclusion into one's existing body of knowledge. The context information necessary from a practical point of view includes all information necessary to judge how well the context of the empirical evaluation matches the project environment at hand, and thereby estimate the risk of transfer.

Evidence The experience-factory model as originally proposed by Basili [Basi89, Basi94b] provides an organizational scheme as well as procedures for experience packaging. This model has since been applied successfully in many industrial environments for building up learning organizations for software knowledge. Experience-factory-based learning organizations transfer the general concept of the learning organization successfully into the software domain.

12.3.8 Conjecture 12

The applicability of empirically based models changes based on learning.

> Empirically based models mature from understanding to explaining and
> predicting capability. **(C12)**

Applicability Very often the expectation from empirically based models is too high. The natural evolution of such models starts with understanding, i.e. phenomena can be clearly distinguished; evolves to explaining, i.e. cause–effect relationships can be identified; and ends with predicting, i.e. the impact of all relevant context variables can be included.

Evidence The experience factory model referred to above [Basi89, Basi94b], provides a scheme for evolving empirically based models from understanding to predicting. More evidence to support this model is being collected.

12.4 More on measurements, experiments, and empirical research

To be able to perform meaningful work in this area, a number of additional aspects have to be considered. We will highlight a few of them. For a more comprehensive coverage we refer the reader to some recent books specializing on this subject, such as [Juri01, Wohl00, Prec01b].

12.4.1 Defining experimental goals

A statement of goals is vital for planning and conducting an experiment. By stating the goal explicitly, all data collection and interpretation activities are based on a clearly documented rationale. A goal may have the following aspects:

■ object of study (e.g. design, coding, testing);
■ purpose of study (e.g. comparison, analysis, prediction);
■ focus of study (e.g. effectiveness, efficiency);
■ point of view (e.g. practitioner, researcher);
■ context (e.g. experience of subjects, objects used, environment).

The context and object aspects determine the independent variables for an experiment; the focus of study the dependent ones. Context may also determine which hypotheses are meaningful at all, for example, if the empirical subjects had no prior experience with a method, the results of the study may be meaningless, unless the criterion measured was learning time. The purpose of the study determines the breadth of analysis.

12.4.2 Deriving testable hypotheses

Each experiment or case study should have at least one testable hypothesis. A hypothesis of the form 'method A is good for task T' is not testable but a hypothesis of the form 'method A requires less time than method B to accomplish task T' is. In order to be able to apply inferential statistics, both a null and an alternate hypothesis should be formulated. The null hypothesis would be accepted if there is no significant difference between two sets of data. In the previous example, a null hypothesis would say 'There is no difference between method A and B as far as the time required for task T is concerned'. Only if the null hypothesis has to be rejected, would it make sense to investigate the alternate hypothesis.

12.4.3 Designing experiments

The cornerstone of empirical studies is credibility. It results from the efforts taken to build up the evidence used to support the experimenter's claims. Before correlations are investigated, the causality of the events has to be clearly determined. *Causality* can only be assumed if there is more than a spurious association between the events, one event always occurs before the other (temporal precedence) and, finally, there is a theory (i.e. model of reality) saying why one event caused the other event.

After causality, internal and external validity of the experiment should be assured. An experiment has *internal validity* only if the relationship between presumed causes and measured effects has been observed. It expresses the degree to which the controlled variables could be kept constant. Typical threads are maturation (people get used to the test), history (time between the experiments influences the result), selection (only such participants were selected that are predisposed to the subject), and mortality (not all participants complete the test). *External validity* is the degree to which results also apply to other environments, and it depends on the choices made for test objects and test participants. A typical question in this respect is whether tests made with students have any relevance for professional environments.

Besides establishing the hypothesis to be verified or falsified, the design of an experiment requires a clear definition of independent and dependent variables. *Independent variables* are the (input) factors that are believed to influence the results. By manipulating or varying the values of the independent variables, different results are produced. *Dependent variables* are the (output) results to be measured. For example, in the study of the relative effectiveness of testing and reading techniques by Basili and Selby [Basi87] the dependent variables included number of defects found and cost of defect finding; the independent variables of choice included the defect detection technique used, the experience of subjects involved, and the type of code analyzed. The programming language was kept constant by the fixed choice of Fortran.

The final point to be considered is the method used to randomize the results. For this purpose, people are assigned to different groups corresponding to different levels of the independent variables. In some cases, one group, called the control group, assumes that all independent variables have base values only.

Overall, there exist a number of experimental designs to choose from. The most important are: one factor experiment/paired comparison; block design; blocked factorial design; factorial design/nested design; and fractional factorial design. They all are applicable under different conditions, including the goal of experimentation, the number of independent variables, the possible alternatives for these independent factors, and the number of undesired variations. For example, blocked factorial design is applicable if we deal with more than one independent variable, more than one alternative per variable, and the possibility of undesired variations. A complete discussion can be found in [Juri01].

12.4.4 Analysis and validation of results

The analysis of measurements can typically be done by use of statistical correlation and/or regression analysis techniques. Analysis methods applied to software engineering data range from traditional statistical methods to AI-oriented pattern analysis to do justice to low-volume software engineering data. The combination of quantitative and qualitative analysis methods is a particular characteristic of the field of software. From data (e.g. effort data), to information (e.g. effort distributions across development phases), to knowledge (e.g. effort distributions with adjustments according to different contexts) the benefits mature from understanding to explaining and predicting. In software development, the analysis of exceptions guarantees improvement as it may explain yet another independent factor.

Empirical results must be validated. This includes interviews with the participants to make sure they understood all questions correctly. Special considerations apply to small data sets, the handling of outliers, and the significance level of all results. Data are the raw material for better understanding. Analysis methods enable the identification of patterns resulting in models. Owing to the specific distributions and low volume of software engineering data as well as to hidden context dependencies, analysis requires great care. Large industry-wide databases of measurement data are of limited value only, although they may allow some benchmarking as to where a specific firm ranks with respect to a heterogeneous community of firms. However, these databases would not reflect the specific characteristics of a given company. Today, many successful companies maintain their private database for internal benchmarking and improvement purposes. A well-known example where internal benefits were gained due to careful data analysis is NASA's Software Engineering Laboratory (SEL) [Basi92].

12.4.5 Replication of experiments

Empirical results have to be published in a way that allows for repetition. This fundamental characteristic of scientific experiments is still often violated in computer science. Repeating measurements is useful to find out whether the results still apply. Repeating them unchanged will increase (or decrease) their confidence. By varying the hypotheses, the respective theory can gradually be extended. This is a valid research target.

Experiments that reproduce known results have one big problem: they are not considered as advancing the state-of-the-art, and therefore are usually not accepted for publication in a scientific journal or conference. This is unfortunate because they could help to increase confidence in existing models. They may also serve as a learning experience for students or as an argument to fight against the Not-Applicable-Here (NAH) syndrome.

12.4.6 Ethical issues

Empirical research requires strict adherence to ethics. People should not participate without their consent, nor should people be deceived or their privacy invaded. If students are asked to participate, the experiment should result in an educational gain. The results should not influence the course grades. The same applies in industry. The results of an experiment or study should have no effect on salary. This does not exclude the possibility to motivate people to participate by means of some small financial recognition. The main method to avoid ethical conflicts is to preserve anonymity. Sometimes this requires that groups of at least six to eight people are formed. If data from several tests have to be associated with the same person, special identifiers can be assigned. The correspondence between identifiers and true identities should not be recorded.

12.4.7 Limitations of the experimental approach

The experimental approach is not without limits. First of all, the costs are high and in some cases may become prohibitive. It is clearly impossible to do an experiment with hundreds of professionals, so smaller groups or case studies will have to suffice. We should not forget, however, that if experimentation is one of the costly ways to learn, it is even more costly to do without learning. The second limitation comes from the use of people. This restricts the type of experiments that can be done. There are different limitations for students than for professionals: students may not have the critical experience; professionals may not be willing to undertake every task. The final limitation is the transferability of results: it is not easy to create experiences that are easily transferable without human expert judgment, as source and target contexts typically vary. In a practical work environment, the project and business contexts may change faster than the experimental studies can support. To overcome some of the limitations of controlled experiments, research is investigating 'smarter' combinations of controlled experiments and case studies as well as integrating experimentation with simulation.

Empirical research has been recognized as a major sub-discipline of computer science since about 1980. A first status report can be found in a 1993 Dagstuhl conference [Romb93]. Some recent book publications [Wohl00, Prec01b, Juri01] have been mentioned before. It requires a certain shift away from the emphasis on mathematical approaches. The majority of the problems encountered in software and system development are not mathematical in nature. They are caused by the nature of human work, particularly mental or intellectual work. That means they cannot be understood by mathematical reasoning alone; they can only be understood and controlled empirically. Many researchers in computing hesitate to analyze these activities by empirical methods: for them it is like applying engineering to scientific writing, poetry and painting (applying mathematics would not make a difference for them).

   Empirical research in software and systems engineering needs to take the specifics of this domain into consideration. This results in specific approaches to empirical research, empirical studies, and measurements. The most important characteristics of the software domain include the non-determinism of most methods because of (allowed and intended) human creativity, variability from project to project, and the resulting low volume measurement data sets. Furthermore, the large number of dependent variables and often sparse volumes of data require sophisticated designs and data analysis procedures. Nevertheless, it is important to apply sound methods in order to perform objective and testable investigations. It is not enough to just argue in favor of some desired behavior. As Bob Glass [Glas94] put it: 'Researchers should investigate, not advocate'.

12.5 Examples and study material

12.5.1 Comparative product evaluation

This example[1] describes the comparative evaluation of three text processing products (P1, P2, P3). The measurement plan, outlined in Fig. 12-2, highlights the difference between independent and dependent variables. Besides the product to be evaluated (M1), two more variations of the study are given as independent variables (M2, M3), i.e. task type and application skill. The task type is determined by the nature and complexity of the document to be processed. There are four documents of different complexity, designated as follows: text only (D1), text with figures (D2), text with figures and formulas (D3), and foils (D4). The application skill expresses the experience of the subjects with electronic text processing. Only two levels (novice, expert) are distinguished.

---

[1] We thank Jurgen Munch for this example.

Independent variables (and their domains)	Dependent variables (and their ranges)
M1: Product (P1, P2, P3)	M4: Number of pages per hour (decimal)
M2: Task type (D1, D2, D3, D4)	M5: Learning effort (< 1 hour, < 6 hours, > 6 hours)
M3: Application skill (novice, expert)	M6: Number of system crashes per hour (integer)
	M7: Input/output filters provided (none, too few, enough, plenty)
	M8: Help function (none, useless, acceptable, useful, excellent)
	M9: Spell-check (none, useless, acceptable, useful, excellent)

Fig. 12-2 Measurement plan for product evaluation

In this exercise, six dependent variables are observed. They are named as parameters M4 through M9. They have either nominal (M7–M9), ordinal (M5), or rational scale (M4, M6).

Fig. 12-3 shows a $m \times n$ design for the experiment. It assigns nine inexperienced and nine experienced persons (subjects) to perform the processing of each document with each product. This setup separates the skill levels and isolates the learning effect. Fig. 12-4 shows sample results for two measurements out of a total of 54 (18×3) measurement points. By analyzing these results carefully, a professional assessment of the products in question can be attempted that will be more reliable than a mere subjective judgment.

Skill	Subjects	P1	P2	P3
Novice	S1–S3	D1	D2	D3
	S4–S6	D2	D3	D1
	S7–S9	D3	D1	D2
Expert	S10–S12	D1	D2	D3
	S13–S15	D2	D3	D1
	S16–S18	D3	D1	D2

Fig. 12-3 Experiment design for product evaluation

Independent variables	Dependent variables	Independent variables	Dependent variables
M1: P3	M4: 2.5	M1: P2	M4: 1.0
M2: D1	M5: > 6 hours	M2: D3	M5: < 1 hour
M3: Novice	M6: 0	M3: Expert	M6: 2
	M7: too few		M7: enough
	M8: useful		M8: acceptable
	M9: none		M9: useful

Fig. 12-4 Sample results of product evaluation

The following example is based on an experiment published by Kamsties and Lott [Kams95] which has been discussed in Chapter 5. It is a well-known case of a repeatable experiment. The programs used and the data produced by this experiment are available as study material from the Fraunhofer Institute for Experimental Software Engineering in Kaiserslautern.[2]

Fig. 12-5 gives the key characteristics of the programs used for this experiment. The first program (*ntree*) implements an abstract data type that inserts and searches elements in an unbounded tree. The second program (*cmdline*) evaluates the parameters inserted in a command line and outputs them as a data structure. The third program (*nametable*) inserts and searches entries in a symbol table. All programs are written in C and are provided with scaffold code to ease their execution by a test driver. Comments in the program text are practically non-existent. They can neither help nor mislead their readers. A total of 22 faults (or errors) are known,[3] and have been classified in a number of ways. Only their classification into 'faults of omission' and 'faults of commission' is repeated here.

Program name	LOC (Including headers)	Lines with comments	Faults of omission	Faults of commission	Total faults
ntree	260	5	4	2	6
cmdline	279	1	2	7	9
nametable	281	11	4	3	7

Fig. 12-5 Test program characteristics

Fig. 12-6 outlines the measurement plan for this example. The three independent variables (M1–M3) are language skill, method skill, and method used. Language skill is the self-reported mastery and experience of the programming language in which the test programs are presented. Method skill is the self-assessed mastery of each of the three methods. For both parameters an ordinal scale is used. The methods used are functional or black-box testing (FT), structured or white-box testing (ST), and code reading or inspections (CR). Although subject to a separate analysis, language and method skills are randomized by assigning subjects to groups.

Of the dependent variables measured, we are only repeating four of them (M4–M7). Typically, the number of failures (M4) depends on the test cases used. A test case may fail because of a test case error, or many (ill-chosen) test cases may indicate the same fault. The number of expected failures is therefore not given. Since the number of faults are known, the relation of expected faults to isolated faults can be expressed as a percentage. Two separate numbers are collected: one for the faults of omission (M5); and one for the faults of com-

---

[2] http://www.iese.fhg.de
[3] Since the specifications of the test programs are very coarse, we rely on what has been defined as failure or fault in the original paper.

Independent variables (and their domains)	Dependent variables (and their ranges)
M1: Language skill (1–5)	M4: Number of failures observed (integer)
M2: Method skill (1–5)	M5: Percent of omission faults isolated (decimal)
M3: Method used (FT, ST, CR)	M6: Percent of commission faults isolated (decimal)
	M7: Time needed per method (minutes)

Fig. 12-6 Measurement plan for method evaluation

mission (M6). Their total is a derived number (M8 = M5 + M6). Suggestions for improvements that normally show up in any verification process are ignored. The time needed for a method (M7) is the total time required for all three programs. As will be seen later, for each program a full day (eight hours) was initially allocated. A group could stop earlier if the members felt that they were done, or when their ideas of how to go about the task had exhausted. No group was allowed to continue indefinitely until all errors were found. This corresponds to the typical situation in practice where a limited and pre-planned time period (maybe of several weeks) is available for verification.

The experiment was conducted in order to test three hypotheses: the primary hypothesis (H1) says that the three methods in question differ with respect to effectiveness (number of failures observed and percentage of faults isolated) and efficiency (number of failures or faults divided by time required to detect them); the secondary hypothesis (H2) says that the three methods differ in the effectiveness at isolating faults of different types (faults of omission versus faults of commission); the third hypothesis tested in the reported experiment (correlation of results with language and method skill) is not repeated here. It happens, anyway, to be the weakest result of the study!

Fig. 12-7 gives a formal representation (operational version) of the two first hypotheses. H1 is split up into four sub-hypotheses: two of them (H1.1, H1.2) deal with effectiveness; and two (H1.3, H1.4) with efficiency. Even in this form, the hypotheses only predict that the results of different methods differ from each other (<> sign). The respective null-hypothesis is that they are the same (= sign). In the lower two cases, efficiency is calculated as E4 = M4/M7 and E8 = M8/M7, respectively. The secondary hypothesis consists of three sub-hypotheses, one for each method. Not shown are the sub-hypotheses that actually lead to what we regard as the essence of the Hetzel–Myers law as introduced in Chapter 5, namely that each method detects different errors.

Primary hypothesis	Secondary hypothesis
H1.1: M4 (FT) <> M4 (ST) <> M4 (CR)	H2.1: M5 (FT) <> M6 (FT)
H1.2: M8 (ST) <> M8 (ST) <> M8 (CR)	H2.2: M5 (ST) <> M6 (ST)
H1.3: E4 (FT) <> E4 (ST) <> E4 (CR)	H2.3: M5 (CR) <> M6 (CR)
H1.4: E8 (FT) <> E8 (ST) <> E8 (CR)	

Fig. 12-7 Operational hypotheses used

Fig. 12-8 describes the assignment of work used in the original study. The permutation of programs and methods is such that all combinations of programs and methods occur, and that all possible orderings of applying the methods can be seen. The experiment is run over three (not necessarily consecutive) days with one program per day. All groups see the same program on the same day to avoid cheating.

Program name	Method FT	Method ST	Method CR
ntree (day 1)	G3, G4	G5, G6	G1, G2
cmdline (day 2)	G1, G6	G2, G4	G3, G5
nametable (day 3)	G2, G5	G1, G3	G4, G6

Fig. 12-8 Experiment design for method evaluation

We will not give the detailed results of the study, as reported by Kamsties and Lott [Kams95]. Some results are stronger than others. We are sure, however, that readers who carefully repeat the part of the study that is described here will find yet another confirmation of the Hetzel–Myers law. Kamsties and Lott are quite cautious in this regard: in the conclusion of their paper, they say: 'The observed differences in effectiveness by fault class among the techniques [methods] suggest that a combination of the techniques might surpass the performance of any single technique.'

Exercises

12-1 Outline the difference between the scientific and the engineering approach of discovering knowledge.

12-2 What are typical measurement errors in empirical software engineering studies? What can be done about them?

12-3 What are the key characteristics of a controlled experiment? Why are controlled experiments advantageous?

12-4 In what situations are case studies and surveys more appropriate than controlled experiments?

12-5 Name the most important threads of validity for experiments. What measures can be taken to protect an experiment against them?

12-6 Why is it necessary to repeat experiments? What types of repetitions are useless from a research perspective?

12-7 Explain Bob Glass' dictum that research should investigate, and not advocate.

12-8 What are the five parameters to specify a measurement goal according to the GQM approach?

12-9 How do you derive dependent and independent variables from a GQM goal specification?

12-10 What are possible scenarios that justify combinations of controlled experiments and case studies?

chapter 13

Conclusions and challenges

Programmers are always surrounded by complexity; we cannot avoid it. Our applications are complex because we are ambitious to use our computers in ever more sophisticated ways.

C.A.R. Hoare [Hoar81]

As has been shown in this book, considerable empirical knowledge exists that can be communicated to computer scientists, and to software and system engineers. To grow as a profession, more work needs to be done on this. In this chapter, we will make some suggestions and point out some future research directions.

13.1 More on the laws and theories covered in the book

The 50 laws, 25 hypotheses and 12 conjectures cited in this book (and listed in Appendix 1), cover important aspects of software and systems engineering. They provide an agenda for empirical computer science and in our opinion, are pillars on which professional work can build, be it in research, development, distribution, installation, evolution and maintenance. They are not only part of the folklore, but are having significant impact in practice as well. They cover general areas, applicable to the entire field, and can be extremely useful if interpreted wisely.

We concede that not everybody can observe in his or her daily practice all the laws in this set, nor would he or she formulate them in exactly the way we did. As with all laws in science, our laws are idealizations. Using a characterization given by Chalmers [Chal99], laws of nature describe a tendency of things to behave in a certain manner. Reality is complex and there are always simultaneous operations at work that include other forces and tendencies. On the other hand, some people may call our laws obvious and trivial. This is unavoidable and it is partially a matter of the different views or paradigms guiding our work. As Kuhn [Kuhn70] in his discussion of paradigms points out: 'A law that cannot be demonstrated to one group of scientists may occasionally seem intuitively obvious to another'. Why should we be better off than science in general?

The laws in our set should not be seen as dogmas: they are not authorita-
tively asserted opinions. If proved wrong by objective and repeatable
observations, they should be reformulated or forgotten. Until this is done,
however, the laws we propose are the best we can come up with. They are
offered as signposts for those who look for orientation. By calling these
rules laws, we are also trying to suggest (perhaps cunningly!) that no professional should be allowed to ignore them. As an analogy consider a legal
situation, where not knowing a law (i.e. a rule of conduct established
through legislation) is not accepted as an argument for pleading non-guilty.
It could at least be considered as an act of professional malpractice if somebody openly works against laws that are well-established in the community.

With Fig. 13-1, we give a comparison of our laws with a list of heuristics
recently published by Boehm and Basili [Boeh01]. They try to summarize
the most important empirical results for which objective and quantitative
data exist. Seven of the ten items have been addressed by laws in this book,
as indicated by the reference in the right-hand column. In three cases, we
deviate somewhat from their assessment.

No.	Defect reduction item	Ref.
1.	Finding and fixing a software problem after delivery is often 100 times more expensive than finding and fixing it during the requirements and design phase	L2
2.	Current software projects spend about 40 to 50% of their effort on avoidable rework	(1)
3.	About 80% of the avoidable rework comes from 20% of the defects	L24
4.	About 80% of the defects come from 20% of the modules and about half the modules are defect free	L24
5.	About 90% of the downtime comes from, at most, 10% of the defects	L24
6.	Peer reviews catch 60% of the defects	L17
7.	Perspective-based reviews catch 35% more defects than non-directed reviews	L19
8.	Disciplined personal practices can reduce defect introduction rates by up to 75%	L35
9.	All other things being equal, it costs 50% more per source instruction to develop high-dependability software products than to develop low-dependability software products. However, the investment is more than worth it if significant operations and maintenance costs are involved	(2)
10.	About 40–50% of user programs contain non-trivial defects	(3)

Fig. 13-1 List of the top ten software defect reduction findings

1. We believe that item 2 is only true in an environment where no emphasis
   is placed on early error prevention. We addressed the error prevention
   concept under hypothesis 9 (H9).
2. Item 9 talks about high-dependability software. We agree that to meet
   high robustness criteria, considerable amounts of additional code may
   be necessary to correctly handle illegal input data. This is not the case
   for high-quality software in the sense of high-reliability, as explained in
   conjunction with hypothesis 8 (H8). The reference to operations and
   maintenance costs is more applicable to high-quality than to high-
   dependability software.

3. Item 10 is a rather pessimistic assessment of the current situation. Considering that a program's size may vary between 50 and 5 million LOC, the statement is not very precise, nor is it helpful in a constructive sense.

A similar list for COTS software [Basi01] was discussed in Chapter 4 under hypothesis 7 (H7). More work in this direction can be expected from an organization called Center for Empirically-Based Software Engineering (CeBASE).[1]

Certainly our theories can and should be improved. We are sure that many readers may have expected a different type of theory. Our theories are derived by digging deeper into the nature of the activity or the role of the intermediate products (as requirements or design) being generated. Frequently, they touch on human models and models of the social world, rather than those of the physical world around us. Only a few of them are mathematical in nature. The better we understand the strengths and weaknesses of human information processing and problem solving (in groups or alone), the better are the theories that we can develop for our field. Some readers may be disappointed that such fields as Shannon's information theory, Wiener's cybernetics, automata theory, formal languages, or the entire field of knowledge engineering and artificial intelligence do not appear. Unfortunately, we are unable to discern any empirical results from those fields that are applicable, either as laws or as theories.

Following Popper [Popp63], we tried to accept only such theories that are scientific in the sense that they are falsifiable. We therefore have no objections if our theories are refuted. Recognizing the importance of having a good theory does not mean that we can wait until we have it. It is not only engineering that precedes science. In medicine, also, it is easier to devise a cure, e.g. for Alzheimers, than to explain why a certain person became infected and others not. If we could know precisely the reason why something happens, we would have a chance to prevent it from occurring. We should also be aware that mono-causal relationships are often assumed where multiple causes may come into play. We should therefore strive for simple and robust theories. Contributions are welcome.

The theories we propose are what some authors call micro-theories. They primarily try to explain the individual laws. We have not attempted to develop a macro-theory that combines all of them. For us, it is debatable whether such a macro-theory really exists, and whether it is needed. Our theories also deviate from what Zendler [Zend01] calls a theory. His theories (a system of hypotheses that are connected) roughly correspond to our laws. Our laws are certainly connected, and could be grouped according to their width of applicability.

Our approach of deriving theories is to ask 'why' in the case of a law. Or, more precisely, what is the rationale for this law, its underlying reason? This usually leads us to a layer of science below the one we are on. This layer may lead to other questions of 'why?'. Many people hope that fewer different theories are needed the lower we get. By digging lower, we supposedly get to

---

[1] http://www.cebase.org/

'broader' theories. This is certainly the view of some physicists who hope that oneday they will find a single (grand unifying) theory of everything. This attitude is often labelled reductionism. As an example, the physicist Feynman [Feyn67] was strongly convinced that nature is simple and of great beauty. Whether the reason for this is a single act of creation or not is a metaphysical question. This belief is seldom found outside physics; it is obviously not popular in biology. Biology exhibits inherent complexity, mainly because it has gone through a lengthy process of evolution. We think that computing has more in common with biology (a science trying to understand a billion years of history) than with physics, although its history as a field is still very short. The social and human efforts involved show signs of historical evolution, however. They are clearly not the result of a single act of creation.

13.2 Frequency and quality of experiments

As stated in the introduction, there is still a scarcity of experiments and more need to be done. As pointed out by Tichy [Tich98], there are good reasons why more experiments should be done. Other sciences, such as physics and pharmacy, spend enormous sums on experiments, provided there is agreement among experts that the knowledge to be gained is important. Many experiments have internal and external validity problems. They are usually done with rather small groups, and often include trivial questions and results that do no more than confirm common sense. We have every reason to encourage people to keep going. By doing more experiments, people learn how to do them better, and then can ask more serious questions. As Bob Glass [Glas94] suggested, eventually academic researchers should strive to do empirical studies in industry. This is part of his vision for the year 2020. We believe that this step is due now.

Experiments usually follow innovations with a certain delay. They are not a substitute for new concepts. They are a necessary complement to new ideas, however, in the sense that they help to evaluate them. A specific point is that the data collected in a study should not be thrown away. Doing this would not only make the study suspicious, but it would deprive later investigations of the reference data they may need.

13.3 Research issues

In this book we have concentrated on those lessons learned which are backed by empirical studies. We have also pointed at some areas for which empirical investigations could be expected, for example, the area of distribution and installation. As pointed out by Tichy [Tich98], there are other very popular areas for which little empirical data exists, such as object-orientation, functional programming, and agile methods. Capers Jones complained two years ago that the multi-billion database industry seems to get along without agreed benchmarks for database systems [Jone00]. He was probably not aware that a partial solution exists through the benchmarks established by the suppliers of ERP software (such as SAP and Peoplesoft). We hope that, in the future, all these areas will be covered by firm knowledge derived from controlled experiments.

Taking the view of a practitioner, we expect that future research will address the following types of questions, which are all relevant to the discussions in this book:

1. How can we better identify both the domain and tacit knowledge for a certain application? How can it be distinguished from the procedural and computer-specific knowledge required for a good solution?
2. Can a better borderline be drawn between informal requirements and their formal representation through models or prototypes? The fact that many people unconsciously seem to cross this line causes many problems.
3. How can designs be evaluated with respect to their adequacy for the problem at hand or their value for the user rather than on their format or structure? Format and structure are less important from a user's point of view than they are for developers.
4. Can validation and verification methods be found that tie in with the requirements definition process? They should not require that a complete formal specification (or even a design) has to be provided before any conflicts can be discovered.
5. What properties of a system can be exhibited through static code analysis? As a complement, an indication should be given as to which properties cannot be determined in a given situation. It is the actual situation that counts, not the general case. Examples are range conflicts or termination problems (more on this below!).
6. Can a testing theory be developed that is constructive? Such a theory would allow us to verify selected properties of a system, and it would give reliable answers with a clearly defined limit.
7. How can experiments and case studies be conducted more easily in an industrial setting answering key questions relevant to a specific organization? This would help to avoid the not-applicable-here (NAH) syndrome.

As stated before, some of the theoretical work in computer science produces solutions in search of a problem. This is not all bad. In some cases, what is not considered a problem today may become a serious problem in ten years time. An example is cryptography. Nobody could expect that with the advent of the Internet, security protection would become the key issue. Good theoretical work often takes the direction of proving certain theoretical limits. The best known example of this type of result is the halting problem. Based on the Turing machine model, it could be shown that 'in the general case' it is impossible to prove that a program halts. For a practitioner, things look exactly the other way round. For any program he or she writes, he or she has to say clearly whether it terminates or not. Anything else is professionally irresponsible. He or she therefore needs help, showing case by case which programs terminate, and which do not. In other words, he or she would benefit from work done in a bottom-up fashion, rather than top-down. The same is true for a related problem, namely the equivalence of programs. Dijkstra's law as quoted in Chapter 6, is another example. The above list is intended to motivate researchers to look at problems whose solution would help practitioners.

13.4 Implications for education and practice

The education of computer professionals is caught in a constant dilemma. On the one hand, the market requires instantly usable knowledge. This is exemplified by the languages of the day: it used to be Fortran and COBOL 30 years ago; it is Java and C++ today. On the other hand, universities try to teach fundamental and lasting knowledge. For lack of genuine computer science content, many schools seem to escape to mathematics, the argument being that what is good for other engineers cannot do any harm (or, in a similar vein, learning Latin may be beneficial for a medical doctor). As a consequence, most computer science curricula still have an unusually high load of mathematics. Some of it could be dropped, because it takes away the students' most valuable resource, namely time. What is really needed is basic knowledge and long-lasting skills related to computing. To become an expert in this field requires more than the command of some notations or tools. We hope that this book has helped to identify such material.

The skills developed through empirical investigations should be transferred to students and professionals alike. Students should participate in repeatable experiments, such as those in physics as suggested by Lott and Rombach [Lott96]. For this we need more packaged experiments. Practitioners should be encouraged to make experiments in their environment to determine which methods are applicable. Looking at curricula for computer science, such as [IEEE01], we get the impression that the following message has not been received yet: software and systems engineering is more than development, nor does it end with development; distribution, installation, administration, and maintenance should also be taught. Today, and in the future, more people will be concerned about these aspects than about development. The same is true for technology assessment and user studies.

The biggest challenge for educators is to prepare people to become true professionals. We tend to train technical specialists only. Denning [Denn01] believes that one reason for this is that academics in our field are not practicing their profession. Most of them do not regularly design or evaluate systems. That is different in some other professions, such as law, medicine, and architecture. People we train should be encouraged to assume full professional responsibilities, and not just for certain technical aspects. To be able to do that they have to rely on proven concepts for the entire field. They have to know their own limitations and those of their methods and tools. They have to know where to get advice and how to evaluate it. They should build on knowledge, not on opinions. What we have called laws represents such knowledge.

13.5 Future of software and systems engineering

The importance of both these fields is likely to grow in the future. However, we should not create expectations that we cannot fulfill, we must be careful that our own aspirations do not grow faster than our abilities; and we should watch out for those simplifiers or charlatans who propagate cures that do not work. One example is those who say we should never write large programs. If these people lived by what they preach they would not use a phone, send an e-mail, drive a car, or fly by airplane. In all these cases the software systems that perform essential functions have grown to several million instructions. Tony Hoare's view, as given in the chapter epigraph, is the only realistic one.

Many people who complain about the disappointing state of software engineering point at the masses of low-skilled people who write software. This is really a strange discussion. Of course we want millions of people to be able to adapt computers to their needs, and industry will continue to support this trend by providing the appropriate tools. Spreadsheets are a good example: they are a great invention that purposely conceals the fact that people who use them are indeed programming. The technical community has therefore to solve two distinct problems: first, it has to tell these people (the layperson programmers) what to watch out for – even in the case of spreadsheets, no user is guarded against programming errors; second, it must provide the professional developers (the expert programmers) with a framework of principles, methods, and tools that allows them to produce high-quality products. The professional developers should be challenged and encouraged to set themselves apart from the layperson. They should have higher targets and should know how to meet them in a predictable way.

The question whether a field is science or not is often answered by pointing to the progress achieved. No doubt, in the professional part of software and systems engineering, progress can be found. However, it moves slowly; it is visible in decades rather than in months. We should achieve agreement what the key accomplishments of the field are. Only then will we know what should be transferred. The best way to transfer knowledge gained is by developing the appropriate skills in people. It is a poorer solution to try to introduce it into an ongoing process by means of regulations and bureaucracy.

Although we have been emphasizing empirical and scientific methods in this book, we want to make it very clear that we do not want to loose the creative or even artistic part of software and systems design. We need many more innovative solutions, even to old and boring problems. We like to have products that we enjoy, and that appeal to our aesthetic feeling. Science, technology, and art need not be in conflict; they can easily form a symbiosis. Its chances are best if we understand our science and master our technology.

13.6 Beyond observations, laws, and theories

Finally, we should like to put the views presented in this book into perspective. We will do this by referring to some ideas put forth by Roger Penrose [Penr89], a British mathematician and physicist. In his opinion, science will severely restrict itself if it only looks for laws that are algorithmic. In that case, we would be able to calculate the future given a certain set of preconditions. This is not only in conflict with the concept of free will, however, but also with reality. Our future is not computable from the past, although it is determined by it. Penrose postulates that science should also consider processes that are essentially lawless. Examples come from the two extremes of a spectrum. One is where large time frames or huge spaces are involved. It starts with cosmology and the biological evolution and ends with the daily weather. The other end of the spectrum is the sub-microscopic part of nature, namely quantum dynamics.

The processes to be observed in quantum dynamics are not computational or algorithmic. They may be deterministic or non-deterministic. The essential point is that they are non-reversible in time. In cosmology, the process of going from the big bang to black holes is certainly non-reversible, because there is information that is lost in a black hole. The entire field of tectonics has this character, leading to volcanism and earthquakes. Mathematical models to describe these types of processes are the subject of chaos theory. Here, processes are studied where small changes of the preconditions have a major influence on the outcome (the famous beat of wings of a butterfly that causes a thunderstorm elsewhere). Their application to systems and software engineering has not yet been fully investigated.

Another point we should like to discuss is what Penrose says about theories. He places them into four categories: superb, useful, tentative, and misguided. As examples of superb theories he quotes Euclidian geometry, Newton's mechanics, Einstein's relativity, and the quantum theory as originated by Planck, Heisenberg, and others. A useful theory of today is the big bang theory. The Ptolomaic world model was a useful one for many centuries, but not at all in the age of space flights. Most newer physical or cosmological theories he labels tentative. For the category misguided he does not give examples, giving as a reason that he does not want to lose half of his friends. As far as superb theories are concerned, Penrose believes that they not only survived the selection process of history, but must have some deep underlying rationale. On this scale, we consider our theories as tentative, or useful at best.

As stated in the Introduction to this book, children and scientists like to ask 'Why?'. We will therefore end this book by quoting the final questions of 'Why?' asked by Penrose at the end of his book. They stem from his preoccupation with cosmology and philosophy and go beyond what physicists normally ask. Some of the questions he leaves us with are: 'Why is there life on earth?' 'Why does human life lead to consciousness?' and 'Why is there a universe in which life (human or other) can actually be?' Penrose does not attempt to answer them by providing a theory. This is clearly beyond what science as we understand it today can do. It may remain so forever.

Summary of laws, hypotheses, and conjectures

In this appendix we give tabular overviews of all the laws, hypotheses, and conjectures cited in the book. The three tables list the 50 laws, 25 hypotheses, and 12 conjectures in the same sequence that they appear in the text. A reference to the page where a law or hypothesis is described, can be found via the Index (using the name as argument).

Summary of laws

No.	Name	Law
1	Glass	Requirement deficiencies are the prime source of project failures.
2	Boehm 1	Errors are most frequent during the requirements and design activities and are the more expensive the later they are removed.
3	Boehm 2	Prototyping (significantly) reduces requirement and design errors, especially for user interfaces.
4	Davis	The value of models depends on the view taken, but none is best for all purposes.
5	Curtis	Good designs require deep application domain knowledge.
6	Simon	Hierarchical structures reduce complexity.
7	Constantine	A structure is stable if cohesion is strong and coupling low.
8	Parnas	Only what is hidden can be changed without risk.
9	Denert	Separation of concerns leads to standard architectures.
10	Fitts– Shneiderman	Screen pointing-time is a function of distance and width.
11	DeRemer	What applies to small systems does not apply to large ones.
12	Corbató	Productivity and reliability depend on the length of a program's text, independent of language level used.
13	Dijkstra– Mills–Wirth	Well-structured programs have fewer errors and are easier to maintain.
14	Lanergan	The larger and more decentralized an organization, the more likely it is that it has reuse potential.
15	McIlroy	Software reuse reduces cycle time and increases productivity and quality.
16	Conway	A system reflects the organizational structure that built it.

No.	Name	Law
17	Fagan	Inspections significantly increase productivity, quality, and project stability.
18	Porter–Votta	Effectiveness of inspections is fairly independent of its organizational form.
19	Basili	Perspective-based inspections are (highly) effective and efficient.
20	Hetzel–Myers	A combination of different V&V methods outperforms any single method alone.
21	Sackman 1	Online debugging is more efficient than offline debugging.
22	Dijkstra	Testing can show the presence but not the absence of errors.
23	Weinberg	A developer is unsuited to test his or her code.
24	Pareto–Zipf	Approximately 80 percent of defects come from 20 percent of modules.
25	Gray–Serlin	Performance testing benefits from system-level benchmarks.
26	Nielsen–Norman	Usability is quantifiable.
27	Lehman 1	A system that is used will be changed.
28	Lehman 2	An evolving system increases its complexity, unless work is done to reduce it.
29	Lehman 3	System evolution is determined by a feedback process.
30	Basili–Möller	Smaller changes have a higher error density than large ones.
31	Sackman 2	Individual developer performance varies considerably.
32	Nelson–Jones	A multitude of factors influence developer productivity.
33	Boehm 3	Development effort is a (non-linear) function of product size.
34	DeMarco–Glass	Most cost estimates tend to be too low.
35	Humphrey	Mature processes and personal discipline enhance planning, increase productivity, and reduce errors.
36	Brooks	Adding manpower to a late project makes it later.
37	Baumol	Products replace services through productivity gains.
38	Kupfmüller	Humans receive most information through the visual system and store it in a spatially organized memory.
39	Gestalt	Humans tend to structure what they see to form cohesive patterns.
40	Miller	Short-term memory is limited to 7 ± 2 chunks of information.
41	Krause	Multimodal information is easier to remember than single mode.
42	Librarian	The more knowledge that is available, the more effort has to be spent on the processes to use it.
43	Apprentice	It takes 5000 hours to turn a novice into an expert.
44	Maslow–Herzberg	Human needs and desires are strictly prioritized.
45	Moore	The price/performance of processors is halved every 18 months.
46	Hoagland	The capacity of magnetic devices increases by a factor of ten every decade.
47	Cooper	Wireless bandwidth doubles every 2.5 years.
48	Morris–Ferguson	Architecture wins over technology.
49	Metcalfe	The value of a network increases with the square of its users.
50	Bayes	The probability that a hypothesis is true increases the more unlikely the new event is that confirms this hypothesis.

No.	Name	Hypothesis
1	Booch 1	Object model reduces communication problems between analysts and users.
2	Booch 2	Object-oriented designs reduce errors and encourage reuse.
3	Bauer–Zemanek	Formal methods significantly reduce design errors, or eliminate them early.
4	Gamma	Reusing designs through patterns yields faster and better maintenance.
5	Dahl–Goldberg	Object-oriented programming reduces errors and encourages reuse.
6	Beck–Fowler	Agile programming methods reduce the impact of requirement changes.
7	Basili–Boehm	COTS-based software does not eliminate the key development risks.
8	Mills–Jones	Quality entails productivity.
9	Mays	Error prevention is better than error removal.
10	Hoare	Proving programs solves the problems of correctness, documentation, and compatibility.
11	Gutjahr	Partition testing is more effective than random testing.
12	Weyuker	The adequacy of a coverage criterion can only be intuitively defined.
13	Endres–Glatthaar	The test suite needed to verify an arithmetic path expression can be determined.
14	Hamlet	Suspicion-based testing can be more effective than most other approaches.
15	McCabe	Complexity metrics are good predictors of post-release reliability and maintainability.
16	Wilde	Object-oriented programs are difficult to maintain.
17	Boehm	Project risks can be resolved or mitigated by addressing them early.
18	McGregor	Motivation requires integration and participation.
19	Hawthorne	Group behavior depends on the level of attention given.
20	Marketer	One unsatisfied customer can hurt more than two satisfied customers can help.
21	Shaw–Garlan	A sound architecture significantly reduces development and maintenance costs.
22	Bayer	In spite of disk capacity increases, data access can be kept efficient.
23	Codd	Databases can be independent of devices and applications.
24	Engelbart	Conceptual integrity is the result of a consistent mental model.
25	Basili–Rombach	Measurements require both goals and models.

No.	Conjecture
1	For COTS products, costs and risks of manufacturing can approach those of development.
2	Distribution ends where the customer wants it to end.
3	Prevention of software piracy by technical means is almost impossible.
4	Installability must be designed in.
5	The larger the system, the greater the administration effort that is needed.
6	Any system can be tuned.
7	Human-based methods can only be studied empirically.
8	Process improvements require action-based feedback.
9	Learning is best accelerated by a combination of controlled experiments and case studies.
10	Measurements are always based on actually used models rather than on desired ones.
11	Empirical results are transferable only if abstracted and packaged with context.
12	Empirically based models mature from understanding to explaining and predicting capability.

Biographies of pioneers and key contributors

In this section, short biographies are given of key contributors to the empirical knowledge in software and systems engineering (as well as of the authors of this book). Their names have been associated with the laws and hypotheses formulated in this book. Pictures are provided for all authors of the epigraphs used in the chapter headings.[1] We shall regard them as the pioneers who moved the empirical aspects of our field forward.

Basili, Victor R.: Professor of Computing Science at the University of Maryland and Executive Director Fraunhofer Center Maryland, College Park, MD. Principal Investigator NSF Center for Empirically Based Software Engineering (CeBASE); Director of the Software Engineering Laboratory; founder and member of International Software Engineering Research Network (ISERN); Editor-in-chief of the Empirical Software Engineering. Ph.D. in computer science from University of Texas at Austin, TX (1970).

Bauer, Friedrich Ludwig: Professor Emeritus in Mathematics and Informatics, Technical University Munich since 1989; Full Professor Informatics (1972–89) and Mathematics (1963–72) Technical University Munich; Full Professor, Applied Mathematics Mainz University (1962–3); Associate Professor, Applied Mathematics Mainz University (1958–62); patents on error detecting and correcting codes (1953) and on the stack principle (1957); organizer (1968) of the Garmisch Conference on Software Engineering, and of the International Summer School Marktoberdorf (1970–91), both sponsored by the NATO Science Committee.

Baumol, William J.: Senior Research Economist and Professor of Economics, Emeritus, Princeton University, since 1992; Professor of Economics and Director, C.V. Starr Center for Applied Economics, New York University, since

---

[1] The photos in this section were either taken by the authors or kindly provided by the subjects themselves. The text originates from publicly available sources, unless stated otherwise.

1971; Professor of Economics, Princeton University (1949–92); Assistant Lecturer, London School of Economics (1947–9); Ph.D. University of London (1949); Past President, American Economic Association (1981), Association of Environmental and Resource Economists (1979), Eastern Economic Association (1978–9), Atlantic Economic Society (1985).

Bayer, Rudolf: Professor of Informatics, Technical University of Munich, Germany, since 1972; Head of research group on knowledge bases in Bavarian research center on Knowledge Based Systems; co-founder of TransAction software company; Associate Professor Purdue University (1970–2); Senior Research Scientist at Boeing Research Labs, Seattle (1966–70); Ph.D. in Mathematics from University of Illinois (1966); recipient ACM/SIGMOD Innovations Award for the development of B-trees (2001); holds two software patents.

Bayes, Thomas: 1702–61, English clergyman and mathematician. Although he wrote on theology, e.g., Divine Benevolence (1731), Bayes is best known for his two mathematical works, *Introduction to the Doctrine of Fluxions* (1736), a defense of the logical foundations of Newton's calculus against the attack of Bishop Berkeley, and *Essay Towards Solving a Problem in the Doctrine of Chances* (1763). The latter, pioneering work attempts to establish that the rule for determining the probability of an event is the same whether or not anything is known antecedently to any trials or observations concerning the event. *Source*: The Columbia Encyclopedia, 6th Edition, 2001.[2]

Beck, Kent: Owns and operates First Class Software, Inc. from a ranch in southern Oregon, near the town of Merlin. Consults with Smalltalk developers, and develops Smalltalk tools. Graduate in Architecture from University of Oregon.

Boehm, Barry W.: Professor Software Engineering and Director Center of Software Engineering University of Southern California, Marina del Rey, CA. Prior to that with US Department of Defense as Director of the DARPA Information Science and Technology Office, and as Director of the Software and Computer Technology Office (1989–92); at TRW (1973–89), culminating as Chief Scientist of the Defense Systems Group, and at the Rand Corporation (1959–73), culminating as Head of the Information Sciences Department; Programmer-Analyst at General Dynamics (1955–9); M.S. and Ph.D. from UCLA (1961 and 1964).

Booch, Grady: With Rational Software Corporation as Chief Scientist since its foundation in 1980. One of the original developers of the Unified Modeling Language (UML) (together with I. Jacobson and J. Rumbaugh) and of Rational's products including Rational Rose. Author of several best-selling books on Object Orientation and UML. MSEE from the University of California at Santa Barbara (1979).

---

[2] http://www.bartleby.com/65/ba/Bayes-Th.html

Brooks, Frederick Phillips, Jr: Professor of Computer Science at University of North Carolina, Chapel Hill, NC. Prior to that with IBM Corporation in Poughkeepsie, New York: Manager of Operating System/360 (1964–5); Manager, System/360 Hardware Development (1961–4); Systems Planning Manager (1960–1). Adjunct Assistant Professor Columbia University (1960-1); Ph.D., Harvard University (1956); holds several patents.

Codd, Edgar F.: IBM Fellow; IBM Research Laboratory Almaden, CA. Joined IBM in 1949 to prepare programs for the Selective Sequence Electronic Calculator; worked later on the IBM 701 and Stretch computers. B.A. and M.A. from Oxford University, England, M.Sc. and Ph.D. from University of Michigan; ACM Turing Award (1981).

Constantine, Larry L.: Professor of Computing Sciences at University of Technology, Sydney; Principal Consultant with consulting firm of Constantine & Lockwood, Ltd. Graduate of the Sloan School of Management at MIT.

Conway, Melvin E.: Was with US Airforce Directorate of Computers at L.G. Hanscom Field, Bedford, MA; co-developed the MUMPS operating system; wrote an assembler for the Burroughs 220 and a COBOL compiler for the Univac computer about 1960.

Cooper, Martin: Chairman and chief executive officer of ArrayComm, San José, CA.

Corbató, Fernando J.: Professor Emeritus Department of Electrical Engineering and Computer Science at MIT since 1996; Professor of Engineering (1965–96); Associate Professor (1962–5); associated with the MIT Computation Center from its organization in 1956 until 1966; led the development of the Compatible Time-Sharing System (CTSS) and was a founding member of Project MAC (1963) which produced the Multics (Multiplexed Information and Computing Service) operating system, the precursor of UNIX; Ph.D. from MIT in Physics (1956); ACM Turing Award (1990).

Curtis, Bill: Senior consultant with Cutter Consortium, Arlington, MA; co-founder and chief scientist of TeraQuest Metrics, a firm that provides consulting and training in process improvement. While at the Software Engineering Institute (SEI), Pittsburgh, PA, he led the team that published the Capability Maturity Model for Software (Software CMM). Prior to that, at MCC Research in Austin, TX, and the ITT Programming Technology Center in Stratford, CT.

Dahl, Ole-Johan: Prior to his death in 2002, Professor of Informatics, Oslo University; invented Simula (together with Kristen Nygaard).

Davis, Alan Michael: Founder and President of Omni-Vista, a software consultant company in Colorado Springs, CO, and Professor of Computer Science at the University of Colorado; Ph.D. in computer science from University of Illinois.

DeMarco, Tom: Principal of the Atlantic Systems Guild, and a Fellow of the Cutter Consortium, Arlington, MA. He had managed real-time projects for CEGOS Informatique in France, and was responsible for distributed online banking systems installed in Sweden, Holland, France and Finland. Before that, he was on the ESS-1 project at Bell Telephone Laboratories; M.S. from Columbia University and a diploma from the University of Paris at the Sorbonne.

Denert, Ernst: General manager IVU Traffic Technologies, Berlin, and Chairman of the Supervisory Board of sd&m, Munich, since 2001. Honorary professor and honorary senator at the Technical University in Munich. In 1982, together with Ulf Maiborn, founded sd&m (Software Design & Management) and turned it into a leading software and consulting company, which currently has approximately 850 employees. Joined Softlab, Munich, in 1976 where he was responsible for large-scale projects (e.g. the travel planning and reservation system START) as well as developing methods and tools for software engineering; Ph.D. in Computer Science (1976) and a Diploma in Telecommunications (1972) from the Technical University in Berlin.

DeRemer, Frank: Chairman, Metaware, San José, CA; University of California in Santa Cruz, CA before that.

Dijkstra, Edsger Wybe: Prior to his death in 2002, Professor of Computer Sciences at University of Texas, Austin, TX. Fellow Burroughs Corporation; Professor of Mathematics University of Eindhoven, Netherlands; Ph.D. (1959) University of Amsterdam, Doctoral degree Theoretical Physics (1956) University of Leyden; Candidate degree Mathematics and Physics (1951); ACM Turing Award (1972).

Endres, Albert: Honorary Professor in Computer Science at the University of Stuttgart (since 1986); full Professor of Computer Science at Technical University of Munich (1993–7). With IBM Germany from 1957 to 1992. From 1965 to retirement, software development manager at the IBM laboratory in Boeblingen, Germany. Responsible for compiler, operating system, and database system developments. Also experience in system architecture, performance evaluation and software tools development. Prior to that, system software developer at the IBM laboratories in La Gaude, France, New York City and Poughkeepsie, NY. From 1957 to 1962, application programmer in Sindelfingen, Germany, and data center manager in Düsseldorf, Germany; Ph.D. from University of Stuttgart (1975); diploma in engineering (Dipl. Ing.) from University of Bonn (1957).

Engelbart, Douglas: Director, Bootstrap Institute, Palo Alto, CA, since 1990; part-time Visiting Scholar at Stanford University; Director, Bootstrap Project, Stanford University (1989–90); Senior Scientist, McDonnell Douglas ISG, San Jose, CA (1984–9); Senior Scientist, Tymshare, Inc., Cupertino, CA (1977–84);

Director, Augmentation Research Center, Stanford Research International (1959–77); Researcher, Stanford Research Institute (1957–9); Assistant Professor electrical engineering, University of California at Berkeley (1955–6); Ph.D. University of California at Berkeley in 1955; ACM Turing Award (1997); IEEE Computer Pioneer Award (1993).

Fagan, Michael: Chairman, Michael Fagan Associates Palo Alto, CA, since 1989; about 20 years with IBM as a line manager of software development, engineering development, and manufacturing. In addition, manager of programming methodology for IBM's DP Product Group (Worldwide); Senior Technical Staff Member at IBM's T.J. Watson Research Laboratory; member of the Corporate Technology Staff; and one of the founder members of the IBM Quality Institute. Visiting Professor, Department of Computer Science, University of Maryland (1983–5)

Ferguson, Charles H.: Lecturer at UC Berkeley Graduate School of Journalism; former Visiting Scholar, Center for International Studies, Massachusetts Institute of Technology (MIT); co-founder and former chairman and CEO, Vermeer Technologies, Cambridge, MA; Senior Staff Member, MIT Commission on Industrial Productivity; Software Technology Analyst, IBM; Ph.D. Massachusetts Institute of Technology (1989).

Fitts, P.M.: Experimental psychologist, associated with the US Airforce, Washington, DC.

Fowler, Martin: Chief Scientist at ThoughtWorks, a software consulting company in Chicago, IL, since 2000; before that, independent consultant (1991–2000) and software practitioner (since 1988).

Gamma, Erich: Senior Object Consultant with IFA, a training company in Zürich, Switzerland, since 2001; lab director of Object Technology International in Zürich, (1999–2001); previously held positions with Taligent, an IBM subsidiary (1993–9), and Union Bank of Switzerland (1988-1991); Ph.D. in Computer Science from University of Zürich (1988).

Garlan, David: Assistant Professor of Computer Science at Carnegie Mellon University, Pittsburgh, PA, since 1990; previously with Textronics, Inc., in Oregon; Ph.D. from Carnegie Mellon University in Pittsburgh, PA.

Glass, Robert L.: President of Computing Trends, a publishing company in Bloomington, IN; active in the field of computing and software for over 40 years, largely in industry (1988–present and 1954–82), but also as an academic (1982–8).

Glatthaar, Wolfgang: Director of information systems and organization at DZ Bank, Frankfurt since 1996; with IBM Germany from 1977 to 1996; last position director of Science and Technology; Ph.D. in Computer Science from University of Stuttgart (1974); Diploma in Mathematics and Physics from University of Tübingen (1972); Vice-president and President of German Informatics Society (1992–4); Honorary Professor University of Chemnitz since 1992.

Goldberg, Adele E.: Joined Xerox PARC in 1973, founded ParcPlace Systems in 1988; President of the ACM (1984–6); ACM Systems Software Award (1987), jointly with Alan Kay and Dan Ingalls.

Gray, Jim: Senior researcher and distinguished engineer in Microsoft's Scaleable Servers Research Group and manager of Microsoft's Bay Area Research Center (BARC) in San Francisco, CA; with Microsoft since 1995; was with Digital Equipment (1990–5) and Tandem Computers in Cupertino, CA (1980–90); prior to that with IBM Research in San José, CA, and Yorktown Heights, NY; Ph.D. in Computer Science from University of California at Berkeley; ACM Turing Award (1998).

Gutjahr, Walter J.: Professor in the Department of Statistics and Decision Support, University of Vienna, Austria, since 1993; with Siemens Austria as Manager of Software Quality Assurance (1980–88); Ph.D. in mathematics (1985).

Hamlet, Richard G.: Professor in the Department of Computer Science at Portland State University; Ph.D. in Computer Science from University of Washington (1971).

Herzberg, Frederick I. (1923–2000): Was professor at the University of Utah's College of Business in Salt Lake City since 1972; before that Professor of Management at Case Western Reserve, Cleveland OH; graduate degrees from the University of Pittsburgh, PA.

Hetzel, William C.: Chairman of Software Quality Engineering, Jacksonville, FL; independent software consultant; author of several books on software testing. Ph.D. in Computer Science from University of North Carolina at Chapel Hill, NC (1976).

Hoagland, Albert S.: Director of the Institute for Information Storage Technology at Santa Clara University, and Professor of Electrical Engineering in the School of Engineering, since his retirement from IBM; with IBM for many years, key responsibilities on the first magnetic disk drive, the RAMAC; held major positions in both research and development, e.g. Director for Technical Planning for the IBM Research Division; Ph.D. from University of California at Berkeley, CA.

Hoare, Sir Charles Anthony Richard (Tony): Professor Emeritus at Oxford University, UK; Leading Researcher at Microsoft Research Cambridge, UK since 1999; Professor in Computing at Oxford University (1977–99); Professor of Computer Science at Queen's University Belfast, Northern Ireland (1968–77); with Elliot Brothers, Ltd (1960–68); Distinguished Fellow of the British Computer Society (1978); ACM Turing Award (1980).

Humphrey, Watts S.: Founded the Software Process Program of the Software Engineering Institute (SEI) at Carnegie Mellon University, Pittsburgh, PA; Fellow of the Institute and a research scientist on its staff (1986–96); was associated with the IBM Corporation from 1959 to 1986 where his last position was Director of Programming Quality and Process; holds five US patents; M.A. in Business Administration from University of Chicago; B.S. in physics from Illinois Institute of Technology.

Jones, Capers: Founder and past chairman of Software Productivity Research (SPR) of Burlington, MA; was with the ITT Programming Technology Center in Stratford, CT, and with IBM in Santa Teresa, CA, before that.

Krause, Werner: Retired Professor of Psychology at the Friedrich Schiller University in Jena, Germany.

Kupfmüller, Karl: Was Professor of Electrical Engineering at the University of Stuttgart, Germany.

Lanergan, R.G.: Head of Information Systems Department at Raytheon Corporation (1979).

Lehman, Meir M. (Manny): Professor of Computing at Imperial College of Science, Technology and Medicine, in London; with IBM research laboratory Yorktown Heights, NY, before that.

Maslow, Abraham: Professor at Brandeis University (1951–69), and then resident fellow of the Laughlin Institute in California; died in 1970; from 1937 to 1951 was on the faculty of Brooklyn College, NY where he found two mentors, anthropologist Ruth Benedict and Gestalt psychologist Max Wertheimer. Before that, he did research at Columbia University, NY, where he had contact with the Freudian psychologist Alfred Adler; Ph.D. and M.A. in Psychology from the University of Wisconsin (1934, 1932).

Mays, Richard: Software developer at the IBM development laboratory in Raleigh, NC.

McCabe, Thomas J.: Founded McCabe & Associates in 1977; providing products and services for software analysis and testing; was with the US Dept of Defense and the National Security Agency at Ft Meade, MD, before that.

McGregor, Douglas: Professor of Management at MIT (1954–64) and management consultant; first full-time psychologist on the faculty of MIT; died in 1964; President of Antioch College (1948–54); district manager for a retail gasoline merchandising firm before that; Ph.D. and M.A. in Psychology at Harvard; B.A. at Wayne State University.

McIlroy, Douglas M.: Adjunct Professor in Department of Computer Science at Dartmouth College, Hanover, NH, since 1996; also Distinguished Member of Technical Staff in the Computing Sciences Research Center at Bell Laboratories (formerly AT&T, now Lucent Technologies); was head of the Computing Techniques Research Department from 1965 to 1986; participated in the design of PL/I, contributed to C++, and has written unusual compilers for Lisp, ALTRAN (an algebraic manipulation system), PL/I, and TMG (a compiler-compiler). He conceived 'pipes' as realized in the UNIX operating system and wrote several of the original Unix routines; joined Bell Laboratories in 1958 after earning a Ph.D. in Applied Mathematics from MIT.

Metcalfe, Robert M.: With International Data Group (IDG) since 1992; vice president of technology since 1993. In 1979, founded 3COM Corporation, a computer networking company; held various positions including Chairman, Chief Executive Officer, President, Division General Manager, and Vice President of Sales and Marketing. Ph.D. in Computer Science from Harvard in 1973. Associate Professor of Electrical Engineering at Stanford University. Since 1972, member of research staff at Xerox Palo Alto Research Center, where he invented the Ethernet.

Miller, George A.: Professor of Psychology, Emeritus, Department of Psychology at Princeton University.

Mills, Harlan D.: At the time of his death in 1996, he was Professor of Computer Science at the Florida Institute of Technology and the Director of the Information Systems Institute, Vero Beach, FL. Was with IBM from 1964 to 1987. He was Director of Software Engineering and Technology for the Federal Systems Division, a member of the IBM Corporate Technical Committee, and an IBM Fellow (1981); best known as the originator of the Cleanroom Development and the Chief Programmer Team concept. Prior to and during his industrial career he served on the faculties of Iowa State, Princeton, New York, Johns Hopkins Universities, and the University of Maryland. Before joining IBM, he worked at GE and RCA; Ph.D. in Mathematics from Iowa State University (1952).

Möller, Karl-Heinz: Formerly with Siemens Corporation in Munich, Germany. Ph.D.

Moore, Gordon E.: Chairman Emeritus of Intel Corporation, since 1997; co-founded Intel in 1968, serving initially as Executive Vice President; was President and Chief Executive Officer from 1975 until 1987; Ph.D. in Chemistry and Physics from the California Institute of Technology.

Morris, C.R.: With Harvard University, Cambridge, MA (1993).

Myers, Glenford J. Co-founder and chairman of RadiSys Corporation in Hillsboro, OR since 1987; Manager of Microprocessor Product Line Architecture and Manager of the Microprocessor Strategic Business Segment at Intel (1981–7). While at Intel responsible for the feasibility and design of Intel's 286 and 80960 microprocesor chips. Various engineering and management positions with IBM (1968–81). Ph.D. from the Polytechnic Institute of New York.

Nelson, Edward A.: With the System Development Corporation (1968).

Nielsen, Jacob: Principal of the Nielsen Norman Group, which he co-founded in 1998 with Donald A. Norman; was a Sun Microsystems Distinguished Engineer before that; holds 61 US patents, mainly on ways of making the Internet easier to use. Ph.D. in computer science from Technical University of Denmark.

Norman, Donald A.: Professor of Computer Science, Northwestern University, Evanston, IL, since 2001; co-founder of the Nielsen Norman Group; Vice President and Apple Fellow, Apple Computer Inc., Cupertino, CA. (1993–7); Lecturer and Research Fellow, Department of Psychology and Center for Cognitive Studies, Harvard University (1962–6); Instructor, Moore School of Electrical Engineering, University of Pennsylvania (1957–9); Ph.D. in Mathematical Psychology (1962) and M.S. in Electrical Engineering (1959), both from University of Pennsylvania.

Pareto, Vilfredo: Italian economist and sociologist (1848–1923), became professor of political economy at the University of Lausanne (in 1893); had studied mathematics and engineering in Turin and worked as an engineer for many years.

Parnas, David Lorge: Professor Computing and Software, McMaster University, Hamilton, Ontario; before that Professor at the University of Victoria, the Technische Hochschule Darmstadt, the University of North Carolina at Chapel Hill, Carnegie Mellon University and the University of Maryland. Also advisor Philips Computer Industry, Apeldoorn (Netherlands), the US Naval Research Laboratory in Washington, DC and the IBM Federal Systems Division. B.S.,
M.S. and Ph.D. in Electrical Engineering from Carnegie Mellon University, Pittsburgh, PA; licensed as a Professional Engineer in the Province of Ontario.

Porter, Adam A.: Associate Professor, Department of Computer Science, University of Maryland, College Park, MD.

Rombach, H. Dieter: Full Professor in the Department of Computer Science at the University of Kaiserslautern, Germany; Director of the Fraunhofer Institute for Experimental Software Engineering (IESE) in Kaiserslautern. Its aim is to shorten the time needed for transferring research technologies into industrial practice. From 1984 to 1991 he held faculty positions with the Computer Science Department at the University of Maryland, College Park, MD, and was project leader in the Software Engineering Laboratory (SEL), a joint venture between NASA, Goddard Space Flight Center, Computer Sciences Corporation, and the University of Maryland. Ph.D. in Computer Science from the University of Kaiserslautern, Germany (1984); M.S. in Mathematics and Computer Science from the University of Karlsruhe (1978).

Sackman, H: Formerly researcher at Rand Corporation, Santa Monica, CA.

Serlin, Omri: Chairman of the Transaction Processing Performance Council (TPC)(1988–2000); founder and principal of ITOM International Co., publisher of an industry newsletter; B.S. and M.S. degrees in Electrical Engineering.

Shaw, Mary: Professor of Computer Science at Carnegie Mellon University, Pittsburgh, PA, since 1987; from 1984–7, Chief Scientist of Carnegie Mellon's Software Engineering Institute.

Shneiderman, Ben: Professor of Computer Science at University of Maryland, College Park, MD; Ph.D. State University of New York, Stony Brook, NY; B.S. City College New York, NY.

Simon, Herbert Alexander: Professor of Computer Science and Psychology at Carnegie Mellon University, Pittsburgh, from 1949 until his death in 2001; proposed, together with Allen Newell, the General Problem Solver, the first AI program (1956); with the Illinois Institute of Technology, Chicago, from 1942 to 1949; Ph.D. from the University of California, Berkeley (1942); M.A. from the University of Chicago (1936) in Economics and Political Science; Nobel Prize in economics (1978); ACM Turing Award (1975).

Votta, Larry G: With Motorola, Schaumburg, IL, USA; before that with Bell Labs, Lucent Technologies, Morristown, NJ.

Weinberg, Gerald M.: Professor of Computer Science, State University of New York in Binghampton, NY; formed consulting firm of Weinberg & Weinberg in 1969.

Weyuker, Elaine J.: Technology Leader in the Large-Scale Programming Research organization at AT&T Labs; was a professor at New York University for 18 years before that; Ph.D. in computer science from Rutgers University (1977); M.S.E. in Computer and Information Sciences from University of Pennsylvania (1968).

Wilde, Norman: Professor in Computer Science at University of West Florida in Pensacola, FL; Ph.D. in Mathematics and Operations Research from MIT.

Wirth, Niklaus: Retired Professor of Computer Science at the Federal Institute of Technology (ETH), Zurich, Switzerland, since 1999. Had obtained that position in 1968. Before that, he was Assistant Professor of Computer Science at Stanford University (1963–7), and then at the University of Zurich (1967–8); Ph.D. from the University of California at Berkeley (1963); M.Sc. from Laval University, Canada (1960); Diploma degree in Electronics Engineering from the ETH in Zurich (1959); ACM Turing Award (1984), IEEE Computer Society's computer pioneer award, IBM Europe Science and Technology Prize.

Zemanek, Heinz: Retired Professor of Computer Science at the Technical University of Vienna and former director IBM Laboratory Vienna (1961–75); later he was IBM Fellow (1975–85). Led the building and programming of the pioneer computer 'Mailüfterl' (1954–61) and the design of the Vienna Definition Language and Method (VDL and VDM). Ph.D. from University of Technology Vienna (1951), the 'venia legendi' (teaching privilege) in 1958 and the title of professor in 1964. From 1947 to 1961, was assistant professor at this university; was Vice-president and President of IFIP (1968–74), and founded the Austrian Computer Society.

Zipf, George Kingsley: Professor in Linguistics at Harvard University (1902–50).

On-going projects/research groups

Since 1998, several academic and industrial research groups worldwide have made the paradigm shift to an experimental software engineering view. Each of these groups is producing software engineering models valid within their local laboratory environments. In order to take the next step towards building the basic models and components of the entire software engineering discipline, we have to be able to abstract from the characteristics of specific environments. No single research group is able to provide the laboratory environment necessary to learn about variations in the effects of technologies across multiple environments and influential factors. These goals led to the formation of the International Software Engineering Research Network (ISERN). whose members are listed here.[1]

Member site	Contact	Address
Blekinge TH, Sweden	C. Wohlin	Blekinge Institute of Technology, S-371 79 Karlskrona, Sweden
Carleton University, Canada	L. C. Briand	Carleton University, Department of System and Computer Engineering, Ottawa, Canada
Central Research Institute of Electric Power Industry, Tokyo, Japan	M. Takahashi	Communication and Information Research Laboratory, Central Research Institute of Electric Power Industry, 2-11-1, Iwado-Kita, Komae, Tokyo 20, Japan
COPPE, Rio de Janeiro, Brazil	G. H. Travassos	Università Federal Rio de Janeiro, Systems Engineering and Computer Science Program, Bloco H, Sl. 319, Centro de Tecnologia Cid. Universitária Rio de Janeiro, Brazil
Daimler-Chrysler Research Center, Germany	F. Houdek	Daimler-Chrysler, Forschung & Technik, Postfach 2360, D-89013 Ulm
Ericsson Radio Systems AB, Linköping, Sweden	K. Sandahl	Ericsson Radio Systems AB, ZeLab – Systems Engineering Lab, Box 12 48, S-581 12 Linköping, Sweden

---

[1] For an update of this list refer to http://www.iese.fhg.de/network/ISERN/pub/

Member site	Contact	Address
Fraunhofer Center, Maryland, USA	M. Zelkowitz	Fraunhofer Center, Maryland, University of Maryland, Ag/Life Sciences Surge Bldg. (296), Room 3115, College Park, MD 20742, USA
Fraunhofer Institute for Experimental Software Engineering, Germany	A. Jedlitschka	Fraunhofer IESE, Sauerwiesen 6, D-67661 Kaiserslautern, Germany
Lucent Technologies – Bell Laboratories, USA	A. Mockus	Lucent Technologies, Bell Laboratories, Room IHC 16-347, 1000 E. Warrenville Road, Naperville, IL 60566, USA
Lund University, Sweden	M. Hoest	Department of Communication Systems, Lund Institute of Technology, Lund University, Box 118, S-221 00 Lund, Sweden
Motorola, USA	L.G. Votta	Motorola , Schaumburg IL, USA
Nara Institute of Science and Technology, Japan	K. Torii	NAIST, Graduate School of Inf. Science, 8916-5, Takayama-cho, Ikoma, Nara 630-01, Japan
National Space Development Agency of Japan	M. Katahira	National Space Development Agency of Japan, Tokyo, Japan
Norwegian University of Technology & Science, Norway	R. Conradi	Dept. of Computer Science and Telematics, NTH, N-7034 Trondheim, Norway
NTT Data Corporation, Japan	T. Hayama	NTT Data Corp., Laboratory for Information Technology, Kowa-Kawasaki-Nishi 9F, 66-2 Horikawa-cho Saiwai-ku, Kawasaki 210, Japan
Politechnico Madrid, Spain	N. Juristo	Universidad Politécnica de Madrid, Departamento de Lenguajes y Sistemas Informáticos e Ingeniería del Software, Madrid, Spain
Quality Laboratories Sweden AB (Q-Labs), Sweden	G. Fagerhus	Q-Labs, Ideon Research Park, S-223 70 Lund, Sweden
Solid Information Technologies, Finland	M. Oivo	Solid Information Technologies, Inc., FIN-90570 Oulu, Finland
Telcordia, USA	C. M. Lott	Telcordia Technologies, Morris Corporate Center, 445 South Street, Morristown, NJ 07960-6438, USA
TU Vienna, Austria	S. Biffl	Technische Universität Wien, Karlsplatz 13, A-1040 Wien, Austria
Univerity of Southern California, USA	B. W. Boehm	University of Southern California, Los Angeles CA, USA
Universitá degli Studi di Roma 'Tor Vergata', Italy	G. Cantone	Universitá degli Studi di Roma 'Tor Vergata', Dipartimento di Informatica, Via della Ricerca Scientifica, I-00133 Roma, Italy
University of Alberta	J. Miller	University of Alberta, Canada
University of Bari, Italy	G. Visaggio	Universitá di Bari, Dipartimento di Informatica, Via Orabona 4, 70126 Bari, Italy

Member site	Contact	Address
University of Calgary	G. Ruhe	University of Calgary, Canada
University of Hawaii, USA	P. Johnson	Department of Information and Computer Sciences, University of Hawaii, 2565 The Mall, Honolulu, HI 96822, USA
University of Kaiserslautern, Germany	H. D. Rombach	AG Software Engineering, FB Informatik, Geb. 57, Universität Kaiserslautern, P.O. 3049, D-67653 Kaiserslautern, Germany
University of Maryland, Baltimore County, USA	C. Seaman	University of Maryland, Baltimore County, 1000 Hilltop Circle, Baltimore, MD 21250, USA
University of Maryland, College Park, MD, USA	V. R. Basili	Institute for Adv. Comp. Studies, Department of Computer Science, University of Maryland, College Park MD 20742, USA
University of New South Wales, Australia	R. Jeffery	University of New South Wales, Department of Information Systems, Sydney 2052, Australia
University of Oslo	D. Sjøberg	University of Oslo, Norway
University of Sao Paulo, Brazil	J. C. Maldonado	University of São Paulo – Campus of São Carlos, Brazil
University of Strathclyde, Scotland, UK	M. Wood	Department of Computer Science, University of Strathclyde, Glasgow G1 1XH, Scotland, UK
VTT Electronics, Finland	S. Komi-Sirviö	VTT Electronics, PO Box 1100, FIN-90571 Oulu, Finland

References

[Abde91]   Abdel-Hamil, T., Madnick, S.: *Software Project Dynamics: An Integrated Approach*. Englewood Cliffs, NJ: Prentice Hall 1991

[Acke96]   Ackermann, P.: *Developing Object-Oriented Multimedia Software – Based on the MET++ Application Framework*. Heidelberg: dpunkt 1996

[Adam84]   Adams, E.N.: Optimizing Preventive Service of Software Products. *IBM J. of Research and Development* 28, 1 (1984), 2–14

[Albr79]   Albrecht, A.J.: Measuring Application Development Productivity. In: *Proc. Joint SHARE/GUIDE/IBM Application Development Symposium 1979*, 83–92

[Alle01]   Allen, J.H.: *The CERT® Guide To System and Network Security Practices*. Upper Saddle River, NJ: Addison-Wesley 2001

[Aron70]   Aron, J.D.: Estimating Resources for Large Programming Systems. In: Buxton, J.N., Randell, B. (eds): *Software Engineering Techniques*. Brussels: NATO Science Committee 1970, 68–79

[Ashc89]   Ashcraft, M.H.: *Human Memory and Cognition*. Glenview, IL: Scott, Foresman and Company 1989

[Bake72]   Baker, F.T.: Chief Programmer Team Management in Production Programming. *IBM Systems J.* 11, 1 (1972), 56–73

[Basi81]   Basili, V.R., Reiter, R.: A Controlled Experiment Quantitatively Comparing Software Development Approaches. *IEEE Trans on Software Engineering* 7, 3 (1981), 299–320

[Basi84]   Basili, V.R., Perricone, B.T.: Software Errors and Complexity: An Empirical Investigation. *Comm. ACM* 27, 1 (1984), 41–52

[Basi86]   Basili, V.R., Selby, R.W., Hutchins, D.H.: Experimentation in Software Engineering. *IEEE Trans on Software Engineering* 12, 7 (1986), 733–743

[Basi87]   Basili, V.R., Selby, R.W.: Comparing the Effectiveness of Software Testing Strategies. *IEEE Trans on Software Engineering* 13, 12 (1987), 1278–1296

[Basi88]   Basili, V.R., Rombach, H.D.: The TAME Project: Towards Improvement-Oriented Software Environments. *IEEE Trans on Software Engineering* 14, 6 (1988), 758–773

[Basi89]   Basili, V.R.: Software Development: A Paradigm of the Future. In: *Proc. International Computer Software and Applications Conference (COMPSAC), Orlando, FL, 1989*, 471–485

[Basi92]   Basili, V.R., Caldiera, G., McGarry, F.E. *et al.*: The Software
            Engineering Laboratory: An Operational Software Experience
            Factory, In: *Proceedings of the 14th International Conference
            on Software Engineering (ICSE 92)*, 1992

[Basi94a]   Basili, V.R., Caldiera, G., Rombach, H.D.: Goal Question
            Metric Paradigm. In: Marciniak, J.J. (ed.): *Encyclopedia of
            Software Engineering*. New York: Wiley 1994, 528–532

[Basi94b]   Basili, V.R., Caldiera, G., Rombach, H.D.: Experience Factory.
            In: Marciniak, J.J. (ed.): *Encyclopedia of Software Engineering*.
            New York: Wiley 1994, 469–476

[Basi96a]   Basili, V.R., Briand, L.C., Welo, W.L.: A Validation of Object-
            Oriented Design Metrics as Quality Indicators. *IEEE Trans. on
            Software Engineering* 22, 10 (1996), 751–761

[Basi96b]   Basili, V.R., Briand, L.C., Melo, W.L.: How Reuse Influences
            Productivity of Object-Oriented Systems. *Comm. ACM* 39, 10
            (1996), 104–116

[Basi96c]   Basili, V.R., Green, S., Laitenberger, O., Lanubile, F., Shull, F.,
            Sørumgård, S., Zelkowitz, M.: The Empirical Investigation of
            Perspective-Based Reading. *Empirical Software Engineering* 1, 2
            (1996), 133–164

[Basi98a]   Basili, V.R., Briand, L.C., Morasca, S.: Defining and Validating
            Measures for Object-Based High-level Designs. Fraunhofer
            Kaiserslautern, Report IESE-018.98/E (1998)

[Basi98b]   Basili, V.R.: Empirical Software Engineering. *Software Process
            Newsletter*, 12 (1998), 1–3

[Basi99]   Basili, V.R., Shull, F., Lanubile, F.: Building Knowledge through
            Families of Experiments. *IEEE Trans on Software Engineering*
            25, 4 (1999), 458–473

[Basi01]   Basili, V.R., Boehm, B.W.: COTS Based Systems Top 10 List.
            IEEE Computer 34, 5 (2001), 91–93

[Baue82]   Bauer, F.L., Wössner, H.: *Algorithmic Language and Program
            Development*. New York: Springer 1982

[Baue93]   Bauer, D.: A Reusable Parts Center. *IBM Systems J.* 32, 4
            (1993), 620–624

[Baum01]   Baumol, W.J., Blinder, A.S.: *Macroeconomics: Principles and
            Policy*. Orlando, FL: Harcourt 2001 (8th edn)

[Baye72]   Bayer, R., McCreight, E.M.: Organization and Maintenance of
            Large Ordered Indexes. *Acta Informatica* 1, 3 (1972), 173–189

[Beck99]   Beck, K.: *Extreme Programming Explained: Embrace Change*.
            Upper Saddle River, NJ: Addison-Wesley 1999

[Beck01]   Beck, K., Fowler, M.: *Planning Extreme Programming*. Upper
            Saddle River, NJ: Addison-Wesley 2001

[Bela76]   Belady, L.A., Lehman, M.M.: A Model of Large Program
            Development. *IBM Syst. J.* 3, (1976), 225–252

[Bern93]   Bernstein, L.: Get the Design Right! *IEEE Software*, 10, 5
            (1993), 61–62

[*Bigg91*] Biggerstaff, T.J., Perlis, A.J. (eds): *Software Reusability: Volume I, Concepts and Models*. Reading, MA: Addison-Wesley 1991

[*Bill94*] Billings, C., Clifton, J., Kolkhorst, B., Lee, E., Wingert, W.B.: Journey to a Mature Software Process. *IBM Systems J*. 23, 1 (1994), 46–61

[*Blas77*] Blasgen, M.W., Eswaran, K.P.: Storage and Access in Relational Data Bases. *IBM Systems J*. 16, 4 (1977), 363–377

[*Boeh75*] Boehm, B.W., McClean, R.K., Urfrig, D.B.: Some Experience with Automated Aids to the Design of Large-Scale Reliable Software. *IEEE Trans on Software Engineering* 1, 1 (1975), 125–133

[*Boeh76*] Boehm, B.W.: Software Engineering. *IEEE Trans on Computers* 25, 12 (1976), 1226–1241

[*Boeh79*] Boehm, B.W.: Software Engineering – As it is. In: *Proc. 4th International Conf. on Software Engineering*, IEEE Cat.79CH1479–5C, IEEE Computer society Press (1979), 11–21

[*Boeh81*] Boehm, B.W.: *Software Engineering Economics*. Englewood Cliffs, NJ: Prentice-Hall 1981

[*Boeh84a*] Boehm, B.W., Gray, T.E., Seewaldt, T.: Prototyping Versus Specifying: A Multiproject Experiment. *IEEE Trans on Software Engineering* 10, 3 (1984), 290–302

[*Boeh84b*] Boehm, B.W.: Software Engineering Economics. *IEEE Trans on Software Engineering* 10, 1 (1984), 4–21

[*Boeh88*] Boehm, B.W.: A Spiral Model of Software Development and Enhancement. *IEEE Computer* 21, 5 (1988), 61–72

[*Boeh89a*] Boehm, B.W.: *Software Risk Management*. Cat. No. EH0291–5, Los Alamitos, CA: IEEE Computer Society Press 1989

[*Boeh89b*] Boehm, B.W., Ross, R.: Theory W Software Project Management: Principles and Examples. *IEEE Trans on Software Engineering* 15, 7 (1989), 902–916

[*Boeh91*] Boehm, B.W.: Software Risk Management: Principles and Practices. *IEEE Software* 8, 1 (1991), 32–41

[*Boeh00a*] Boehm, B.W., Basili, V.R.: Gaining Intellectual Control of Software Development. *IEEE Computer* 33, 5 (2000), 27–33

[*Boeh00b*] Boehm, B.W: Unifiying Software Engineering and Systems Engineering. *IEEE Computer* 33, 3 (2000), 114–116

[*Boeh00c*] Boehm, B.W., Abts, C., Brown, A.W., Chulani, S., Clark, B.K., Horowitz, E., Madachy, R., Reifer, D., Steece, B.: *Software Cost Estimation with COCOMO II*. Upper Saddle River, NJ: Prentice Hall 2000

[*Boeh01*] Boehm, B.W., Basili, V.R.: Software Defect Reduction Top 10 List. *IEEE Computer* 34, 1 (2001), 135–137

[*Booc91*] Booch, G.: *Object Oriented Design with Applications*. Redwood City, CA: Benjamin/Cummings 1991

[*Bria96*] Briand, L.C., Devanbu, P., Melo, W.: An Investigation Into Coupling Measures for C++. Fraunhofer-Institut Kaiserslautern, Report IESE-006–96 (1996)

[*Bria98*]   Briand, L.C., Daly, J., Porter, V. Wüst, J.: A Comprehensive
           Empirical Evaluation of Product Measures for Object-Oriented
           Systems. Fraunhofer Kaiserslautern, Report IESE-021.98/E (1998)

[*Bria99*]   Briand, L.C., Arisholm, E., Counsell, S., Houdek, F., Thévenod-
           Fosse, P.: *Empirical Studies of Object-Oriented Artifacts,
           Methods, and Processes: State of The Art and Future
           Directions.* Techn. Report ISERN-99–12 (1999)

[*Broo75*]   Brooks, F.P.: *The Mythical Man-Month – Essays on Software
           Engineering.* Reading, MA: Addison-Wesley 1975 (Extended
           version as Anniversary Edition 1995)

[*Broo87*]   Brooks, F.P.: No Silver Bullet: Essence and Accidents of
           Software Engineering. *IEEE Computer* 20, 4 (1987), 10–19

[*Broy80*]   Broy, M.: Zur Spezifikation von Programmen für die
           Textverarbeitung. In: Wossidlo, P.R. (ed.): Textverarbeitung und
           Informatik. Informatik-Fachberichte 30, Heidelberg: Springer
           1980, 75–93

[*Broy01*]   Broy, M.: Toward a Mathematical Foundation of Software
           Engineering Methods. *IEEE Trans on Software Engineering* 27,
           1 (2001), 42–57

[*BSA00*]   BSA Business Software Alliance: Sixth Annual BSA Global
           Software Piracy Study. 2000. *http://www.bsa.org/*

[*Buxt70*]   Buxton, J.N., Randell, B. (eds): *Software Engineering
           Techniques.* Brussels: NATO Science Committee 1970

[*Card87*]   Card, D.N., McGarry, F.E., Page, G.T.: Evaluating Software
           Engineering Technologies. *IEEE Trans on Software Engineering*
           13, 7 (1987), 845–851

[*Chal99*]   Chalmers, A.F.: *What is This Thing Called Science?* St. Lucia,
           Queensland: University of Queensland Press, 1999 (3rd edition)

[*Chen76*]   Chen, P.: The Entity Relationship Model – Towards a Unified
           View of Data. *ACM Transactions on Database Systems* 1, 1
           (1976), 1–36

[*Chid94*]   Chidamber, S.R., Kemerer, C.F.: A Metrics Suite for Object-
           Oriented Design. *IEEE Trans on Software Engineering* 20, 6
           (1994), 476–493

[*Chil92*]   Chillarege, R., Bhandari, I., Chaar, J., Halliday, M., Moebus,
           D., Ray, B., Wong, M.Y.: Orthogonal Defect Classification – A
           Concept for In-Process Measurement. *IEEE Trans on Software
           Engineering* 18, 11 (1992), 943–956

[*Clar94*]   Clarke, E.M., Grumberg, O., Long, D.E.: Model Checking and
           Abstraction. *ACM Trans on Programming Languages and
           Systems* 16, 5 (1994), 1512–1542

[*Cobb90*]   Cobb, R.H., Mills, H.D.: Engineering Software under Statistical
           Quality Control. *IEEE Software* 7, 6 (1990), 44–54

[*Codd70*]   Codd, E.F.: A Relational Model of Data for Large Shared Data
           Banks. *Comm. ACM* 13, 6 (1970), 377–387

312

[*Codd82*]   Codd, E.F.: Relational Database: A Practical Foundation for Productivity. *Comm. ACM* 25, 2 (1982), 109–117

[*Cons01*]   Constantine, L.L.: Back to the Future. *Comm. ACM* 44, 3 (2001), 126–129

[*Conw68*]   Conway, M.E.: How Do Committees Invent? *Datamation* 14, 4 (1968), 28–31

[*Coop01*]   Cooper, M.: Bandwidth and the Creation of Awareness. *Comm. ACM* 44, 3 (2001), 55–57

[*Corb69*]   Corbató, F.J.: PL/I as a Tool for System Programming. *Datamation* 15, 5 (1969), 66–76

[*Cros79*]   Crosby, P.B.: *Quality Is Free: The Art of Making Quality Certain.* New York: McGraw-Hill 1979

[*Curt88*]   Curtis, B., Krasner, H., Iscoe, N.: A Field Study of the Software Design Process for Large Systems. *Comm. ACM* 31, 11 (1988), 1268–1287

[*Curt90*]   Curtis, B.: Empirical Studies of the Software Design Process. In: *Proc. Human Computer Interaction Interact '90.* Amsterdam: North Holland 1990, xxxv–xl

[*Cusu95*]   Cusumano, M.A., Selby, R.W.: *Microsoft Secrets.* New York: Free Press 1995

[*Dahl67*]   Dahl, O.J., Nygaard, K.: Class and Subclass declarations. In: Buxton, J.N. (ed.): *Simulation Programming Languages.* Amsterdam: North Holland 1967, 158–174

[*Daly77*]   Daly, E.: Management of Software Development. *IEEE Trans on Software Engineering* 3, 3 (1977), 229–242

[*Daly96*]   Daly, J., Brooks, A., Miller, J., Roper, M., Wood, M.: Evaluating Inheritance Depth on the Maintainability of Object-Oriented Software. *Empirical Software Engineering* 1, 2 (1996),102–132

[*Davi90*]   Davis, A.: *Software Requirements: Objects, Functions, and States.* Upper Saddle River, NJ: Prentice Hall 1990

[*Davi95*]   Davis, A.: *201 Principles of Software Development.* New York: McGraw Hill 1995

[*Davi96*]   Davis, R., Samuelson, P., Kapor, M., Reichman, J.: A New View of Intellectual Property and Software. *Comm. ACM* 39, 3 (1996), 21–30

[*Dege00*]   Degele, N.: *Informiertes Wissen.* Frankfurt: Campus 2000

[*DeMa78*]   DeMarco, T.: *Structured Analysis and System Specification.* New York: Yourdon 1978

[*DeMa82*]   DeMarco, T.: *Controlling Software Projects.* Englewood Cliffs, NY: Yourdon 1982

[*DeMa87*]   DeMarco, T., Lister, T.: *Peopleware: Productive Projects and Teams.* New York: Dorset House 1987

[*DeMa95*]   DeMarco, T.: *Why Does Software Cost So Much? And Other Puzzles of Information Age.* New York: Dorset House 1995

[*DeMa01*]   DeMarco, T.: Invited Talk at sd&m Software Pioneers Conference. Bonn June 2001

[Dene91]   Denert, E.: *Software Engineering.* Heidelberg: Springer 1991

[Denn84]   Denning, P.J., Brown, R.L.: *Operating Systems. Scientific American* 251, 3 (1984), 94–106

[Denn01]   Denning, P.J.: Crossing the Chasm. *Comm. ACM* 44, 4 (2001), 21–25

[DeRe75]   DeRemer, F., Kron, H.: Programming In-the-Large versus Programming In-the Small. Proc. *Int. Conf. Reliable Software*, IEEE Computer Society Press, IEEE Cat.75CH0940-7 (1975), 114–121

[Dewa00]   Dewal, S., Schnichels, L.: Bank2010: Eine fachliche und technische Vision. In: Mehlhorn, K., Snelting, G.(eds): *Informatik 2000.* Heidelberg: Springer 2000, 337–355

[Diaz97]   Diaz, M., Sligo, J.: How Software Process Improvement Helped Motorola. *IEEE Software* 14, 5 (1997), 75–81

[Diff01]   Diffie, W.: Ultimate Cryptography. *Comm. ACM* 44, 3 (2001), 84–86

[Dijk68]   Dijkstra, E.W.: GO TO Statement Considered Harmful. Letter to the Editor. *Comm. ACM* 11, 3 (1968), 147–148

[Dijk69]   Dijkstra, E.W.: Notes on Structured Programming. *Report EWD 249*, Eindhoven Technical University 1969

[Dijk70]   Dijkstra, E.W.: Structured Programming. In: [Buxt70], 84–88

[Duns80]   Dunsmore, H.E., Gannon, J.D.: Analysis of Effects of Programming Factors on Programming Effort. *J of Systems and Software* 1 (1980), 143–153

[Dura84]   Duran, J., Ntafos, S.: An Evaluation of Random Testing. *IEEE Trans on Software Engineering* 10, 7 (1984), 438–444

[Dvor94]   Dvorak, J.: Conceptual Entropy and Its Effect on Class Hierarchies. *IEEE Computer* 27, 6 (1994), 59–63

[Ebbi85]   Ebbinghaus, H.: *Über das Gedächtnis.* Leipzig: Duncker und Humblot 1885

[Elsh76]   Elshoff, J.L.: An Analysis of Some Commercial PL/I Programs. *Trans on Software Engineering* 2, 6 (1976), 113–120

[Endr75]   Endres, A.: An Analysis of Errors and Their Causes in System Programs. *IEEE Trans on Software Engineering* 1, 2 (1975), 140–149

[Endr77]   Endres, A.: *Analyse und Verifikation von Programmen.* München: Oldenbourg 1977

[Endr78]   Endres, A., Glatthaar, W.: A Complementary Approach to Program Analysis and Testing. In: Bracchi, G., Lockemann, P. (eds): *Information Systems Methodology*, Lecture Notes in Computer Science 65, Heidelberg: Springer 1978, 380–401

[Endr88]   Endres, A.: Software-Wiederverwendung: Ziele, Wege und Erfahrungen. *Informatik-Spektrum* 11, 2 (1988), 85–95

[Endr93a] Endres, A.: Lessons Learned in an Industrial Software Lab. *IEEE Software* 10, 5 (1993), 58–61

[*Endr93b*]　Endres, A.: Model Reuse and Technology Transfer. In: Rombach, H.D., Basili, V.R., Selby, R.W.: *Experimental Software Engineering Issues: Critical Assessment and Future Directions*. LNCS 706. Heidelberg: Springer 1993, 202–205

[*Endr00*]　Endres, A., Fellner, D.: *Digitale Bibliotheken*. Heidelberg: dpunkt 2000

[*Enge68*]　Engelbart, D.C., English, W.K.: A Research Center for Augmenting Human Intellect. *AFIPS Proceeding, Fall Joint Computer Conference* 33 (1968), 395–410. Reprinted in: Greif, I. (ed.): *Computer-Supported Cooperative Work: A Book of Readings*. Palo Alto, CA: Morgan Kaufmann 1988

[*Faga76*]　Fagan, M.E.: Design and Code Inspections to Reduce Errors in Program Development. *IBM Systems J.* 15, 3 (1996), 182–211

[*Faga86*]　Fagan, M.E.: Advances in Software Inspections. *IEEE Trans on Software Engineering* 12, 7 (1986), 744–751

[*Fent93*]　Fenton, N.E.: Objectives and Context of Measurement/ Experimentation. In: Rombach, H.D., Basili, V.R., Selby, R.W.: *Experimental Software Engineering Issues: Critical Assessment and Future Directions*. LNCS 706. Heidelberg: Springer 1993, 82–86

[*Fent94*]　Fenton, N.E., Pfleeger, S.L., Glass, R.L.: Science and Substance: A Challenge to Software Engineers. *IEEE Software* July 1994, 86–95

[*Fent99*]　Fenton, N.E., Neil, M.: A Critique of Software Defect Prediction Models. *IEEE Trans on Software Engineering* 25, 5 (1999), 675–689

[*Fent00*]　Fenton, N.E., Ohlsson, N.: Quantitative Analysis of Faults and Failures in a Complex Software System. *IEEE Trans on Software Engineering* 26, 8 (2000), 797–814

[*Ferg97*]　Ferguson, P., Humphrey, W.S., Khajenoori, S., Macke, S., Matvya, A.: Results of Applying the Personal Software Process. *IEEE Computer* 30, 5 (1997), 24–31

[*Feyn67*]　Feynman, R.P.: *The Character of Physical Law* Cambridge, MA: MIT Press 1967

[*Fitt54*]　Fitts, P.M.: The Information Capacity of the Human Motor System in Controlling the Amplitude of Movement. *Journal of Experimental Psychology* 47 (1954), 381–391

[*Fowl01*]　Fowler, M.: The New Methodology. *http://www.martinfowler.com/ newMethodology.html/*

[*Frak94*]　Frakes, W.B. (ed.): Software Reuse: Advances in Software Reusability. In: *Proc. 3rd International Conf. on Software Reuse*, Los Alimitos, CA: IEEE CS Press 1994

[*Fran93*]　Frankl, P.G., Weyuker, E.J.: A Formal Analysis of the Fault-Detecting Ability of Testing Methods. *IEEE Trans on Software Engineering* 19, 3 (1993), 202–213

[*Gamm95*] Gamma, E., Helm, R., Johnson, R., Vlissides, J.: *Design Patterns: Elements of Reusable Object-Oriented Software.* Reading, MA: Addison-Wesley 1995

[*Gamm01*] Gamma, E.: Invited Talk at sd&m Software Pioneers Conference. Bonn June 2001

[*Gann77*] Gannon, J.D.: An Experimental Evaluation of Data Type Conventions. *Comm. ACM* 20, 8 (1977), 584–595

[*Gatz83*] Gatzhammer, P.P.: Distributed Data Processing with Small System Executive/VSE. IBM Böblingen Techn. Report TR 05.291 (1983)

[*Gilb88*] Gilb, T.: *Principles of Software Engineering Management.* Reading, MA: Addison Wesley 1988

[*Glas94*] Glass, R.L.: The Software Research Crisis. *IEEE Software* 11, 6 (1994), 42–47

[*Glas98*] Glass, R.L.: *Software Runaways. Lessons Learned from Massive Software Project Failures.* Upper Saddle River, NJ: Prentice Hall 1998

[*Glas01*] Glass, R.L.: Frequently Forgotten Fundamental Facts about Software Engineering. *IEEE Software* 18, 3 (2001), 110–112

[*Gold89*] Goldberg, A., Robson, D.: *Smalltalk-80: The Language.* Reading, MA. Addison-Wesley 1989

[*Gomb98*] Gomberg, M., Evard, R., Stacey, C.: A Comparison of Large-Scale Software Installation Methods on NT and UNIX. In: *USENIX Conference on Large Installation System Administration of Windows NT*, 1998. *http://www.usenix.org/ publications/library/proceedings/lisa-nt98/gomberg.html*

[*Good75*] Goodenough, J.B., Gerhart, S.L.: Towards a Theory of Test Data Selection. *IEEE Trans on Software Engineering* 1, 2 (1975), 156–173

[*Grad94*] Grady, R.B., Van Slack, T.: Key Lessons in Achieving Widespread Inspection Use. *IEEE Software*, July 1994, 46–57

[*Gray91*] Gray, J.: The Benchmark Handbook for Database and Transaction Processing Systems. San Mateo, CA: Morgan Kaufmann 1991

[*Gray93*] Gray, J., Reuter, A.: *Transaction Processing: Concepts and Techniques.* San Mateo, CA: Morgan Kaufmann 1993

[*Gris93*] Griss, M.L: Software Reuse: From Library to Factory. *IBM Systems J.* 32, 4 (1993), 548–566

[*Gupt96*] Gupta, D., Jalote, P., Barua, G.: A Formal Framework for On-line Software Version Change. *IEEE Trans on Software Engineering* 22, 2 (1996), 120–131

[*Gutj99*] Gutjahr, W.: Partition vs Random Testing: The Influence of Uncertainty. *IEEE Trans on Software Engineering* 25, 5 (1999), 661–667

[*Hall90*] Hall, A.: Seven Myth of Formal Methods. *IEEE Software* 7, 5 (1990), 11–19

References

[Halp99]   Halprin, G.: Maturing System Administration. In: *Proc. Usenix LISA-NT'99 Technical Conference 1999. http://www.usenix.org/ publications/library/proceedings/lisa-nt99/index.html*

[Haml90]   Hamlet, R.G., Taylor, R.: Partition Testing Does Not Inspire Confidence. *IEEE Trans on Software Engineering* 16, 12 (1990), 1402–1411

[Hare88]   Harel, D.: On Visual Formalisms. *Comm. ACM* 31, 5 (1988), 514–530

[Haye85]   Hayes, I.J.: Applying Formal Specification to Software Development in Industry. *IEEE Trans on Software Engineering* 11, 2 (1985), 169–178

[Hers99]   Hersleb, J.D., Grinter, R.E.: Splitting the Organisation and Integrating of Code: Conway's Law Revisited. In: *Proc. 21st Intl. Conf. on Software Engineering (ICSE)*. New York: ACM 1999, 85–95

[Herz66]   Herzberg, F.: *Work and the Nature of Man*. Cleveland: World Publishing 1966

[Hetz76]   Hetzel, W.C.: *An Experimental Analysis of Program Verification Methods*. Ph.D. Thesis, University of North Carolina, Chapel Hill, 1976

[Hiem74]   Hiemann, P.: A New Look at the Program Development Process. In: Hackl, C. (ed.): *Programming Methodology*. LNCS 23, Heidelberg: Springer 1974

[Hoar69]   Hoare, C.A.R.: An Axiomatic Basis for Computer Programming. *Comm. ACM* 12, 10 (1969), 576–580, 583

[Hoar71]   Hoare, C.A.R.: Proof of a Program: Find. *Comm. ACM* 14, 1 (1971), 39–45

[Hoar72]   Hoare, C.A.R.: Proof of Correctness of Data Representations. *Acta Informatica* 1, 4 (1972), 271–281

[Hoar81]   Hoare, C.A.R.: The Emperor's Old Clothes; 1980 Turing Award Lecture. *Comm. ACM* 24, 2 (1981), 75–83

[Hoch00]   Hoch, D.J., Roeding, C.R., Purkert, G., Lindner, S.K., Müller, R.: *Secrets of Software Success*. Boston: Harvard Business School Press 2000

[Hofm01]   Hofmann, H.F., Lehner, F.: Requirements Engineering as a Success Factor in Software Projects. *IEEE Software* 18, 4 (2001), 58–66

[Howd76]   Howden, W.E.: Reliability of the Path Analysis Testing Strategy. *IEEE Trans on Software Engineering* 2, 3 (1976), 140–149

[Hump89]   Humphrey, W.S.: *Managing the Software Process*. Reading, MA.: Addison-Wesley 1989

[Hump96]   Humphrey, W.S.: Using a Defined and Measured Personal Software Process. *IEEE Software* 13, 3 (1996), 77–88

[Hump97a] Humphrey, W.S.: *Introduction to the Personal Software Process*. Reading, MA: Addison-Wesley 1997

[Hump97b] Humphrey, W.S.: *Managing Technical People*. Reading, MA: Addison-Wesley 1997

[*IEEE84*] *IEEE Guide to Software Requirements Specifications.* IEEE   317
Computer Society, IEEE Std 830–1984, 1984
[*IEEE90*] *IEEE Standard Glossary of Software Engineering Terminology,*
IEEE Computer Society, IEEE Std 610.12–1990 (Revision and
Redesignation of IEEE Std 729–1983), 1990
[*IEEE01*] IEEE/ACM Computing Curriculum. Final Draft December 15,
2001. *http://www.computer.org/education/cc2001/final/*

[*Jaco92*] Jacobson, I., Christerson, M., Jonsson, P., Övergaard, G.:
Object-Oriented Software Engineering. Reading, MA: Addison-
Wesley 1992
[*Jalo98*] Jalote, P., Haragopal, M.: Overcoming the NAH Syndrome for
Inspection Deployment. In: *Proc. 20th Intl Conf. on Software
Engineering (ICSE).* Los Alamitos, CA: IEEE CS Press 1998,
371–378
[*Jone90*] Jones, C.B.: *Systematic Software Development Using VDM.*
London: Prentice Hall International 1990
[*Jone94*] Jones, C.: Gaps in the Object-Oriented Paradigm. *IEEE
Computer* 27, 6 (1994), 90–91
[*Jone96*] Jones, C.: *Applied Software Measurement, Assuring
Productivity and Quality.* New York: McGraw-Hill 1996
[*Jone00*] Jones, C.: *Software Assessments, Benchmarks, and Best
Practices.* Boston: Addison-Wesley 2000
[*Juri01*] Juristo, N., Moreno, A.: *Basics of Software Engineering
Experimentation,* Boston: Kluwer Academic 2001

[*Kams95*] Kamsties, E., Lott, C.M.: An Empirical Evaluation of Three
Defect-DetectionTechniques. In: Schäfer, W., Botella, P. (eds)
Proc. 5th European Software Engineering Conference (ESEC),
LNCS 989, Heidelberg: Springer 1995
[*Kan95*] Kan, S.H.: *Metrics and Models in Software Quality
Engineering.* Reading, MA: Addison-Wesley 1995
[*Kauf97*] Kaufmann, M., Moore, J.: An Industrial Strength Theorem
Prover for a Logic Based on Common Lisp. *IEEE Trans on
Software Engineering* 23, 4 (1997), 214–223
[*Keeh74*] Keehn, D.G., Lacy, J.O.: VSAM Data Set Design Parameters.
IBM Systems J. 13, 3 (1974), 186–212
[*Krau00*] Krause, W.: *Denken und Gedächtnis aus naturwissenschaft-
licher Sicht.* Göttingen: Hogefe 2000
[*Kuhn70*] Kuhn, T.S.: *The Structure of Scientific Revolutions.* Chicago:
University of Chicago Press 1970 (2nd Edition)
[*Kupf71*] Kupfmüller, K.: Grundlagen der Informationstheorie und
Kybernetik. In: Grauer, O.H., Kramer, K., Jug, R. (eds):
Physiologie des Menschen. Band 10. München: Urban und
Schwarzenberg 1971

[*Lait97*]   Laitenberger, O., DeBaud, J.M.: Perspective-Based Reading of Code Documents at Robert Bosch GmbH. Fraunhofer-Institut Kaiserslautern, Report IESE-049.97 (1997)

[*Lait98*]   Laitenberger, O.: Studying the Effect of Code Inspection and Structural Testing on Software Quality. Fraunhofer-Institut Kaiserslautern, Report IESE-024.98 (1998)

[*Lane79*]   Lanergan, R.G., Poynton, B.: Reusable Code – The Application Development Technique of the Future. *Proc. IBM GUIDE/SHARE Application Symposium*, Oct. 1979, 127–136

[*Lane84*]   Lanergan, R.G., Grasso, C.A.: Software Engineering with Reusable Design and Code. *IEEE Trans on Software Engineering* 10, 5 (1984), 498–501

[*Lehm80*]   Lehman, M.M.: On Understanding Laws, Evolution, and Conservation in the Large-Program Life Cycle. *J. of Systems and Software* 1, 3 (1980), 213–231

[*Lehm94*]   Lehman, M.M.: Software Evolution. In: Marciniak, J.J. (ed.): *Encyclopedia of Software Engineering*. New York: J. Wiley 1994, 1202–1208

[*Lehm01*]   Lehman, M.M., Ramil, J.F., Kahen, G.: Thoughts on the Role of Formalisms in Studying Software Evaluation. *Proc. Formal Foundations of Software Evolution*, Lisbon 2001

[*Lenz87*]   Lenz, M., Schmid, H.A., Wolf, P.F.: Software Reuse Through Building Blocks. *IEEE Software* 4, 4 (1987), 34–42

[*Lieb00*]   Lieberman, H.: Programming by Example. *Comm. ACM* 43, 3 (2000), 73–74

[*Lott96*]   Lott, C.M., Rombach, H.D.: Repeatable Software Engineering Experiments for Comparing Defect-Detection Techniques. *Empirical Software Engineering* 1, 3 (1996), 241–277

[*Luer98*]   Luerkens, C.D., Cole, H.J., Legg, D.R.: Software Distribution to PC Clients in an Enterprise Network. In: *USENIX Conference on Large Installation System Administration of Windows NT, 1998*. *http://www.usenix.org/publications/library/proceedings/lisa-nt98/luerkens.html*

[*Marm74*]   Marmier, E.: A Program Verifier for Pascal. *IFIP Congress 74*. Amsterdam: North Holland 1974

[*Mart81*]   Martin, J.: *Application Development Without Programmers*. Upper Saddle River, NJ: Prentice Hall 1981

[*Masl54*]   Maslow, A.H., Frager, R., Fadiman, J.: *Motivation and Personality*. New York: Harper and Row 1954

[*Mats87*]   Matsumoto, Y.: A Software Factory: An Overall Approach to Software Production. In: Freeman, P. (ed.): *Tutorial: Software Reusability*. IEEE Computer Society Cat. No. EH0256–8 (1987), 155–178

[*Mays90*]   Mays, R., Jones, C., Holloway, G., Studinsky, D.: Experiences with Defect Prevention. *IBM Systems J.* 29, 1 (1990), 4–32

[McCa62] McCarthy, J.: Towards a Mathematical Theory of Computation. *Proc. IFIP Congress Munich 1962*

[McCa76] McCabe, T.J.: A Complexity Measure. *IEEE Trans on Software Engineering* 2, 12 (1976), 308–320

[McCa89] McCabe, T.J. , Butler, C.W.: Design Complexity Measurement and Testing. *Comm. ACM* 32, 12 (1989), 1415–1425

[McCu78] McCue, G.M.: IBM's Santa Teresa Laboratory – Architectural Design for Program Development. *IBM Systems J.* 17, 1 (1978), 4–25

[McGr60] McGregor, D.: *The Human Side of Enterprise*. New York: McGraw-Hill 1960

[Metc73] Metcalfe, R.M.: *Packet Communication*. Ph.D. Thesis, Harvard University, Project MAC TR-114, December 1973

[Metc96] Metcalfe, R.M.: The Internet After the Fad. Monticello Memoirs, May 1996. *http://americanhistory.si.edu/csr/comphist/montic/metcalfe.htm – me7*

[Mill56] Miller, G.A.: The Magical Number Seven, Plus or Minus Two: Some Limitations of Our Capability of Information Processing. *Psychol. Review* 63 (1956), 81–97

[Mill71] Mills, H.D.: Top Down Programming in Large Systems. In: Rustin, R. (ed.): *Debugging Techniques in Large Systems*. Courant Computer Science Symposium 1, New York University (1971), 41–55

[Mill83] Mills, H.D.: Software Productivity in the Enterprise. In: *Software Productivity*. New York: Little Brown 1983

[Mill87] Mills, H.D., Dyer, M., Linger, R.C.: Cleanroom Software Engineering. *IEEE Software* 4, 5 (1987), 19–25

[Misr88] Misra, S., Jalics, P.J.: Third-Generation versus Fourth-Generation Software Development. *IEEE Software* 5, 4 (1988), 6–14

[Moel85] Möller, K.H.: Fehlerverteilung als Hilfsmittel zur Qualitätsverbesserung und Fehlerprognose. In: *VDE- Fachtagung Technische Zuverlässigkeit*. Berlin: VDE-Verlag 1985

[Moor65] Moore, G.E.: Cramming More Components Onto Integrated Circuits. *Electronics Magazine*, 38, 8 (April 1965)

[Moor97] Moore, G.E.: Interview with Gordon Moore. *Scientific American*, September 1997. *http://www.sciam.com/interview/moore/092297moore1.html*

[Morr93] Morris, C. R., Ferguson, C. H.: How Architecture Wins the Technology Wars. *Harvard Business Review*, March–April 1993, 86–96

[Moyn96] Moynihan, T.: An Experimental Comparison of Object-Orientation and Functional Decomposition as Paradigms for Communicating System Functionality to Users. *J. of Systems and Software* 33, 2 (1996), 163–169

[Müll99] Müller, G., Ranneberg, K.: *Multilateral Security in Communications*. Reading, MA: Addison-Wesley 1999

[*Musa93*] Musa, J.D.: Operational Profiles in Software-Reliability Engineering. *IEEE Software*, March (1993), 14–32

[*Myer75*] Myers, G.J.: *Reliable Software Through Composite Design*. New York: Petrocelli 1975

[*Myer78*] Myers, G.J.: A Controlled Experiment in Program Testing and Code Walkthroughs/Inspections. *Comm. ACM* 21, 9 (1978), 760–768

[*Myer79*] Myers, G.J.: *The Art of Software Testing*. New York: Wiley and Sons 1979

[*Naur69a*] Naur, P.: Programming by Action Clusters. *BIT* 9, 3 (1969), 250–258

[*Naur69b*] Naur, P., Randell, B.: *Software Engineering*. Brussels: NATO Science Committee 1969

[*Neig84*] Neighbors, J.M.: The Draco Approach to Constructing Software from Reusable Components. *IEEE Trans on Software Engineering* 10, 5 (1984), 564–574

[*Nels66*] Nelson, E.A.: Management Handbook for the Estimation of Computer Programming Cost. Syst. Dev. Corp. Report Ad-A648750 (1966)

[*Niel94*] Nielsen, J.: *Usability Engineering*. San Mateo, CA: Morgan Kaufmann 1994

[*Niel00*] Nielsen, J., Norman, D.A.: Usability on the Web isn't a Luxury. *Information Week Online* 1/14/2000. *http://www.information-week.com/773/web.htm*

[*Niod83*] Niodusch, S.: A Comparison and the Result of Two Tools Which Measure the Complexity of Programs Using the Theories of Halstead and McCabe. IBM Technical Report GTR 05.300 IBM Böblingen 1983

[*Norm93*] Norman, D.A.: *Things That Make Us Smart*. Reading, MA: Perseus Books 1993

[*Pare97*] Pareto, V.: *Cours d'économie politique*. Lausanne: Rouge 1897

[*Parn72*] Parnas, D.L.: On the Criteria To Be Used in Decomposing Systems into Modules. *Comm. ACM* 15, 12 (1972), 1053–1058

[*Parn74*] Parnas, D.L.: On a 'Buzzword': Hierarchical Structure. *IFIP Congress 74*. Amsterdam: North Holland 1974, 336–339

[*Parn01*] Parnas, D.L.: Invited Talk at sd&m Software Pioneers Conference. Bonn June 2001

[*Pars74*] Parsons, H.M.: What happened at Hawthorne? *Science* 183, (1974), 929–932

[*Peng98*] *The Penguin Dictionary of Economics*, 1998. *http://www.xfer.com/entry/444673*

[*Penr89*] Penrose, R.: *The Emperor's New Mind*. Oxford: Oxford University Press 1989

[*Pfle97*] Pfleeger, S.L., Hatton, L.: Investigating the Influence of Formal Methods. *IEEE Computer* 30, 2 (1997), 33–42

[Popp63]   Popper, K.R.: *Conjectures and Refutations: The Growth of Scientific Knowledge*. London: Routledge & Kegan Paul 1963

[Port95]   Porter, A.A., Votta, L.G., Basili, V.R.: Comparing Detection Methods for Software Requirements Inspections: A Replicated Experiment. *IEEE Trans on Software Engineering* 21, 6 (1995), 563–575

[Port97a]   Porter, A.A., Johnson, P.M.: Assessing Software Review Meetings: Results of a Comparative Analysis of Two Experimental Studies. *IEEE Trans on Software Engineering* 23, 3 (1997), 129–145

[Port97b]   Porter, A.A., Siy, H.P., Toman, C.A. Votta, L.G.: An Experiment to Assess the Cost-Benefits of Code Inspections in Large Scale Software Development. *IEEE Trans on Software Engineering* 23, 6 (1997), 329–346

[Port97c]   Porter, A.A., Votta, L.G.: What Makes Inspections Work? *IEEE Software* 14, 6 (1997), 99–102

[Prec98]   Prechelt, L., Tichy, W.F.: A Controlled Experiment to Assess the Benefits of Procedure Argument Type Checking. *Trans on Software Engineering* 24, 4 (1998), 302–312

[Prec99]   Prechelt, L., Unger, B.: Methodik und Ergebnisse einer Experimentreihe über Entwurfsmuster. *Informatik – Forschung und Entwicklung* 14, 2 (1999), 74–82

[Prec00]   Prechelt, L.: An Empirical Comparison of Seven Programming Languages. *IEEE Computer* 33, 10 (2000), 23–29

[Prec01a]   Prechelt, L., Unger, B.: An Experiment Measuring the Effect of Personal Software Process (PSP) Training. *IEEE Trans on Software Engineering* 27, 5 (2001), 465–472

[Prec01b]   Prechelt, L.: *Kontrollierte Experimente in der Softwaretechnik*. Heidelberg: Springer 2001

[Pugh91]   Pugh, E.W., Johnson, L.R., Palmer, J.H.: *IBM's 360 and Early 370 Systems*. Cambridge, MA: MIT Press 1991

[Raim00]   Raimond, E.S.: *The Cathedral and the Bazaar*; 2000 revision. *http://www.tuxedo.org/~esr/writings/cathedral-bazaar/*

[Rati97]   Rational Software Corporation: *Unified Modeling Language (UML) 1.0*. Santa Clara, CA: Rational Software Corporation 1997. *http://www.rational.com/uml*

[Reif95]   Reif, W.: The KIV approach to Software Verification. In: Broy, M., Jähnichen, S. (eds): KORSO: *Methods, Languages and Tools for the Construction of Correct Software*. LNCS 1009, Heidelberg: Springer 1995

[Reif99]   Reif, W.: Formale Methoden für sicherheitskritische Software – Der KIV-Ansatz. *Informatik – Forschung und Entwicklung* 14, 4 (1999), 193–202

[Romb87]   Rombach, H.D.: A Controlled Experiment on the Impact of Software Structure on Maintainability. *IEEE Trans on Software Engineering* 13, 3 (1987), 344–354

[*Romb93*] Rombach, H.D., Basili, V.R., Selby, R.W. (eds): *Experimental Software Engineering Issues: Critical Assessment and Future Directions*. Lecture Notes in Computer Science # 706, Heidelberg: Springer 1993

[*Romb02*] Rombach, H.D.: IESE Overview. In: Marciniak, J.J. (ed.): *Encyclopedia of Software Engineering*. (2nd edition). New York: Wiley 2002

[*Royc70*] Royce, W.W.: Managing the Development of Large Software Systems: *Proc. Westcon August 1970* (reprinted in *Proc. ICSE 9*, IEEE Computer Society Press 1987), 328–338

[*Rube68*] Rubey, R.J., *et al.*: Comparative Evaluation of PL/I. USAF Rep. ESD-TR-68–150, 1968

[*Rumb91*] Rumbaugh, J., Blaha, M., Premerlani, W., Eddy, F., Lorensen, W.: *Object-Oriented Modeling and Design*. Englewood Cliffs, NJ: Prentice Hall 1991

[*Sack68*] Sackman, H., Erikson, W.J., Grant, E.E.: Exploratory Experimental Studies Comparing Online and Offline Programming Performance. *Comm. ACM* 11, 1 (1968), 3–11

[*Samu01*] Samuelson, P.: Intellectual Property for an Information Age. *Comm. ACM* 44, 2 (2001), 67–68

[*Sche01*] Schechter, B., Ross, M.: Leading the Way in Storage. IBM Think Research 2001. *http://domino.research.ibm.com/comm/ wwwr_thinkresearch.nsf/pages/storage297.html*

[*Sega93*] Segal, M.E., Frieder, O.: On-The-Fly Program Modification: Systems for Dynamic Updating. *IEEE Software* 10, 2 (1993), 53–65

[*Selb87*] Selby, R.W., Basili, V.R., Baker, F.T.: Cleanroom Software Development: An Empirical Investigation. *IEEE Trans on Software Engineering* 13, 9 (1987), 1027–1037

[*Selb88*] Selby, R.: Empirically Analyzing Software Reuse in a Production Environment. In: Tracz, W. (ed.) *Software Reuse: Emerging Technology*. IEEE Computer Society Cat. No. EH0278–2 (1988), 176–189

[*Shar93*] Sharble, R.C., Cohen, S.S.: The Object-Oriented Brewery: A Comparison of Two Object Oriented Development Methods. *ACM SIGSOFT Software Engineering Notes*, 18, 2 (1993), 60–73

[*Shaw90*] Shaw, M.: Prospects for an Engineering Discipline of Software. *IEEE Software* 7, 6 (1990), 15–24

[*Shaw96*] Shaw, M., Garlan, D.: *Software Architecture. Perspectives of an Emerging Discipline*. Upper Saddle River, NJ: Prentice Hall 1996

[*Shne98*] Shneiderman, B.: *Designing the User Interface*. Reading, MA: Addison-Wesley 1998 (3rd edition)

[*Shul00*] Shull, F., Rus, I., Basili, V.R.: How Perspective-Based Reading Can Improve Requirements Inspections. *IEEE Computer* 33, 7 (2000), 73–79

[Shla88]   Shlaer, S., Mellor, S.: *Object-Oriented Analysis: Modeling the World in Data*. New York: Prentice Hall 1988

[Simo62]   Simon, H.A.: The Architecture of Complexity. *Proc. American Philosophical Society* 106 (1962), 467–482. Reprinted in [Simo69]

[Simo69]   Simon, H.A.: *The Sciences of the Artificial*. Cambridge, MA: MIT Press 1969

[Simo74]   Simon, H.A.: How Big is a Chunk? *Science* 183 (1974) 482–488

[Snee87]   Sneed, H., Jandrasics, G.: Software Recycling. *Proc. IEEE Conference on Software Maintenance*, 1987, 82–90

[Spiv89]   Spivey, J.M.: *The Z Notation: A Reference Manual*. London: Prentice Hall International 1989

[Stev74]   Stevens, W.P., Myers, G.J., Constantine, L.L.: Structured Design. *IBM Systems J.* 13, 2 (1974), 115–139

[Stut94]   Stutzke, R.D.: A Mathematical Expression of Brooks' Law. In: *Ninth International Forum on COCOMO and Cost Modeling, Los Angeles 1994*

[Tich98]   Tichy, W.: Should Computer Scientists Experiment More? *IEEE Computer* 31, 5 (1998), 32–40

[Trav99]   Travassos, G.H., Shull, F., Fredericks, M., Basili, V.R.: Detecting Defects in Object Oriented Designs: Using Reading Techniques to Increase Software Quality. In: *Proc. Conf. on Object-Oriented Programming, Systems, Languages, and Applications (OOPSLA), Denver, CO 1999*

[Tril98]   Trilk, J.: *Skalierbare Visualisierung objectorientierter Software*. Ph.D. Thesis, Technical University of Munich 1998

[Turn93]   Turner, C.D., Robson, D.J.: The State-Based Testing of Object-Oriented Programs. *Proc. IEEE Conf. on Software Maintenance 1993*, 302–310

[Unge98]   Unger, B., Prechelt, L.: The Impact of Inheritance Depth on Maintenance Tasks. Techn. Report 18/1998, Fakultät Informatik, Universität Karlsruhe 1998

[Walk99]   Walker, R.J., Baniassad, E.L.A., Murphy, G.C.: An Initial Assessment of Aspect-Oriented Programming. In: *Proc. 21st Intl. Conf. on Software Engineering (ICSE)*. New York: ACM 1999, 120–130

[Wals77]   Walston, C.E., Felix; C.P.: A Method of Programming Measurement and Estimation. *IBM Systems J.* 16, 1 (1977)

[Wein71]   Weinberg, G.M.: *The Psychology of Computer Programming*. New York: Van Nostrand Reinhold 1971

[Well83]   Weller, E.F.: Lessons from Three Years of Inspection Data. *IEEE Software* 10, 5 (1993) 38–45

[Wert23]   Wertheimer, M.: Untersuchungen zur Lehre von der Gestalt I + II, *Psychologische Forschung*, 1 (1923), 47–58 and 4 (1923), 301–350. Translation published in Ellis, W.: *A Source Book of Gestalt Psychology*. London: Routledge & Kegan Paul 1938

[*Weyu80*] Weyuker, E.J., Ostand, T.J.: Theories of Program Testing and the Application of Revealing Subdomains. *IEEE Trans on Software Engineering* 6, 3 (1980), 236–246

[*Weyu88*] Weyuker, E.J.: The Evaluation of Program-based Software Test Adequacy Criteria. *Comm. ACM* 31, 6 (1988), 668–675

[*Weyu93*] Weyuker, E.J.: More Experience with Dataflow Testing. *IEEE Trans on Software Engineering* 19, 9 (1993), 912–919

[*Wild93*] Wilde, N., Matthews, P., Huitt, R.: Maintaining Object-Oriented Programs. *IEEE Software* 10, 1 (1993), 75–80

[*Wirf90*] Wirfs-Brock, R., Wilkerson, B., Wiener, L.: *Designing Object-Oriented Software.* New York: Prentice Hall 1990

[*Wirt71*] Wirth, N.: Program Development by Stepwise Refinement. *Comm. ACM* 14, 4 (1971), 221–227

[*Wirt85*] Wirth, N.: From Programming Language Design to Computer Construction. *ACM* 28, 2 (1985), 160–164

[*Wohl00*] Wohlin, C. *et al.*: *Experimentation in Software Engineering: An Introduction.* Boston: Kluwer Academic 2000

[*Wolv74*] Wolverton, R.W.: The Cost of Developing Large-Scale Software. *IEEE Trans on Computers* June 1974, 282–303

[*Wood97*] Wood, M., Roper, M., Brooks, A., Miller, J.: Comparing and Combining Software Defect-Detection Techniques. In: Jazayeri, M., Schauer, H. (eds): *Proc. 6th European Software Engineering Conference (ESEC)*, LNCS 1301, Heidelberg: Springer 1997, 262–277

[*Wu01*] Wu, M.W., Lin, Y.D.: Open Source Software Development: An Overview. *IEEE Computer* 34, 6 (2001), 33–38

[*Your97*] Yourdon, E.: *Death March: Managing 'Mission Impossible' Projects.* Upper Saddle River, NJ: Prentice Hall 1997

[*Zelk98*] Zelkowitz, M.V., Wallace, D.: Experimental Models for Validating Technology. *IEEE Computer* 31, 5 (1998), 23–31

[*Zema68*] Zemanek, H.: Abstrakte Objekte. *Elektronische Rechenanlagen* 10, 5 (1968), 208–216

[*Zend01*] Zendler, A.: A Preliminary Software Engineering Theory as Investigated by Published Experiments. *Empirical Software Engineering* 6, 2 (2001), 161–180

[*Zhan99*] Zhang, Z., Basili, V.R., Shneiderman, B.: Perspective-based Usability Inspection: An Empirical Validation of Efficacy. *Empirical Software Engineering* 4, 1 (1999), 43–69

[*Zweb95*] Zweben, S.H., Edwards, S.H., Weide, B.W., Hollingsworth, J.E.: The Effects of Layering and Encapsulation on Software Development Cost and Quality. *IEEE Trans on Software Engineering* 21, 3 (1995), 200–208